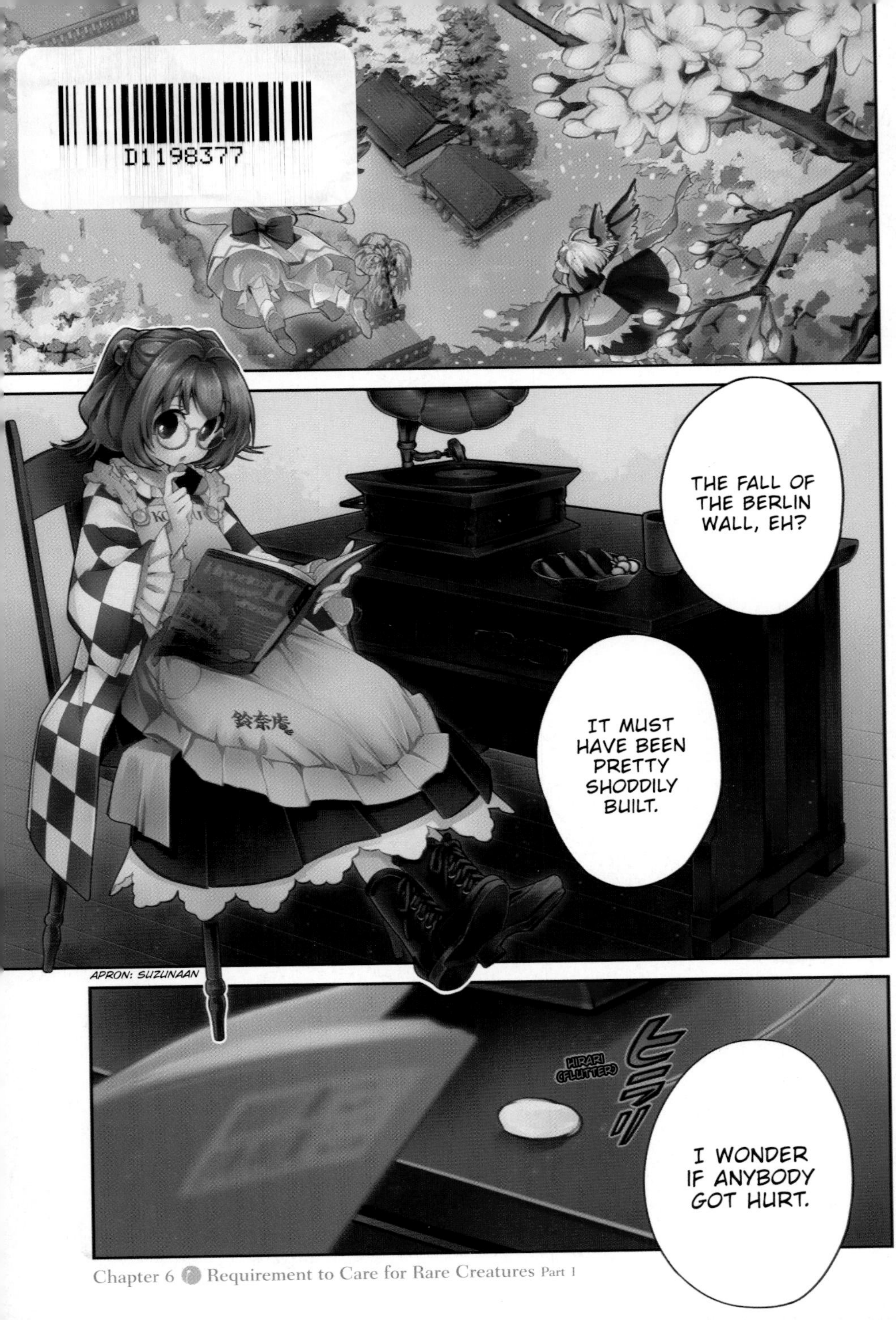
THE FALL OF THE BERLIN WALL, EH?
IT MUST HAVE BEEN PRETTY SHODDILY BUILT.
鈴奈庵
APRON: SUZUNAAN
HIRARI (FLUTTER)
I WONDER IF ANYBODY GOT HURT.

Chapter 6 Requirement to Care for Rare Creatures Part 1

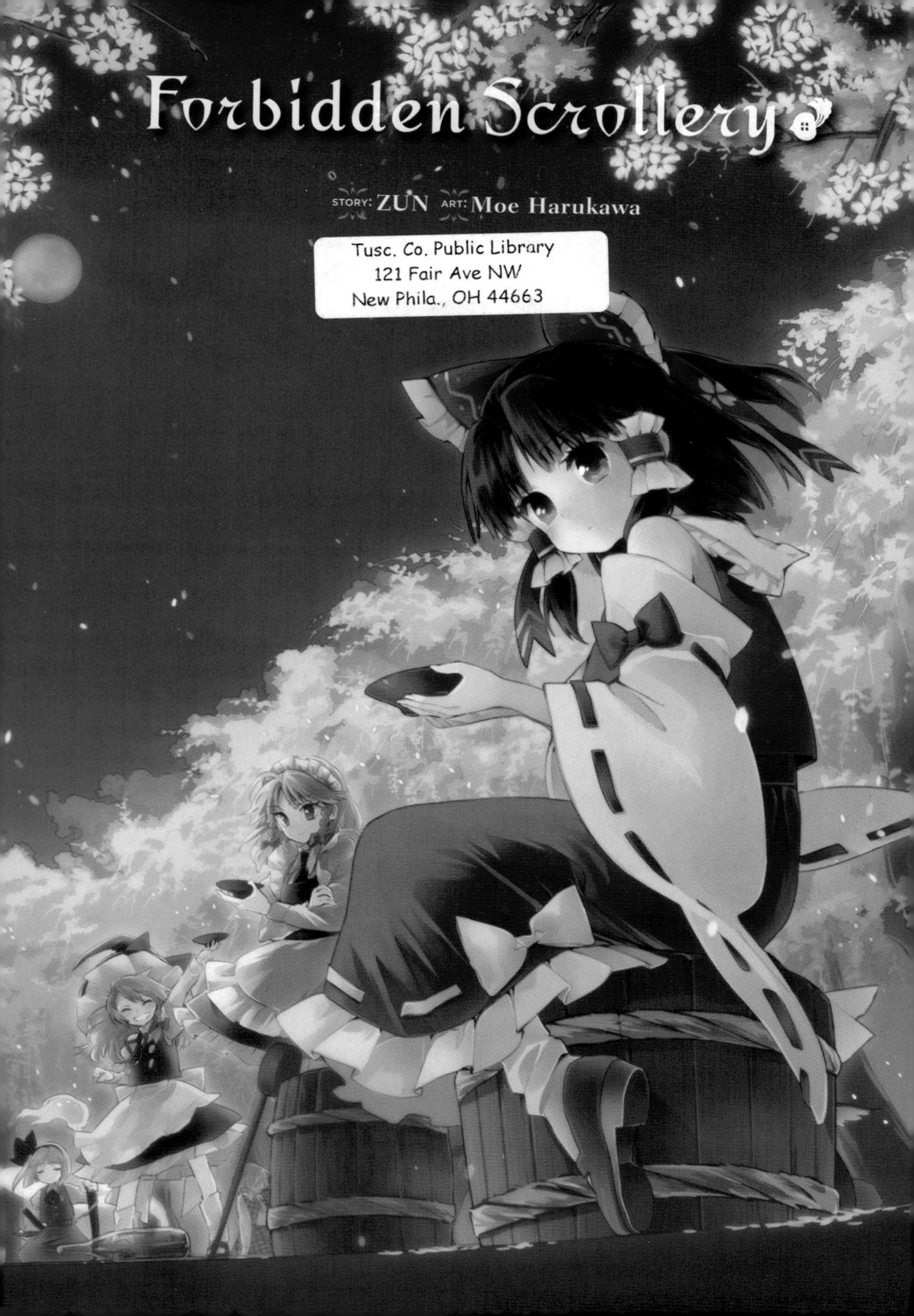
Forbidden Scrollery
STORY: ZUN ART: Moe Harukawa

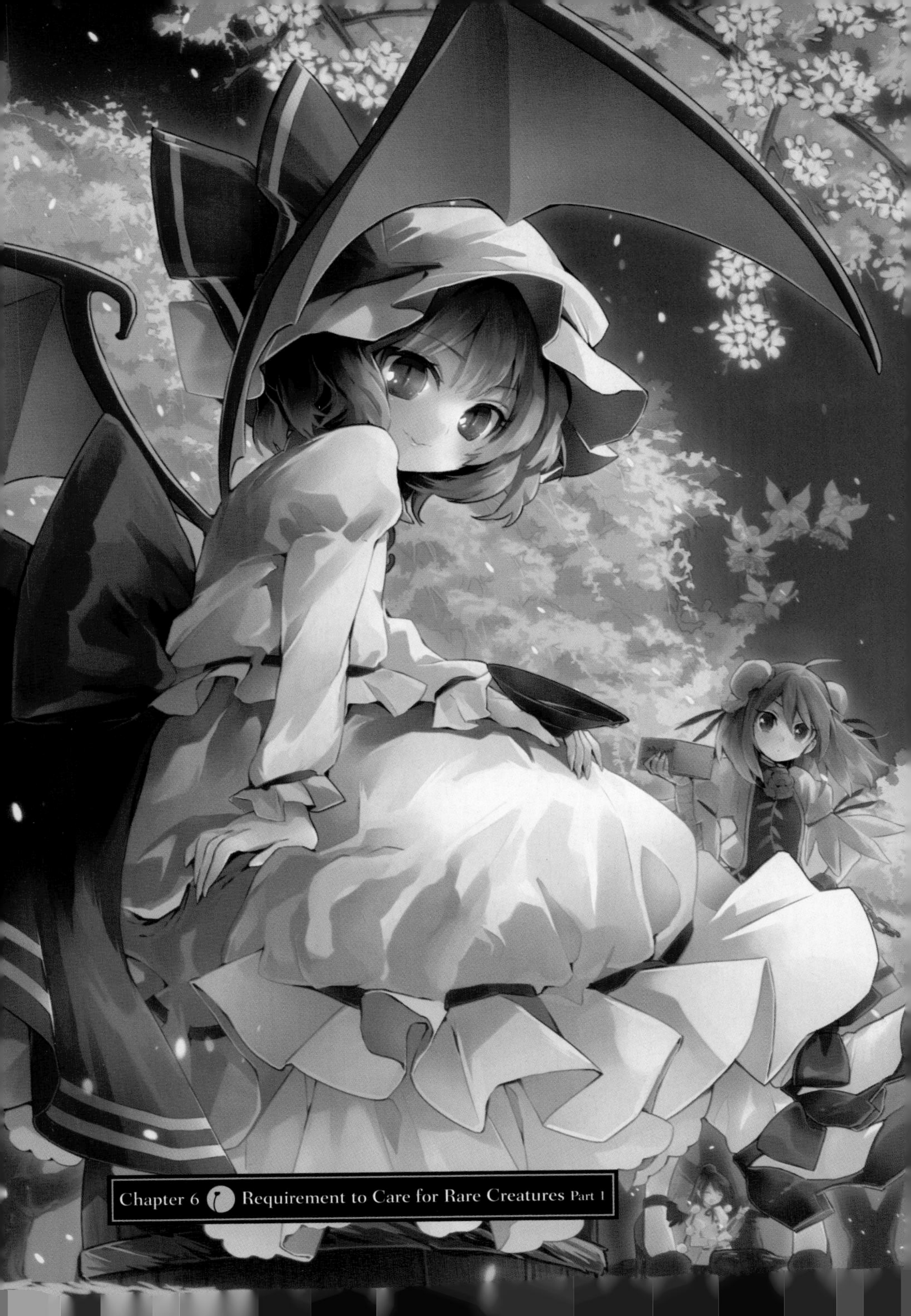

Chapter 6 Requirement to Care for Rare Creatures Part 1

CONTENTS

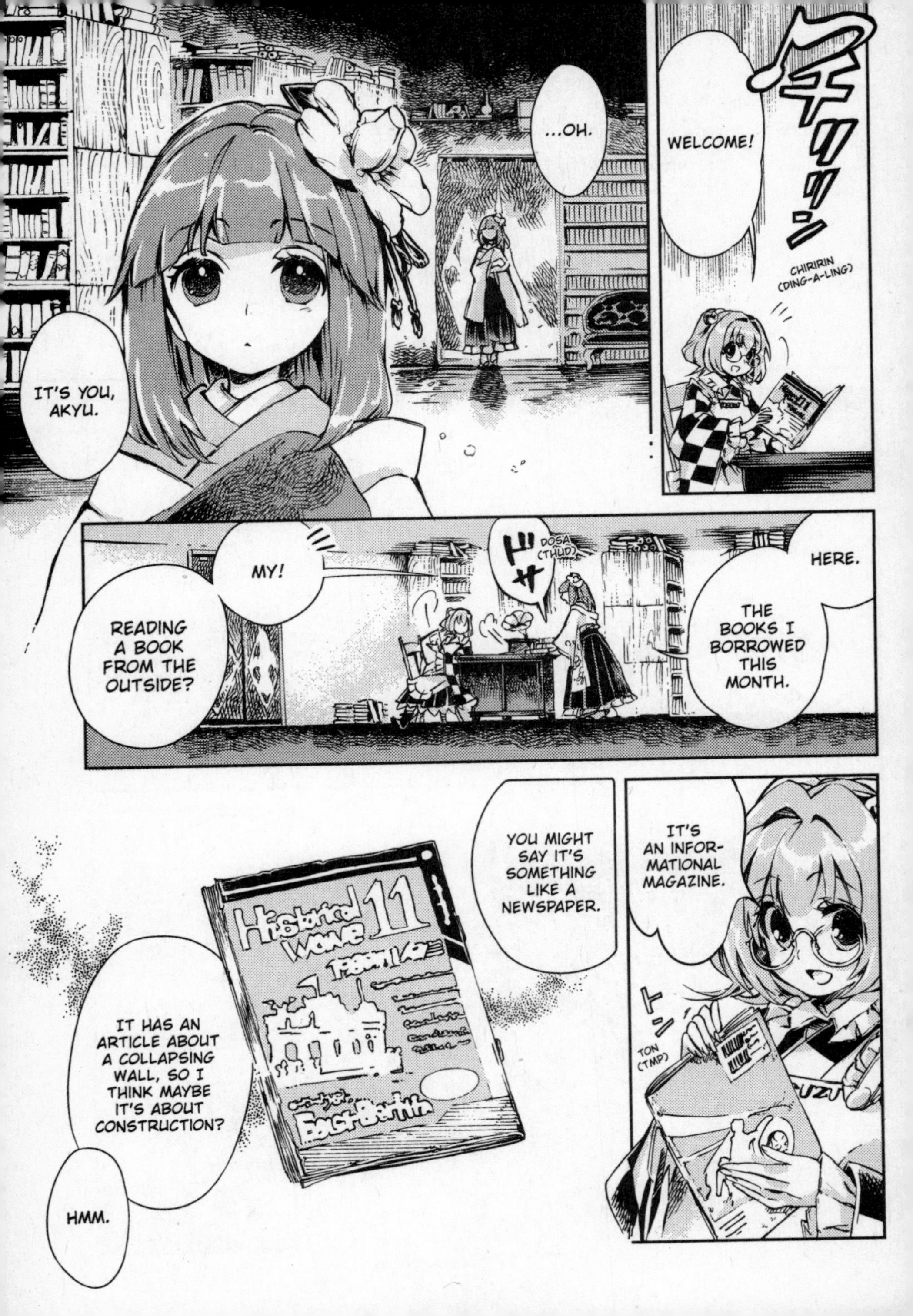
CHIRIRIN (DING-A-LING)
WELCOME!
...OH.
IT'S YOU, AKYU.
HERE.
THE BOOKS I BORROWED THIS MONTH.
DOSA (THUD)
MY!
READING A BOOK FROM THE OUTSIDE?
IT'S AN INFOR-MATIONAL MAGAZINE.
TON (TMP)
YOU MIGHT SAY IT'S SOMETHING LIKE A NEWSPAPER.
Historical Wave 11
IT HAS AN ARTICLE ABOUT A COLLAPSING WALL, SO I THINK MAYBE IT'S ABOUT CONSTRUCTION?
HMM.

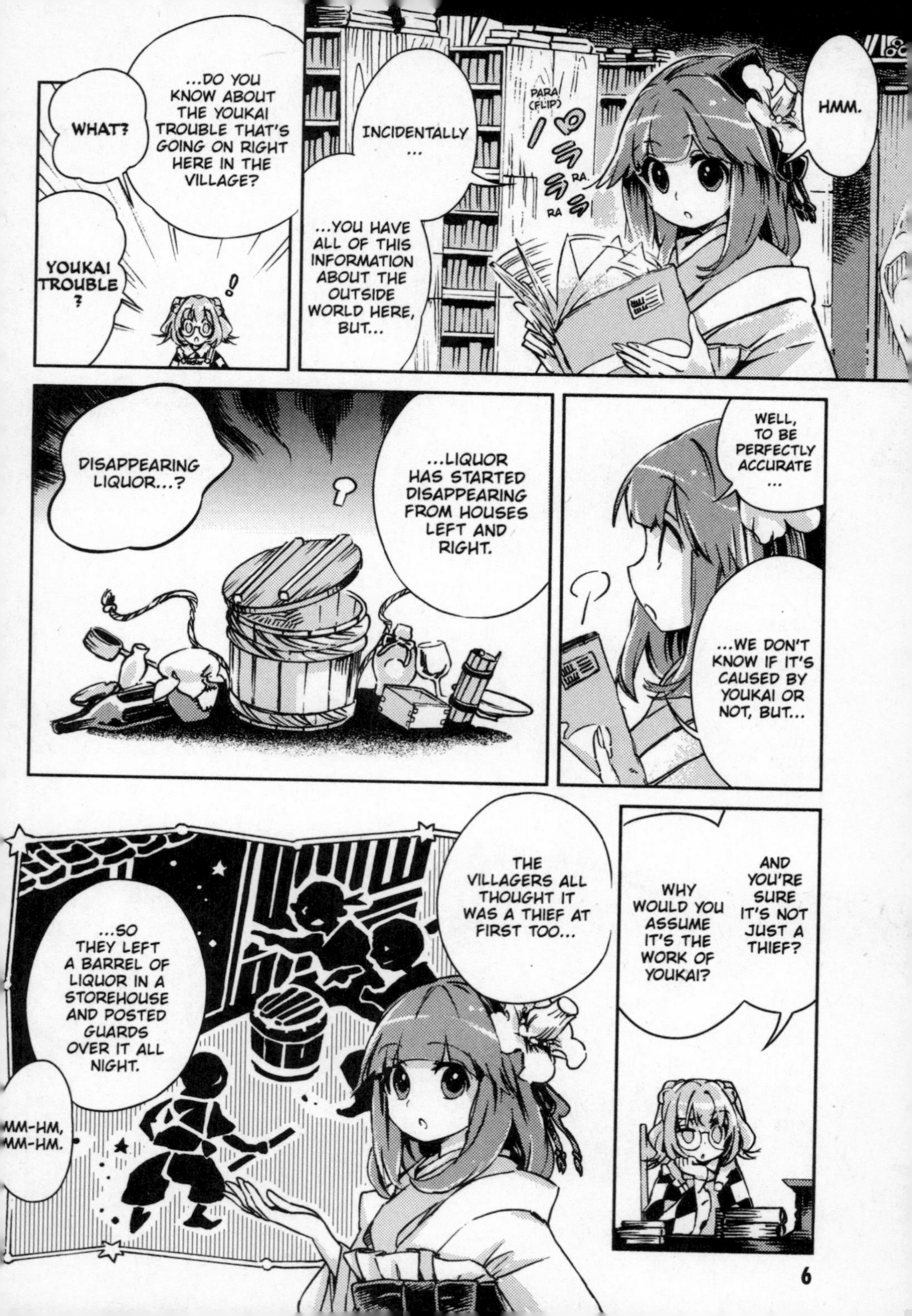
HMM.
PARA (FLIP)
RA. RA
INCIDENTALLY...
...YOU HAVE ALL OF THIS INFORMATION ABOUT THE OUTSIDE WORLD HERE, BUT...
...DO YOU KNOW ABOUT THE YOUKAI TROUBLE THAT'S GOING ON RIGHT HERE IN THE VILLAGE?
WHAT?
YOUKAI TROUBLE?
!
WELL, TO BE PERFECTLY ACCURATE...
...WE DON'T KNOW IF IT'S CAUSED BY YOUKAI OR NOT, BUT...
...LIQUOR HAS STARTED DISAPPEARING FROM HOUSES LEFT AND RIGHT.
DISAPPEARING LIQUOR...?
AND YOU'RE SURE IT'S NOT JUST A THIEF?
WHY WOULD YOU ASSUME IT'S THE WORK OF YOUKAI?
THE VILLAGERS ALL THOUGHT IT WAS A THIEF AT FIRST TOO...
...SO THEY LEFT A BARREL OF LIQUOR IN A STOREHOUSE AND POSTED GUARDS OVER IT ALL NIGHT.
MM-HM, MM-HM.

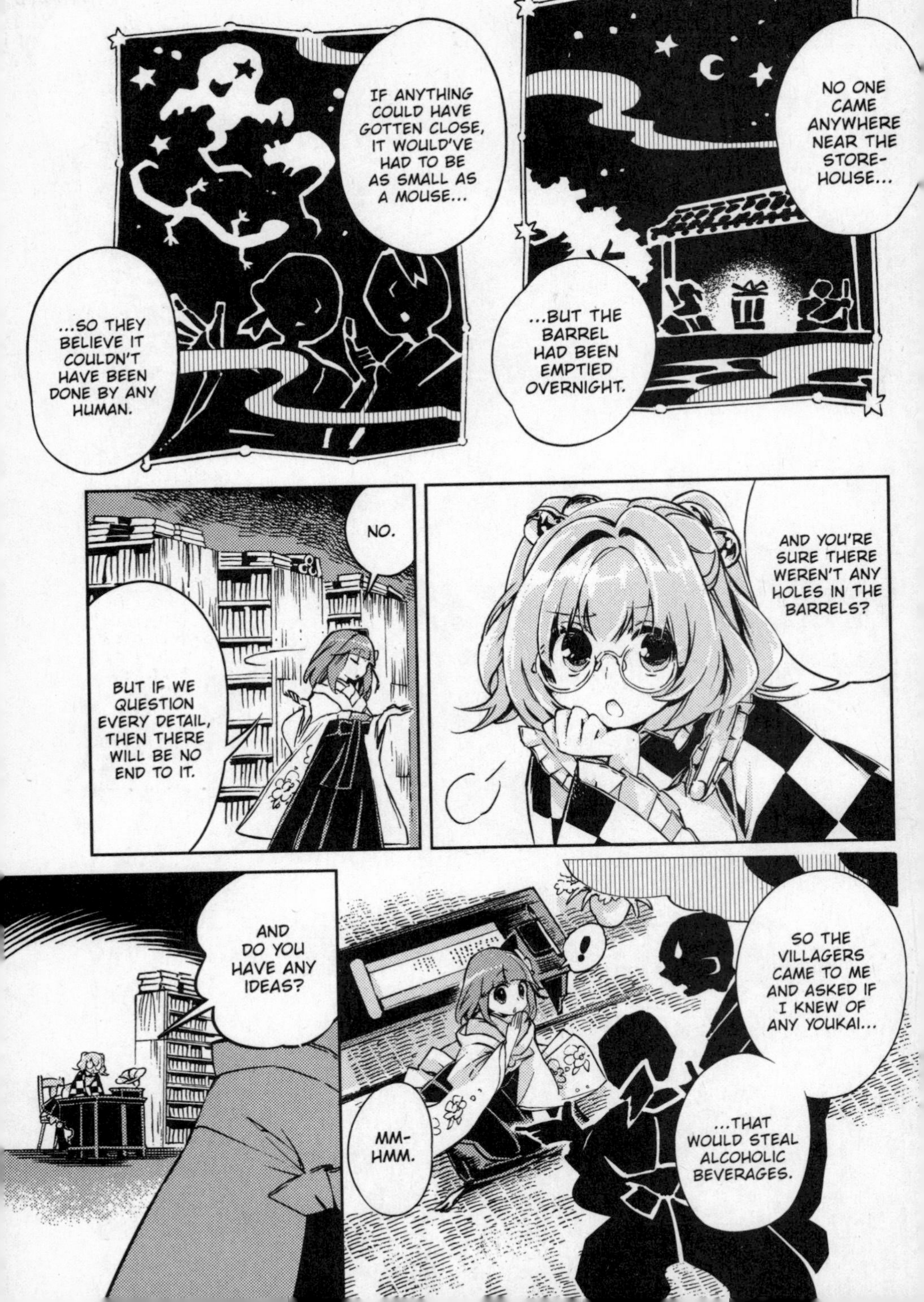
NO ONE CAME ANYWHERE NEAR THE STORE-HOUSE...
...BUT THE BARREL HAD BEEN EMPTIED OVERNIGHT.
IF ANYTHING COULD HAVE GOTTEN CLOSE, IT WOULD'VE HAD TO BE AS SMALL AS A MOUSE...
...SO THEY BELIEVE IT COULDN'T HAVE BEEN DONE BY ANY HUMAN.
AND YOU'RE SURE THERE WEREN'T ANY HOLES IN THE BARRELS?
NO.
BUT IF WE QUESTION EVERY DETAIL, THEN THERE WILL BE NO END TO IT.
SO THE VILLAGERS CAME TO ME AND ASKED IF I KNEW OF ANY YOUKAI...
...THAT WOULD STEAL ALCOHOLIC BEVERAGES.
!
MM-HMM.
AND DO YOU HAVE ANY IDEAS?

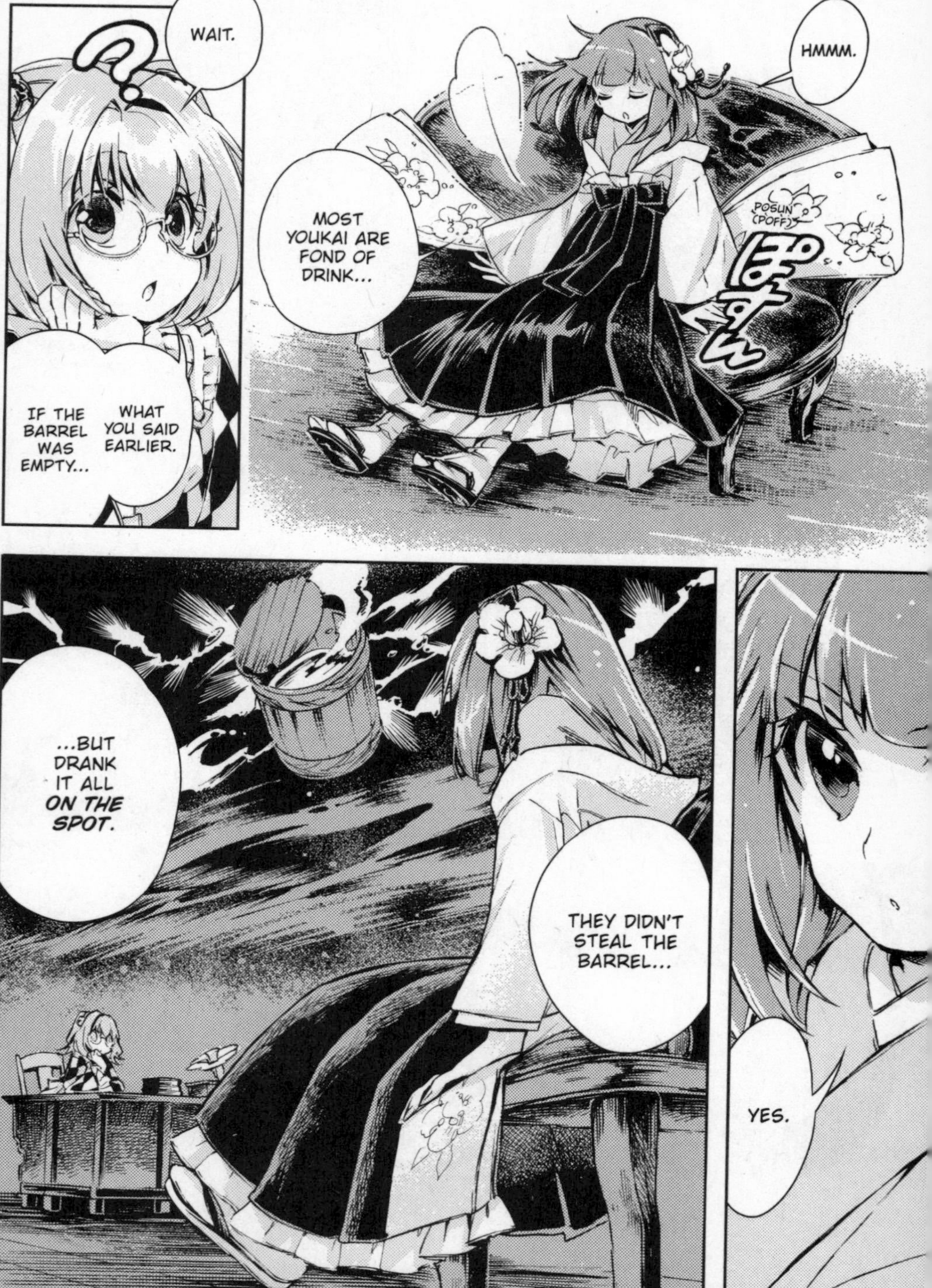
HMMM.
POSUN (POFF)
ぽすん
MOST YOUKAI ARE FOND OF DRINK...
WAIT.
WHAT YOU SAID EARLIER.
IF THE BARREL WAS EMPTY...
YES.
THEY DIDN'T STEAL THE BARREL...
...BUT DRANK IT ALL *ON THE SPOT*.

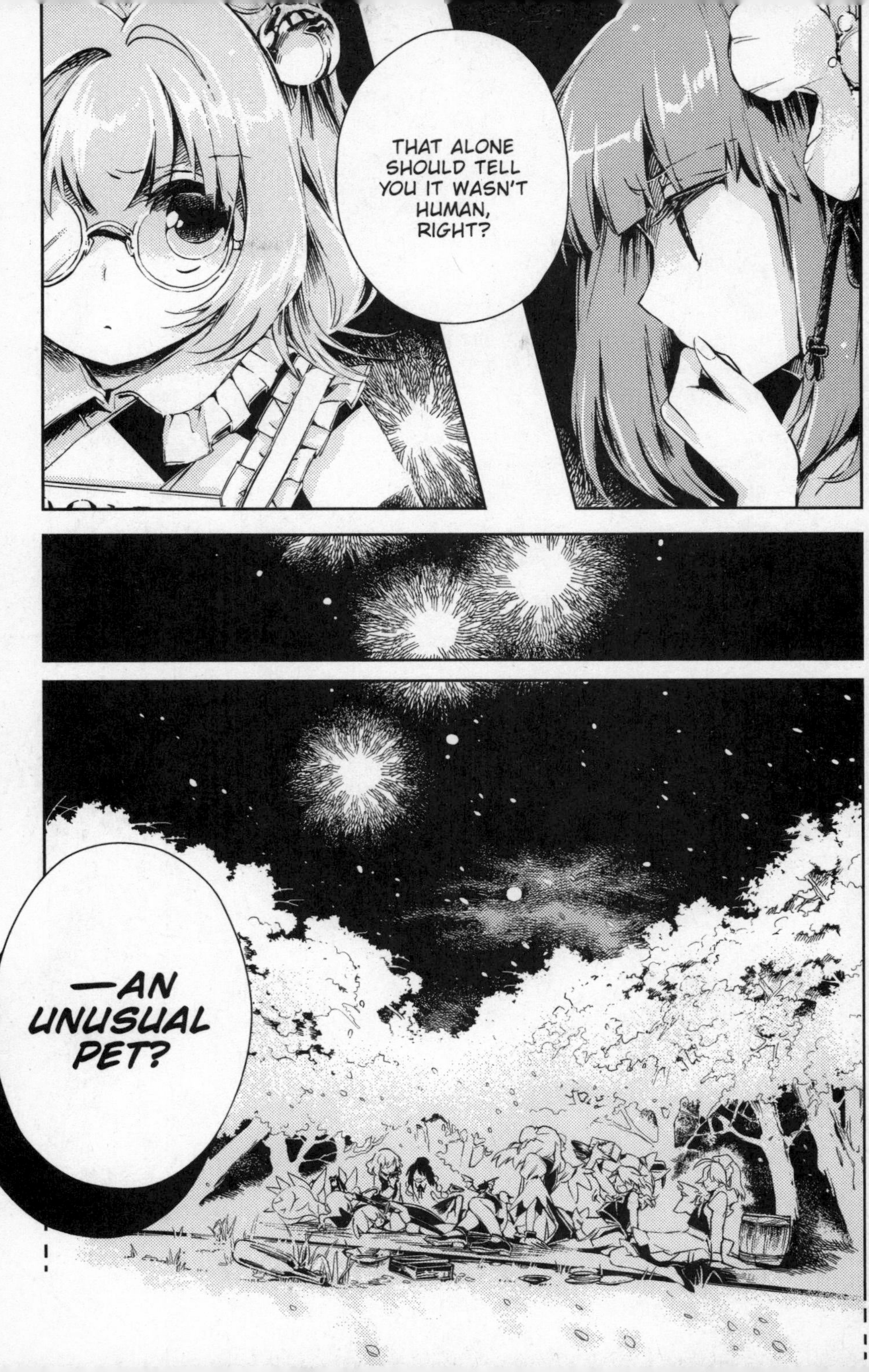
THAT ALONE SHOULD TELL YOU IT WASN'T HUMAN, RIGHT?
—AN UNUSUAL PET?

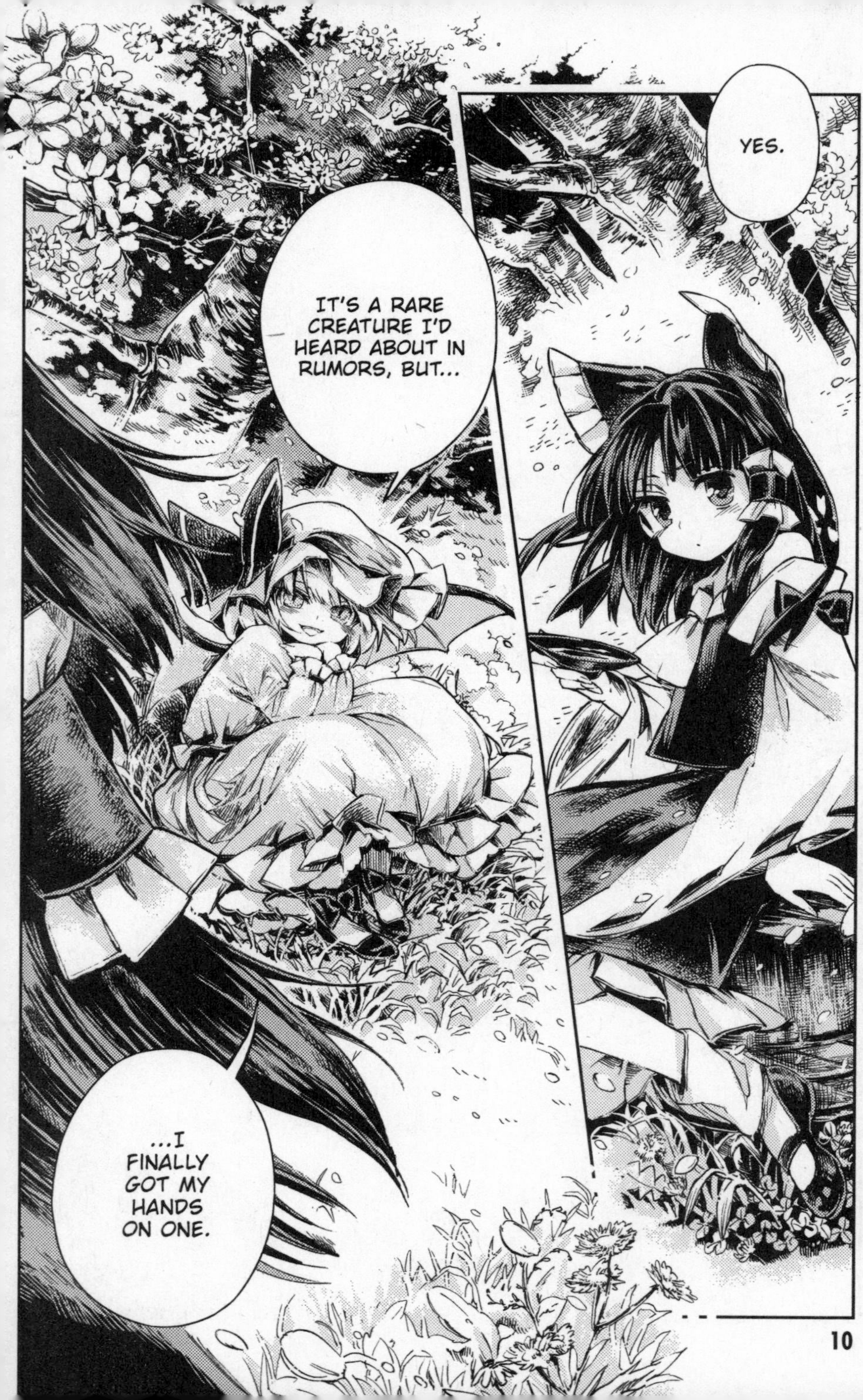
YES.
IT'S A RARE CREATURE I'D HEARD ABOUT IN RUMORS, BUT...
...I FINALLY GOT MY HANDS ON ONE.

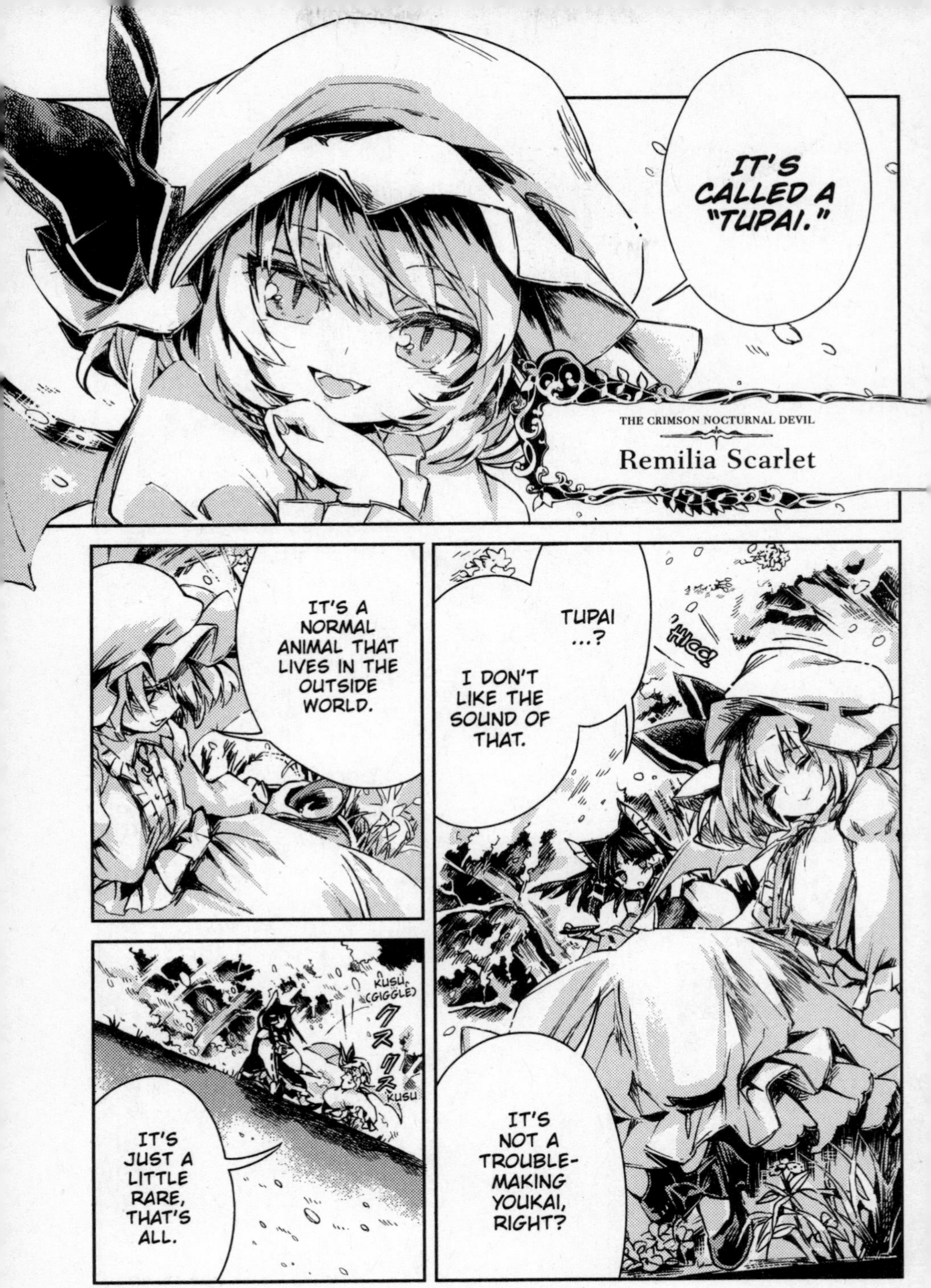
IT'S CALLED A "TUPAI."
THE CRIMSON NOCTURNAL DEVIL
Remilia Scarlet
TUPAI ...?
I DON'T LIKE THE SOUND OF THAT.
HICC!
IT'S NOT A TROUBLE-MAKING YOUKAI, RIGHT?
IT'S A NORMAL ANIMAL THAT LIVES IN THE OUTSIDE WORLD.
KUSU (GIGGLE)
クスクス
KUSU
IT'S JUST A LITTLE RARE, THAT'S ALL.

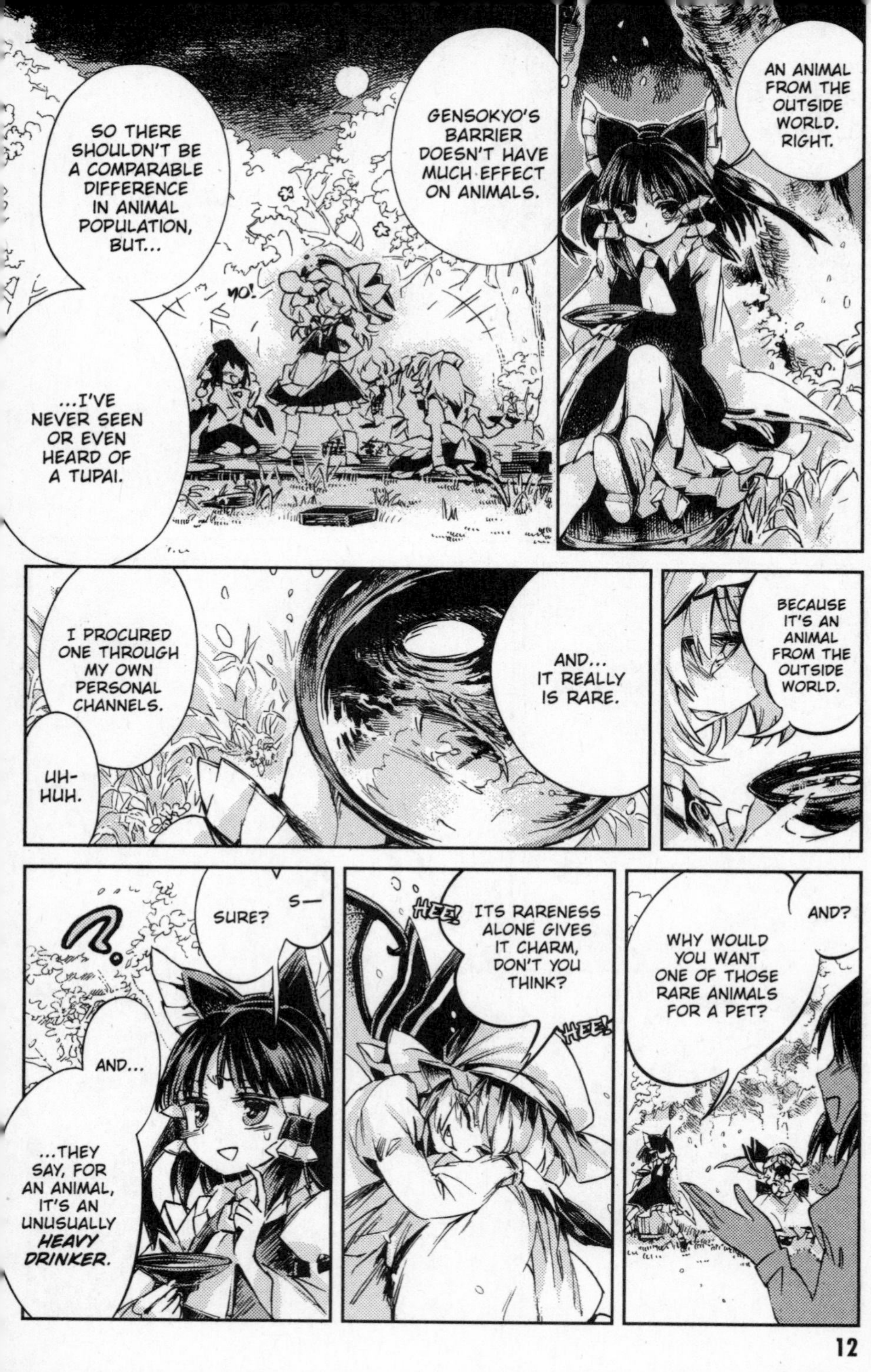
AN ANIMAL FROM THE OUTSIDE WORLD. RIGHT.
GENSOKYO'S BARRIER DOESN'T HAVE MUCH EFFECT ON ANIMALS.
SO THERE SHOULDN'T BE A COMPARABLE DIFFERENCE IN ANIMAL POPULATION, BUT...
NO!
...I'VE NEVER SEEN OR EVEN HEARD OF A TUPAI.
BECAUSE IT'S AN ANIMAL FROM THE OUTSIDE WORLD.
AND... IT REALLY IS RARE.
I PROCURED ONE THROUGH MY OWN PERSONAL CHANNELS.
UH-HUH.
AND?
WHY WOULD YOU WANT ONE OF THOSE RARE ANIMALS FOR A PET?
HEE!
ITS RARENESS ALONE GIVES IT CHARM, DON'T YOU THINK?
HEE!
S—
SURE?
AND...
...THEY SAY, FOR AN ANIMAL, IT'S AN UNUSUALLY *HEAVY DRINKER*.

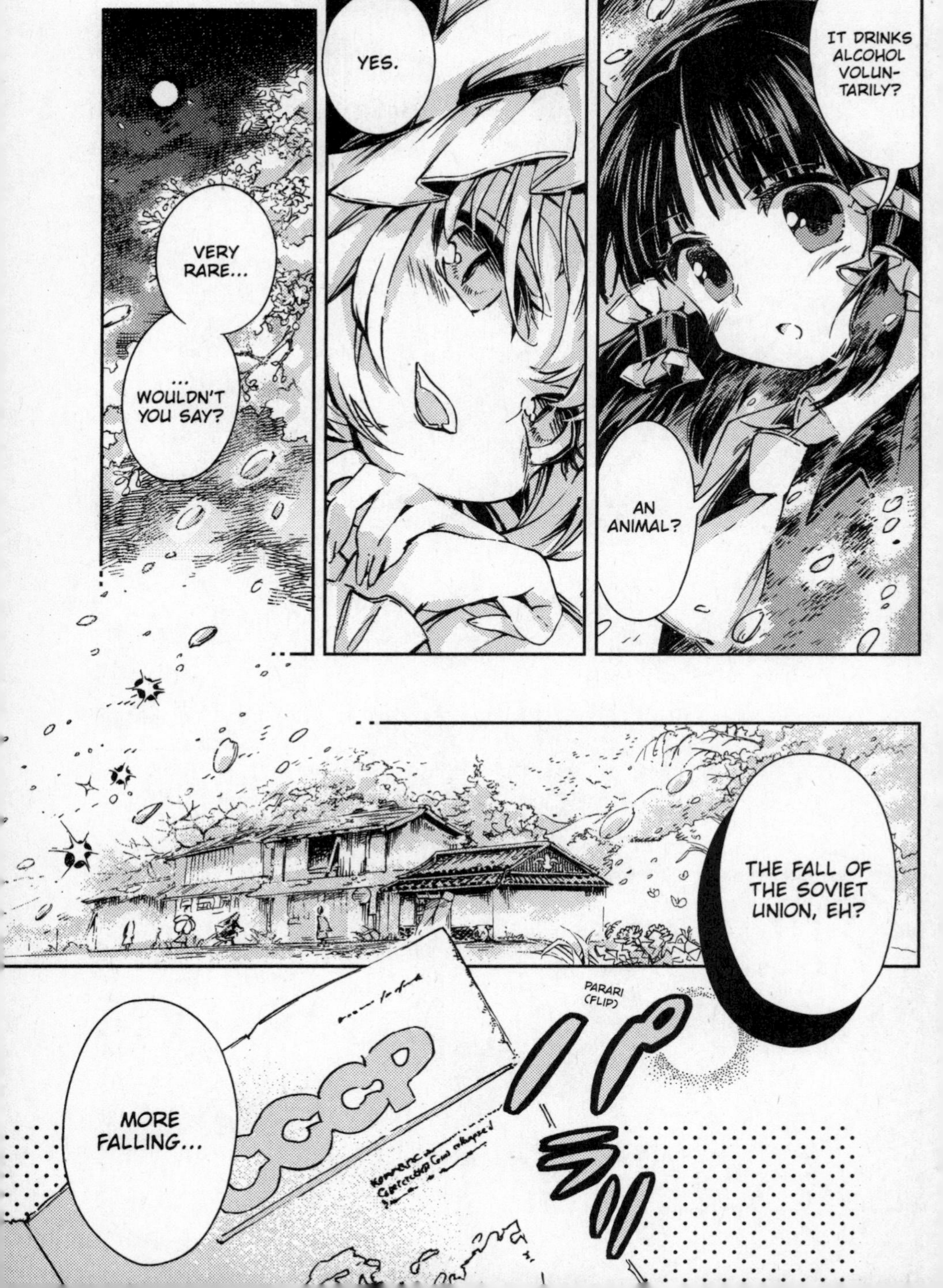
IT DRINKS ALCOHOL VOLUNTARILY?
AN ANIMAL?
YES.
VERY RARE...
...WOULDN'T YOU SAY?
THE FALL OF THE SOVIET UNION, EH?
PARARI (FLIP)
CCCP
MORE FALLING...

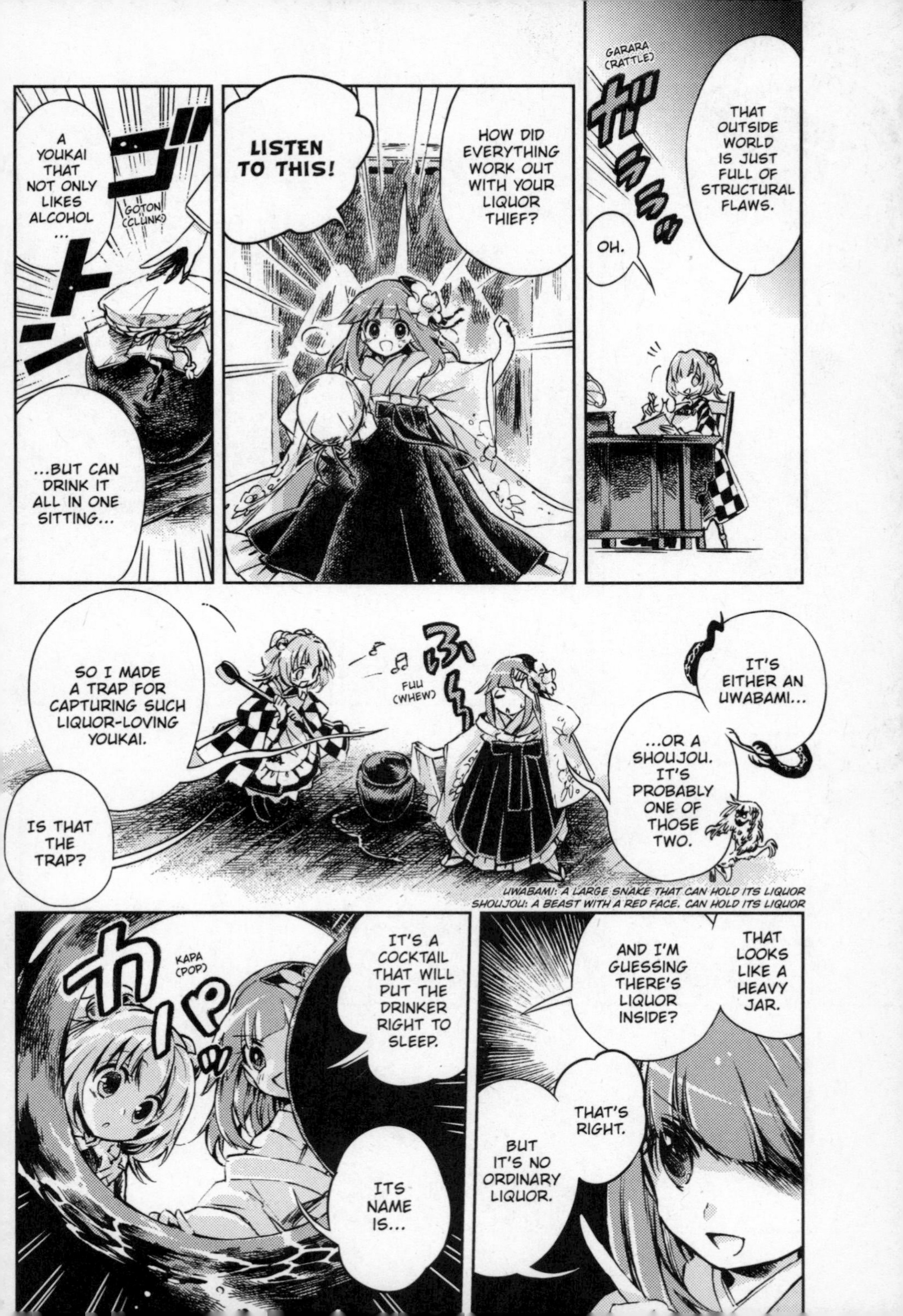
GARARA (RATTLE)
THAT OUTSIDE WORLD IS JUST FULL OF STRUCTURAL FLAWS.
OH.
HOW DID EVERYTHING WORK OUT WITH YOUR LIQUOR THIEF?
LISTEN TO THIS!
A YOUKAI THAT NOT ONLY LIKES ALCOHOL ...
GOTON (CLUNK)
...BUT CAN DRINK IT ALL IN ONE SITTING...
IT'S EITHER AN UWABAMI...
...OR A SHOUJOU. IT'S PROBABLY ONE OF THOSE TWO.
FUU (WHEW)
SO I MADE A TRAP FOR CAPTURING SUCH LIQUOR-LOVING YOUKAI.
IS THAT THE TRAP?
UWABAMI: A LARGE SNAKE THAT CAN HOLD ITS LIQUOR
SHOUJOU: A BEAST WITH A RED FACE. CAN HOLD ITS LIQUOR
THAT LOOKS LIKE A HEAVY JAR.
AND I'M GUESSING THERE'S LIQUOR INSIDE?
THAT'S RIGHT.
BUT IT'S NO ORDINARY LIQUOR.
IT'S A COCKTAIL THAT WILL PUT THE DRINKER RIGHT TO SLEEP.
KAPA (POP)
ITS NAME IS...

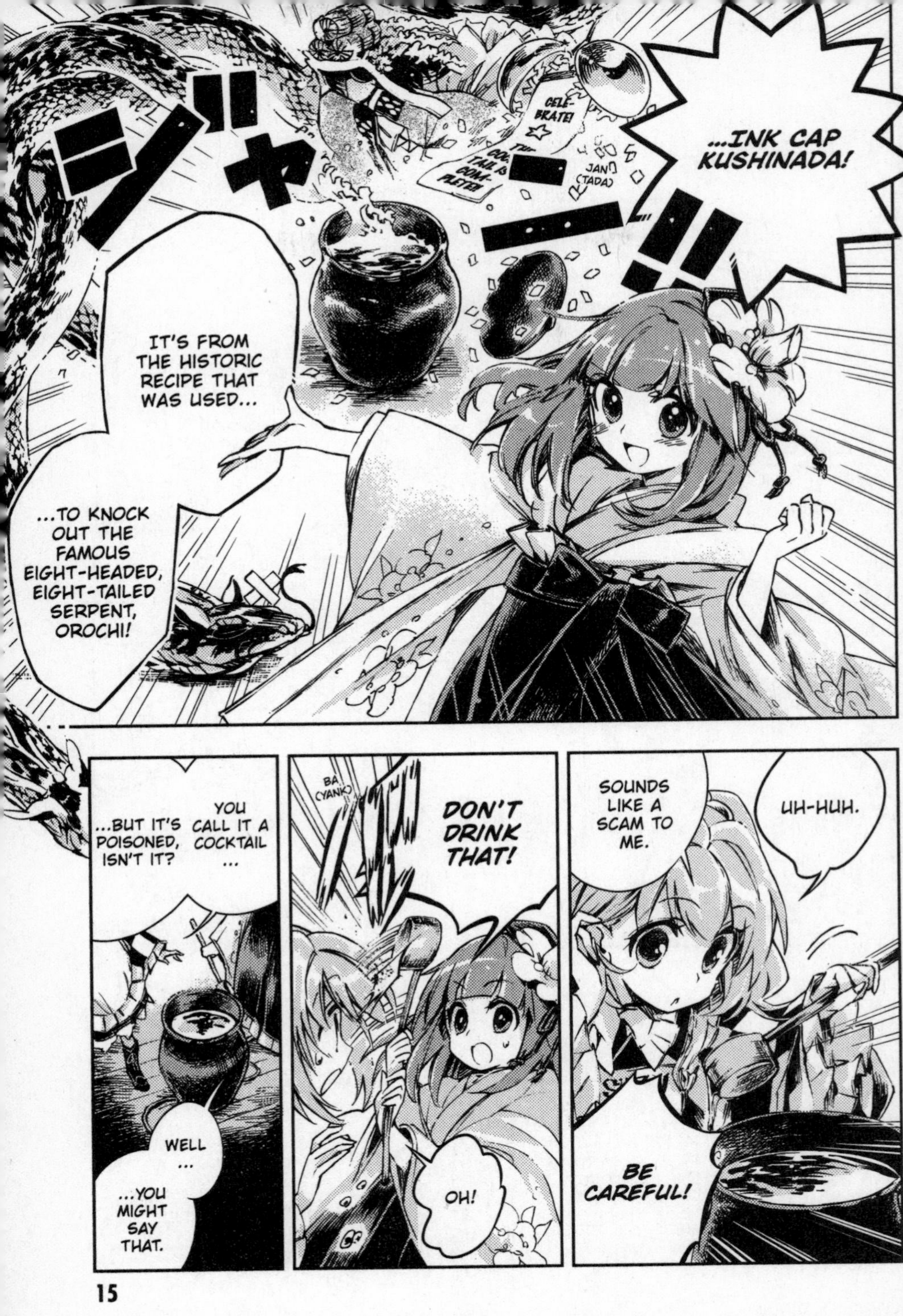

...INK CAP KUSHINADA!
ジャーー!!
JAN (TADA)
CELEBRATE! ☆ THE COCKTAIL IS COMPLETE!!
IT'S FROM THE HISTORIC RECIPE THAT WAS USED...
...TO KNOCK OUT THE FAMOUS EIGHT-HEADED, EIGHT-TAILED SERPENT, OROCHI!
UH-HUH.
SOUNDS LIKE A SCAM TO ME.
BE CAREFUL!
BA (YANK)
DON'T DRINK THAT!
OH!
YOU CALL IT A COCKTAIL ...
...BUT IT'S POISONED, ISN'T IT?
WELL ...
...YOU MIGHT SAY THAT.

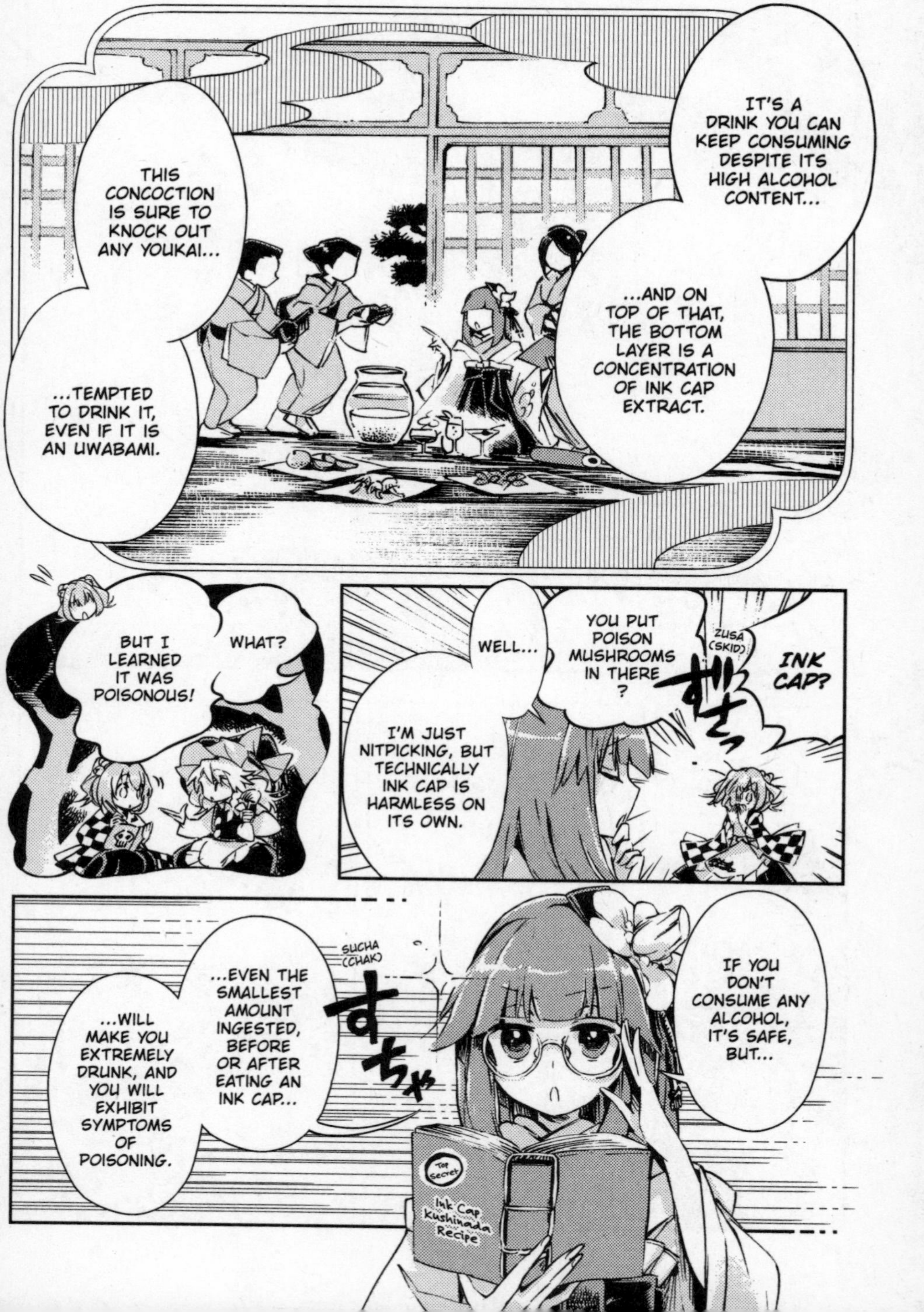
IT'S A DRINK YOU CAN KEEP CONSUMING DESPITE ITS HIGH ALCOHOL CONTENT...
...AND ON TOP OF THAT, THE BOTTOM LAYER IS A CONCENTRATION OF INK CAP EXTRACT.
THIS CONCOCTION IS SURE TO KNOCK OUT ANY YOUKAI...
...TEMPTED TO DRINK IT, EVEN IF IT IS AN UWABAMI.
INK CAP?
ZUSA (SKID)
YOU PUT POISON MUSHROOMS IN THERE?
WELL...
I'M JUST NITPICKING, BUT TECHNICALLY INK CAP IS HARMLESS ON ITS OWN.
WHAT?
BUT I LEARNED IT WAS POISONOUS!
IF YOU DON'T CONSUME ANY ALCOHOL, IT'S SAFE, BUT...
SUCHA (CHAK)
...EVEN THE SMALLEST AMOUNT INGESTED, BEFORE OR AFTER EATING AN INK CAP...
...WILL MAKE YOU EXTREMELY DRUNK, AND YOU WILL EXHIBIT SYMPTOMS OF POISONING.
Top Secret
Ink Cap Kushinada Recipe

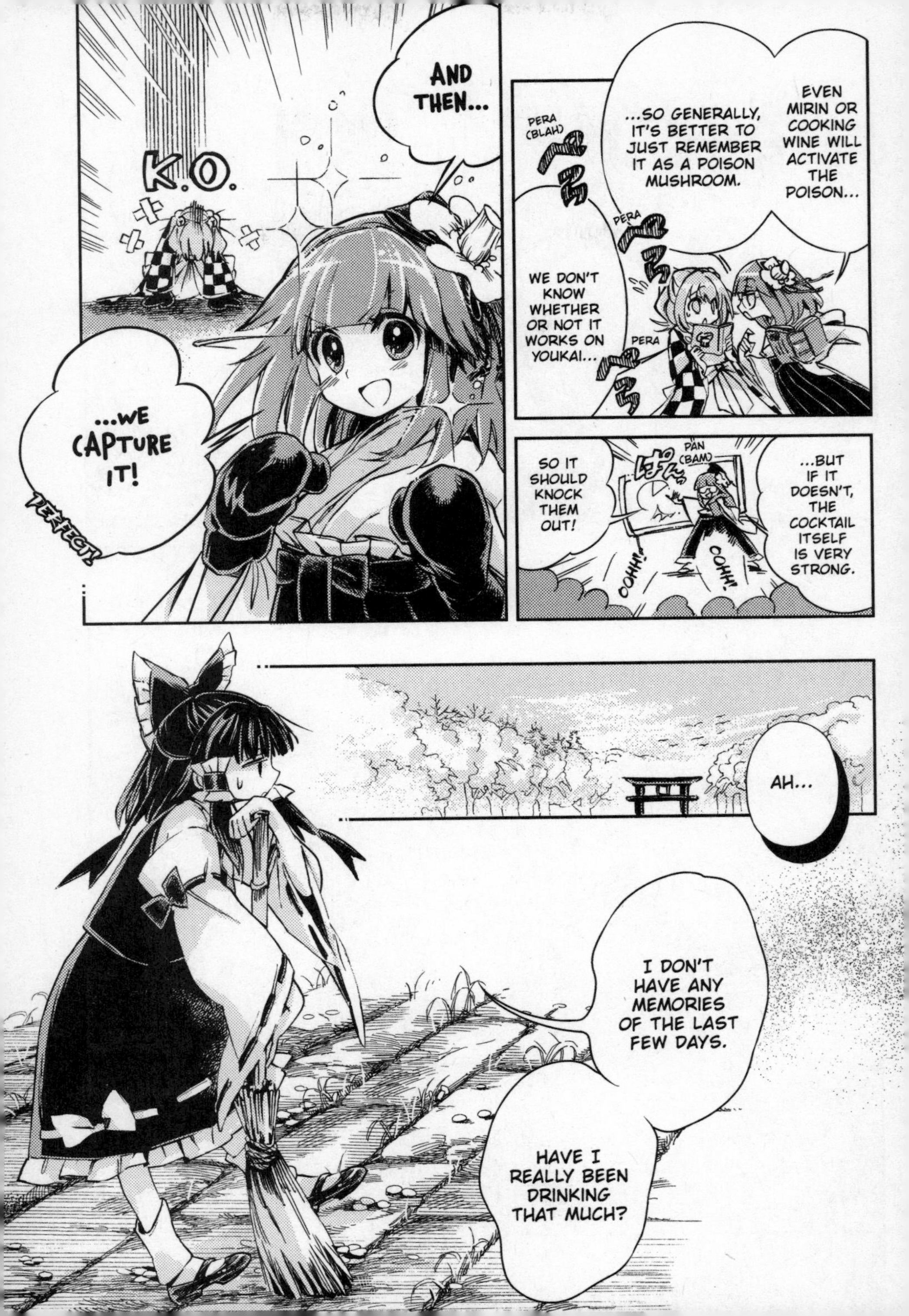
EVEN MIRIN OR COOKING WINE WILL ACTIVATE THE POISON...
...SO GENERALLY, IT'S BETTER TO JUST REMEMBER IT AS A POISON MUSHROOM.
PERA (BLAH)
PERA
WE DON'T KNOW WHETHER OR NOT IT WORKS ON YOUKAI...
PERA
...BUT IF IT DOESN'T, THE COCKTAIL ITSELF IS VERY STRONG.
PAN (BAM)
SO IT SHOULD KNOCK THEM OUT!
OOHH!
OOHH!
AND THEN...
K.O.
...WE CAPTURE IT!
PERFECT!
AH...
I DON'T HAVE ANY MEMORIES OF THE LAST FEW DAYS.
HAVE I REALLY BEEN DRINKING THAT MUCH?

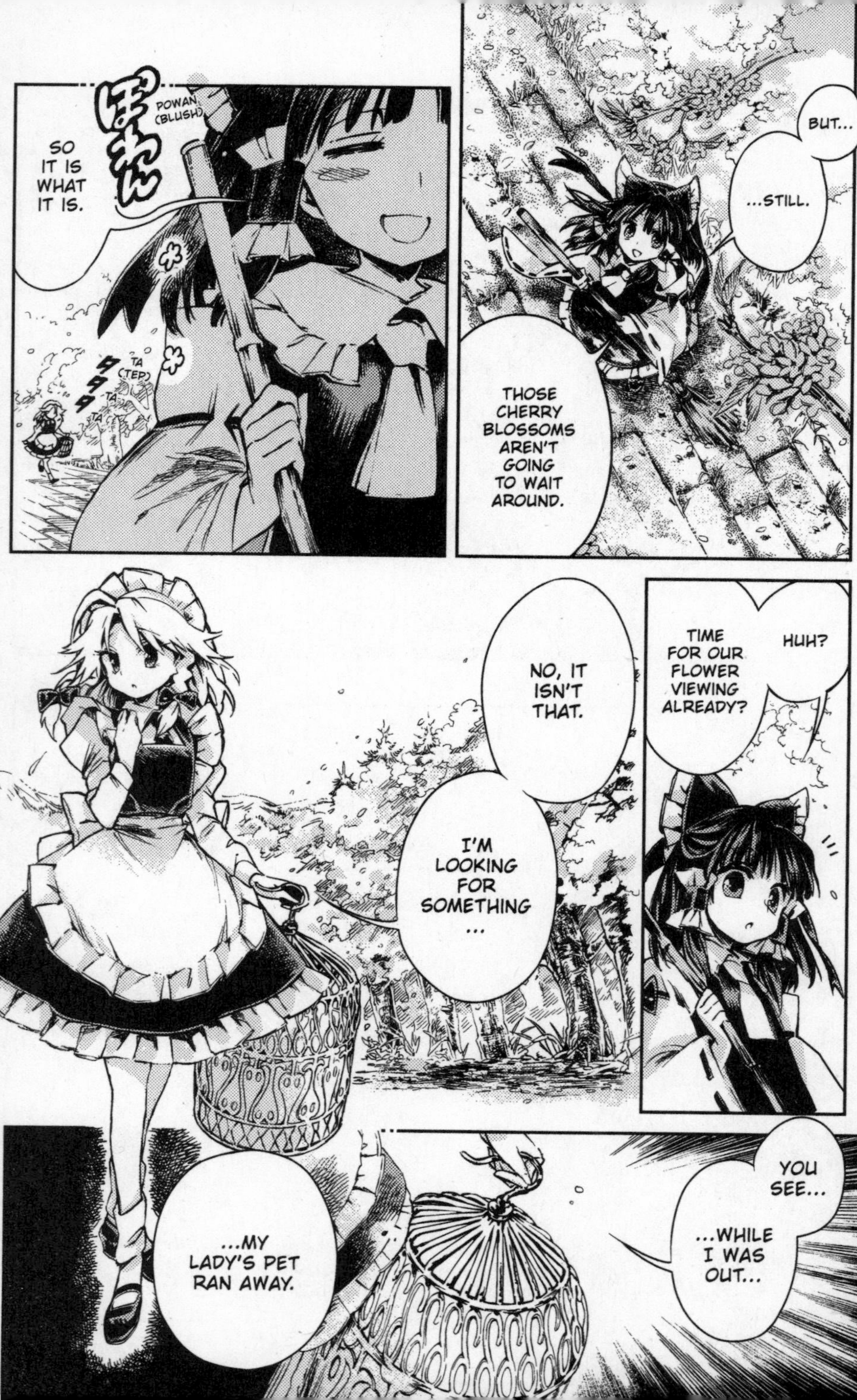
BUT...
...STILL.
THOSE CHERRY BLOSSOMS AREN'T GOING TO WAIT AROUND.
POWAN (BLUSH)
SO IT IS WHAT IT IS.
TA TA TA (TEP)
HUH?
TIME FOR OUR FLOWER VIEWING ALREADY?
NO, IT ISN'T THAT.
I'M LOOKING FOR SOMETHING...
YOU SEE...
...WHILE I WAS OUT...
...MY LADY'S PET RAN AWAY.

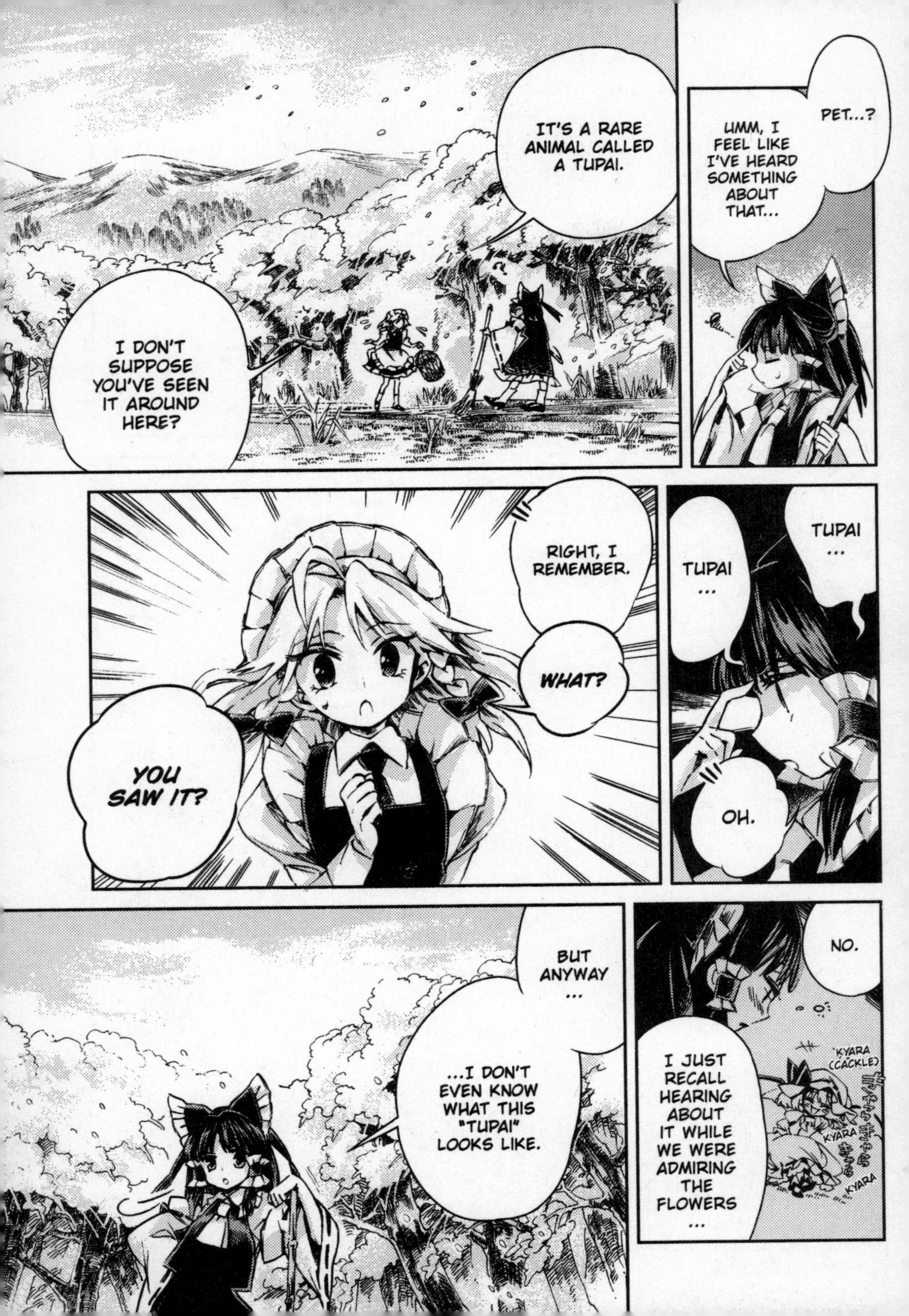
PET...?
UMM, I FEEL LIKE I'VE HEARD SOMETHING ABOUT THAT...
IT'S A RARE ANIMAL CALLED A TUPAI.
I DON'T SUPPOSE YOU'VE SEEN IT AROUND HERE?
TUPAI ...
TUPAI ...
OH.
RIGHT, I REMEMBER.
WHAT?
YOU SAW IT?
NO.
I JUST RECALL HEARING ABOUT IT WHILE WE WERE ADMIRING THE FLOWERS ...
KYARA (CACKLE)
KYARA
KYARA
BUT ANYWAY ...
...I DON'T EVEN KNOW WHAT THIS "TUPAI" LOOKS LIKE.

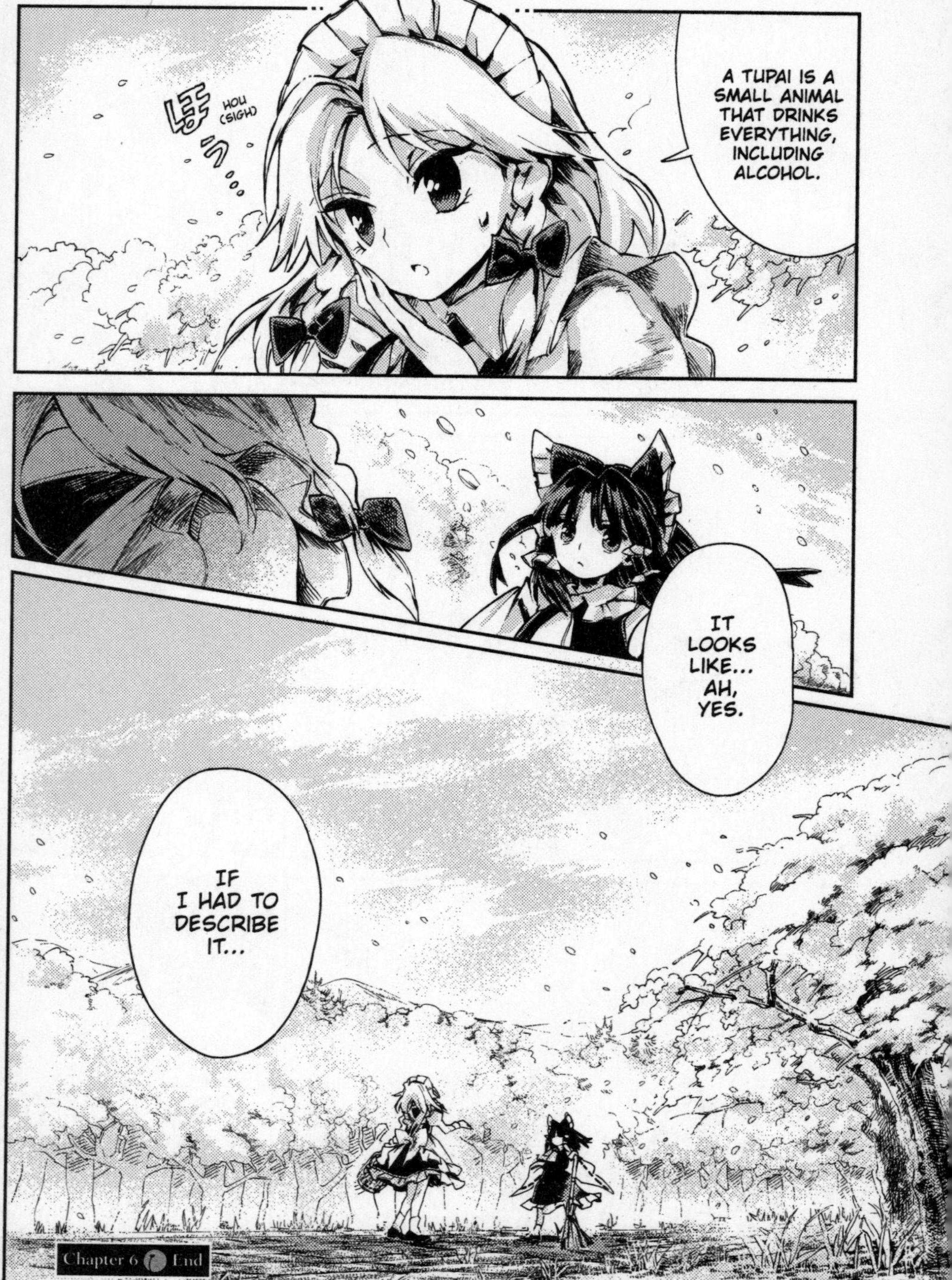
A TUPAI IS A SMALL ANIMAL THAT DRINKS EVERYTHING, INCLUDING ALCOHOL.
HOU (SIGH)
IT LOOKS LIKE... AH, YES.
IF I HAD TO DESCRIBE IT...
Chapter 6 End

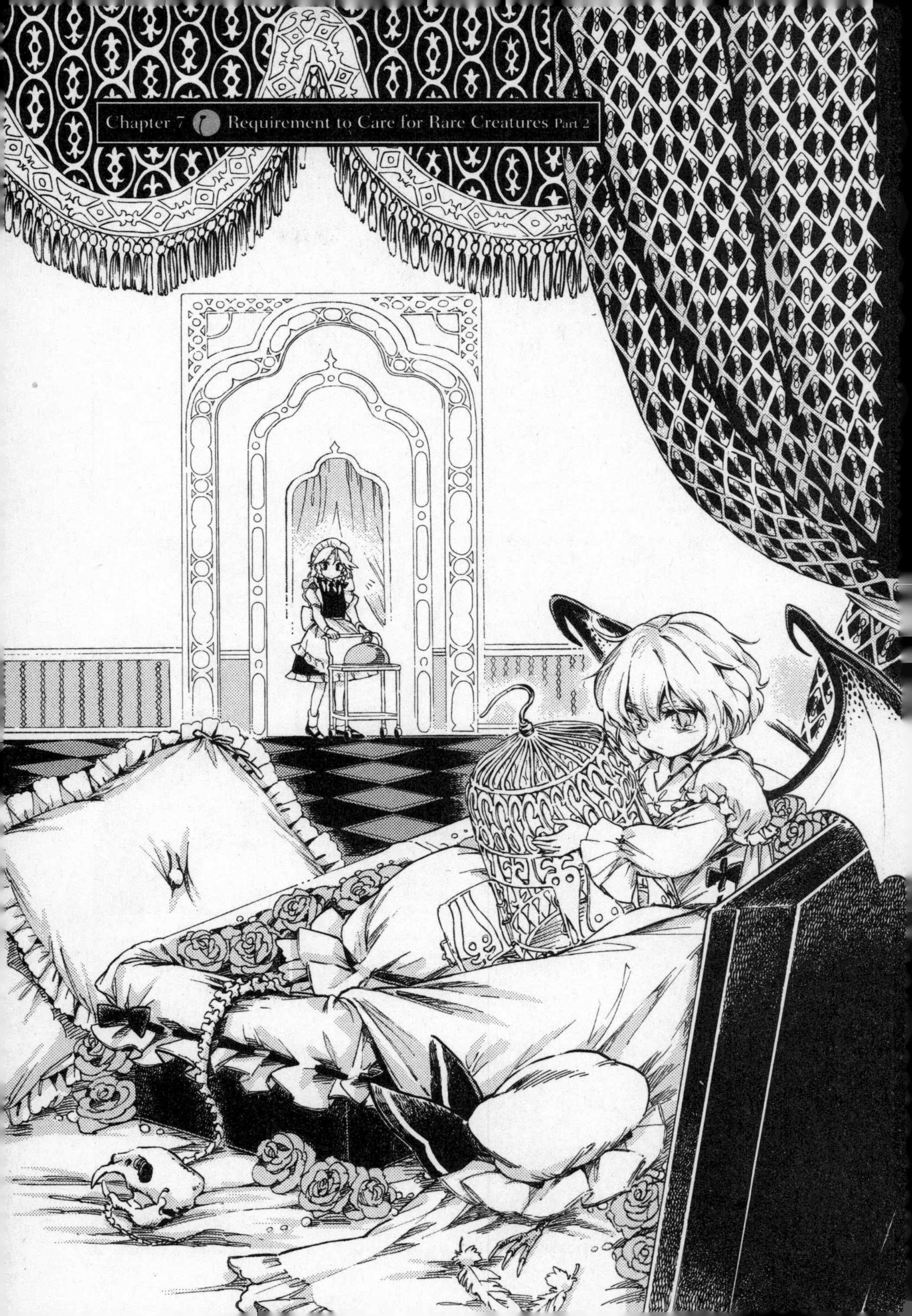
Chapter 7 Requirement to Care for Rare Creatures Part 2

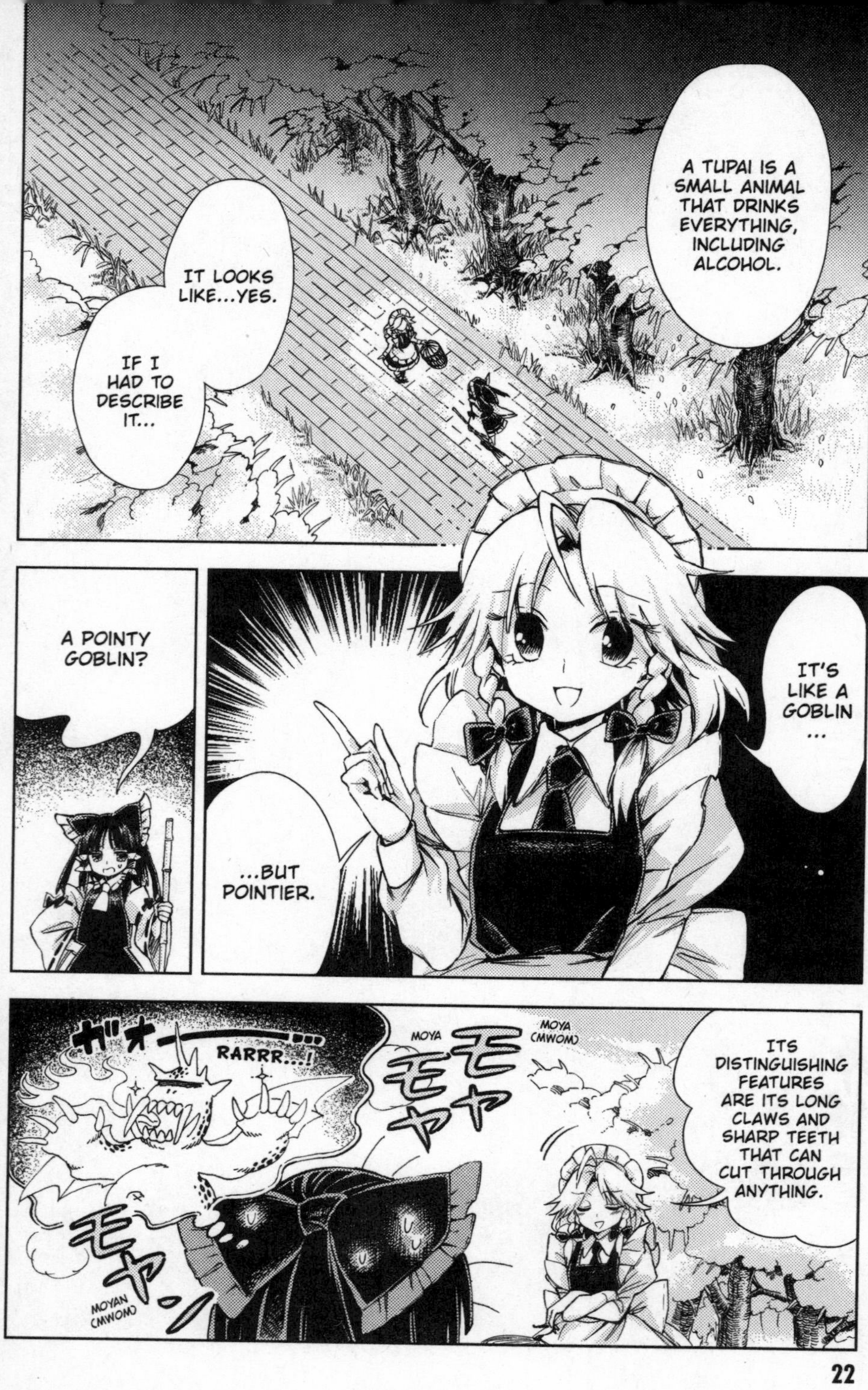
A TUPAI IS A SMALL ANIMAL THAT DRINKS EVERYTHING, INCLUDING ALCOHOL.
IT LOOKS LIKE...YES.
IF I HAD TO DESCRIBE IT...
IT'S LIKE A GOBLIN ...
...BUT POINTIER.
A POINTY GOBLIN?
ITS DISTINGUISHING FEATURES ARE ITS LONG CLAWS AND SHARP TEETH THAT CAN CUT THROUGH ANYTHING.
モヤ
MOYA (MWOM)
モヤ
MOYA
ガオー
RARRR...!
モヤン
MOYAN (MWOM)

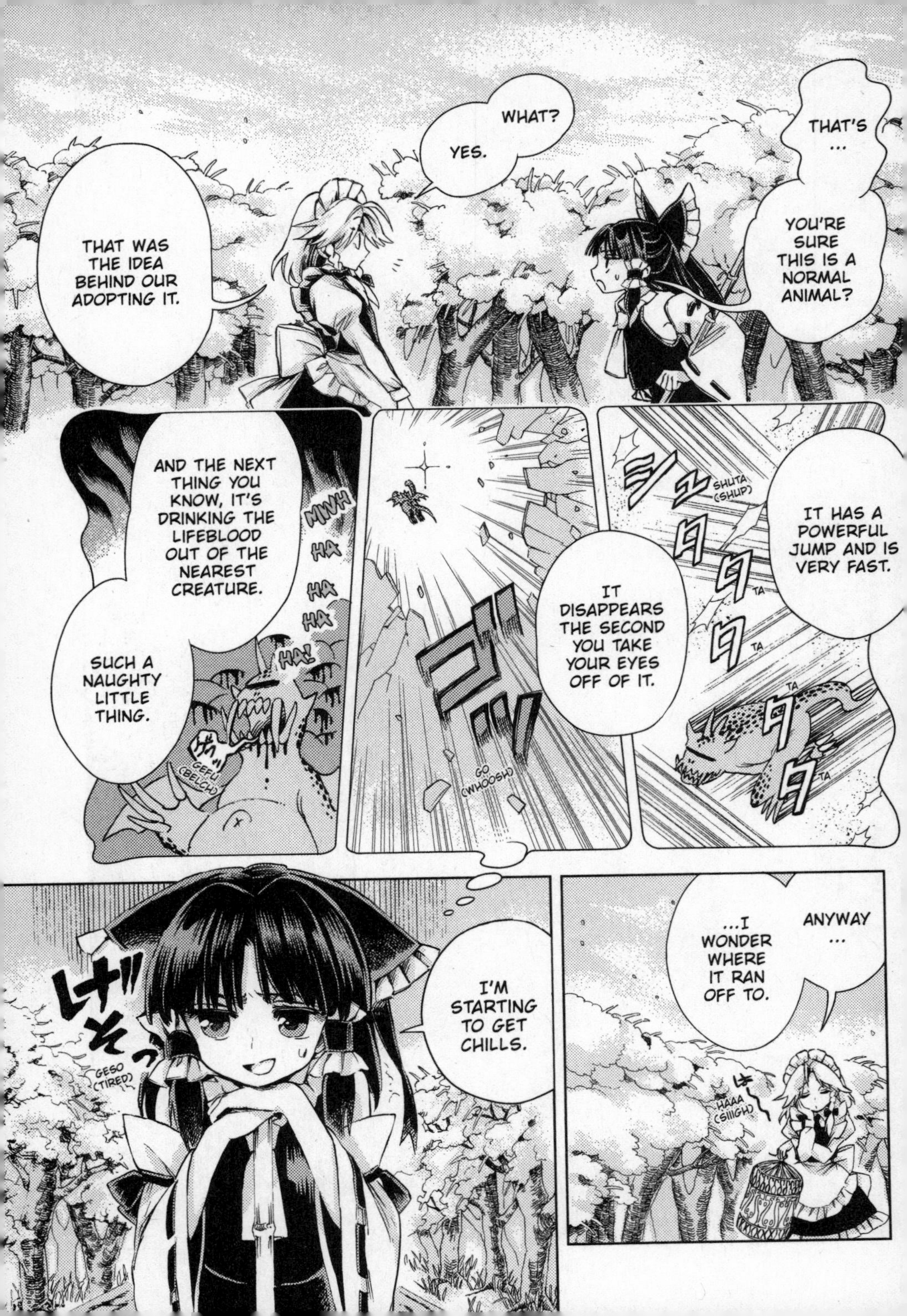
THAT'S ...
YOU'RE SURE THIS IS A NORMAL ANIMAL?
WHAT?
YES.
THAT WAS THE IDEA BEHIND OUR ADOPTING IT.
SHUTA (SHUP)
TA
TA
TA
TA
IT HAS A POWERFUL JUMP AND IS VERY FAST.
IT DISAPPEARS THE SECOND YOU TAKE YOUR EYES OFF OF IT.
GO (WHOOSH)
AND THE NEXT THING YOU KNOW, IT'S DRINKING THE LIFEBLOOD OUT OF THE NEAREST CREATURE.
MWH HA HA HA HA!
SUCH A NAUGHTY LITTLE THING.
GEFU (BELCH)
ANYWAY ...
...I WONDER WHERE IT RAN OFF TO.
HAAA (SIIIGH)
I'M STARTING TO GET CHILLS.
GESO (TIRED)

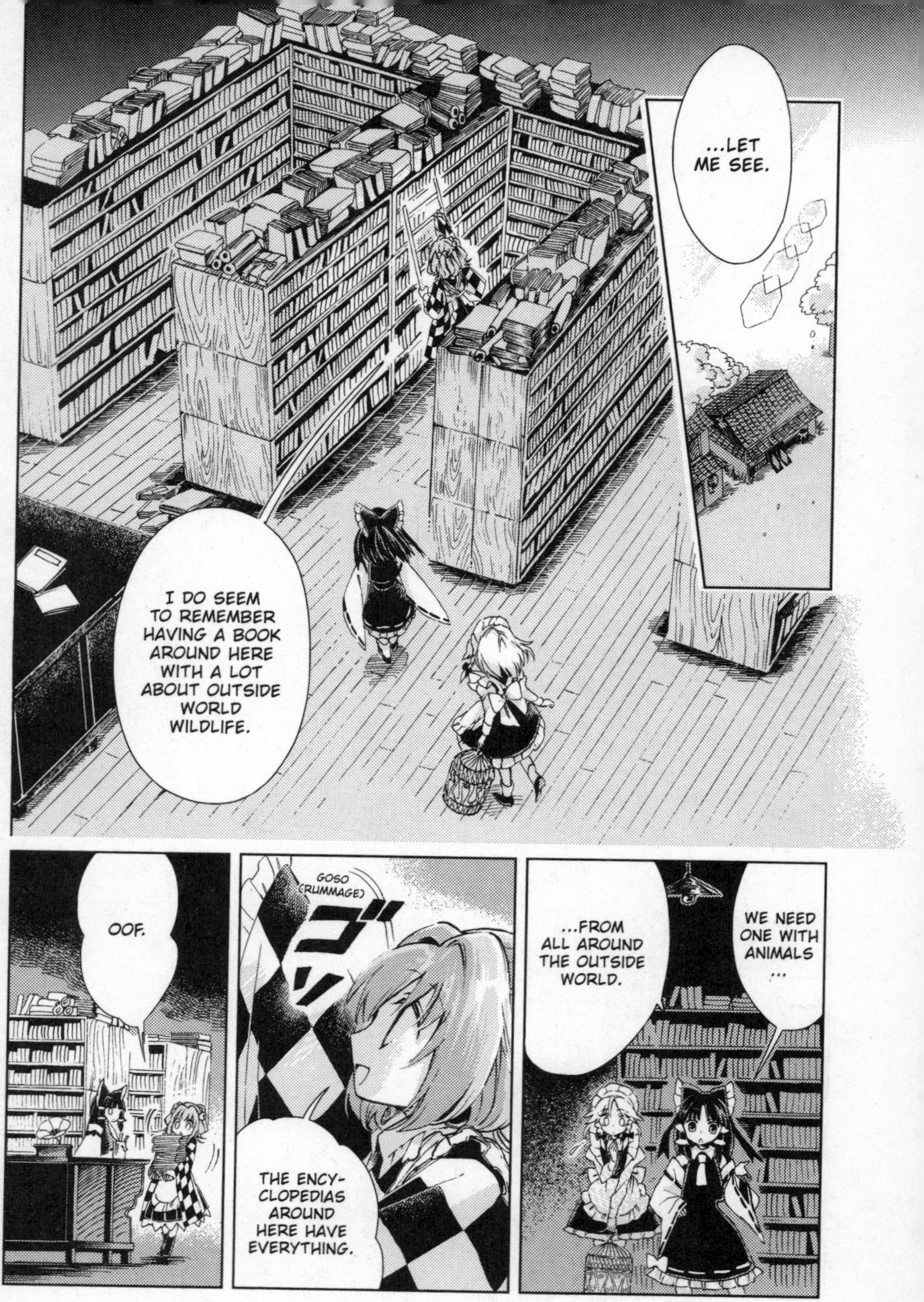
...LET ME SEE.
I DO SEEM TO REMEMBER HAVING A BOOK AROUND HERE WITH A LOT ABOUT OUTSIDE WORLD WILDLIFE.
WE NEED ONE WITH ANIMALS ...
...FROM ALL AROUND THE OUTSIDE WORLD.
GOSO (RUMMAGE)
THE ENCY-CLOPEDIAS AROUND HERE HAVE EVERYTHING.
OOF.

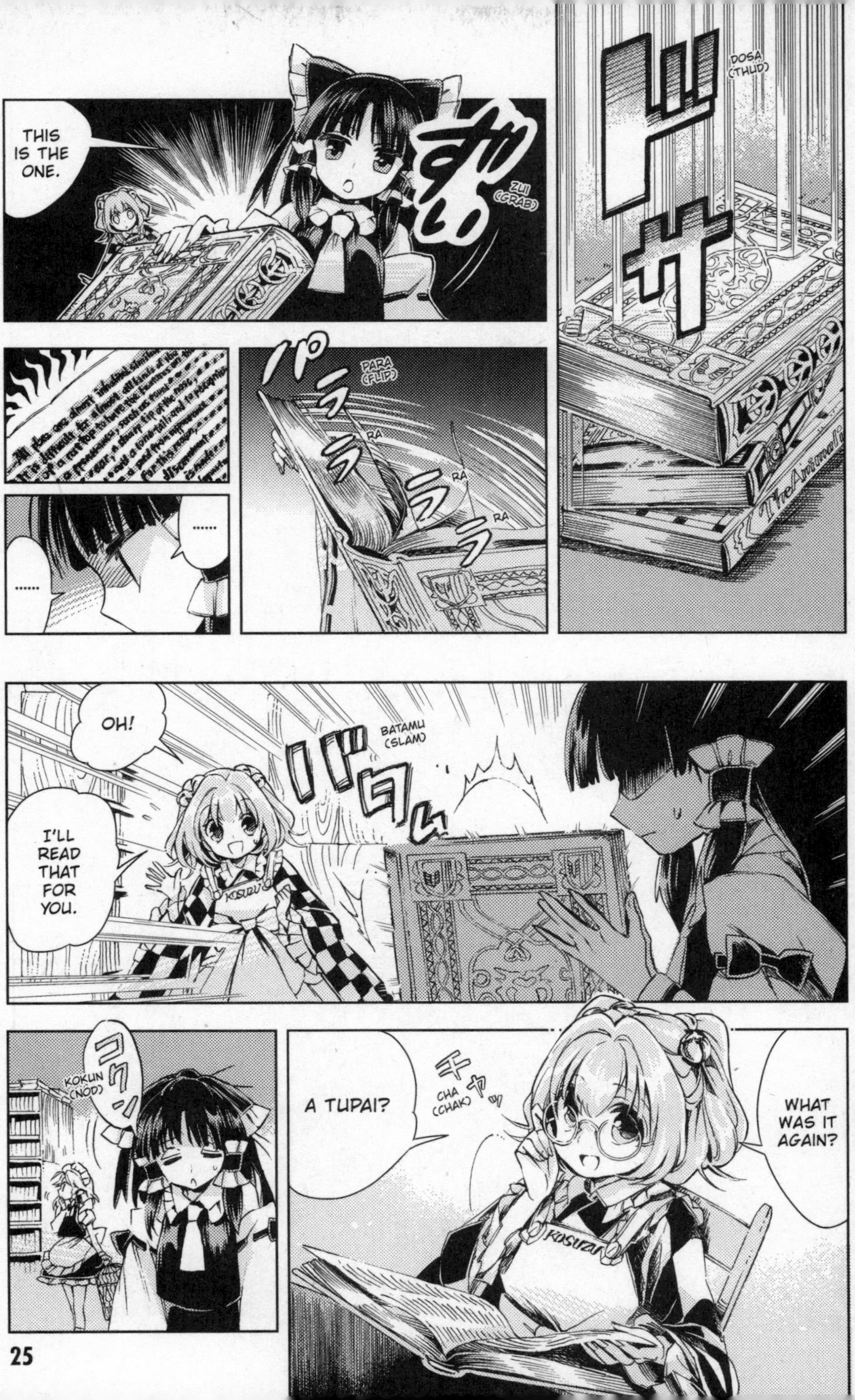
DOSA (THUD)
THIS IS THE ONE.
ZUI (GRAB)
PARA (FLIP)
RA
RA
RA
......
......
BATAMU (SLAM)
OH!
I'LL READ THAT FOR YOU.
WHAT WAS IT AGAIN?
CHA (CHAK)
A TUPAI?
KOKUN (NOD)

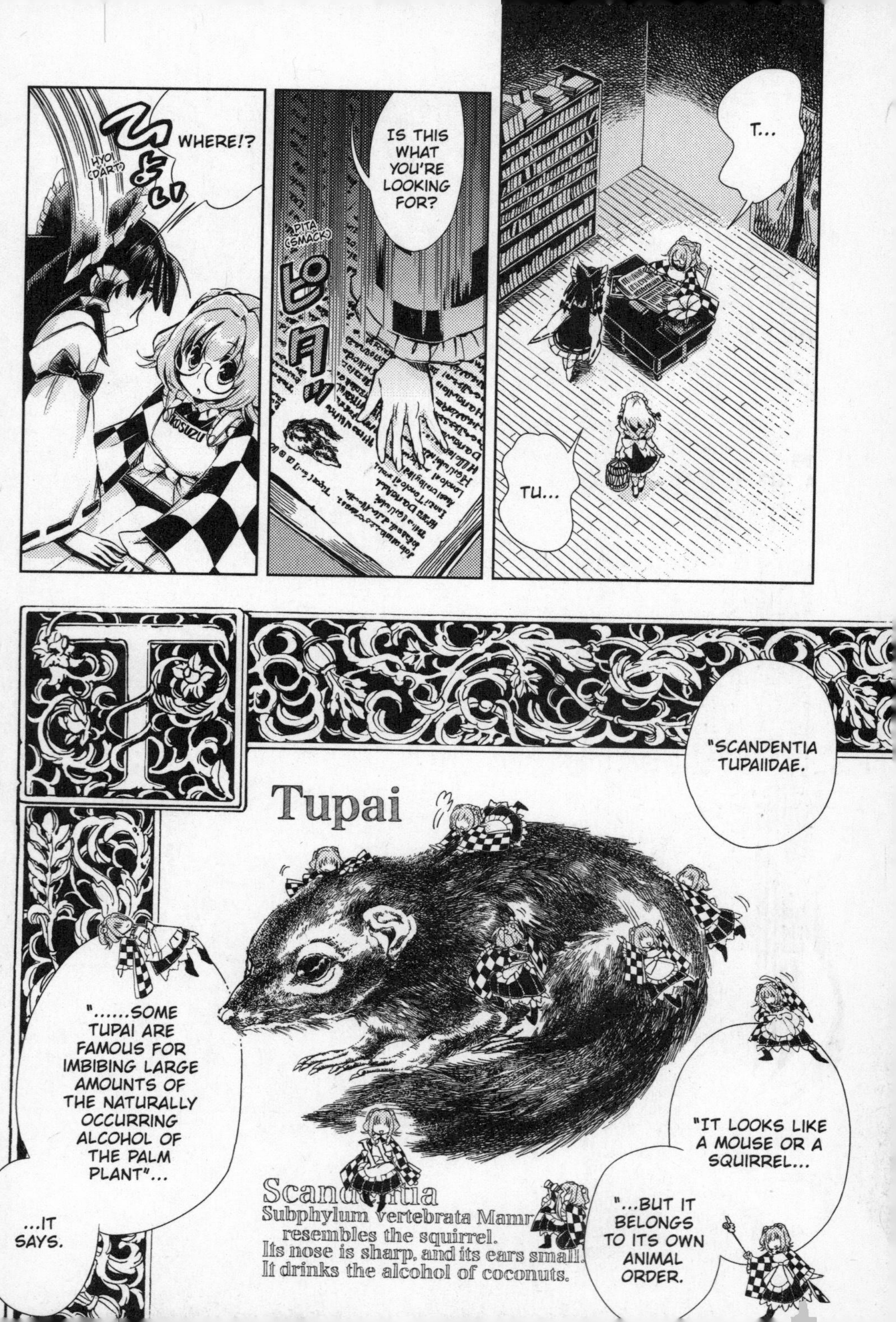
T...
TU...
IS THIS WHAT YOU'RE LOOKING FOR?
PITA (SMACK)
WHERE!?
HYOI (DART)
Tupai
"SCANDENTIA TUPAIIDAE.
"IT LOOKS LIKE A MOUSE OR A SQUIRREL...
"...BUT IT BELONGS TO ITS OWN ANIMAL ORDER.
"......SOME TUPAI ARE FAMOUS FOR IMBIBING LARGE AMOUNTS OF THE NATURALLY OCCURRING ALCOHOL OF THE PALM PLANT"...
...IT SAYS.
Subphylum vertebrata Mamr
resembles the squirrel.
Its nose is sharp, and its ears small.
It drinks the alcohol of coconuts.

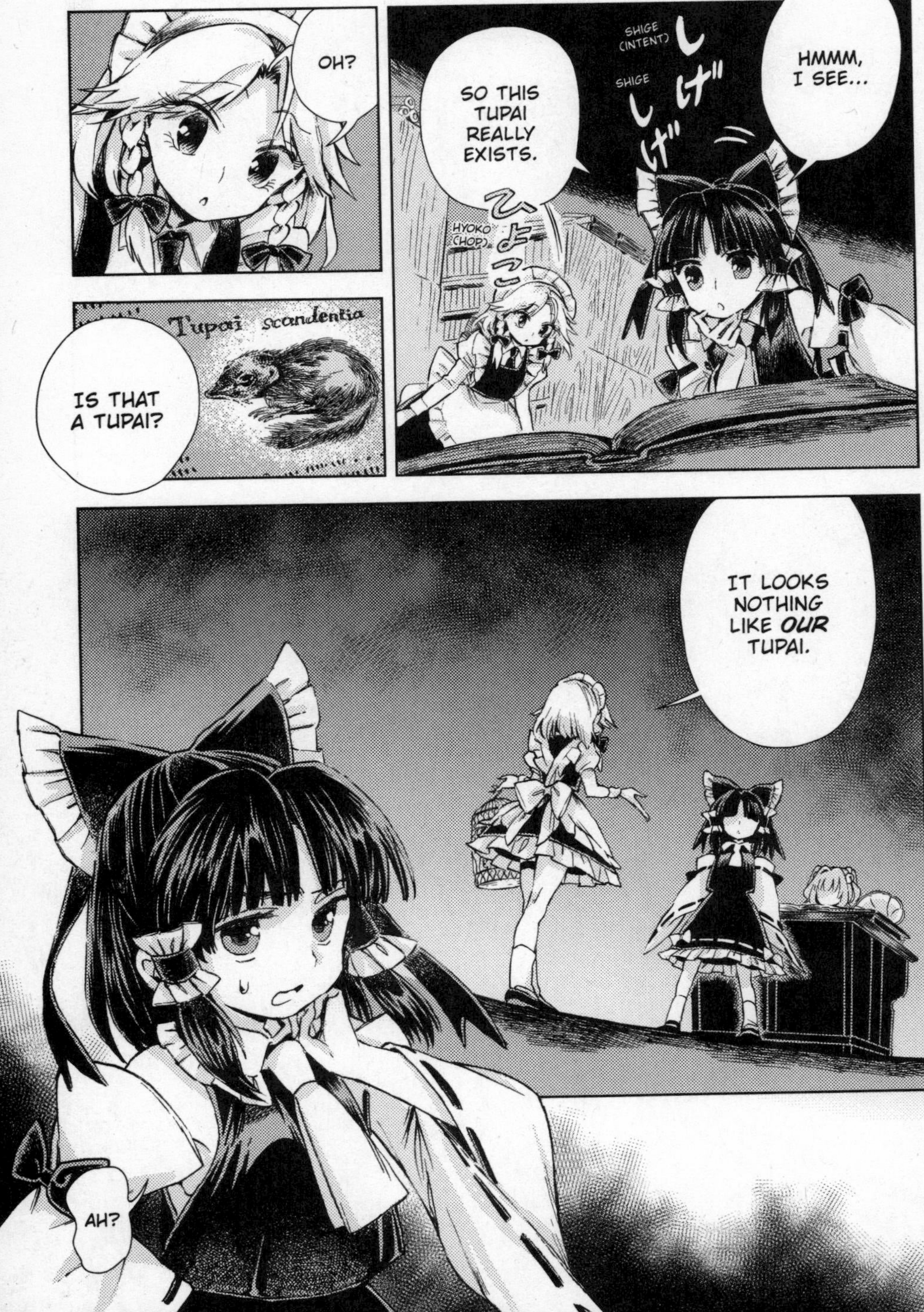

HMMM, I SEE...
SHIGE (INTENT)
SHIGE
しげしげ
SO THIS TUPAI REALLY EXISTS.
ひょこ
HYOKO (CHOP)
OH?
Tupai scandentia
IS THAT A TUPAI?
IT LOOKS NOTHING LIKE *OUR* TUPAI.
AH?

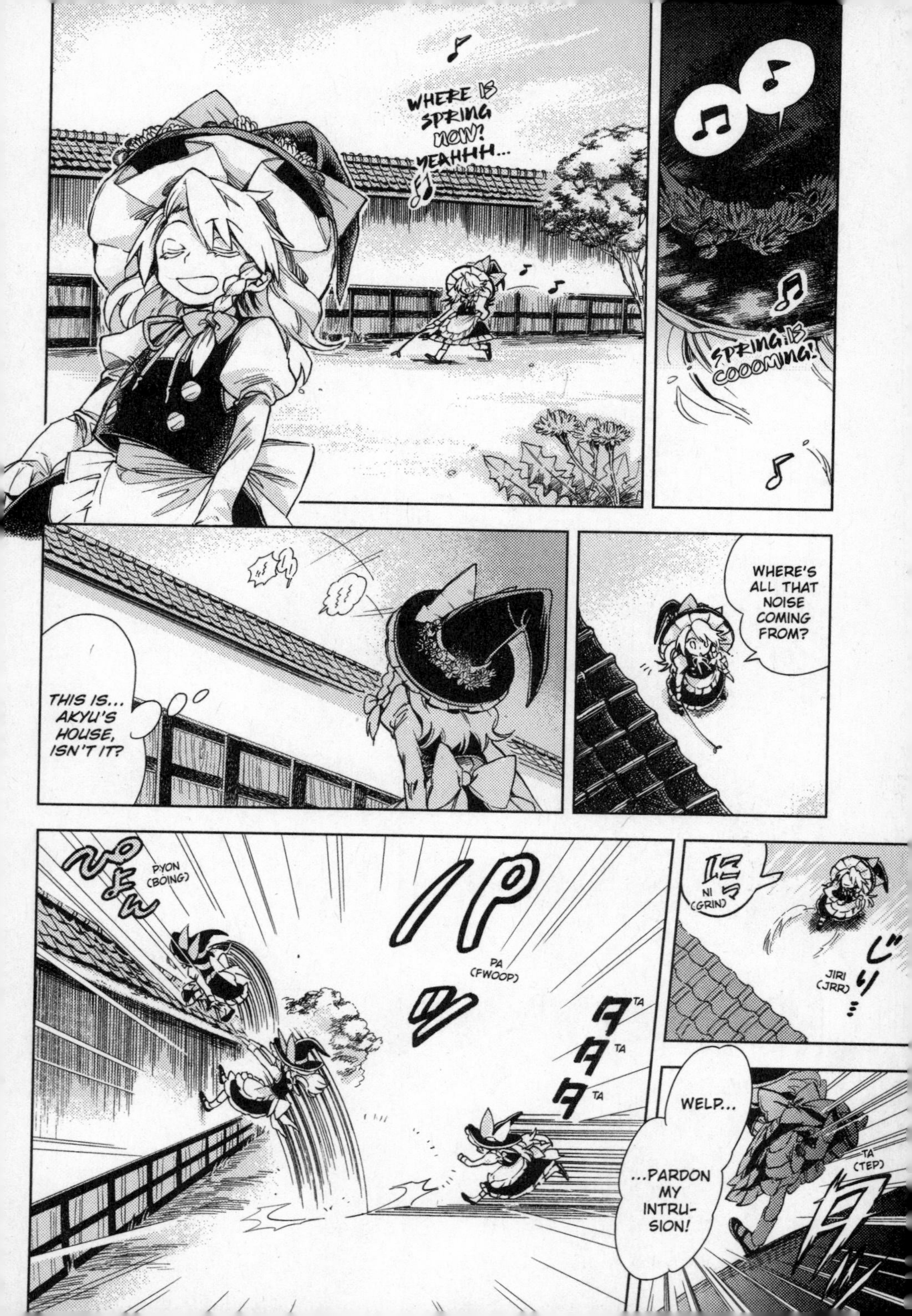

SPRING IS COOOMING!
WHERE IS SPRING NOW? YEAHHH...
WHERE'S ALL THAT NOISE COMING FROM?
THIS IS... AKYU'S HOUSE, ISN'T IT?
NI (GRIN)
JIRI (JRR)
WELP...
...PARDON MY INTRUSION!
TA (TEP)
PA (FWOOP)
PYON (BOING)
TA TA TA

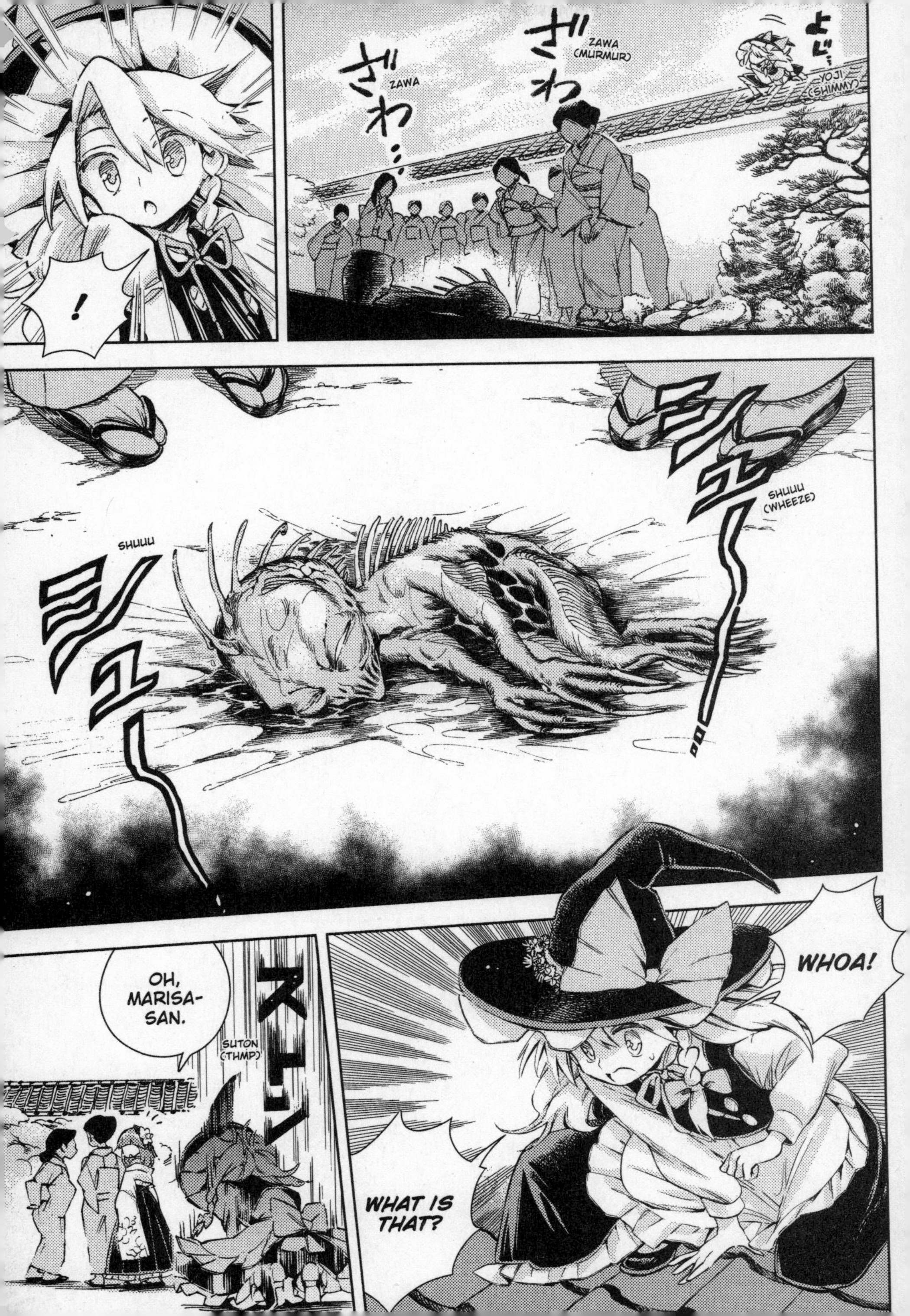
よじ
YOJI (SHIMMY)
ざわ
ZAWA (MURMUR)
ざわ…
ZAWA
!
シュー…
SHUUU (WHEEZE)
シュー
SHUUU
WHOA!
WHAT IS THAT?
ストン
SUTON (THMP)
OH, MARISA-SAN.

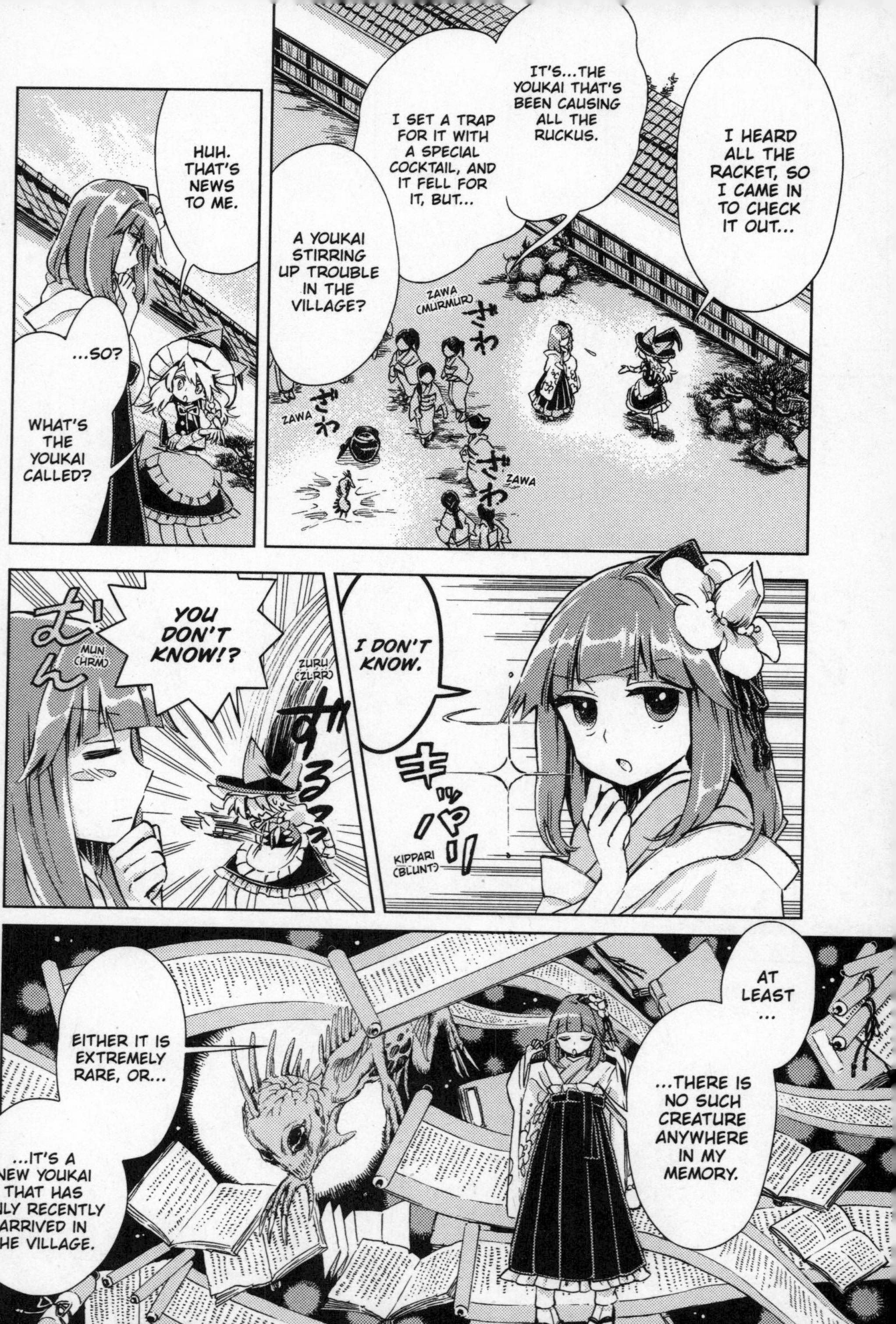
I HEARD ALL THE RACKET, SO I CAME IN TO CHECK IT OUT...
IT'S...THE YOUKAI THAT'S BEEN CAUSING ALL THE RUCKUS.
I SET A TRAP FOR IT WITH A SPECIAL COCKTAIL, AND IT FELL FOR IT, BUT...
A YOUKAI STIRRING UP TROUBLE IN THE VILLAGE?
ざわ
ZAWA (MURMUR)
ざわ
ZAWA
ざわ
ZAWA
HUH. THAT'S NEWS TO ME.
...SO?
WHAT'S THE YOUKAI CALLED?
I DON'T KNOW.
キッパリ
KIPPARI (BLUNT)
むん
MUN (HRM)
YOU DON'T KNOW!?
ずるっ
ZURU (ZLRR)
AT LEAST...
...THERE IS NO SUCH CREATURE ANYWHERE IN MY MEMORY.
EITHER IT IS EXTREMELY RARE, OR...
...IT'S A NEW YOUKAI THAT HAS ONLY RECENTLY ARRIVED IN THE VILLAGE.

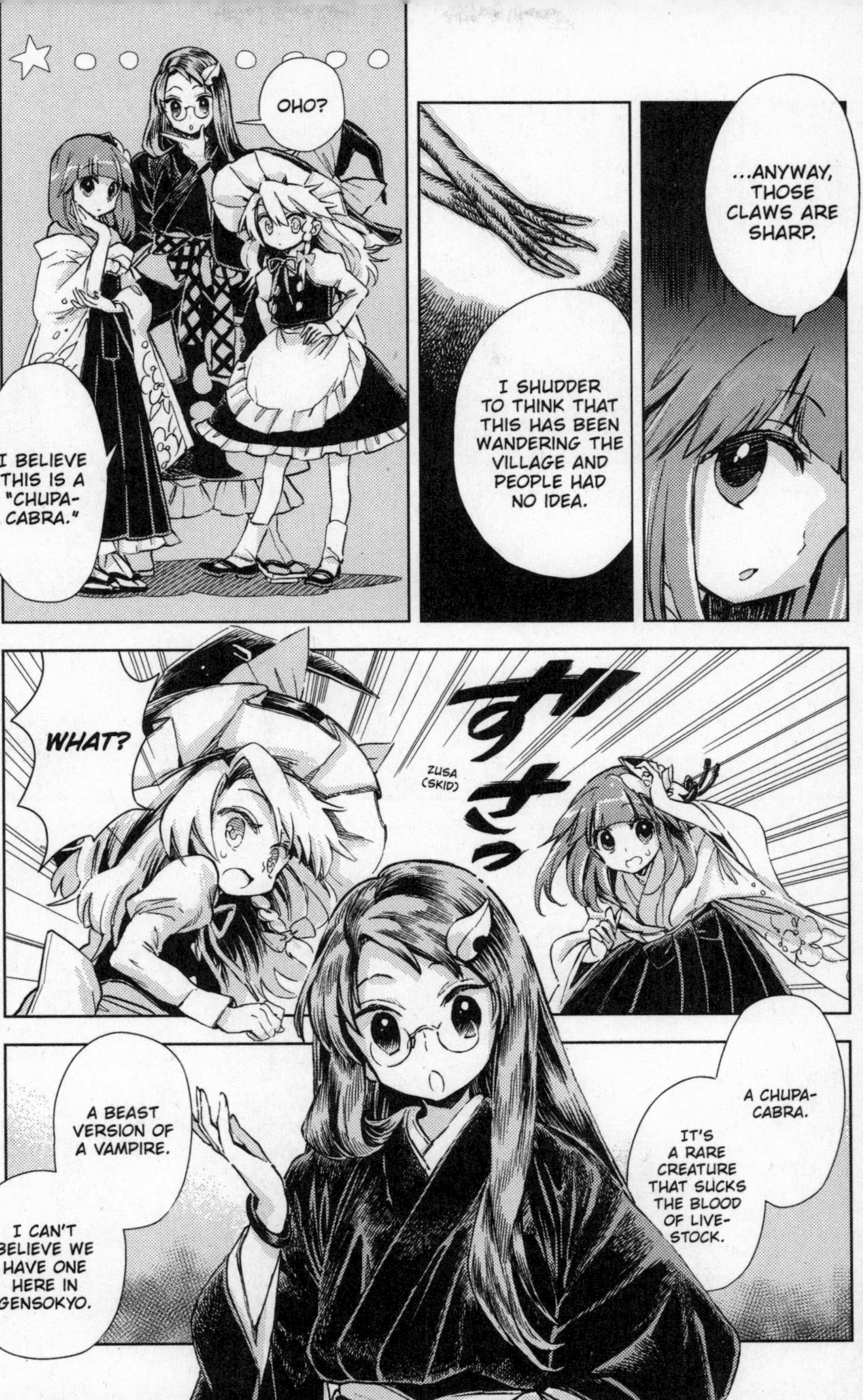
...ANYWAY, THOSE CLAWS ARE SHARP.
I SHUDDER TO THINK THAT THIS HAS BEEN WANDERING THE VILLAGE AND PEOPLE HAD NO IDEA.
OHO?
I BELIEVE THIS IS A "CHUPA-CABRA."
ずさっ
ZUSA (SKID)
WHAT?
A CHUPA-CABRA.
IT'S A RARE CREATURE THAT SUCKS THE BLOOD OF LIVE-STOCK.
A BEAST VERSION OF A VAMPIRE.
I CAN'T BELIEVE WE HAVE ONE HERE IN GENSOKYO.

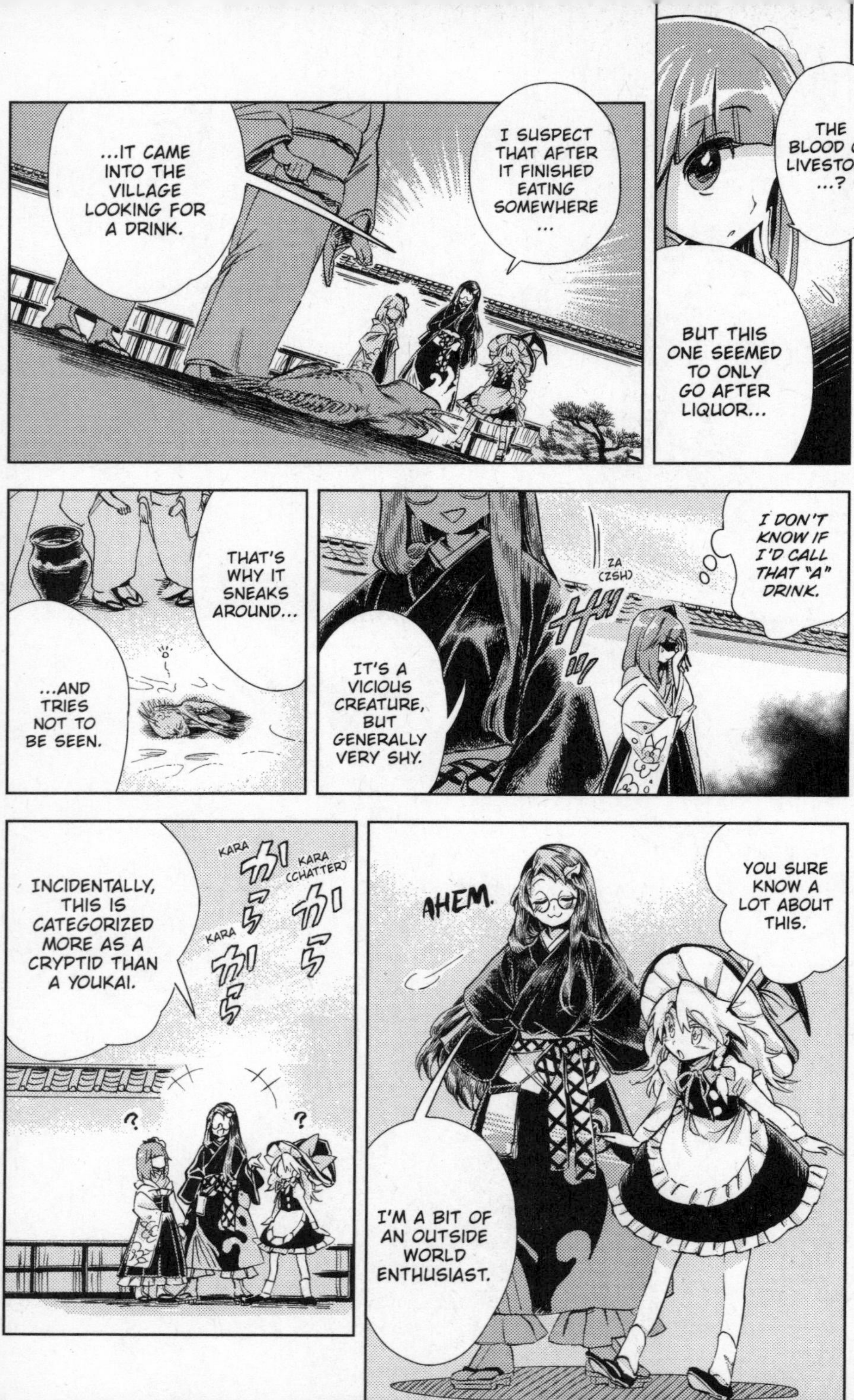
THE BLOOD OF LIVESTOCK ...?
BUT THIS ONE SEEMED TO ONLY GO AFTER LIQUOR...
I SUSPECT THAT AFTER IT FINISHED EATING SOMEWHERE ...
...IT CAME INTO THE VILLAGE LOOKING FOR A DRINK.
I DON'T KNOW IF I'D CALL THAT "A" DRINK.
ZA (ZSH)
IT'S A VICIOUS CREATURE, BUT GENERALLY VERY SHY.
THAT'S WHY IT SNEAKS AROUND...
...AND TRIES NOT TO BE SEEN.
YOU SURE KNOW A LOT ABOUT THIS.
AHEM.
I'M A BIT OF AN OUTSIDE WORLD ENTHUSIAST.
KARA KARA (CHATTER)
KARA
INCIDENTALLY, THIS IS CATEGORIZED MORE AS A CRYPTID THAN A YOUKAI.

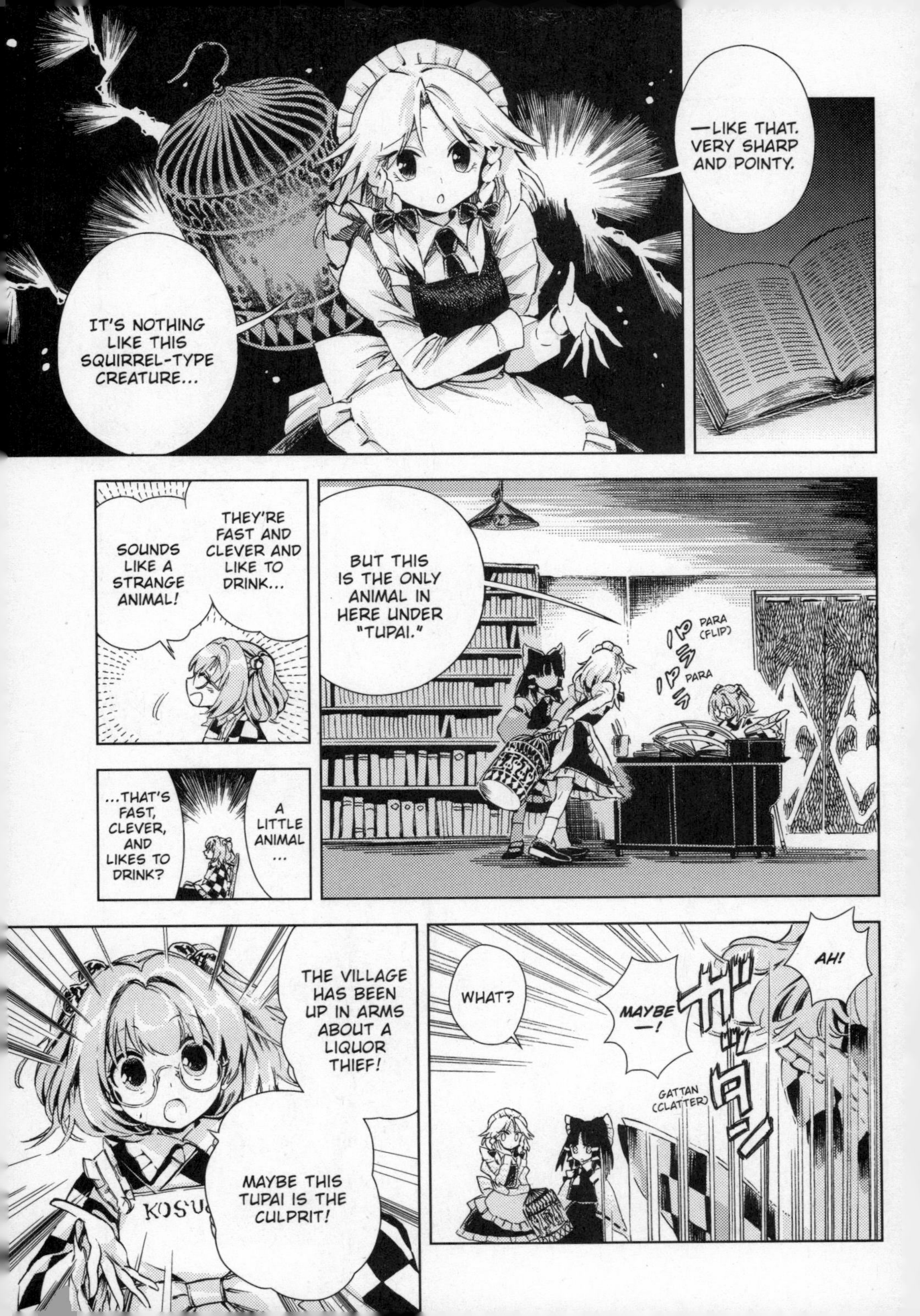
—LIKE THAT. VERY SHARP AND POINTY.
IT'S NOTHING LIKE THIS SQUIRREL-TYPE CREATURE...
BUT THIS IS THE ONLY ANIMAL IN HERE UNDER "TUPAI."
パラ PARA (FLIP)
パラ PARA
THEY'RE FAST AND CLEVER AND LIKE TO DRINK...
SOUNDS LIKE A STRANGE ANIMAL!
A LITTLE ANIMAL...
...THAT'S FAST, CLEVER, AND LIKES TO DRINK?
AH!
MAYBE—!
WHAT?
ガタッ GATTAN (CLATTER)
THE VILLAGE HAS BEEN UP IN ARMS ABOUT A LIQUOR THIEF!
MAYBE THIS TUPAI IS THE CULPRIT!
KOSU

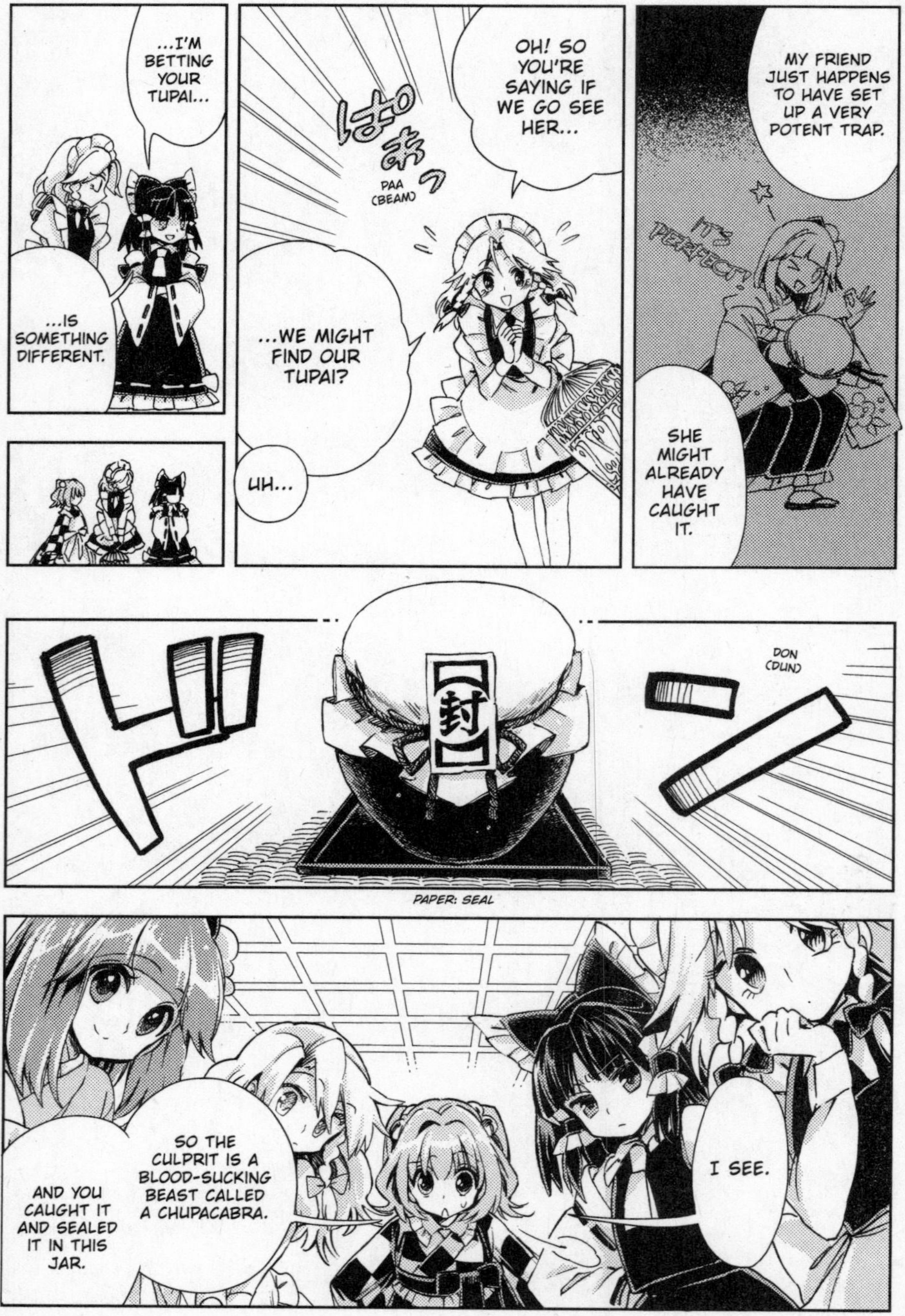
MY FRIEND JUST HAPPENS TO HAVE SET UP A VERY POTENT TRAP.
IT'S PERFECT!
SHE MIGHT ALREADY HAVE CAUGHT IT.
OH! SO YOU'RE SAYING IF WE GO SEE HER...
ぱぁっ
PAA (BEAM)
...WE MIGHT FIND OUR TUPAI?
UH...
...I'M BETTING YOUR TUPAI...
...IS SOMETHING DIFFERENT.
ドーン
DON (DUN)
封
PAPER: SEAL
I SEE.
SO THE CULPRIT IS A BLOOD-SUCKING BEAST CALLED A CHUPACABRA.
AND YOU CAUGHT IT AND SEALED IT IN THIS JAR.

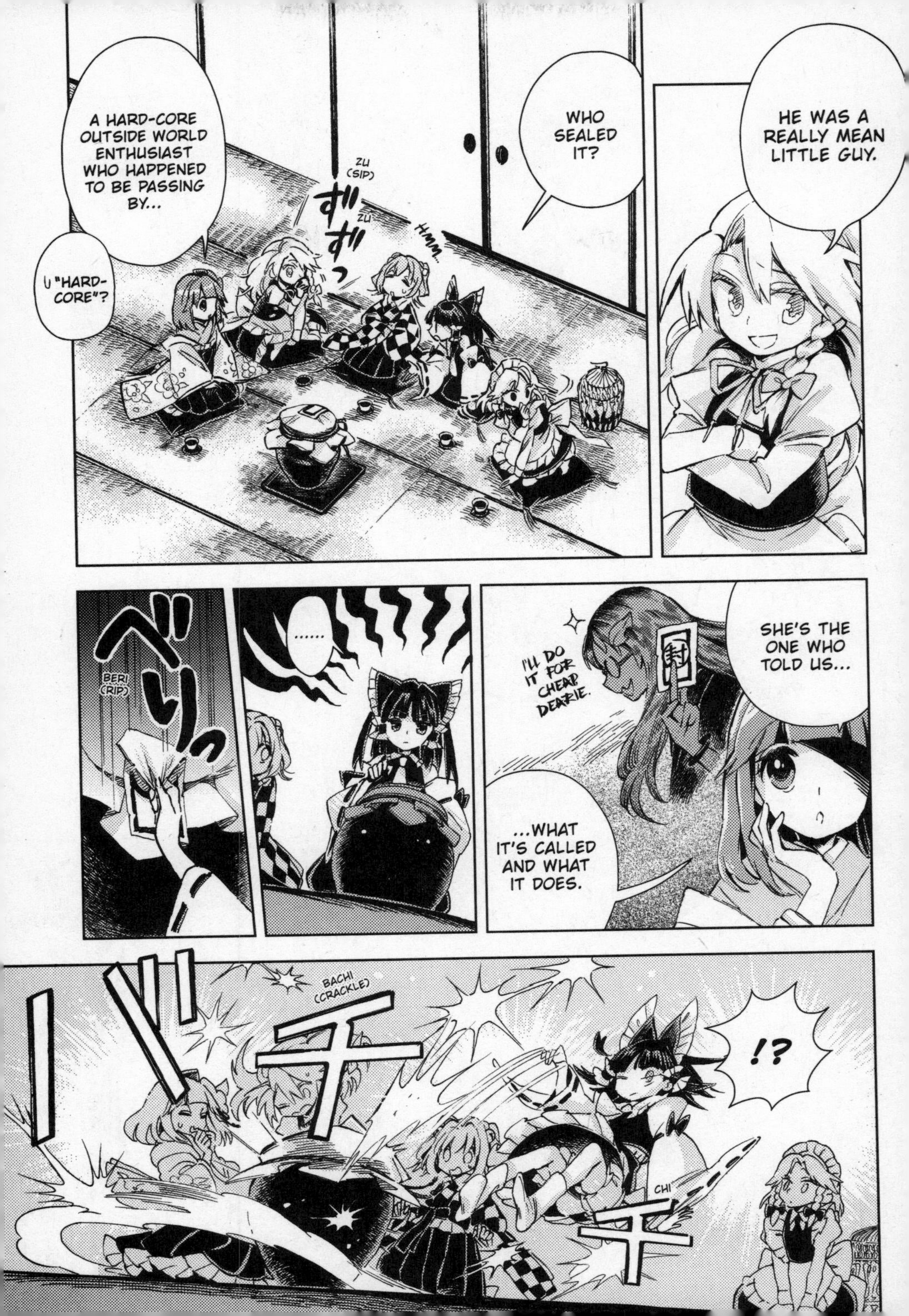
HE WAS A REALLY MEAN LITTLE GUY.
WHO SEALED IT?
ZU (SIP)
ZU
HMM...
A HARD-CORE OUTSIDE WORLD ENTHUSIAST WHO HAPPENED TO BE PASSING BY...
U "HARD-CORE"?
SHE'S THE ONE WHO TOLD US...
I'LL DO IT FOR CHEAP, DEARIE.
...WHAT IT'S CALLED AND WHAT IT DOES.
......
BERI (RIP)
!?
BACHI (CRACKLE)
CHI

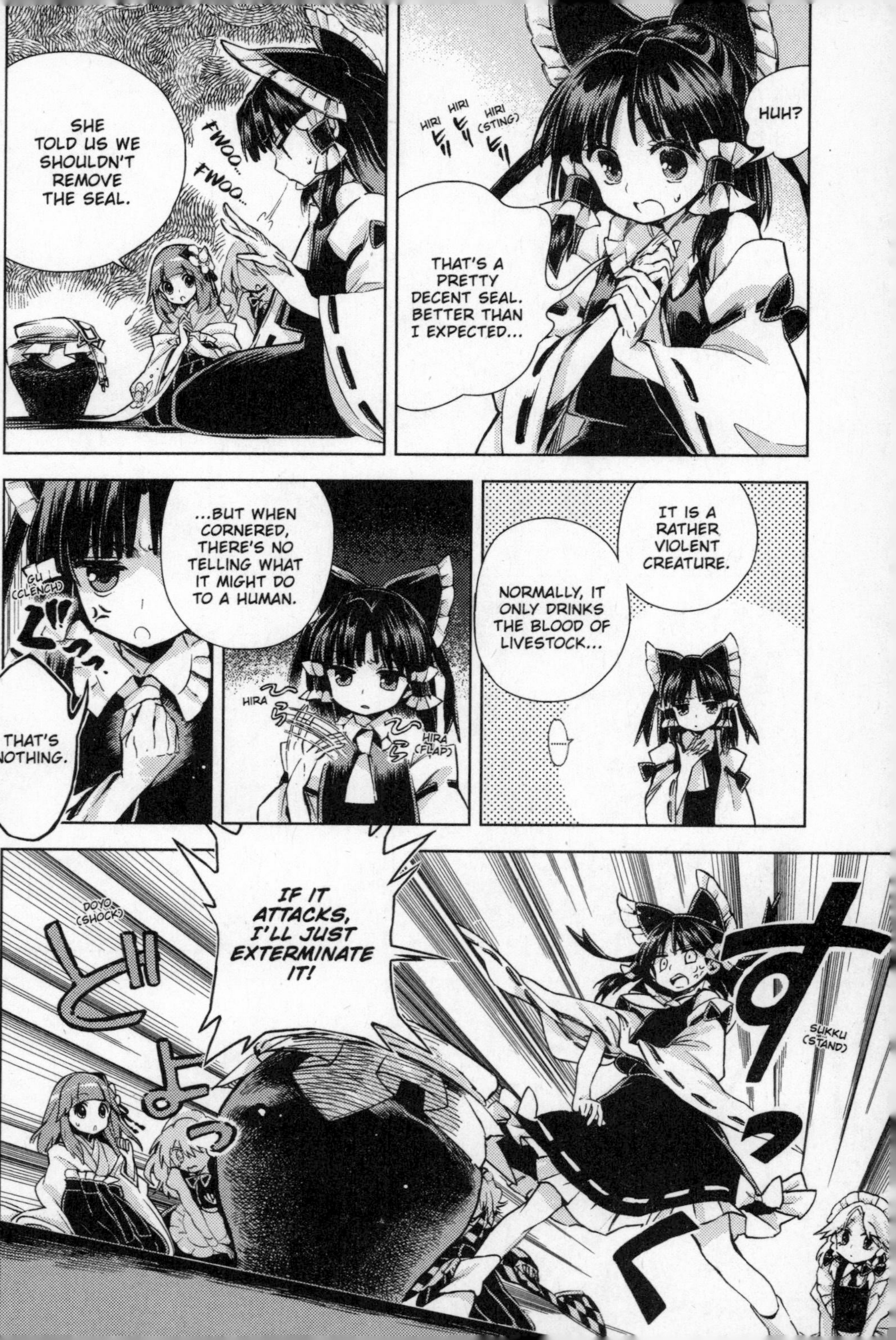
HUH?
HIRI HIRI HIRI (STING)
THAT'S A PRETTY DECENT SEAL. BETTER THAN I EXPECTED...
FWOO... FWOO...
SHE TOLD US WE SHOULDN'T REMOVE THE SEAL.
IT IS A RATHER VIOLENT CREATURE.
NORMALLY, IT ONLY DRINKS THE BLOOD OF LIVESTOCK...
......
...BUT WHEN CORNERED, THERE'S NO TELLING WHAT IT MIGHT DO TO A HUMAN.
HIRA HIRA (FLAP)
GU (CLENCH)
THAT'S NOTHING.
SUKKU (STAND)
IF IT ATTACKS, I'LL JUST EXTERMINATE IT!
DOYO (SHOCK)

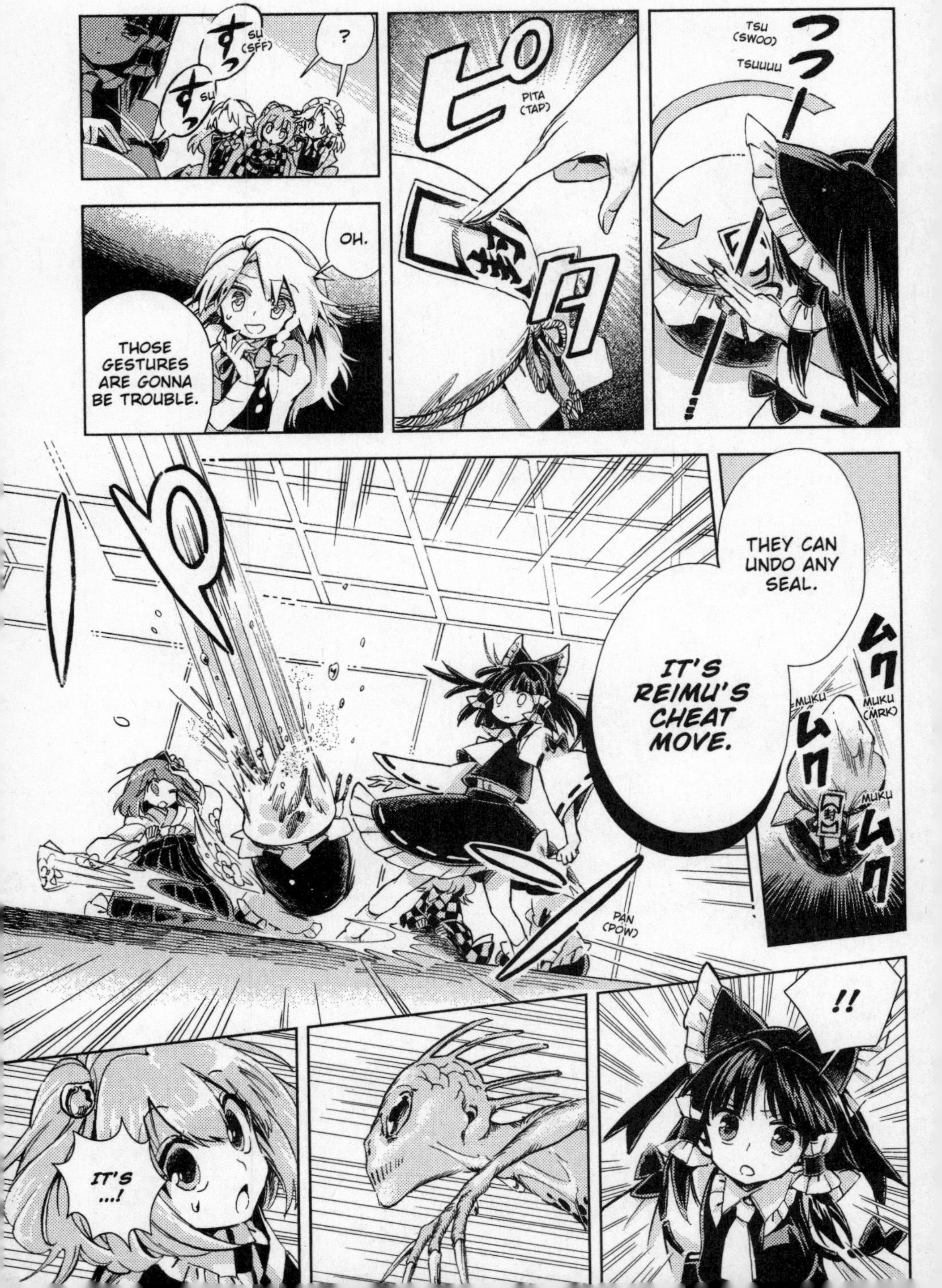
TSU (SWOO)
TSUUUU
PITA (TAP)
SU (SFF)
SU
?
OH.
THOSE GESTURES ARE GONNA BE TROUBLE.
MUKU (MRK)
MUKU
MUKU
THEY CAN UNDO ANY SEAL.
IT'S REIMU'S CHEAT MOVE.
PAN (POW)
!!
IT'S ...!

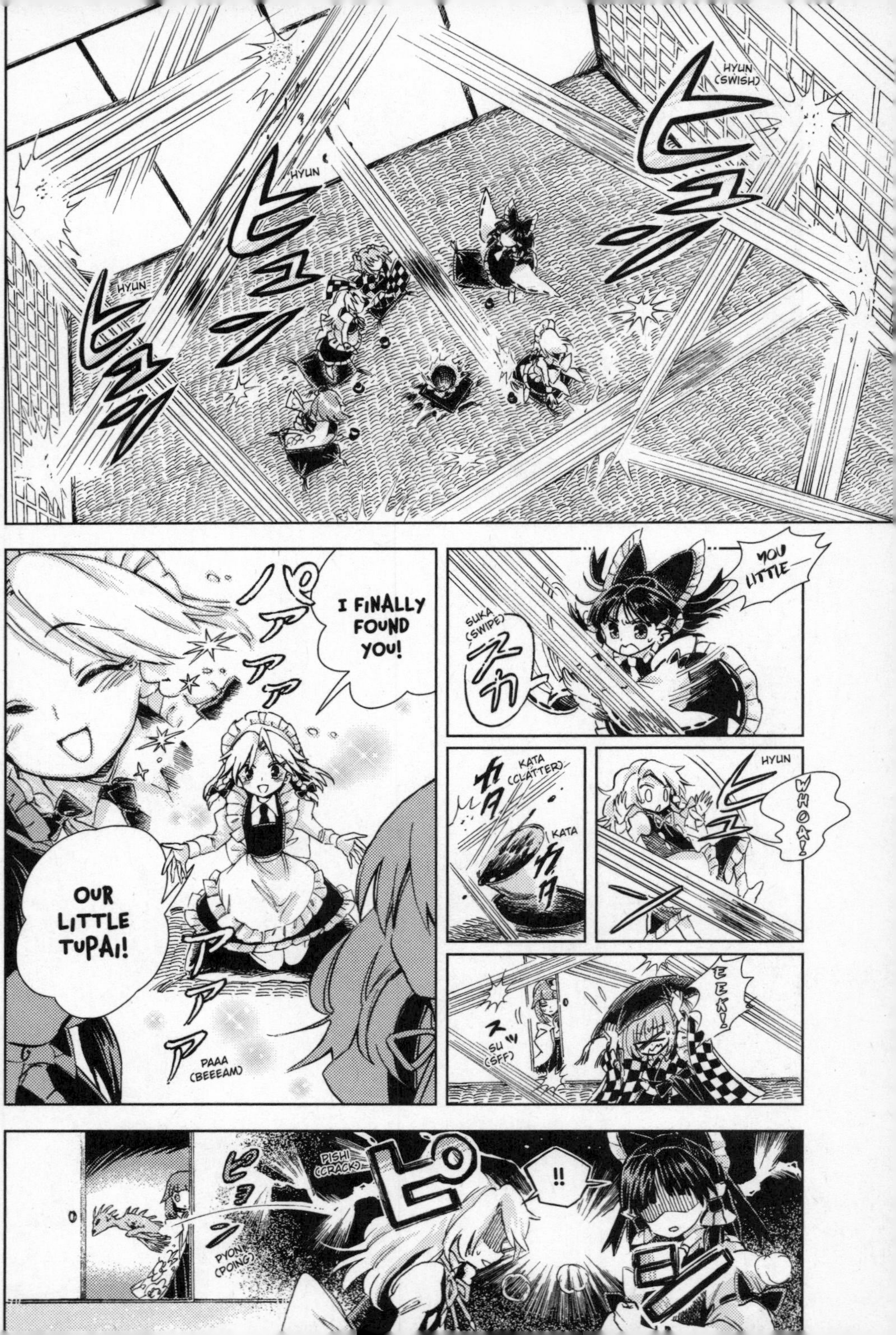
HYUN (SWISH)
HYUN
HYUN
YOU LITTLE—
SUKA (SWIPE)
HYUN
WHOA!
KATA (CLATTER)
KATA
EEEK!
SU (SFF)
I FINALLY FOUND YOU!
OUR LITTLE TUPAI!
PAAA (BEEEAM)
!!
PISHI (CRACK)
PYON (POING)

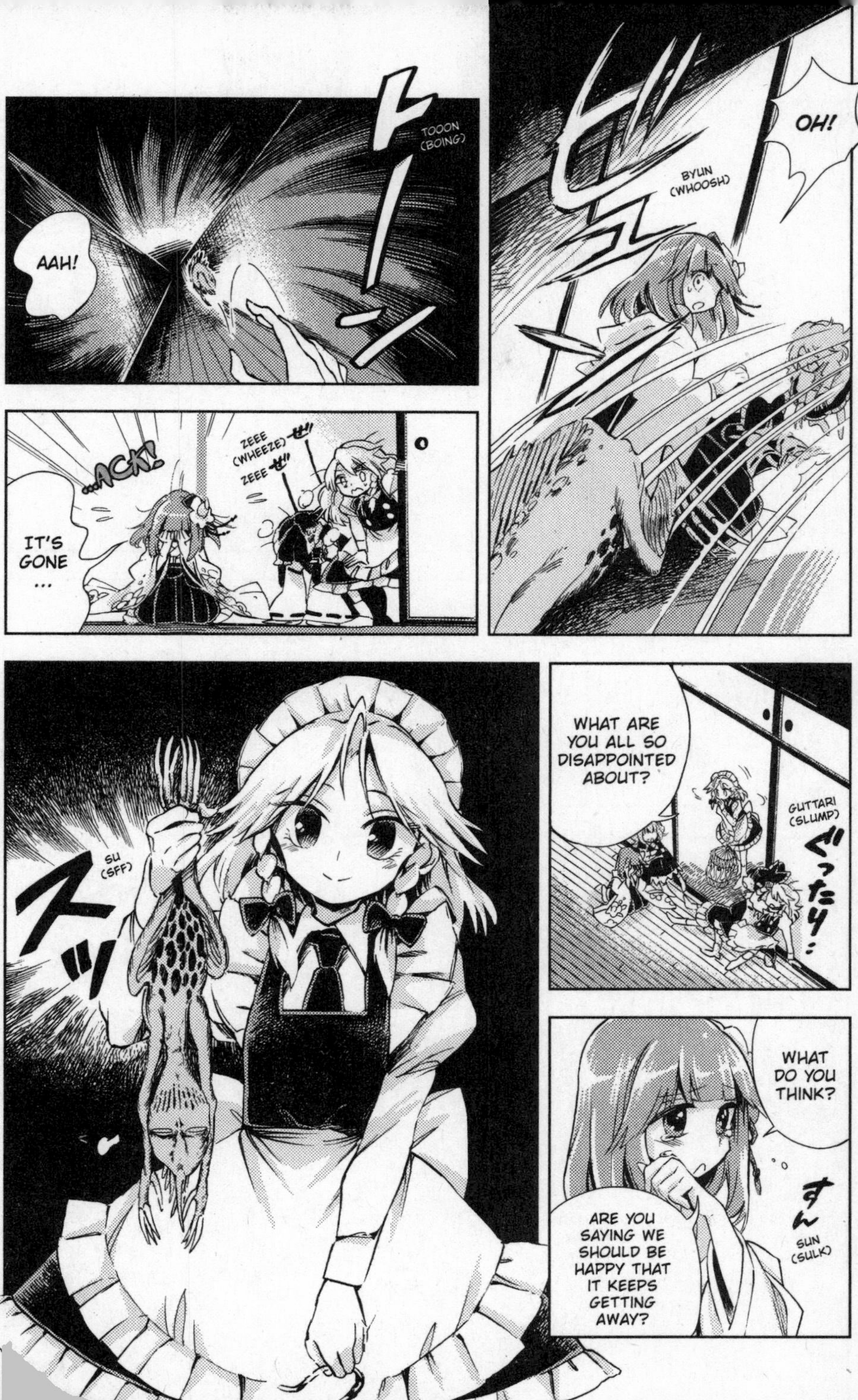
OH!
BYUN (WHOOSH)
TOOON (BOING)
AAH!
...ACK!
ZEEE (WHEEZE)
ZEEE
IT'S GONE ...
WHAT ARE YOU ALL SO DISAPPOINTED ABOUT?
GUTTARI (SLUMP)
ぐったり
WHAT DO YOU THINK?
ARE YOU SAYING WE SHOULD BE HAPPY THAT IT KEEPS GETTING AWAY?
すん
SUN (SULK)
SU (SFF)

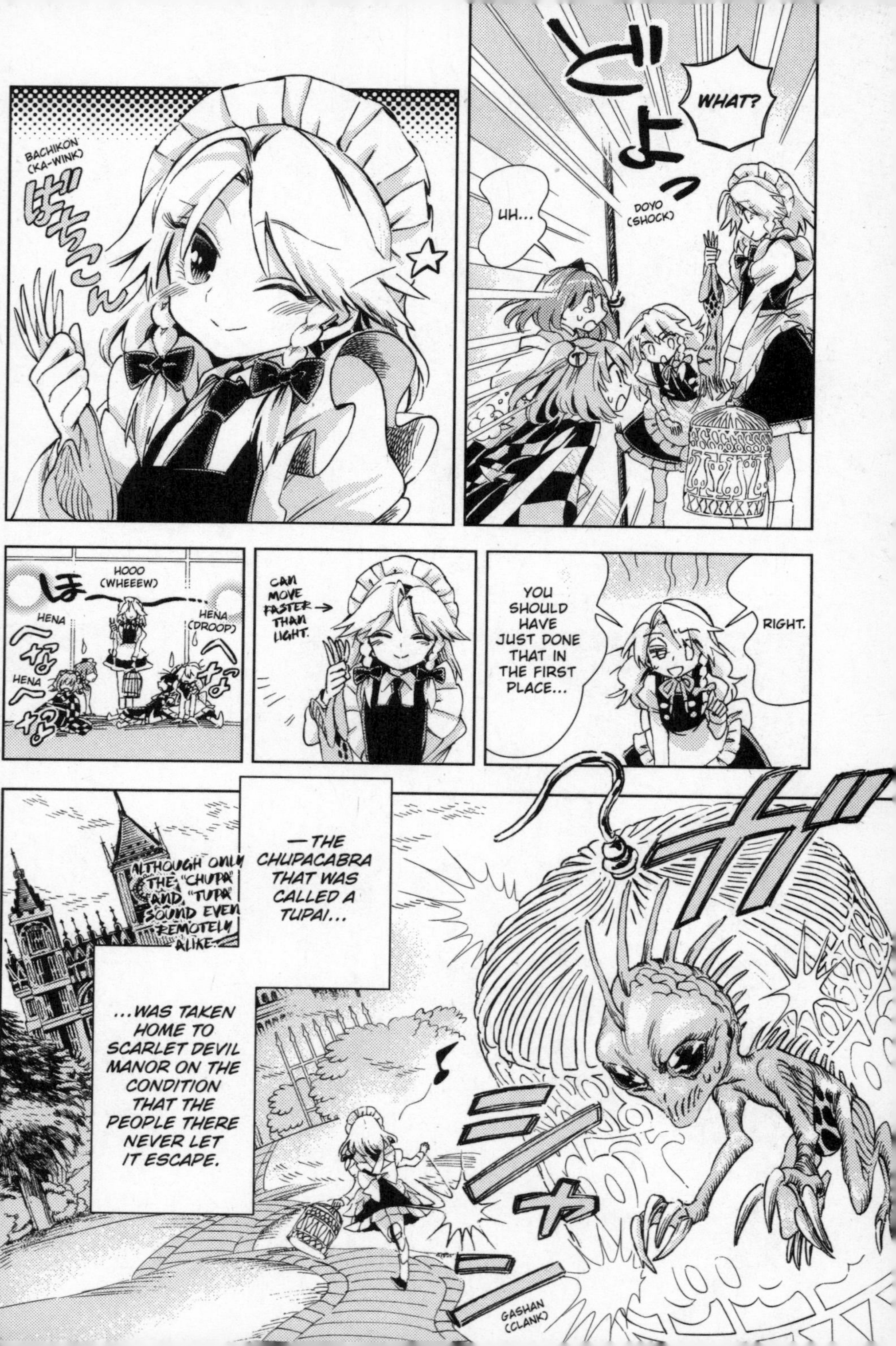

どよっ
WHAT?
DOYO (SHOCK)
UH...
ばちこん
BACHIKON (KA-WINK)
YOU SHOULD HAVE JUST DONE THAT IN THE FIRST PLACE...
RIGHT.
CAN MOVE FASTER THAN LIGHT.
ほー
HOOO (WHEEEW)
へな
HENA (DROOP)
へな
HENA
へな
HENA
—THE CHUPACABRA THAT WAS CALLED A TUPAI...
ALTHOUGH ONLY THE "CHUPA" AND "TUPA" SOUND EVEN REMOTELY ALIKE.
...WAS TAKEN HOME TO SCARLET DEVIL MANOR ON THE CONDITION THAT THE PEOPLE THERE NEVER LET IT ESCAPE.
GASHAN (CLANK)

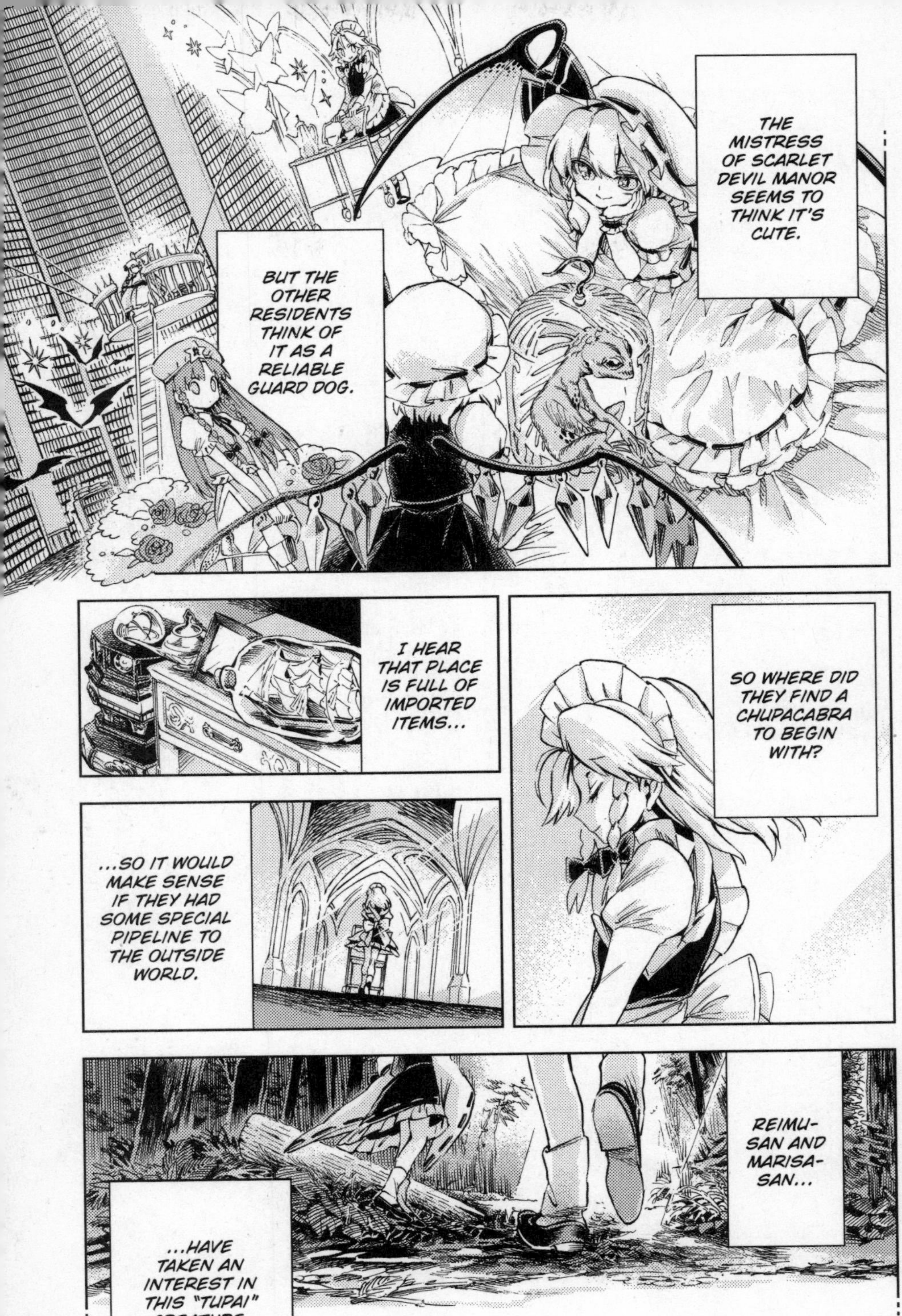
THE MISTRESS OF SCARLET DEVIL MANOR SEEMS TO THINK IT'S CUTE.
BUT THE OTHER RESIDENTS THINK OF IT AS A RELIABLE GUARD DOG.
SO WHERE DID THEY FIND A CHUPACABRA TO BEGIN WITH?
I HEAR THAT PLACE IS FULL OF IMPORTED ITEMS...
...SO IT WOULD MAKE SENSE IF THEY HAD SOME SPECIAL PIPELINE TO THE OUTSIDE WORLD.
REIMU-SAN AND MARISA-SAN...
...HAVE TAKEN AN INTEREST IN THIS "TUPAI" CREATURE.

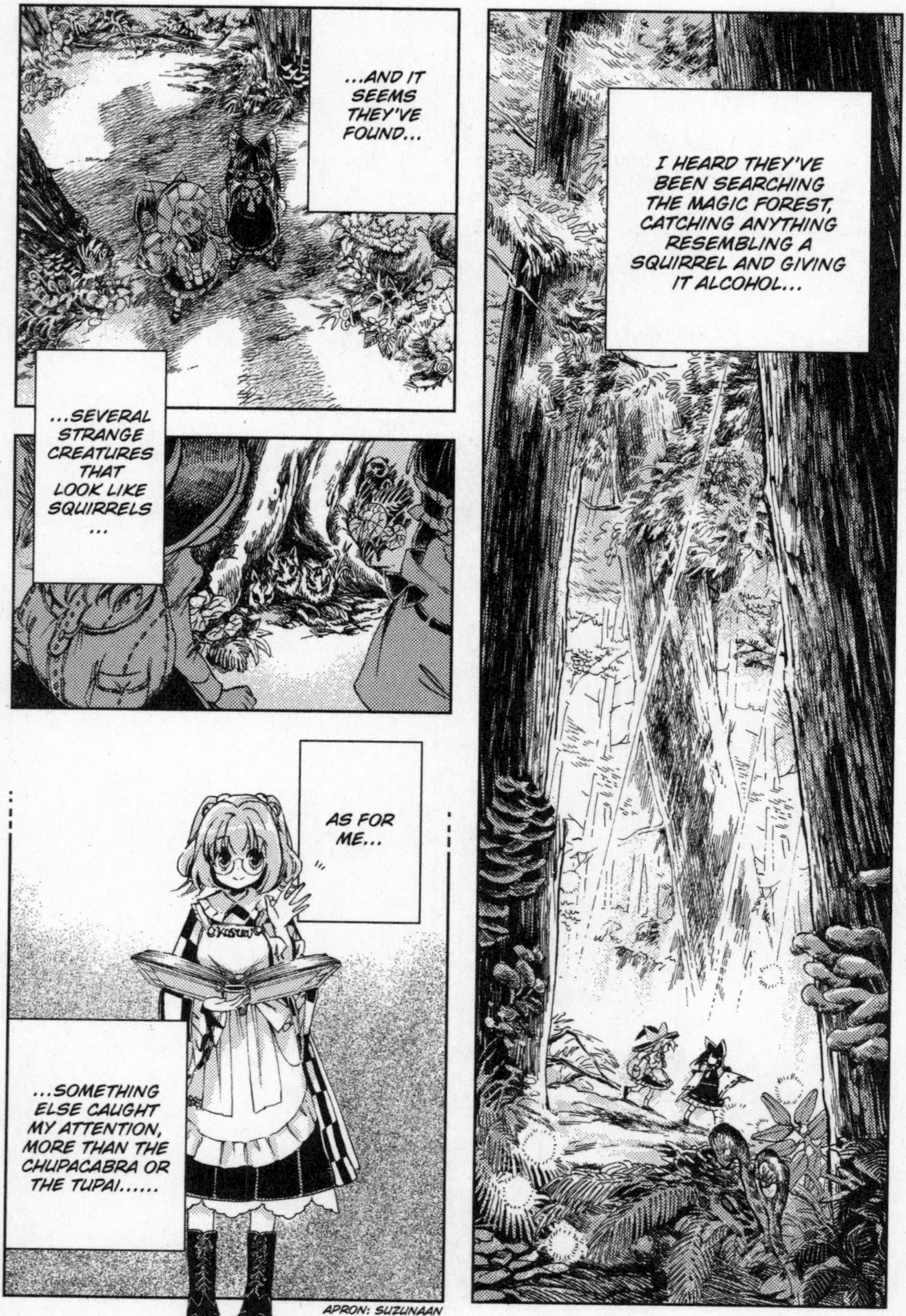
I HEARD THEY'VE BEEN SEARCHING THE MAGIC FOREST, CATCHING ANYTHING RESEMBLING A SQUIRREL AND GIVING IT ALCOHOL...
...AND IT SEEMS THEY'VE FOUND...
...SEVERAL STRANGE CREATURES THAT LOOK LIKE SQUIRRELS ...
AS FOR ME...
...SOMETHING ELSE CAUGHT MY ATTENTION, MORE THAN THE CHUPACABRA OR THE TUPAI......
APRON: SUZUNAAN

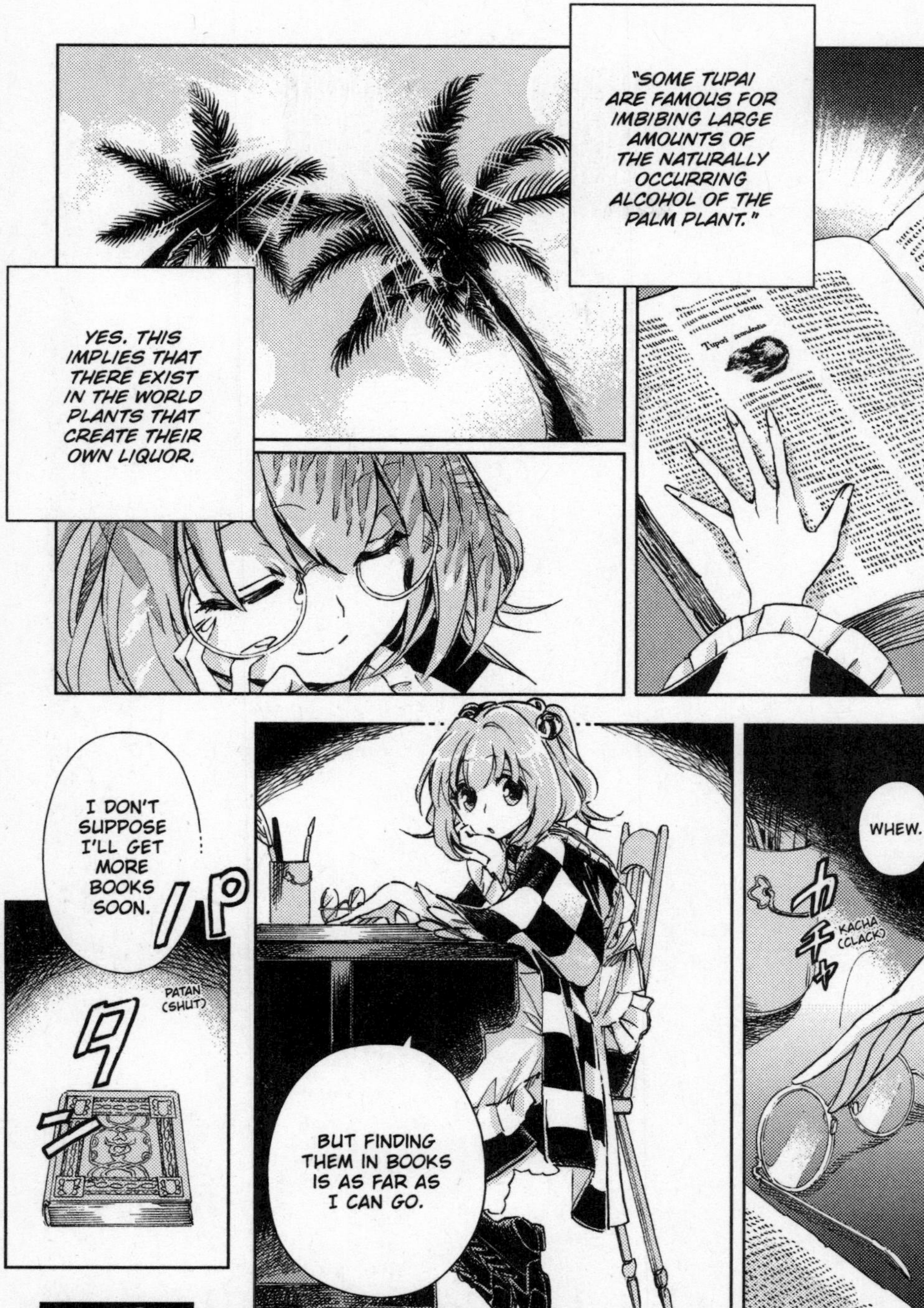
"SOME TUPAI ARE FAMOUS FOR IMBIBING LARGE AMOUNTS OF THE NATURALLY OCCURRING ALCOHOL OF THE PALM PLANT."
YES. THIS IMPLIES THAT THERE EXIST IN THE WORLD PLANTS THAT CREATE THEIR OWN LIQUOR.
WHEW.
KACHA (CLACK)
I DON'T SUPPOSE I'LL GET MORE BOOKS SOON.
BUT FINDING THEM IN BOOKS IS AS FAR AS I CAN GO.
PATAN (SHUT)

Chapter 7 End

Forbidden Scrollery

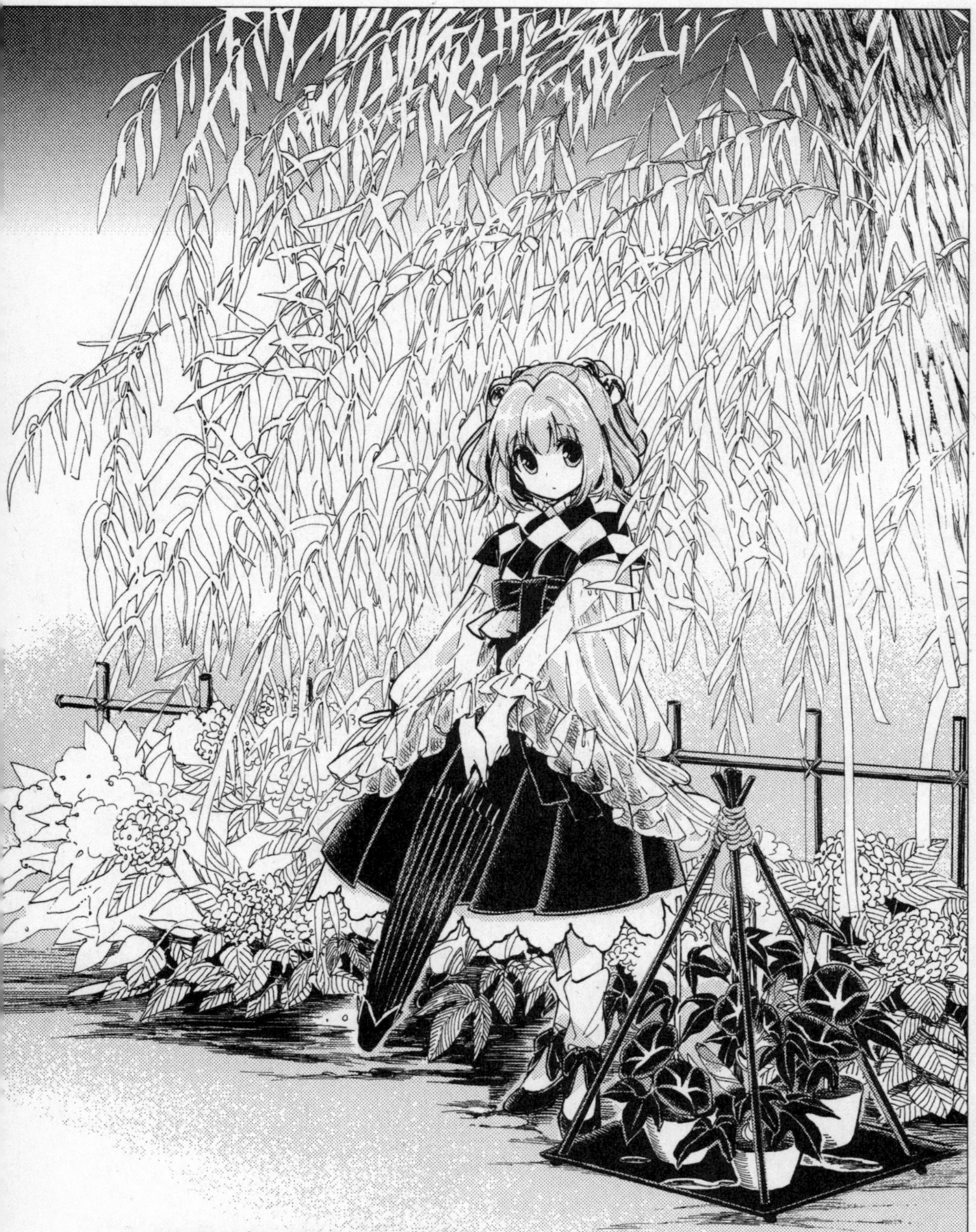

Chapter 8 Oinari-san's Hood Part 1

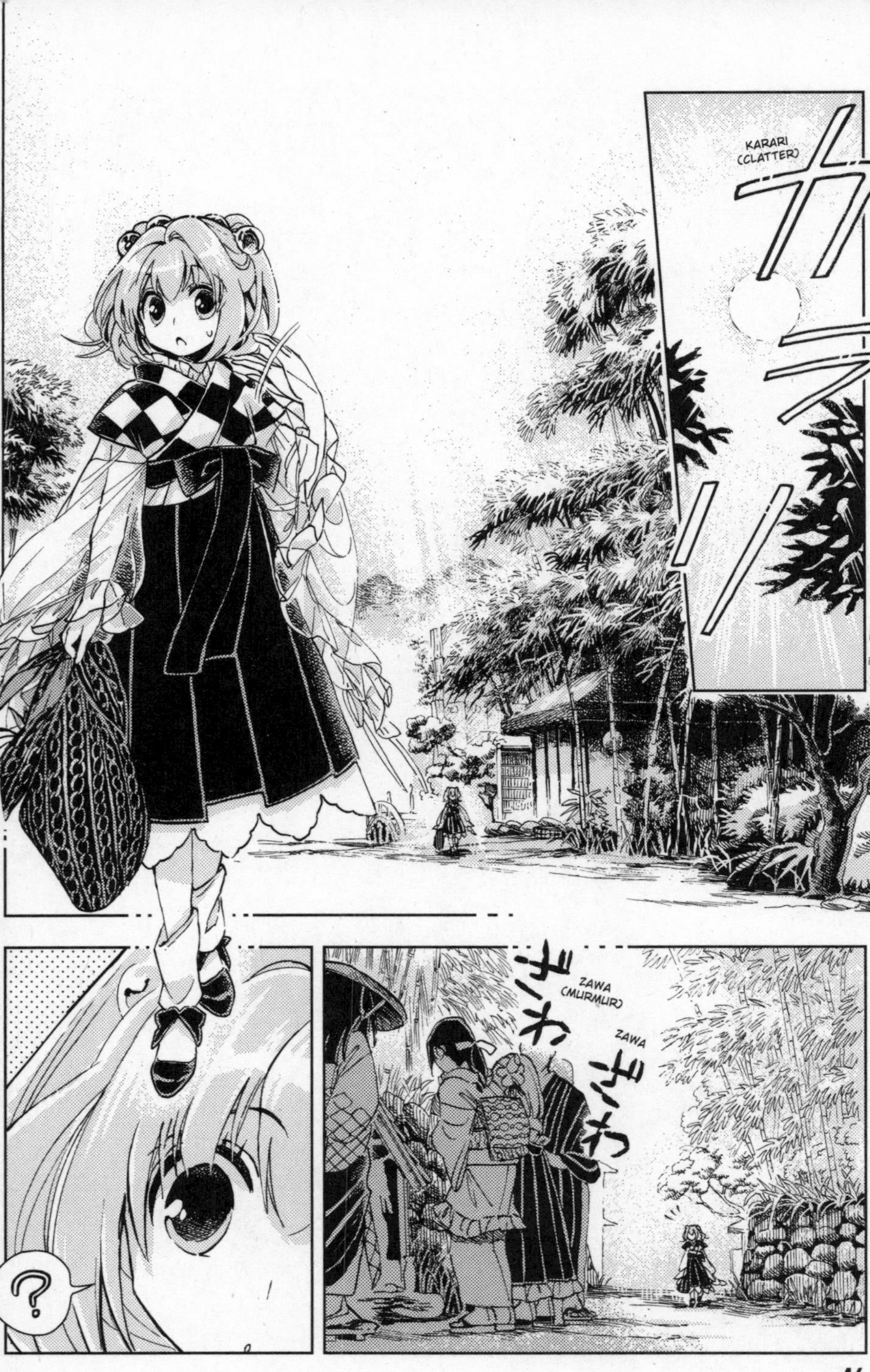
KARARI (CLATTER)
カラリ
ZAWA (MURMUR)
ZAWA
ざわ ざわ
?

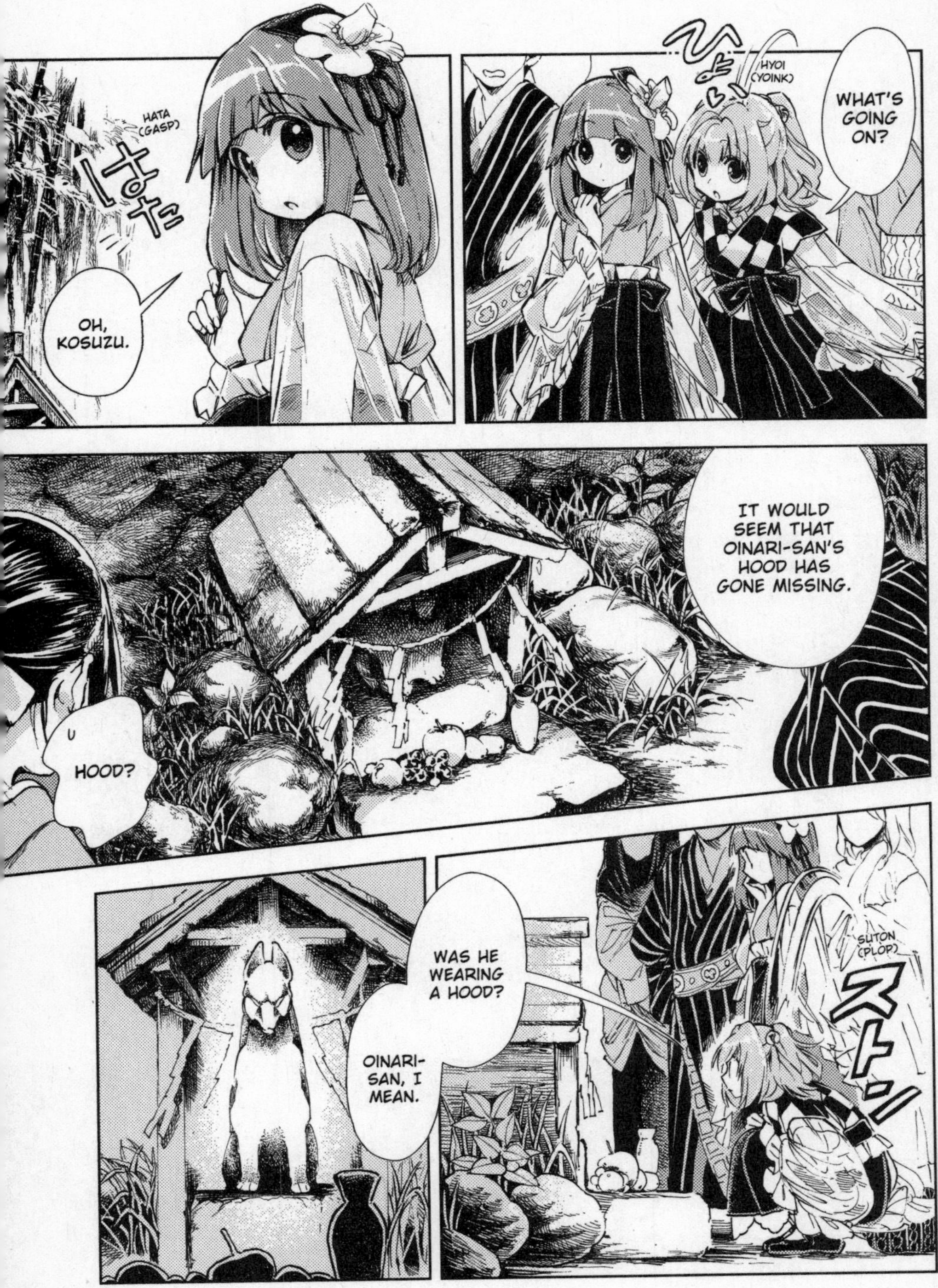
WHAT'S GOING ON?
ひょい
HYOI (YOINK)
HATA (GASP)
はた
OH, KOSUZU.
IT WOULD SEEM THAT OINARI-SAN'S HOOD HAS GONE MISSING.
U HOOD?
SUTON (PLOP)
ストン
WAS HE WEARING A HOOD?
OINARI-SAN, I MEAN.

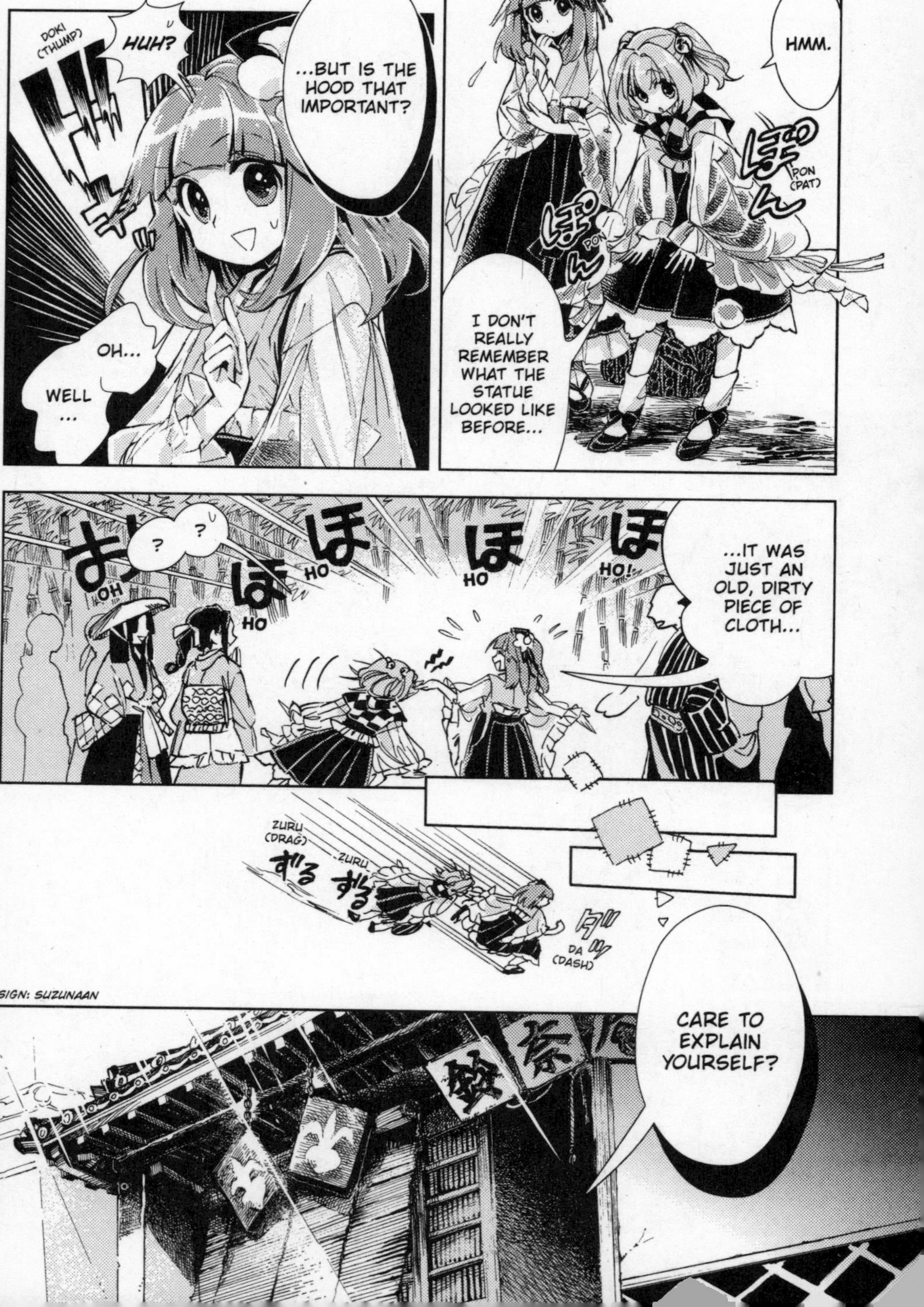
HMM.
ぽん
PON (PAT)
ぽん
PON
I DON'T REALLY REMEMBER WHAT THE STATUE LOOKED LIKE BEFORE...
...BUT IS THE HOOD THAT IMPORTANT?
HUH?
DOKI (THUMP)
OH...
WELL...
...IT WAS JUST AN OLD, DIRTY PIECE OF CLOTH...
ほ
HO!
ほ
HO
ほ
HO
ほ
HO
お
OH
?
?
ZURU (DRAG)
ずる
ZURU
ずる
ダッ
DA (DASH)
SIGN: SUZUNAAN
CARE TO EXPLAIN YOURSELF?

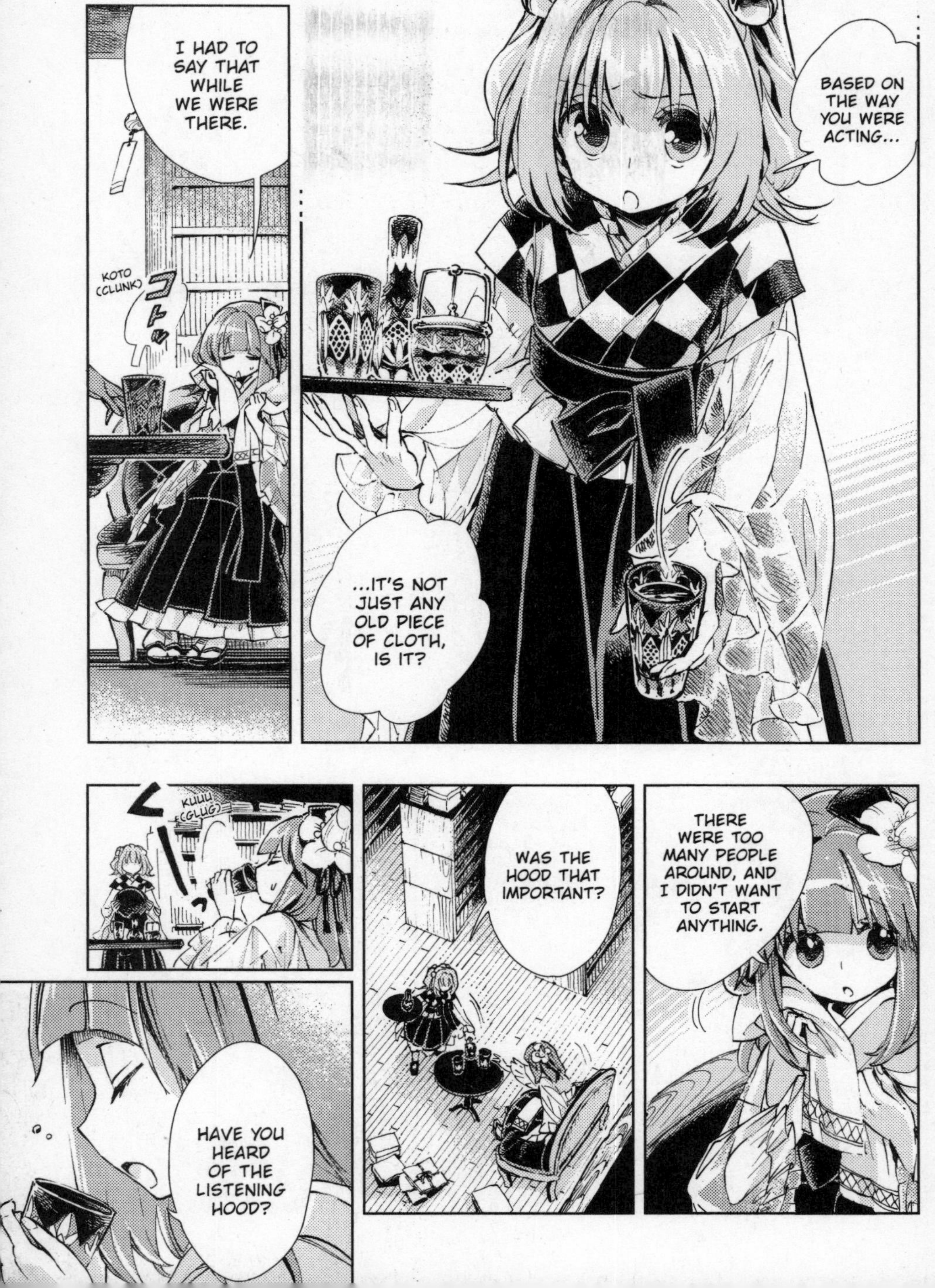
BASED ON THE WAY YOU WERE ACTING...
...IT'S NOT JUST ANY OLD PIECE OF CLOTH, IS IT?
I HAD TO SAY THAT WHILE WE WERE THERE.
KOTO (CLUNK)
THERE WERE TOO MANY PEOPLE AROUND, AND I DIDN'T WANT TO START ANYTHING.
WAS THE HOOD THAT IMPORTANT?
KUUU (GLUG)
HAVE YOU HEARD OF THE LISTENING HOOD?

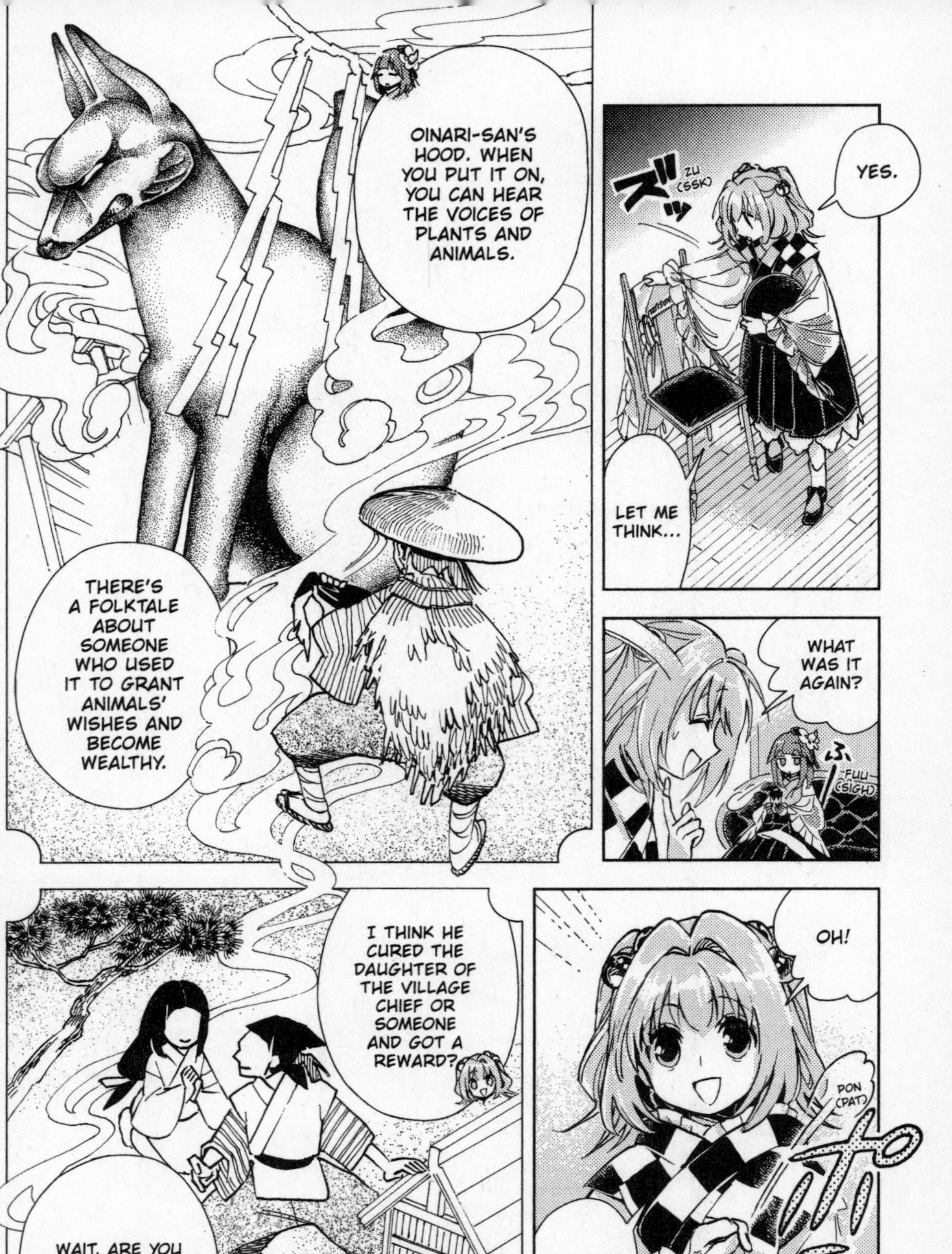

YES.
ZU (SSK)
LET ME THINK...
WHAT WAS IT AGAIN?
FUU (SIGH)
OINARI-SAN'S HOOD. WHEN YOU PUT IT ON, YOU CAN HEAR THE VOICES OF PLANTS AND ANIMALS.
THERE'S A FOLKTALE ABOUT SOMEONE WHO USED IT TO GRANT ANIMALS' WISHES AND BECOME WEALTHY.
OH!
PON (PAT)
I KNOW WHAT YOU'RE TALKING ABOUT.
I THINK HE CURED THE DAUGHTER OF THE VILLAGE CHIEF OR SOMEONE AND GOT A REWARD?
WAIT, ARE YOU SAYING THAT THE LOST HOOD IS THAT HOOD?

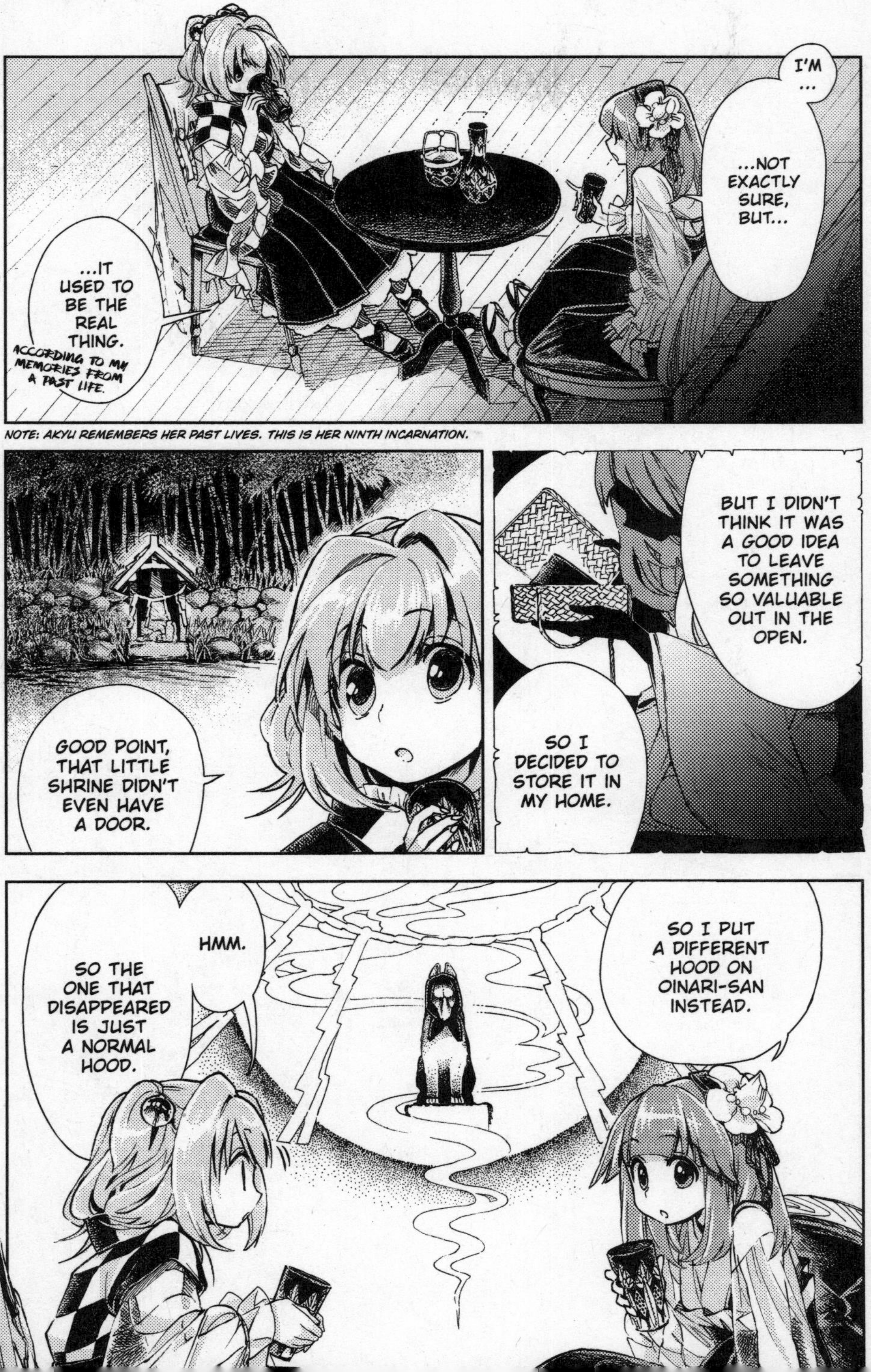
I'M ...
...NOT EXACTLY SURE, BUT...
...IT USED TO BE THE REAL THING.
ACCORDING TO MY MEMORIES FROM A PAST LIFE.
NOTE: AKYU REMEMBERS HER PAST LIVES. THIS IS HER NINTH INCARNATION.
BUT I DIDN'T THINK IT WAS A GOOD IDEA TO LEAVE SOMETHING SO VALUABLE OUT IN THE OPEN.
SO I DECIDED TO STORE IT IN MY HOME.
GOOD POINT, THAT LITTLE SHRINE DIDN'T EVEN HAVE A DOOR.
SO I PUT A DIFFERENT HOOD ON OINARI-SAN INSTEAD.
HMM.
SO THE ONE THAT DISAPPEARED IS JUST A NORMAL HOOD.

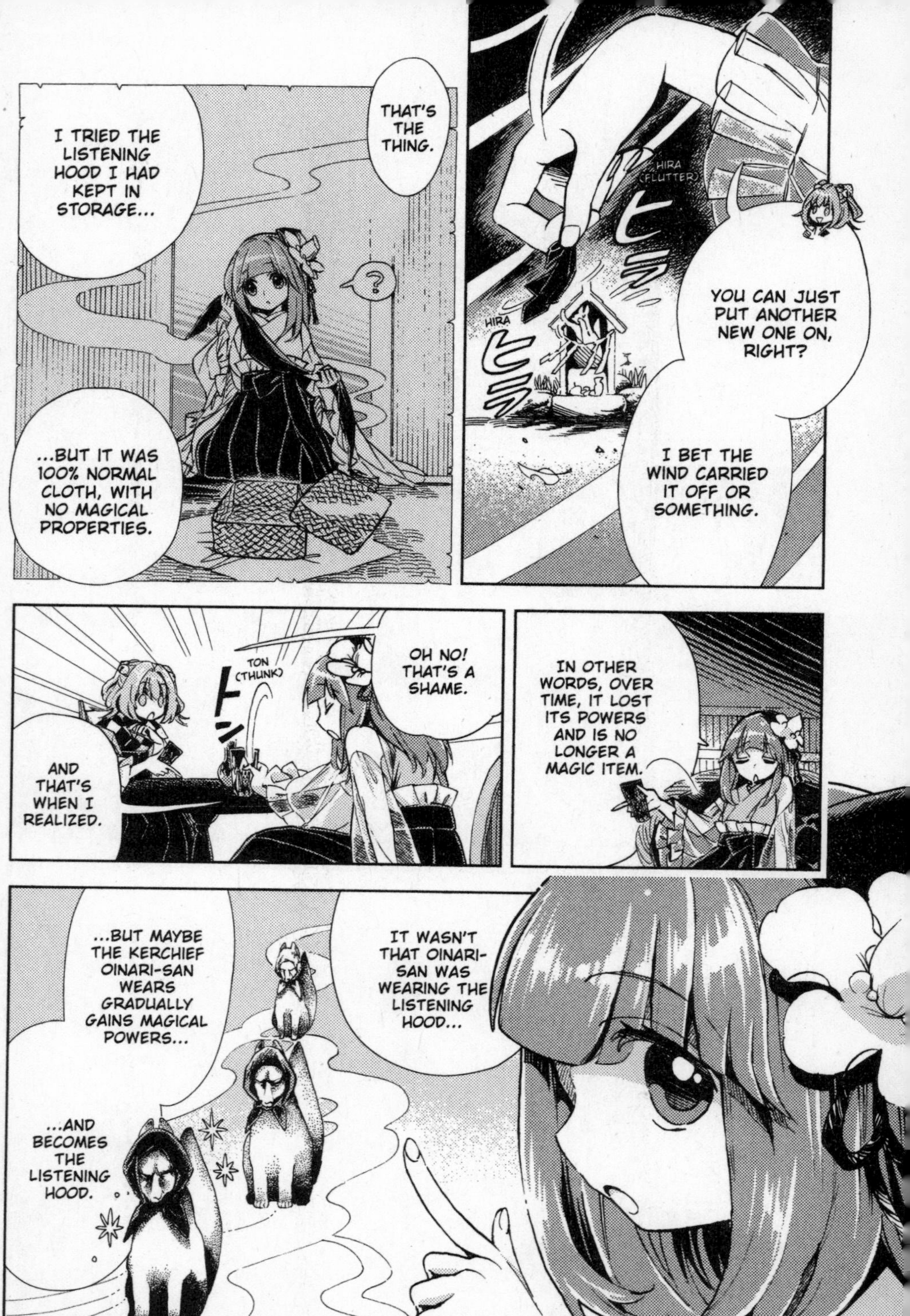

YOU CAN JUST PUT ANOTHER NEW ONE ON, RIGHT?
HIRA (FLUTTER)
HIRA
I BET THE WIND CARRIED IT OFF OR SOMETHING.
THAT'S THE THING.
I TRIED THE LISTENING HOOD I HAD KEPT IN STORAGE...
?
...BUT IT WAS 100% NORMAL CLOTH, WITH NO MAGICAL PROPERTIES.
IN OTHER WORDS, OVER TIME, IT LOST ITS POWERS AND IS NO LONGER A MAGIC ITEM.
OH NO! THAT'S A SHAME.
TON (THUNK)
AND THAT'S WHEN I REALIZED.
IT WASN'T THAT OINARI-SAN WAS WEARING THE LISTENING HOOD...
...BUT MAYBE THE KERCHIEF OINARI-SAN WEARS GRADUALLY GAINS MAGICAL POWERS...
...AND BECOMES THE LISTENING HOOD.

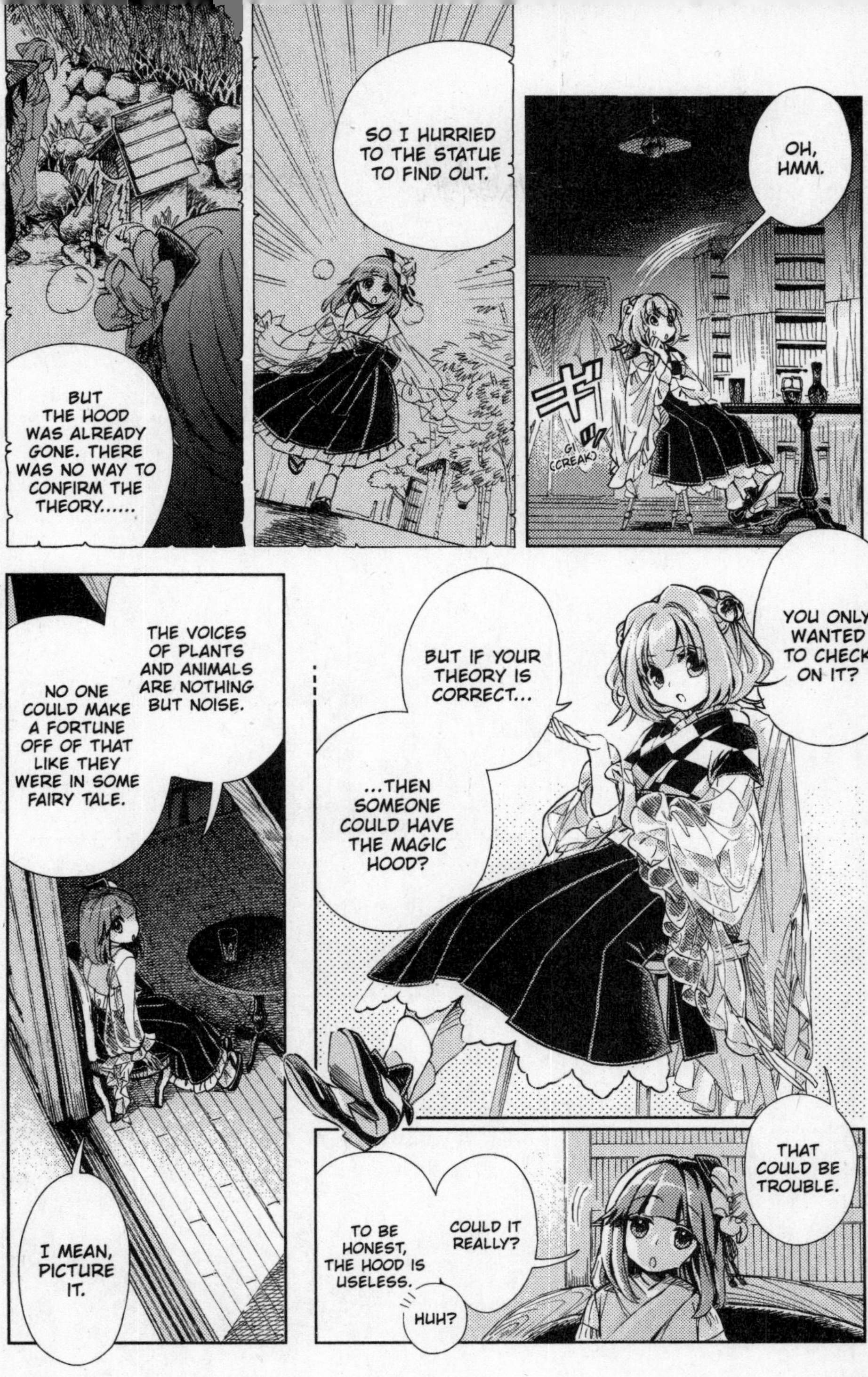
OH, HMM.
ギ
GI (CREAK)
SO I HURRIED TO THE STATUE TO FIND OUT.
BUT THE HOOD WAS ALREADY GONE. THERE WAS NO WAY TO CONFIRM THE THEORY......
YOU ONLY WANTED TO CHECK ON IT?
BUT IF YOUR THEORY IS CORRECT...
...THEN SOMEONE COULD HAVE THE MAGIC HOOD?
THAT COULD BE TROUBLE.
COULD IT REALLY?
TO BE HONEST, THE HOOD IS USELESS.
HUH?
THE VOICES OF PLANTS AND ANIMALS ARE NOTHING BUT NOISE.
NO ONE COULD MAKE A FORTUNE OFF OF THAT LIKE THEY WERE IN SOME FAIRY TALE.
I MEAN, PICTURE IT.

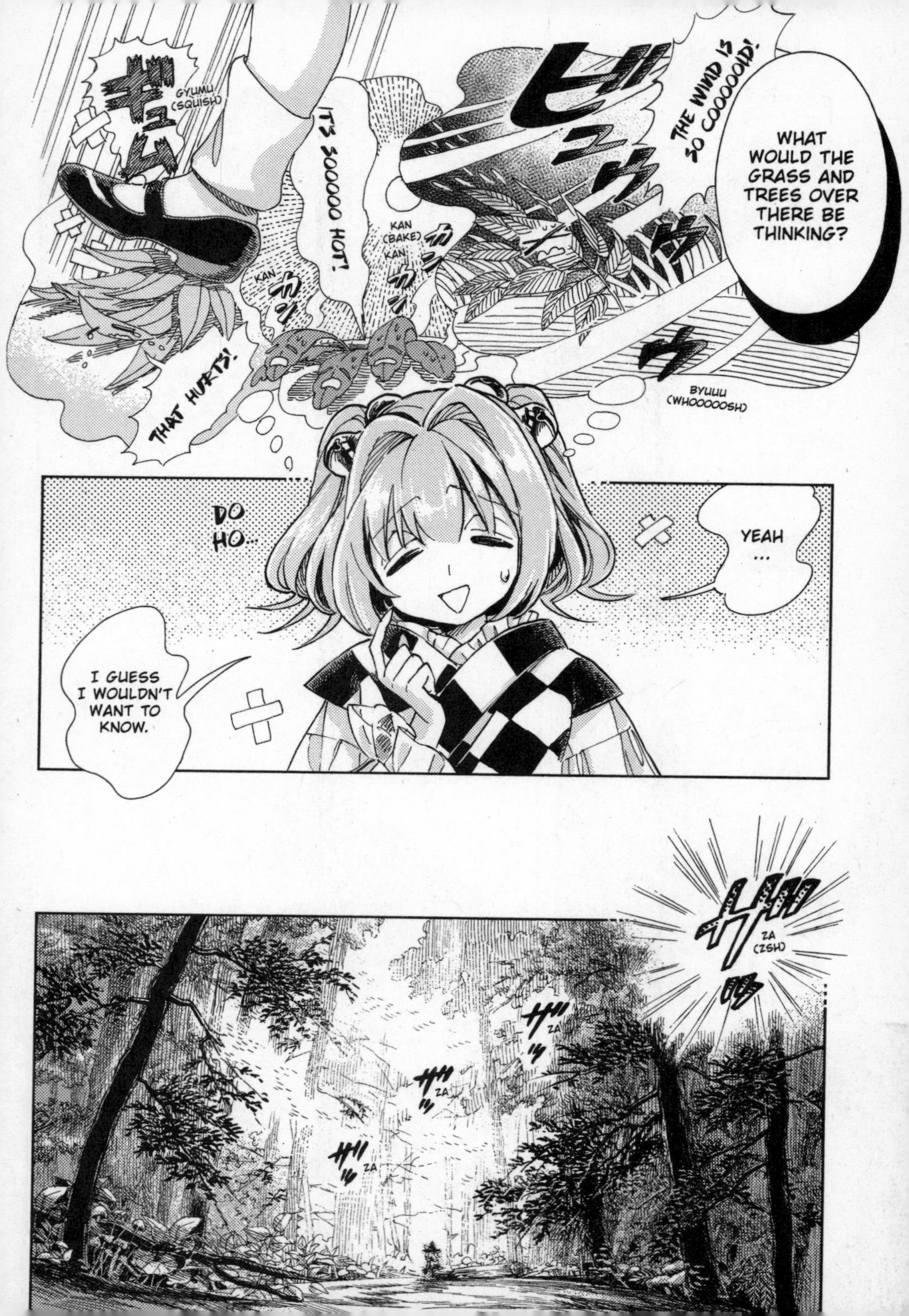

WHAT WOULD THE GRASS AND TREES OVER THERE BE THINKING?
THE WIND IS SO COOOOOLD!
BYUUU (WHOOOOOSH)
IT'S SOOOOO HOT!
KAN (BAKE) KAN
KAN
GYUMU (SQUISH)
THAT HURTS!
YEAH ...
DO HO...
I GUESS I WOULDN'T WANT TO KNOW.
ZA (ZSH)
ZA
ZA
ZA

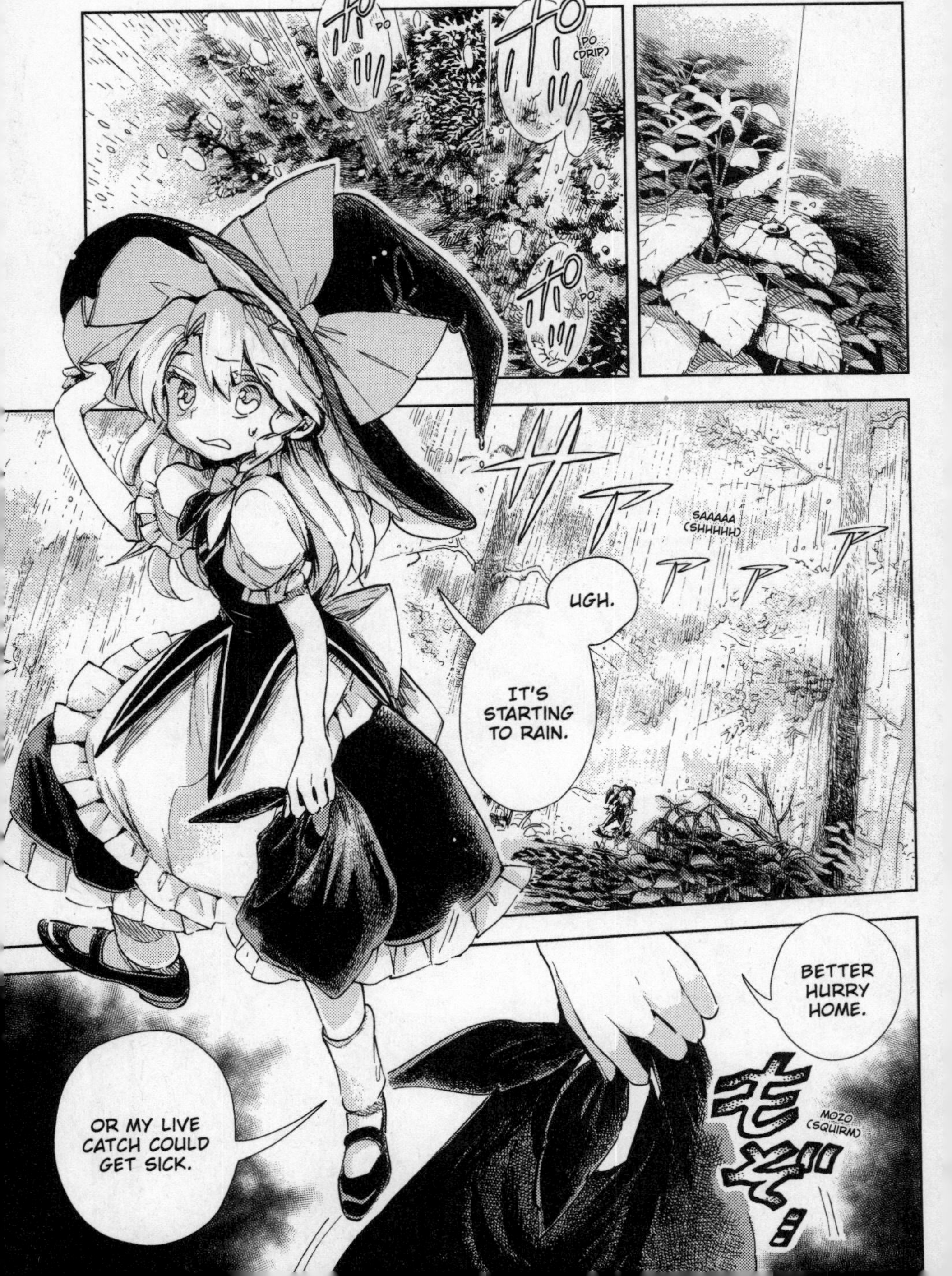

PO (DRIP)
PO
PO
SAAAAA (SHHHHH)
UGH.
IT'S STARTING TO RAIN.
BETTER HURRY HOME.
MOZO (SQUIRM)
OR MY LIVE CATCH COULD GET SICK.

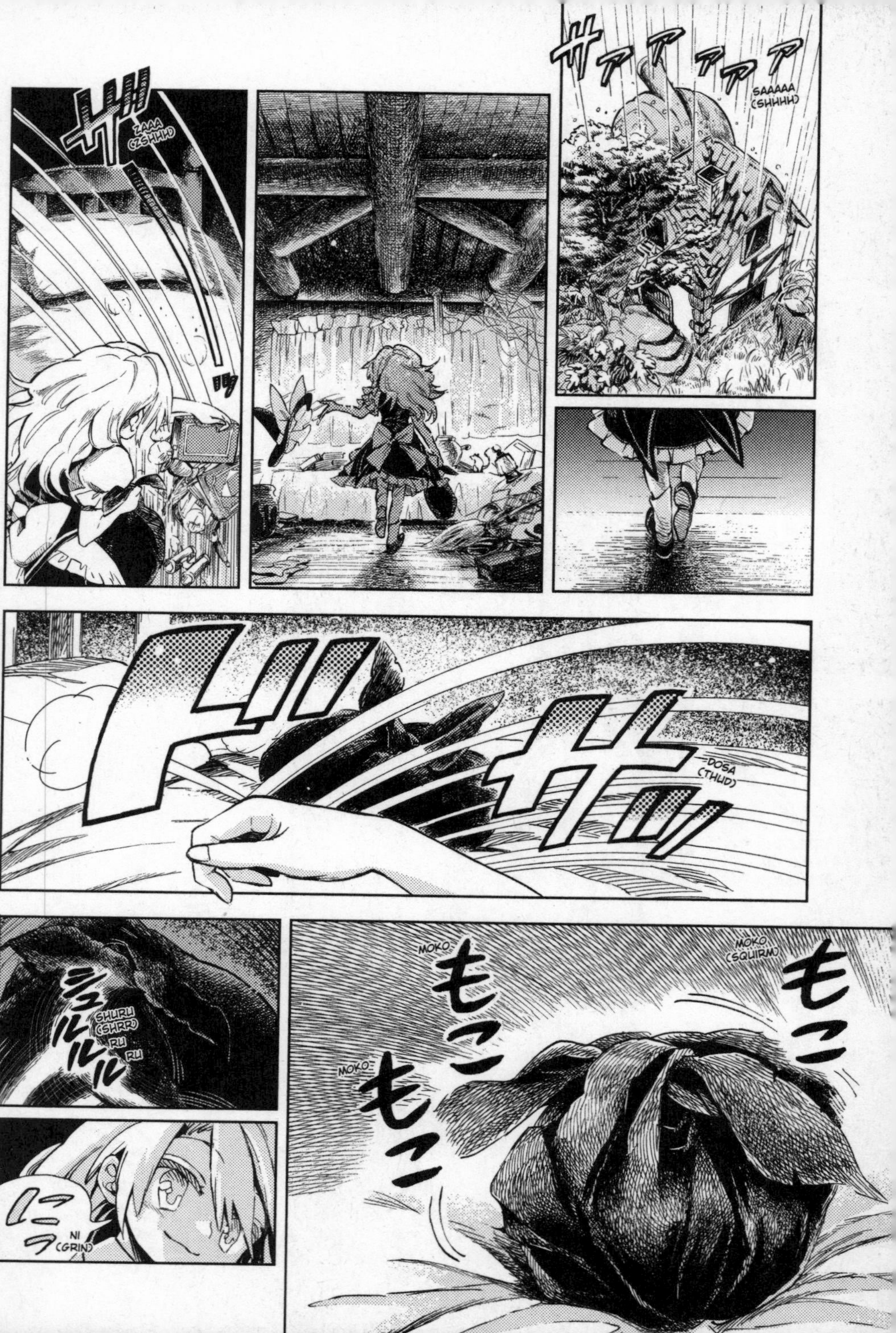

ザァァァァァ
SAAAAA (SHHHH)
ZAAA (ZSHHH)
DOSA (THUD)
もこ
MOKO (SQUIRM)
もこもこ
MOKO
MOKO
シュルルル
SHURU (SHRR) RU RU
にっ
NI (GRIN)

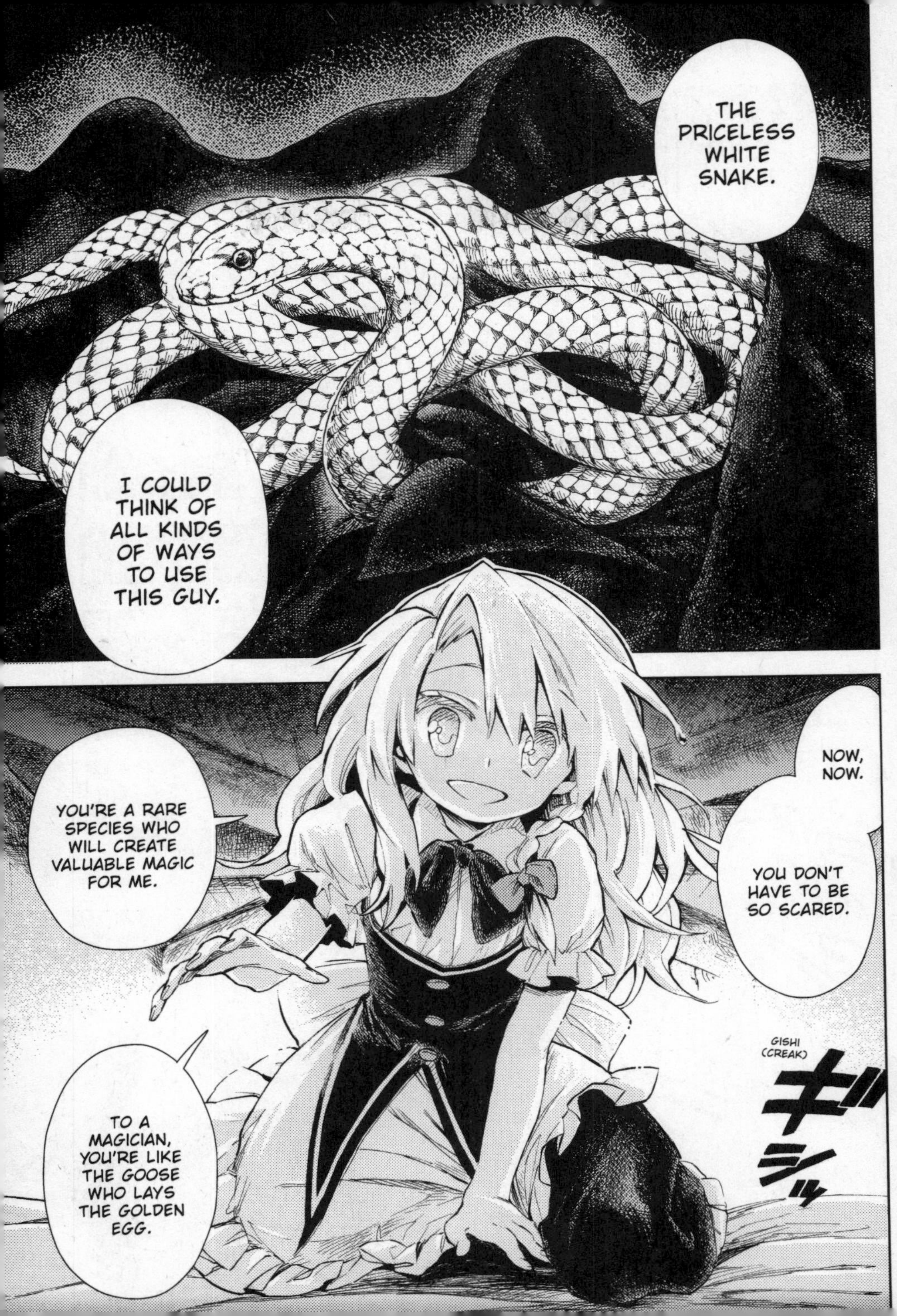
THE PRICELESS WHITE SNAKE.
I COULD THINK OF ALL KINDS OF WAYS TO USE THIS GUY.
NOW, NOW.
YOU DON'T HAVE TO BE SO SCARED.
GISHI (CREAK)
ギシッ
YOU'RE A RARE SPECIES WHO WILL CREATE VALUABLE MAGIC FOR ME.
TO A MAGICIAN, YOU'RE LIKE THE GOOSE WHO LAYS THE GOLDEN EGG.

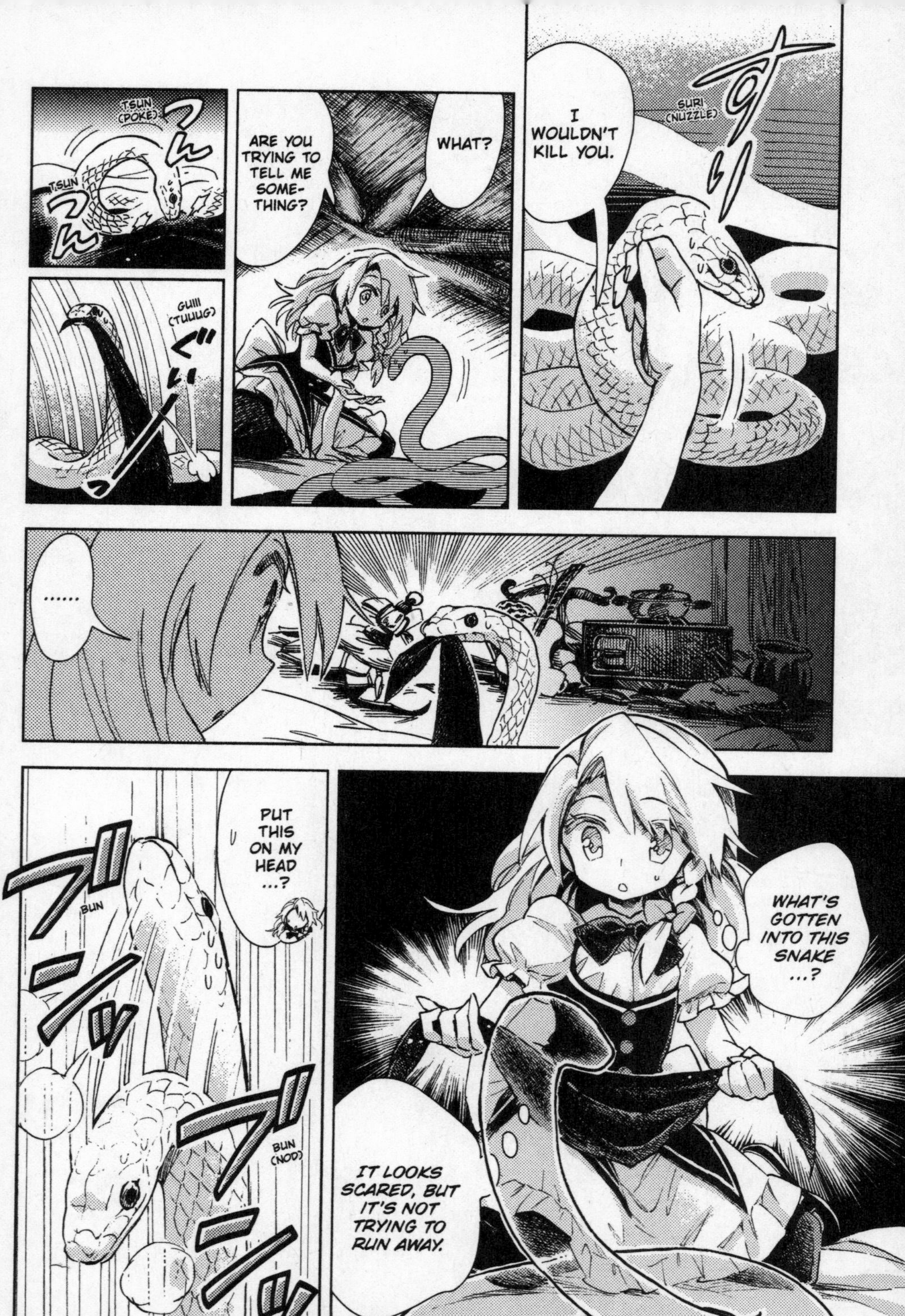
SURI (NUZZLE)
I WOULDN'T KILL YOU.
WHAT?
ARE YOU TRYING TO TELL ME SOME-THING?
TSUN (POKE)
TSUN
GUIII (TUUUG)
......
WHAT'S GOTTEN INTO THIS SNAKE ...?
IT LOOKS SCARED, BUT IT'S NOT TRYING TO RUN AWAY.
PUT THIS ON MY HEAD ...?
BUN
BUN (NOD)

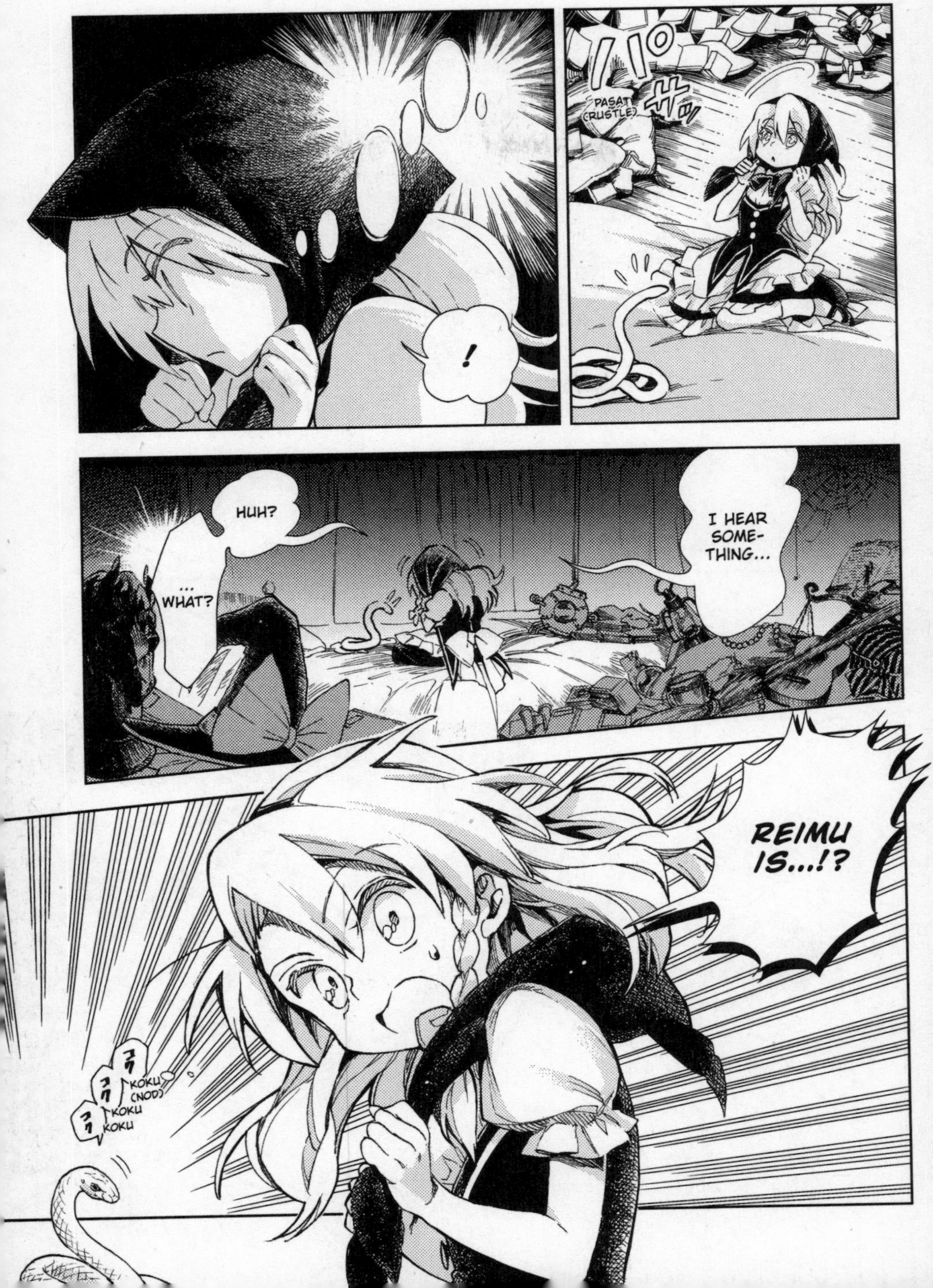
PASA (RUSTLE)
!
I HEAR SOME-THING...
HUH?
... WHAT?
REIMU IS...!?
KOKU (NOD)
KOKU
KOKU

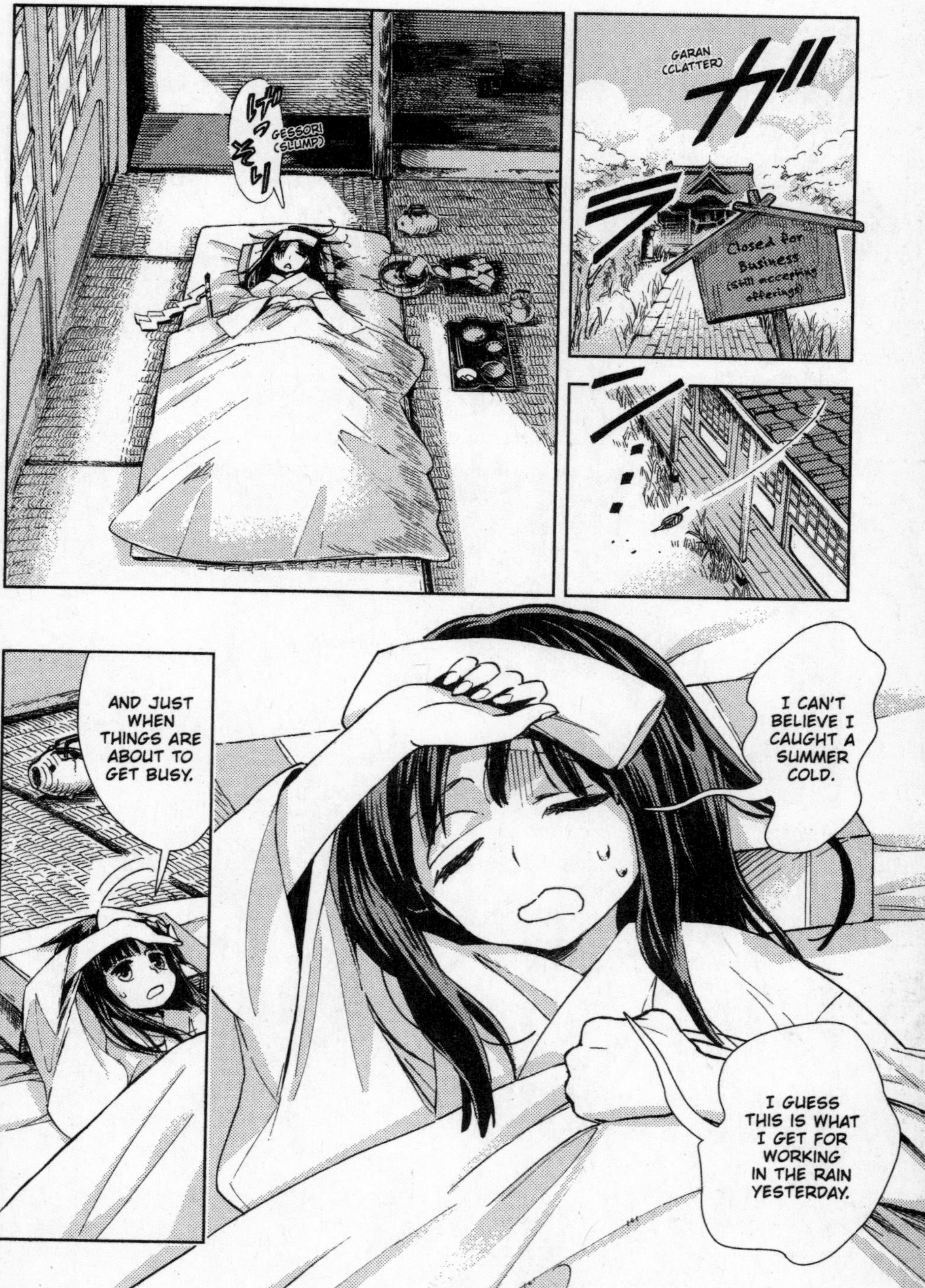
GARAN (CLATTER)
Closed for Business (still accepting offerings)
GESSORI (SLUMP)
I CAN'T BELIEVE I CAUGHT A SUMMER COLD.
I GUESS THIS IS WHAT I GET FOR WORKING IN THE RAIN YESTERDAY.
AND JUST WHEN THINGS ARE ABOUT TO GET BUSY.

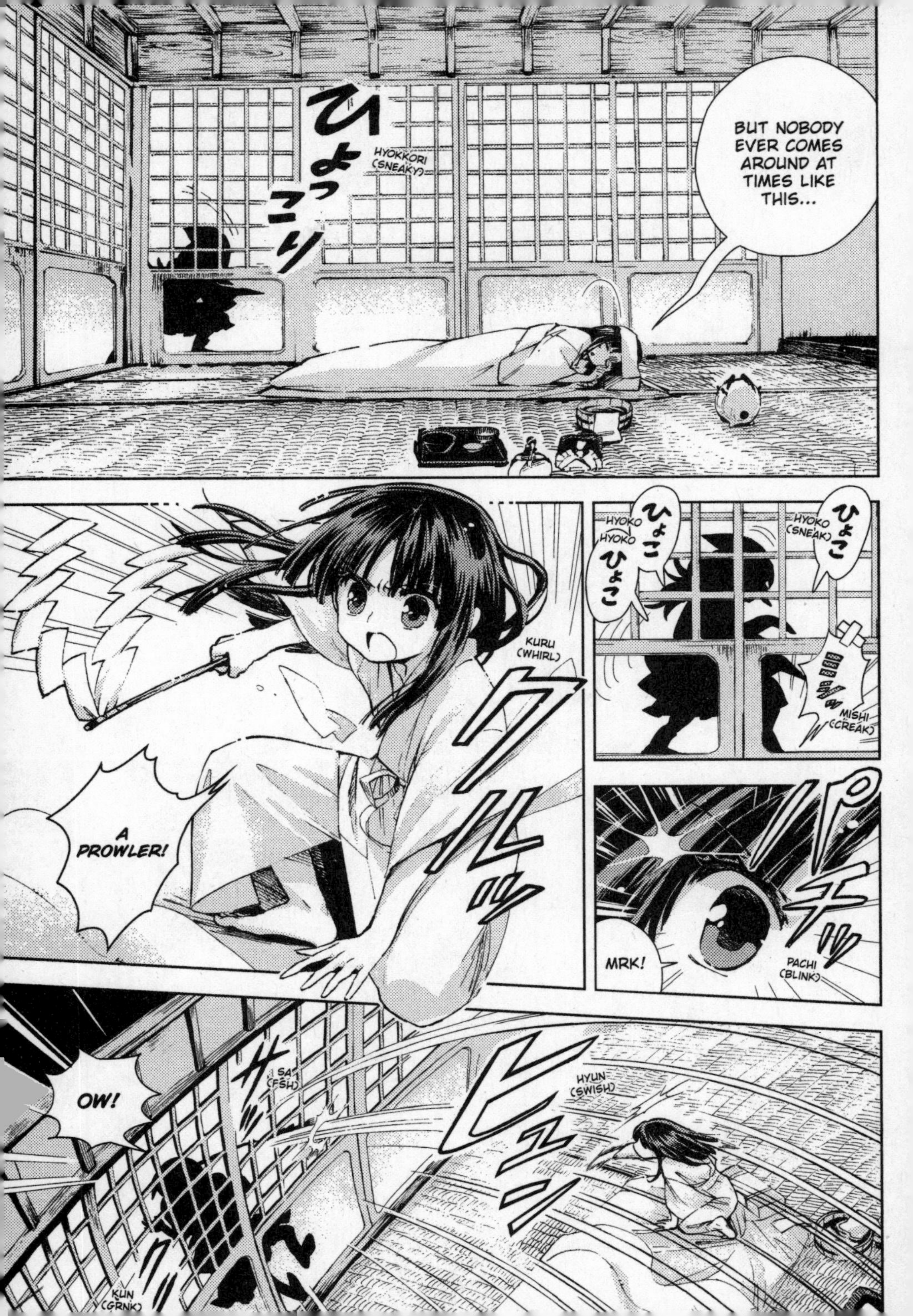
BUT NOBODY EVER COMES AROUND AT TIMES LIKE THIS...
ひょっこり
HYOKKORI (SNEAKY)
ひょこ
HYOKO (SNEAK)
ひょこ
HYOKO
ひょこ
HYOKO
MISHI (CREAK)
PACHI (BLINK)
MRK!
KURU (WHIRL)
A PROWLER!
HYUN (SWISH)
SA (FSH)
OW!
KUN (GRNK)

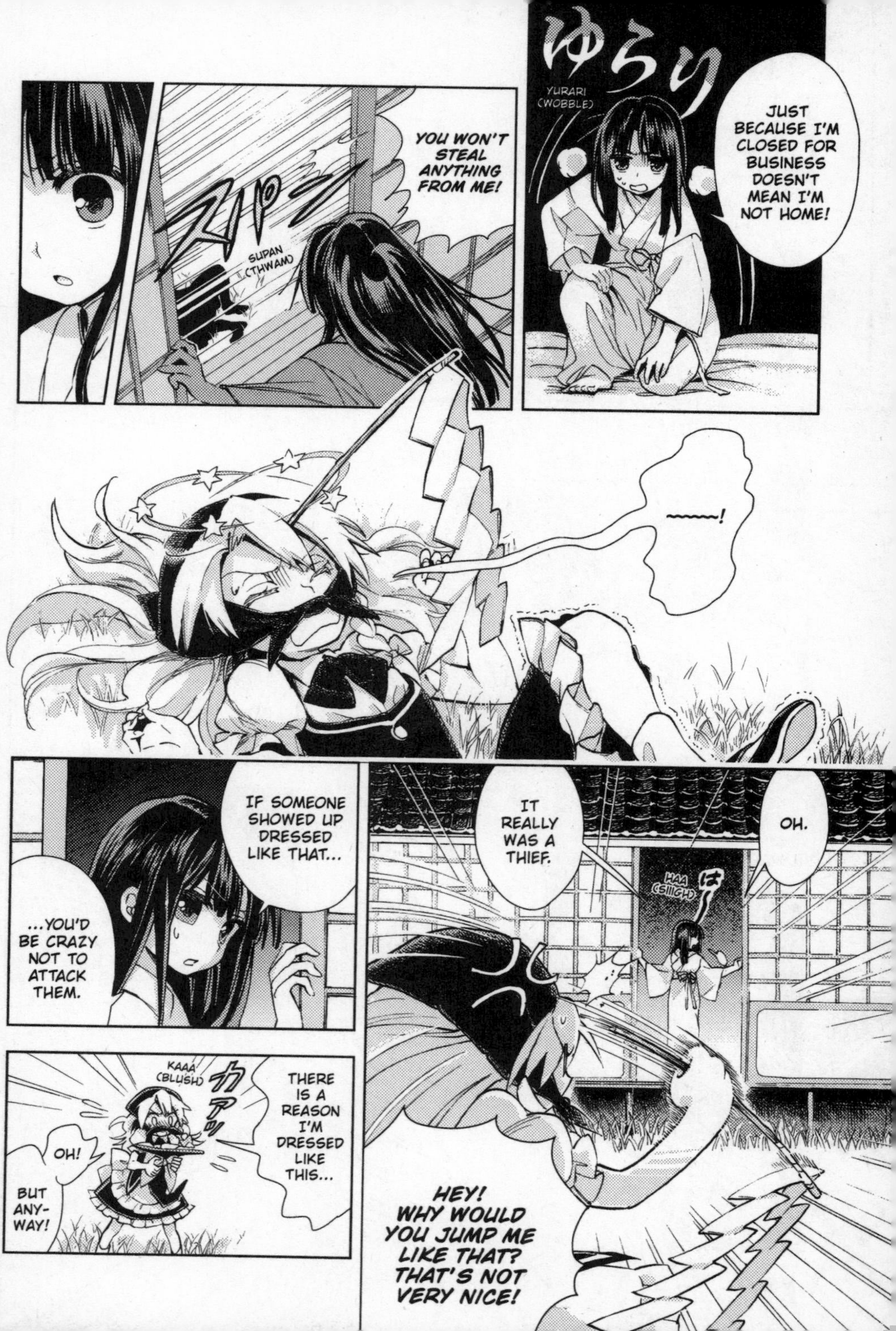
ゆらり
YURARI (WOBBLE)
JUST BECAUSE I'M CLOSED FOR BUSINESS DOESN'T MEAN I'M NOT HOME!
YOU WON'T STEAL ANYTHING FROM ME!
スパン
SUPAN (THWAM)
~~~~!
OH.
はー
HAA (SIIIGH)
IT REALLY WAS A THIEF.
HEY! WHY WOULD YOU JUMP ME LIKE THAT? THAT'S NOT VERY NICE!
IF SOMEONE SHOWED UP DRESSED LIKE THAT...
...YOU'D BE CRAZY NOT TO ATTACK THEM.
THERE IS A REASON I'M DRESSED LIKE THIS...
カアッ
KAAA (BLUSH)
OH!
BUT ANY-WAY!
~~~~

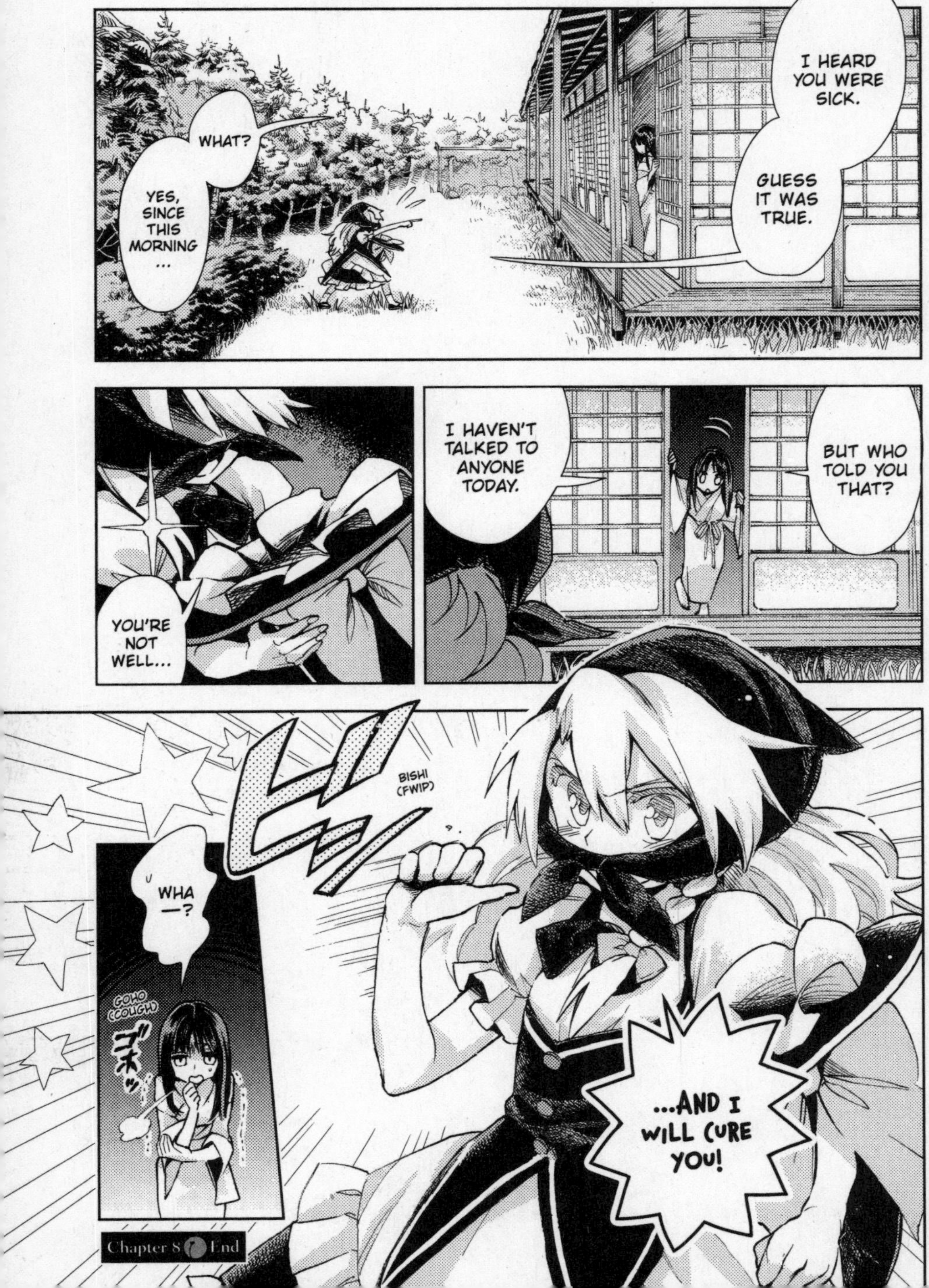
I HEARD YOU WERE SICK.
GUESS IT WAS TRUE.
WHAT?
YES, SINCE THIS MORNING...
BUT WHO TOLD YOU THAT?
I HAVEN'T TALKED TO ANYONE TODAY.
YOU'RE NOT WELL...
BISHI (FWIP)
...AND I WILL CURE YOU!
WHA—?
GOHO (COUGH)
Chapter 8 End

Forbidden Scrollery

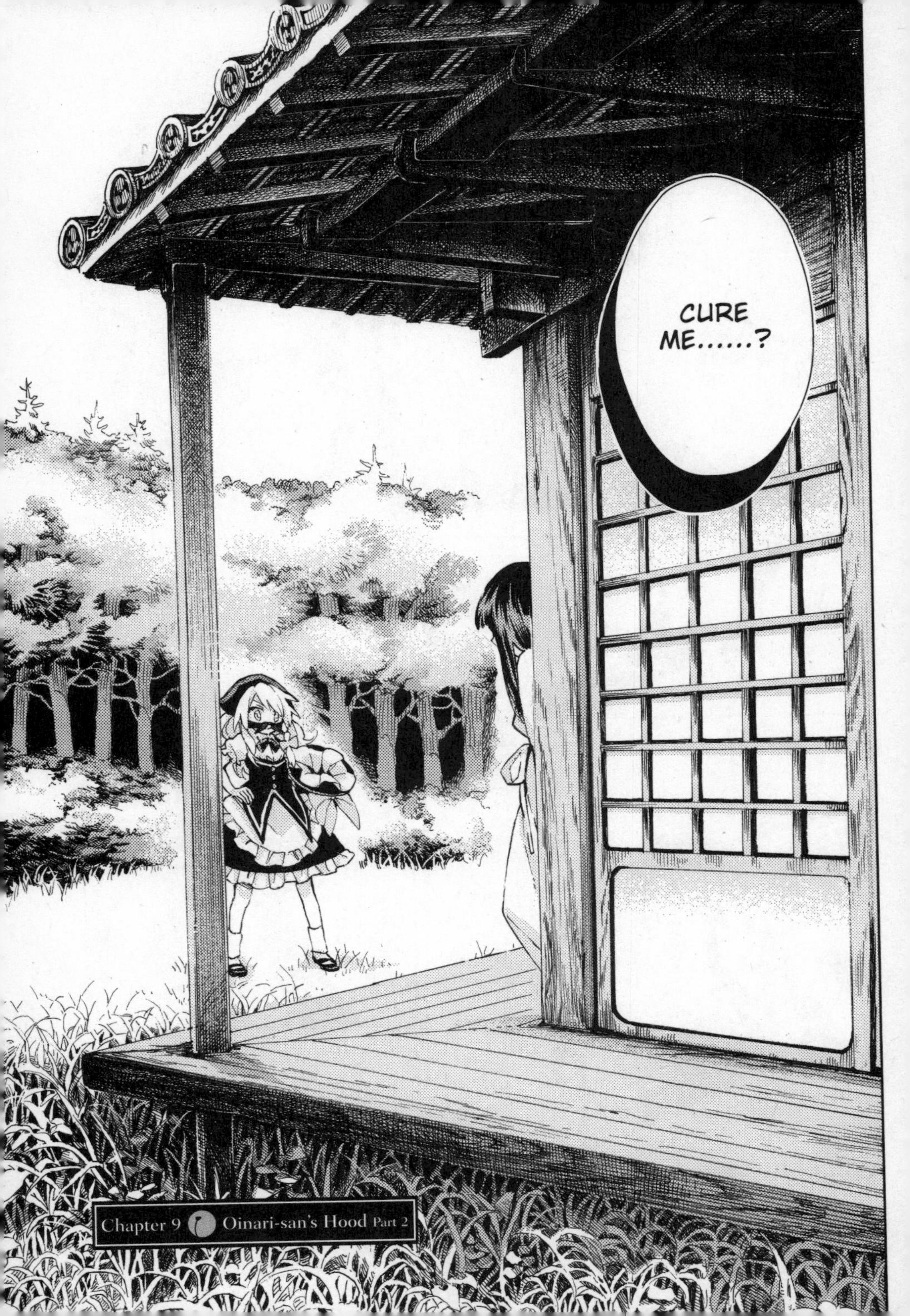
CURE ME......?
Chapter 9 Oinari-san's Hood Part 2

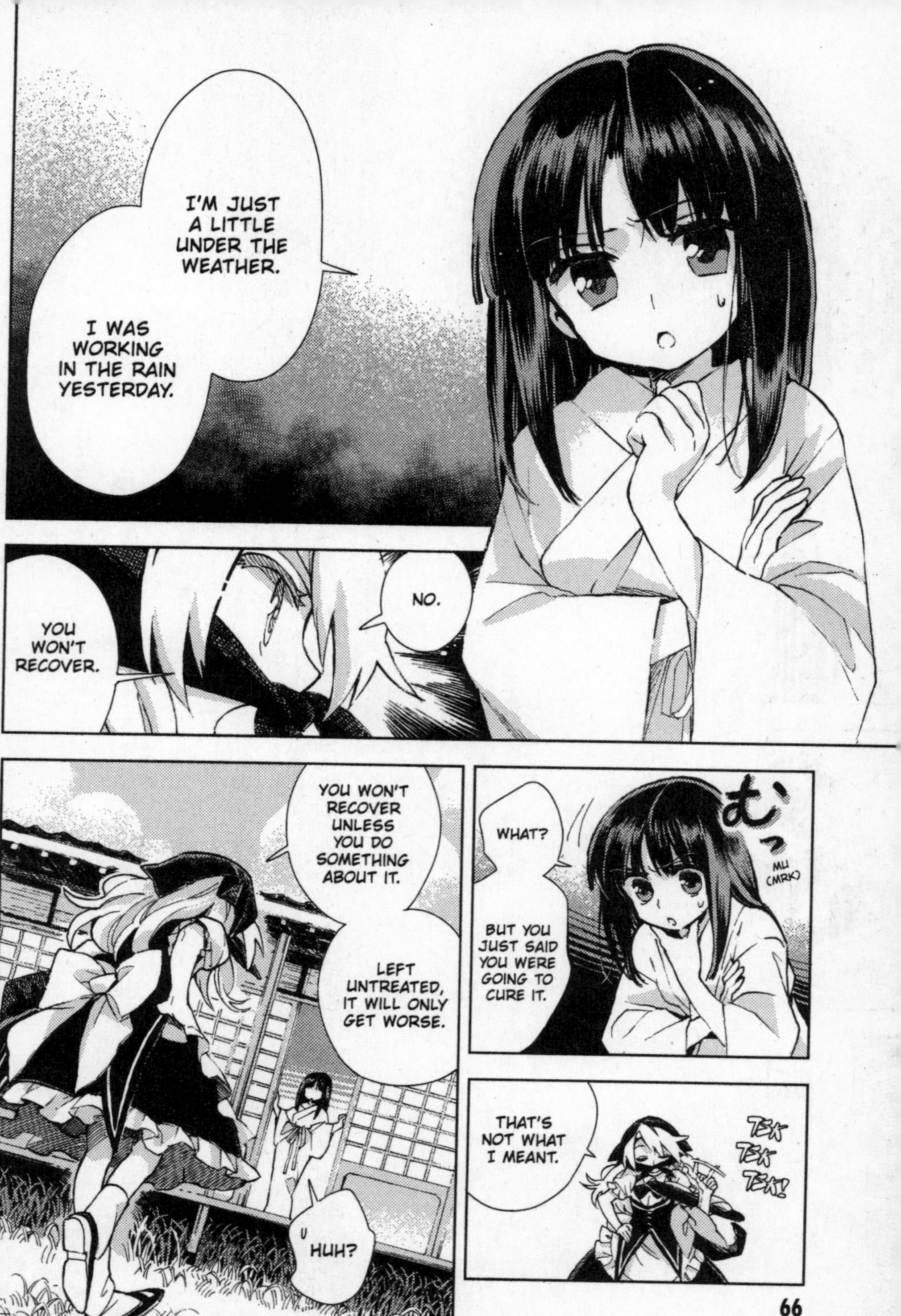
I'M JUST A LITTLE UNDER THE WEATHER.
I WAS WORKING IN THE RAIN YESTERDAY.
NO.
YOU WON'T RECOVER.
WHAT?
むっ
MU (MRK)
BUT YOU JUST SAID YOU WERE GOING TO CURE IT.
THAT'S NOT WHAT I MEANT.
TSK TSK TSK!
YOU WON'T RECOVER UNLESS YOU DO SOMETHING ABOUT IT.
LEFT UNTREATED, IT WILL ONLY GET WORSE.
HUH?

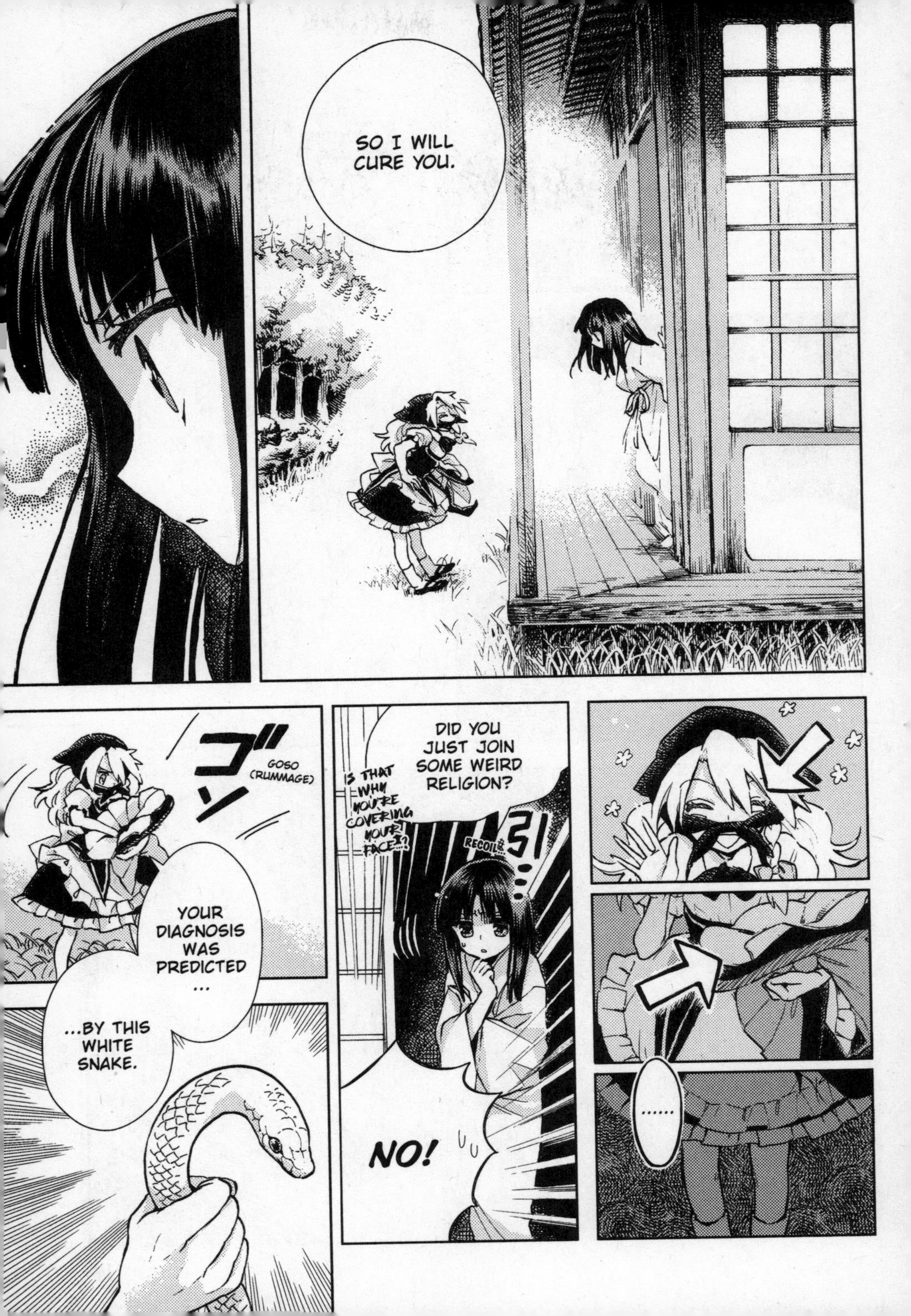
SO I WILL CURE YOU.
......
DID YOU JUST JOIN SOME WEIRD RELIGION?
IS THAT WHY YOU'RE COVERING YOUR FACE...!?
RECOIL
NO!
GOSO (RUMMAGE)
YOUR DIAGNOSIS WAS PREDICTED ...
...BY THIS WHITE SNAKE.

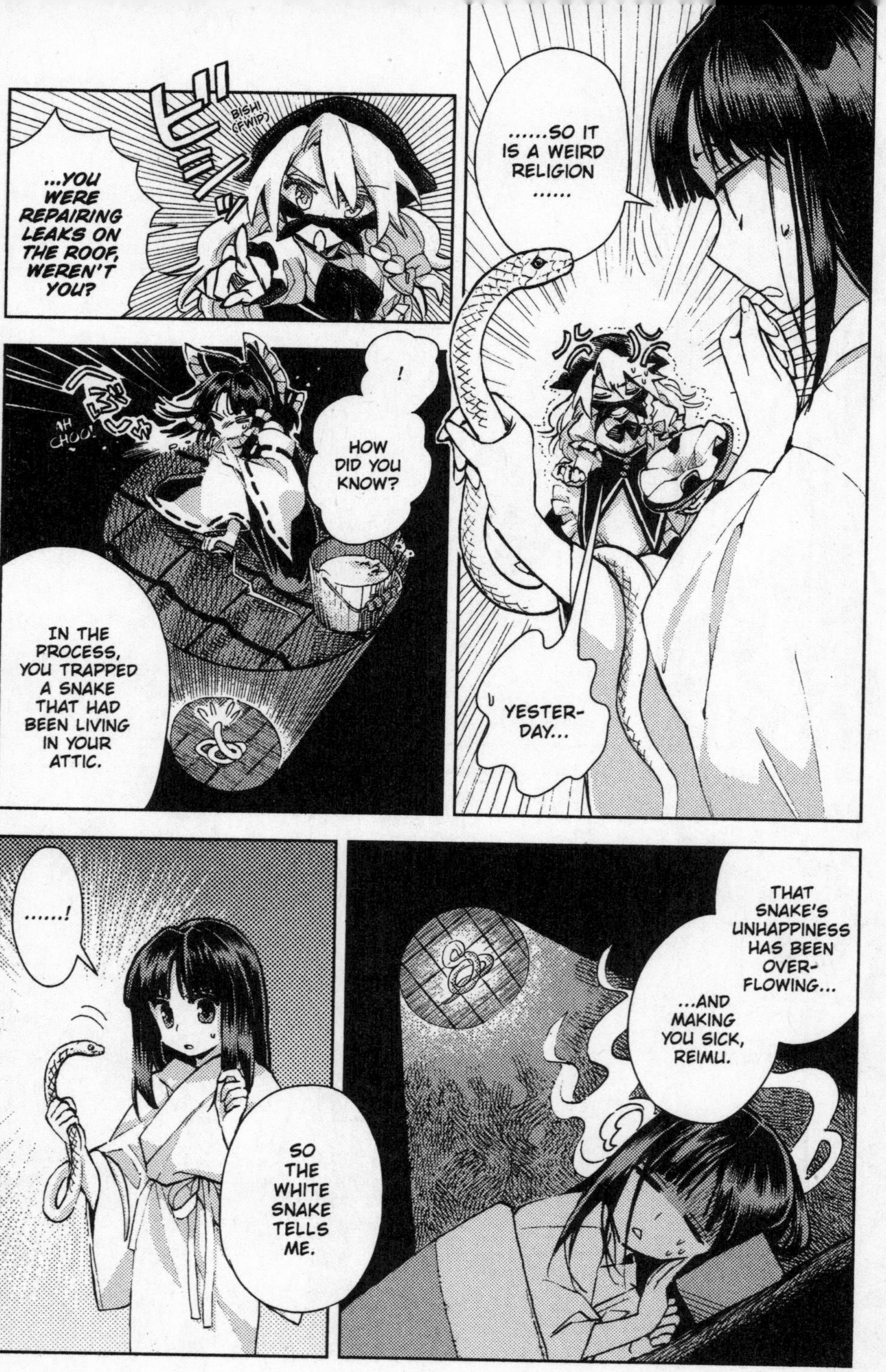
......SO IT IS A WEIRD RELIGION ......
YESTER-DAY...
BISHI (FWIP)
...YOU WERE REPAIRING LEAKS ON THE ROOF, WEREN'T YOU?
!
HOW DID YOU KNOW?
AH CHOO!
IN THE PROCESS, YOU TRAPPED A SNAKE THAT HAD BEEN LIVING IN YOUR ATTIC.
THAT SNAKE'S UNHAPPINESS HAS BEEN OVER-FLOWING...
...AND MAKING YOU SICK, REIMU.
......!
SO THE WHITE SNAKE TELLS ME.

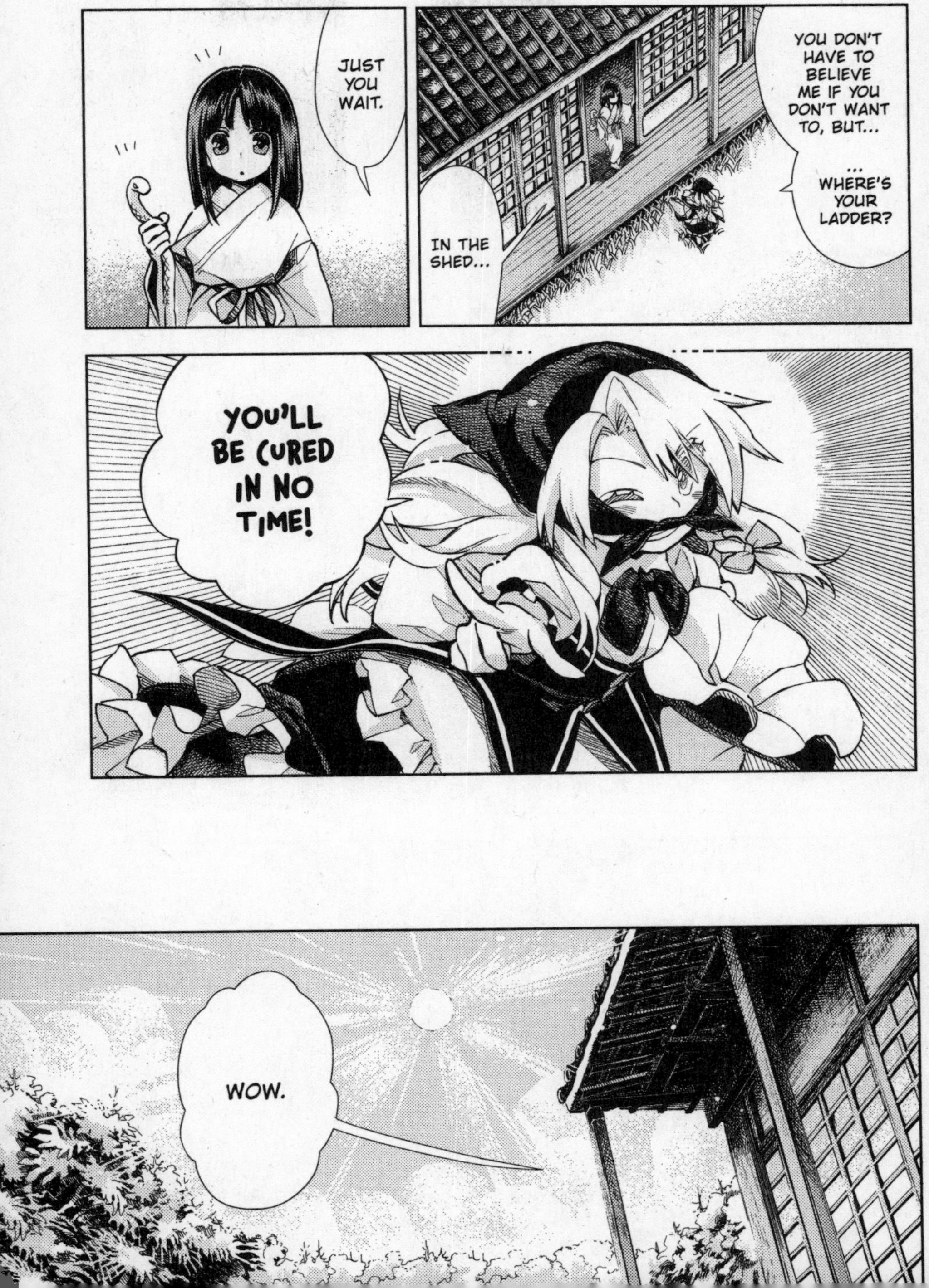
YOU DON'T HAVE TO BELIEVE ME IF YOU DON'T WANT TO, BUT...
... WHERE'S YOUR LADDER?
IN THE SHED...
JUST YOU WAIT.
YOU'LL BE CURED IN NO TIME!
WOW.

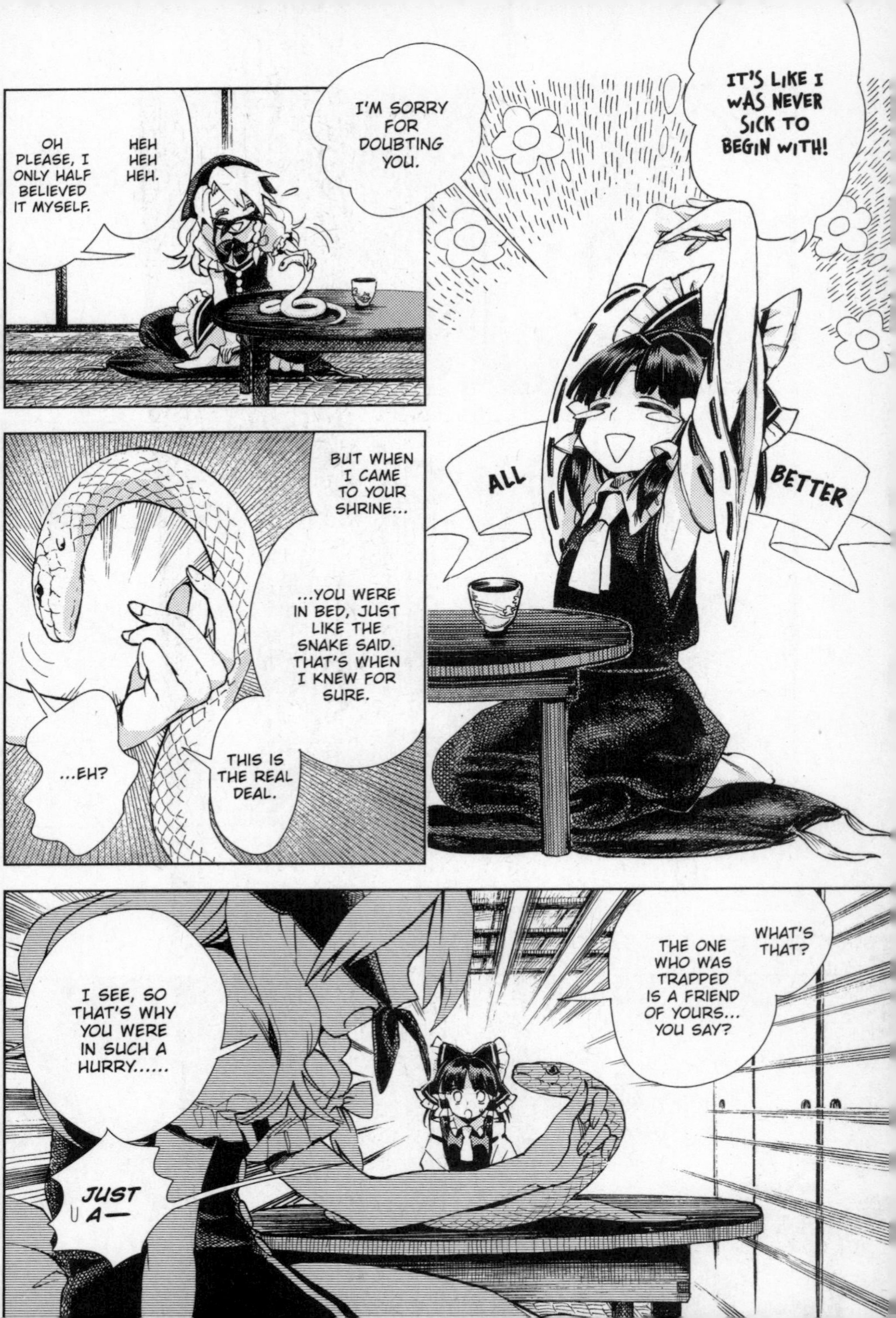
IT'S LIKE I WAS NEVER SICK TO BEGIN WITH!
ALL BETTER
I'M SORRY FOR DOUBTING YOU.
HEH HEH HEH.
OH PLEASE, I ONLY HALF BELIEVED IT MYSELF.
BUT WHEN I CAME TO YOUR SHRINE...
...YOU WERE IN BED, JUST LIKE THE SNAKE SAID. THAT'S WHEN I KNEW FOR SURE.
THIS IS THE REAL DEAL.
...EH?
WHAT'S THAT?
THE ONE WHO WAS TRAPPED IS A FRIEND OF YOURS... YOU SAY?
I SEE, SO THAT'S WHY YOU WERE IN SUCH A HURRY......
JUST A—

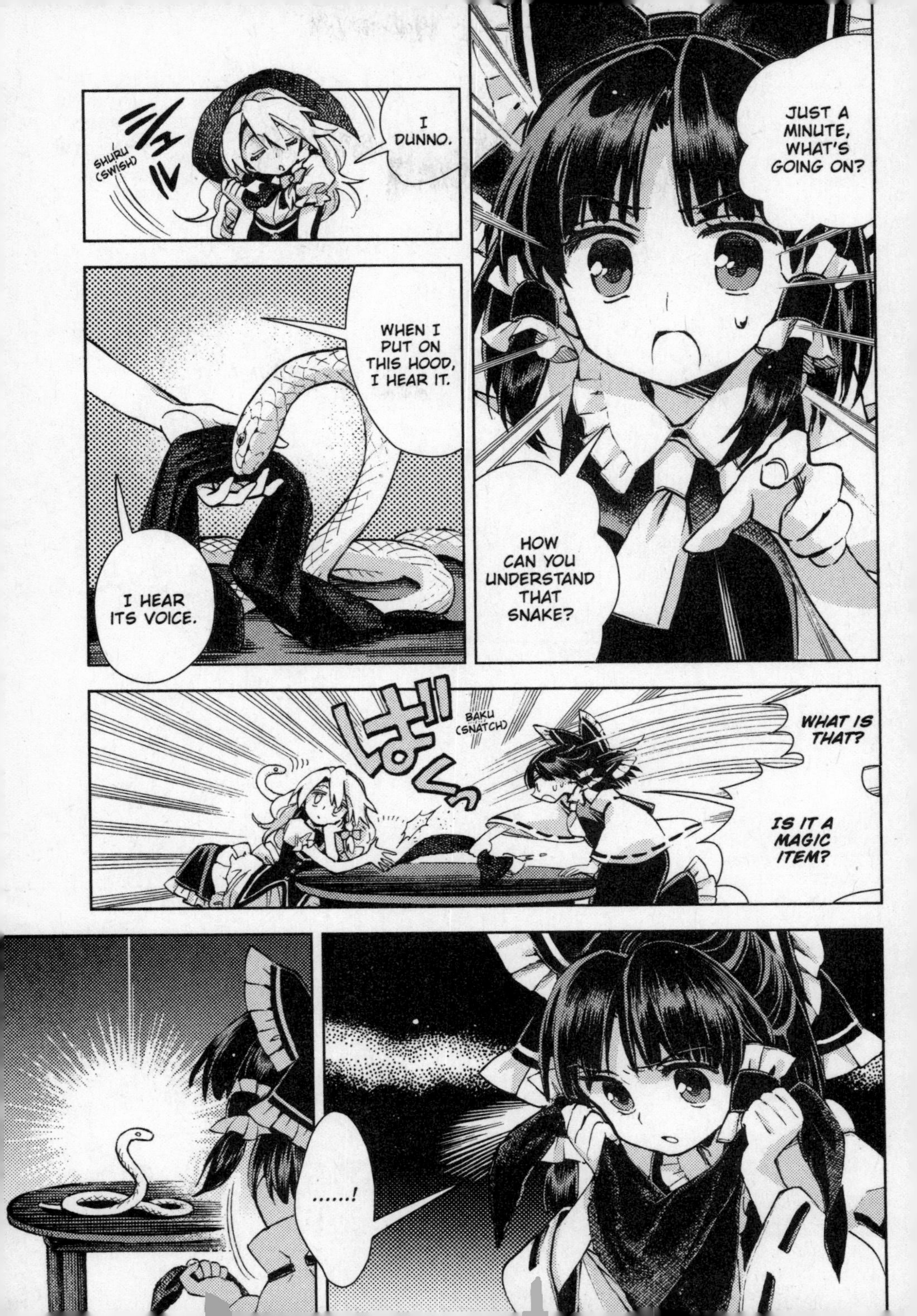
JUST A MINUTE, WHAT'S GOING ON?
HOW CAN YOU UNDERSTAND THAT SNAKE?
シュル
SHURU (SWISH)
I DUNNO.
WHEN I PUT ON THIS HOOD, I HEAR IT.
I HEAR ITS VOICE.
WHAT IS THAT?
IS IT A MAGIC ITEM?
ばくっ
BAKU (SNATCH)
......!

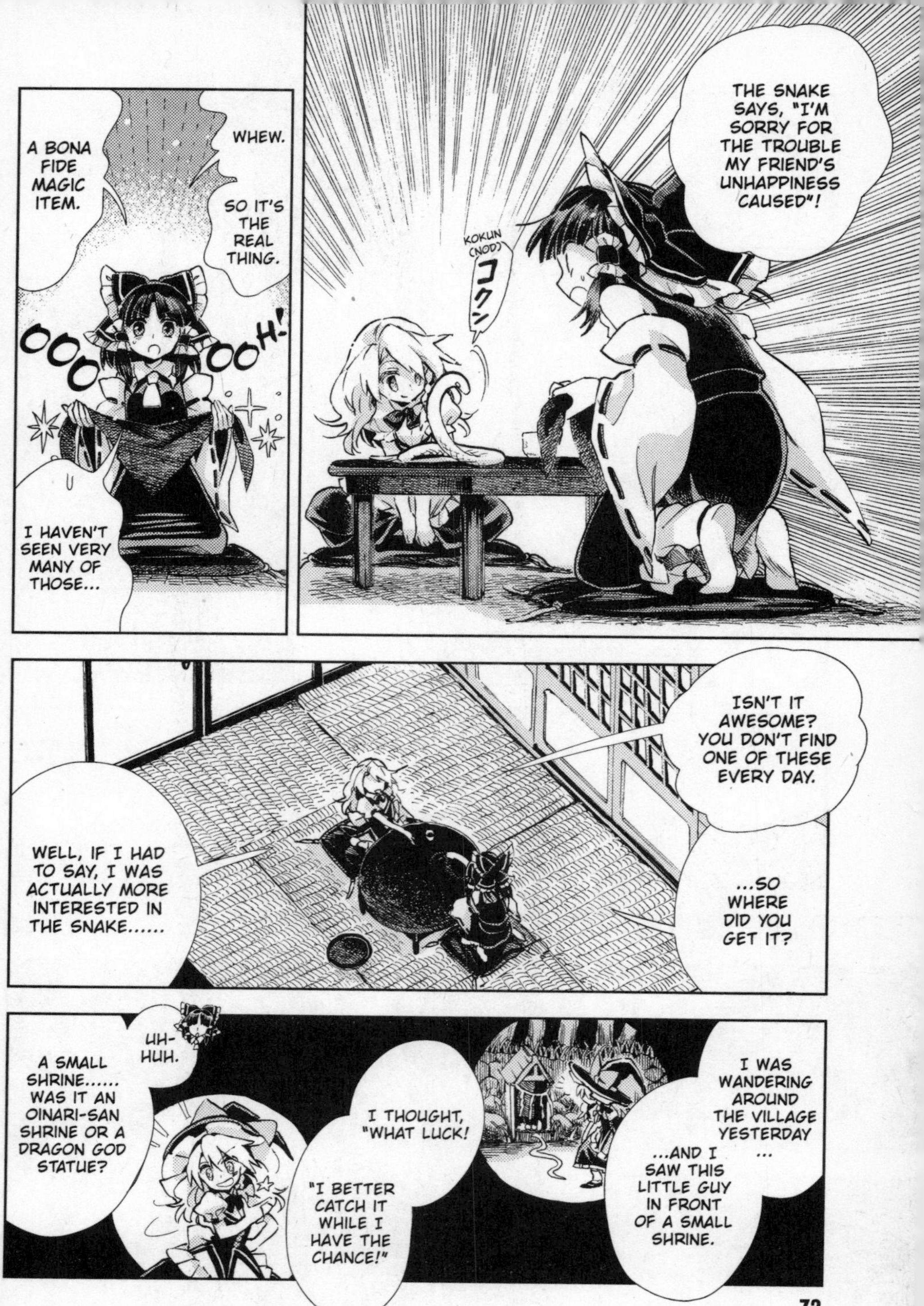
THE SNAKE SAYS, "I'M SORRY FOR THE TROUBLE MY FRIEND'S UNHAPPINESS CAUSED"!
KOKUN (NOD) コクン
WHEW.
SO IT'S THE REAL THING.
A BONA FIDE MAGIC ITEM.
OOOOOH!
I HAVEN'T SEEN VERY MANY OF THOSE...
ISN'T IT AWESOME? YOU DON'T FIND ONE OF THESE EVERY DAY.
...SO WHERE DID YOU GET IT?
WELL, IF I HAD TO SAY, I WAS ACTUALLY MORE INTERESTED IN THE SNAKE......
I WAS WANDERING AROUND THE VILLAGE YESTERDAY ...
...AND I SAW THIS LITTLE GUY IN FRONT OF A SMALL SHRINE.
I THOUGHT, "WHAT LUCK!
"I BETTER CATCH IT WHILE I HAVE THE CHANCE!"
UH-HUH.
A SMALL SHRINE...... WAS IT AN OINARI-SAN SHRINE OR A DRAGON GOD STATUE?

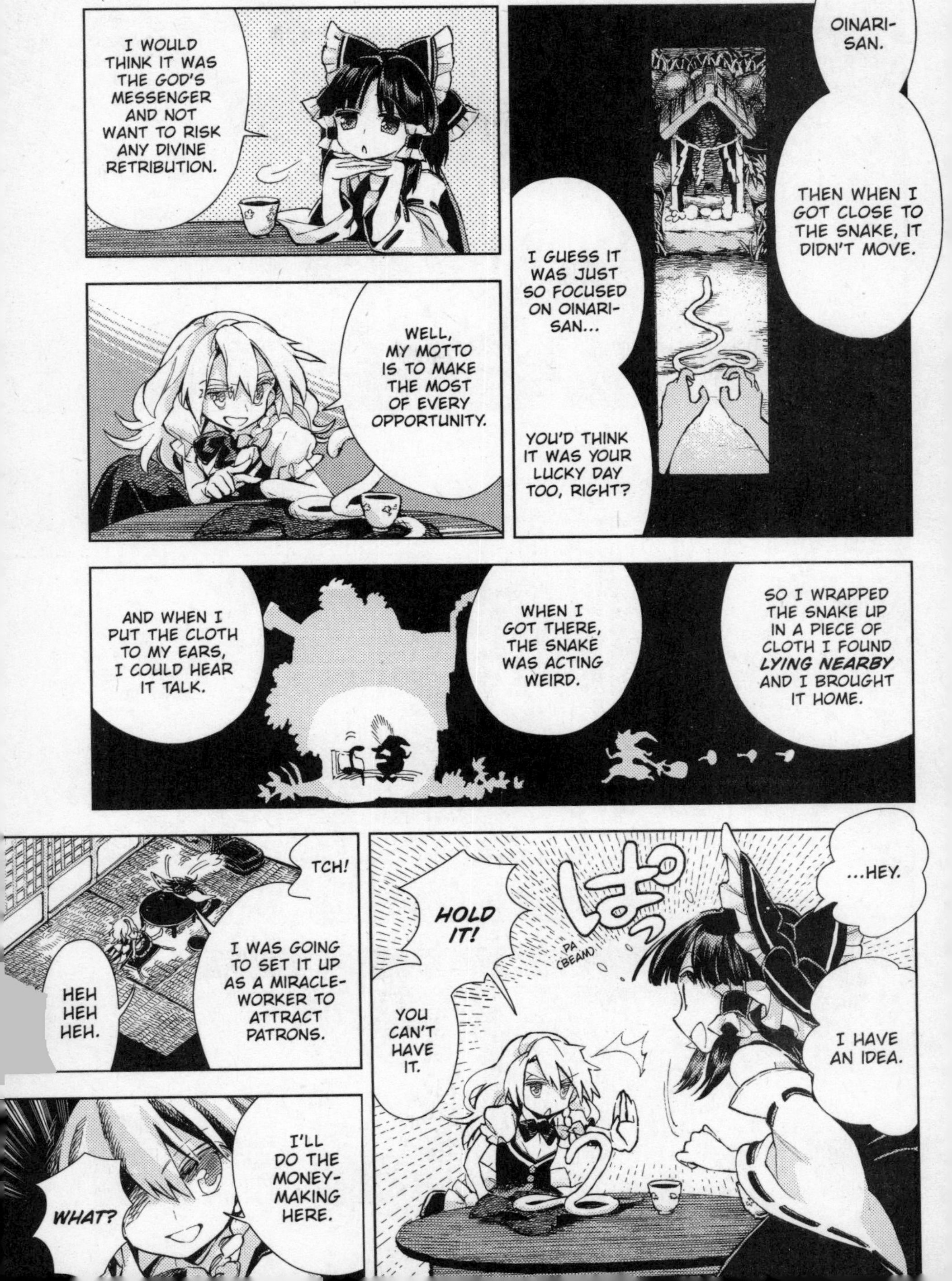
OINARI-SAN.
THEN WHEN I GOT CLOSE TO THE SNAKE, IT DIDN'T MOVE.
I GUESS IT WAS JUST SO FOCUSED ON OINARI-SAN...
YOU'D THINK IT WAS YOUR LUCKY DAY TOO, RIGHT?
I WOULD THINK IT WAS THE GOD'S MESSENGER AND NOT WANT TO RISK ANY DIVINE RETRIBUTION.
WELL, MY MOTTO IS TO MAKE THE MOST OF EVERY OPPORTUNITY.
SO I WRAPPED THE SNAKE UP IN A PIECE OF CLOTH I FOUND *LYING NEARBY* AND I BROUGHT IT HOME.
WHEN I GOT THERE, THE SNAKE WAS ACTING WEIRD.
AND WHEN I PUT THE CLOTH TO MY EARS, I COULD HEAR IT TALK.
...HEY.
I HAVE AN IDEA.
ぱっ
PA (BEAM)
HOLD IT!
YOU CAN'T HAVE IT.
TCH!
I WAS GOING TO SET IT UP AS A MIRACLE-WORKER TO ATTRACT PATRONS.
HEH HEH HEH.
I'LL DO THE MONEY-MAKING HERE.
WHAT?

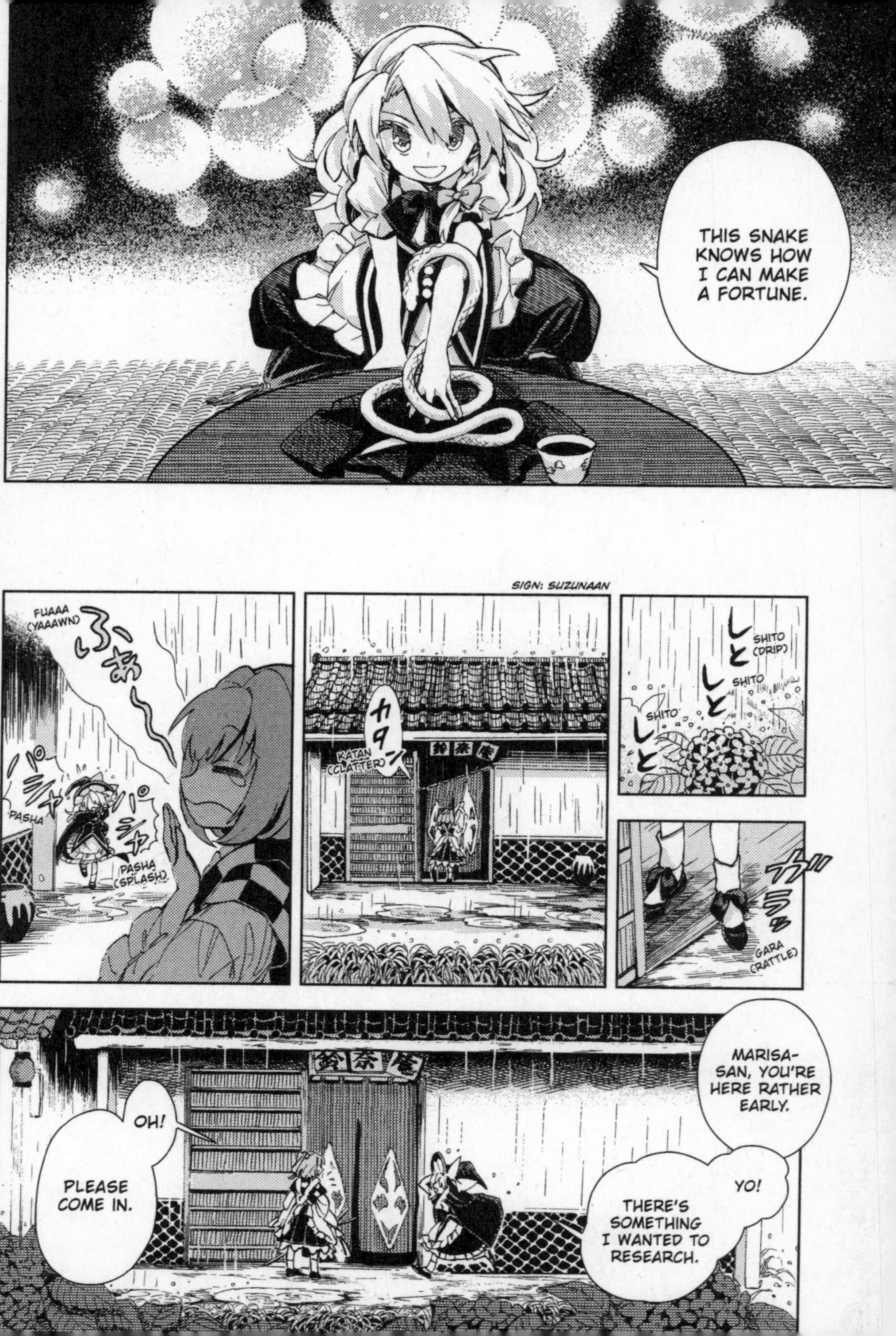
THIS SNAKE KNOWS HOW I CAN MAKE A FORTUNE.
しと
SHITO (DRIP)
しと
SHITO
しと
SHITO
ガラッ
GARA (RATTLE)
SIGN: SUZUNAAN
カタン
KATAN (CLATTER)
ふあ~
FUAAA (YAAAWN)
パシャ
PASHA
パシャ
PASHA (SPLASH)
MARISA-SAN, YOU'RE HERE RATHER EARLY.
YO!
THERE'S SOMETHING I WANTED TO RESEARCH.
OH!
PLEASE COME IN.

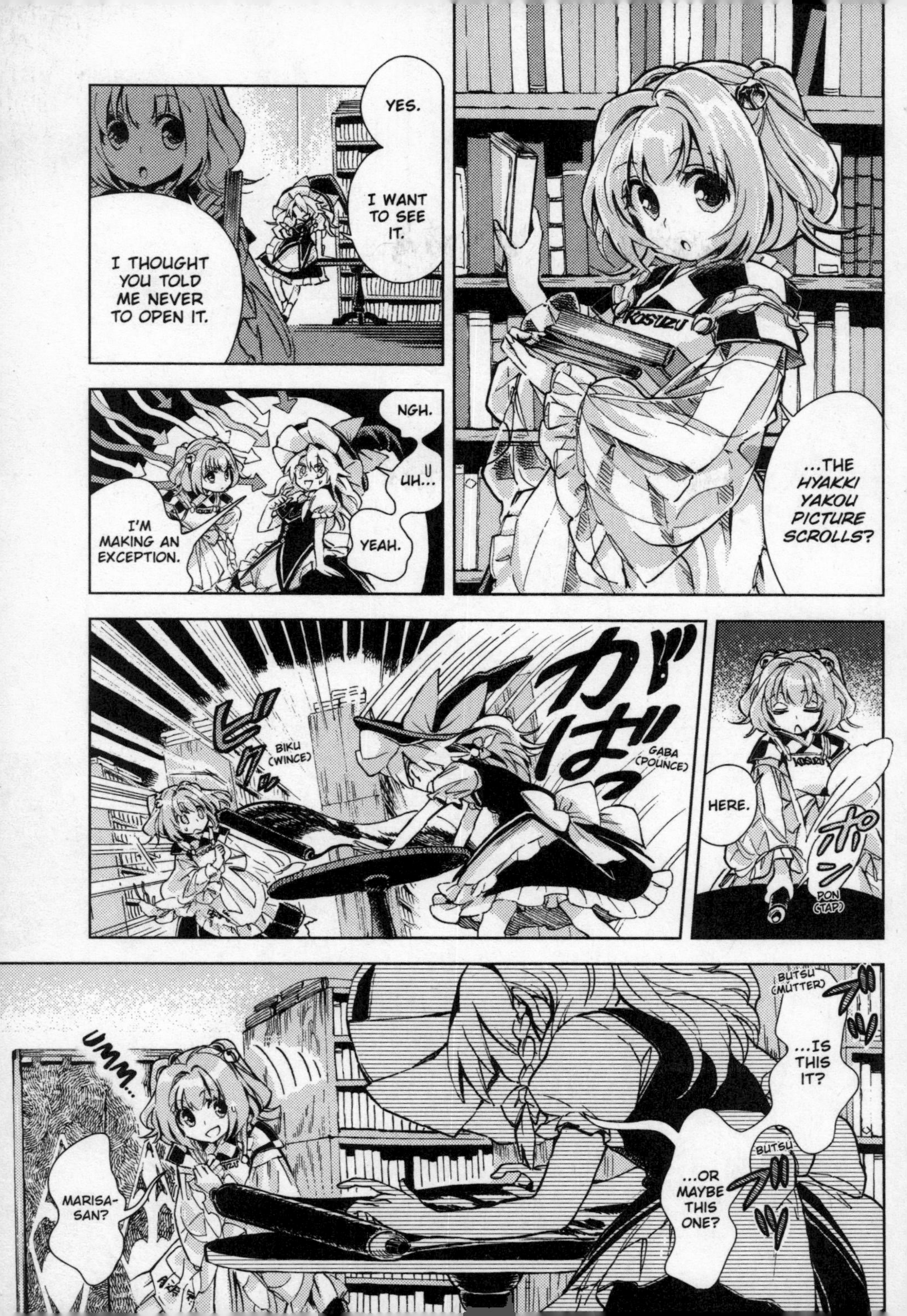
...THE HYAKKI YAKOU PICTURE SCROLLS?
YES.
I WANT TO SEE IT.
I THOUGHT YOU TOLD ME NEVER TO OPEN IT.
NGH.
UH...
YEAH.
I'M MAKING AN EXCEPTION.
HERE.
ポン
PON (TAP)
がばっ
GABA (POUNCE)
BIKU (WINCE)
BUTSU (MUTTER)
...IS THIS IT?
BUTSU
...OR MAYBE THIS ONE?
UMM...
MARISA-SAN?

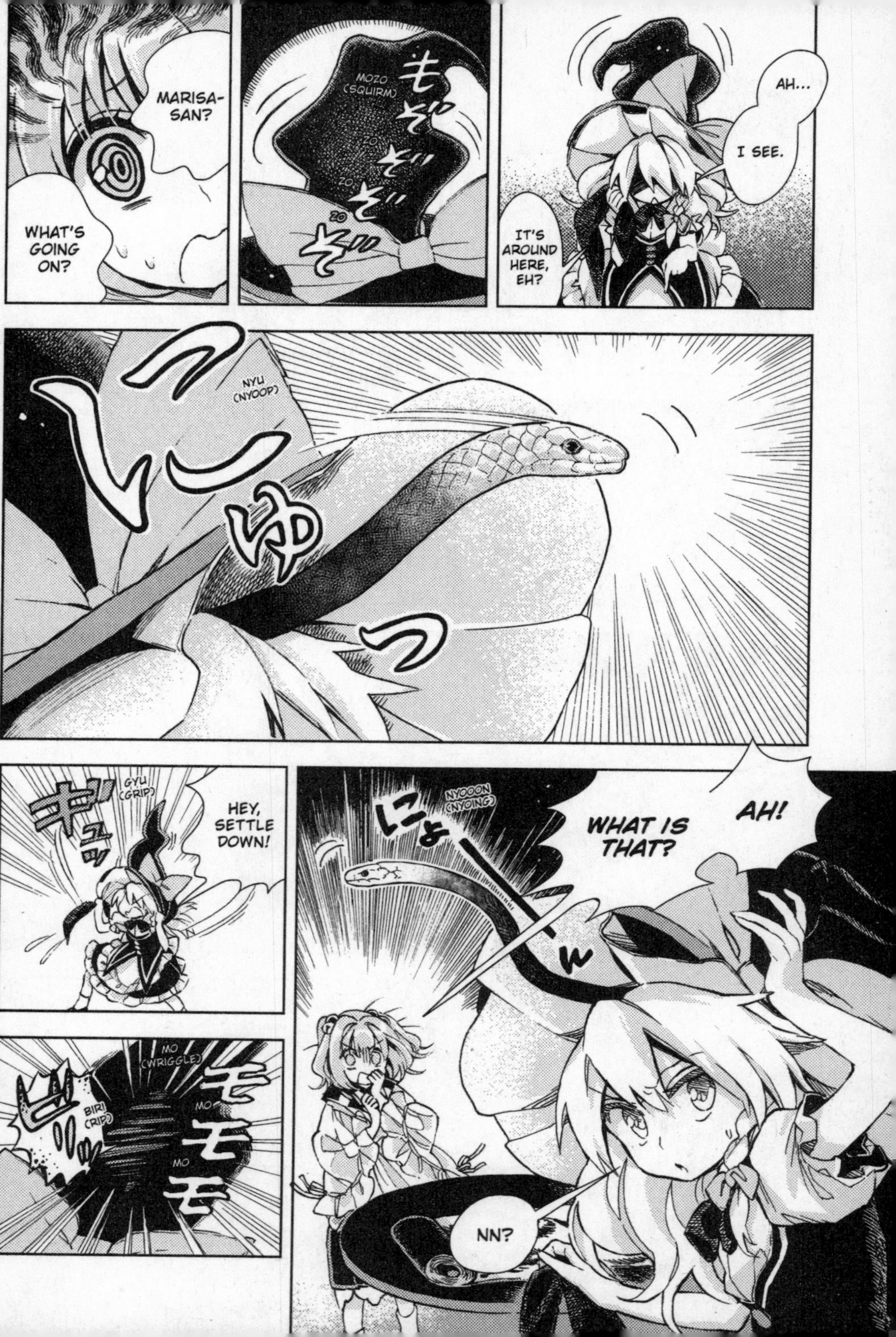
AH...
I SEE.
IT'S AROUND HERE, EH?
MOZO (SQUIRM)
ZO
ZO
ZO
MARISA-SAN?
WHAT'S GOING ON?
NYU (NYOOP)
AH!
WHAT IS THAT?
NYOOON (NYOING)
NN?
GYU (GRIP)
HEY, SETTLE DOWN!
MO (WRIGGLE)
MO
MO
BIRI (RIP)

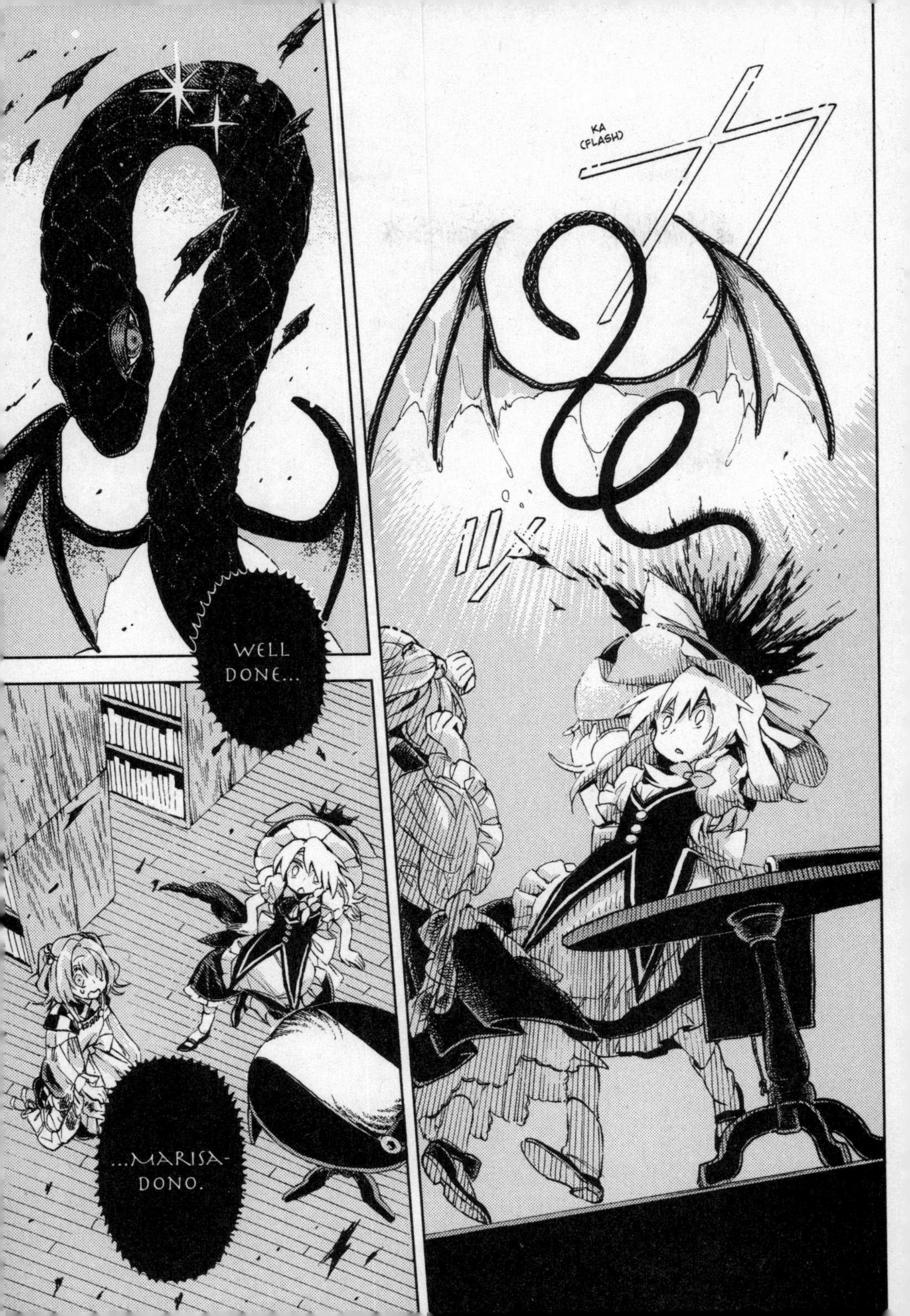
KA (FLASH)
WELL DONE...
...MARISA-DONO.

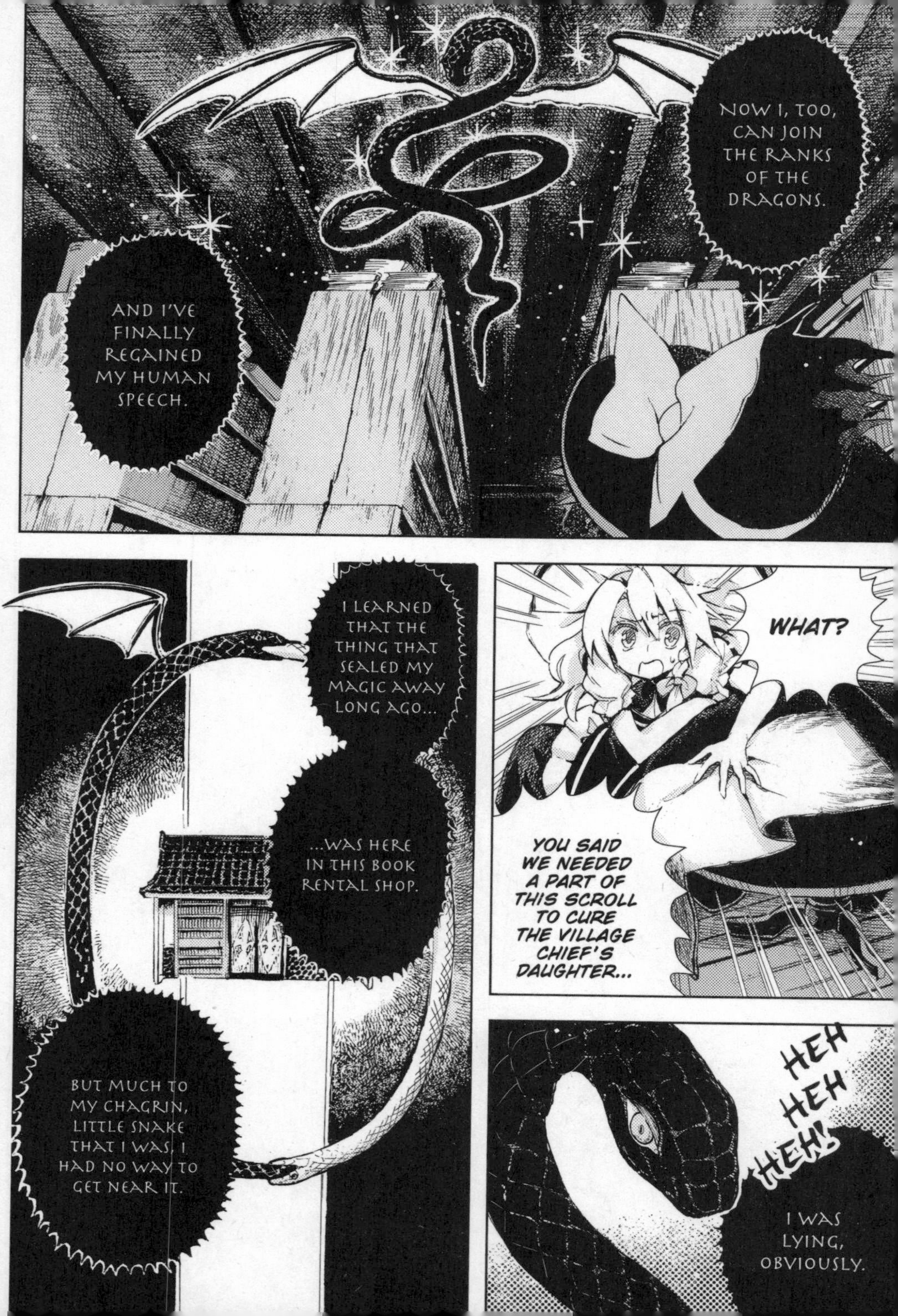
NOW I, TOO, CAN JOIN THE RANKS OF THE DRAGONS.
AND I'VE FINALLY REGAINED MY HUMAN SPEECH.
WHAT?
YOU SAID WE NEEDED A PART OF THIS SCROLL TO CURE THE VILLAGE CHIEF'S DAUGHTER...
HEH HEH HEH!
I WAS LYING, OBVIOUSLY.
I LEARNED THAT THE THING THAT SEALED MY MAGIC AWAY LONG AGO...
...WAS HERE IN THIS BOOK RENTAL SHOP.
BUT MUCH TO MY CHAGRIN, LITTLE SNAKE THAT I WAS, I HAD NO WAY TO GET NEAR IT.

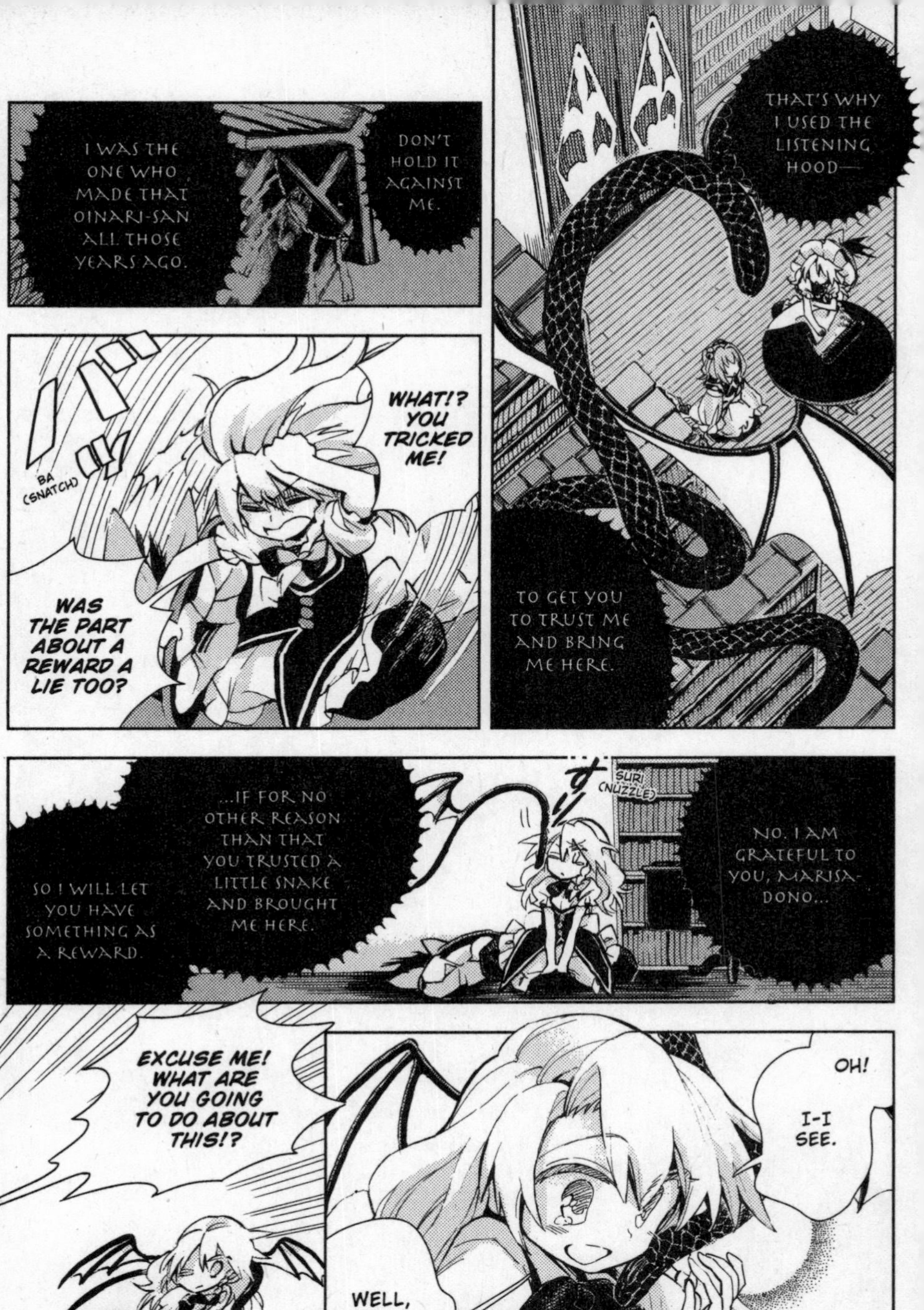
THAT'S WHY I USED THE LISTENING HOOD—
TO GET YOU TO TRUST ME AND BRING ME HERE.
DON'T HOLD IT AGAINST ME.
I WAS THE ONE WHO MADE THAT OINARI-SAN ALL THOSE YEARS AGO.
WHAT!? YOU TRICKED ME!
BA (SNATCH)
WAS THE PART ABOUT A REWARD A LIE TOO?
NO. I AM GRATEFUL TO YOU, MARISA-DONO...
SURI (NUZZLE)
...IF FOR NO OTHER REASON THAN THAT YOU TRUSTED A LITTLE SNAKE AND BROUGHT ME HERE.
SO I WILL LET YOU HAVE SOMETHING AS A REWARD.
OH!
I-I SEE.
WELL, OKAY, THEN.
EXCUSE ME! WHAT ARE YOU GOING TO DO ABOUT THIS!?

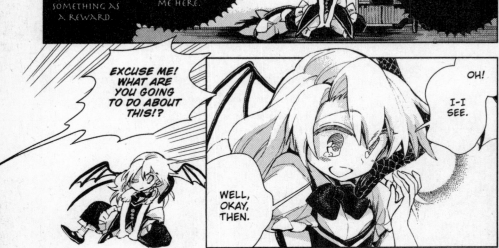

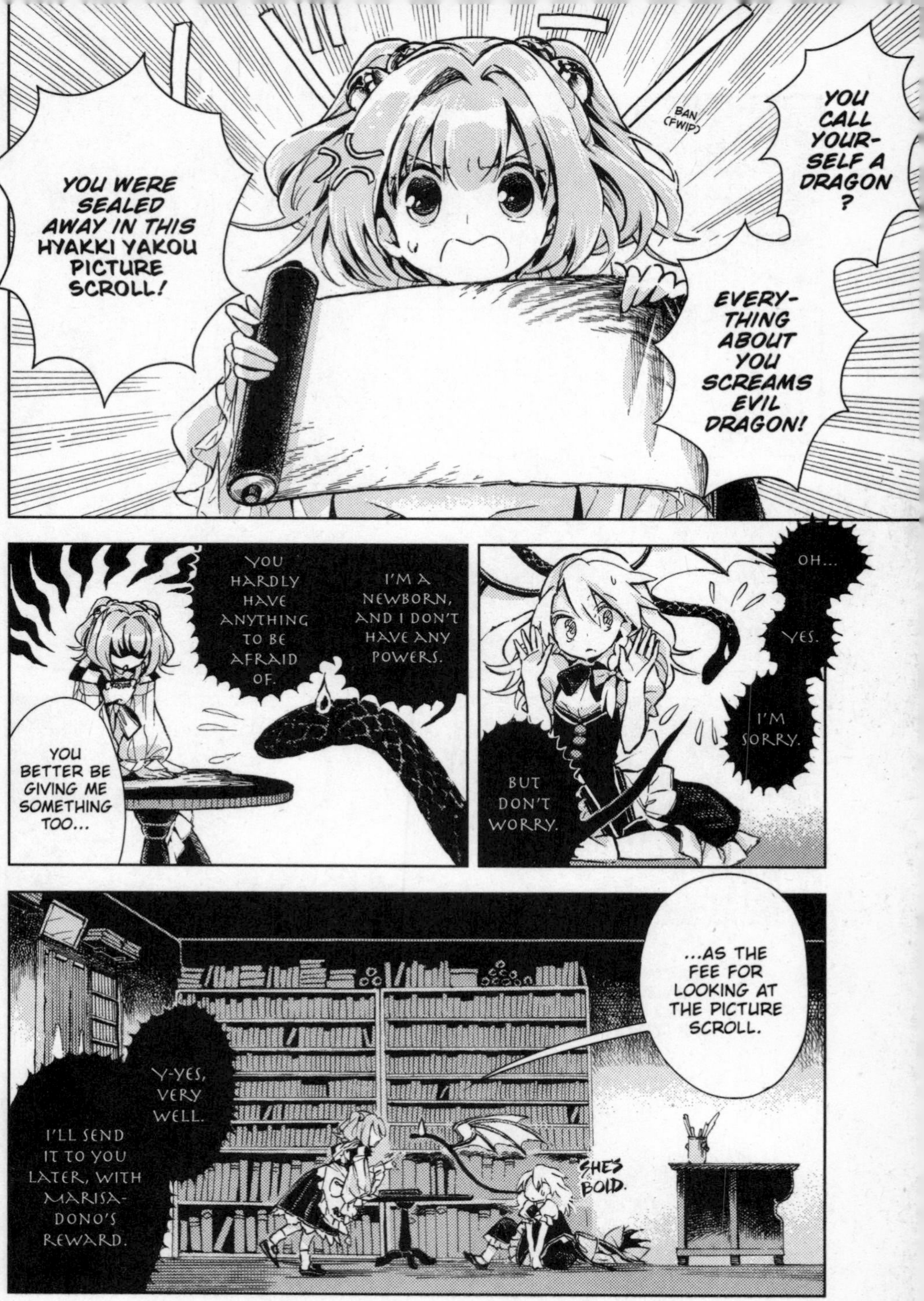
YOU CALL YOURSELF A DRAGON?
BAN (FWIP)
EVERYTHING ABOUT YOU SCREAMS EVIL DRAGON!
YOU WERE SEALED AWAY IN THIS HYAKKI YAKOU PICTURE SCROLL!
OH... YES.
I'M SORRY.
BUT DON'T WORRY.
I'M A NEWBORN, AND I DON'T HAVE ANY POWERS.
YOU HARDLY HAVE ANYTHING TO BE AFRAID OF.
YOU BETTER BE GIVING ME SOMETHING TOO...
...AS THE FEE FOR LOOKING AT THE PICTURE SCROLL.
SHE'S BOLD.
Y-YES, VERY WELL.
I'LL SEND IT TO YOU LATER, WITH MARISA-DONO'S REWARD.

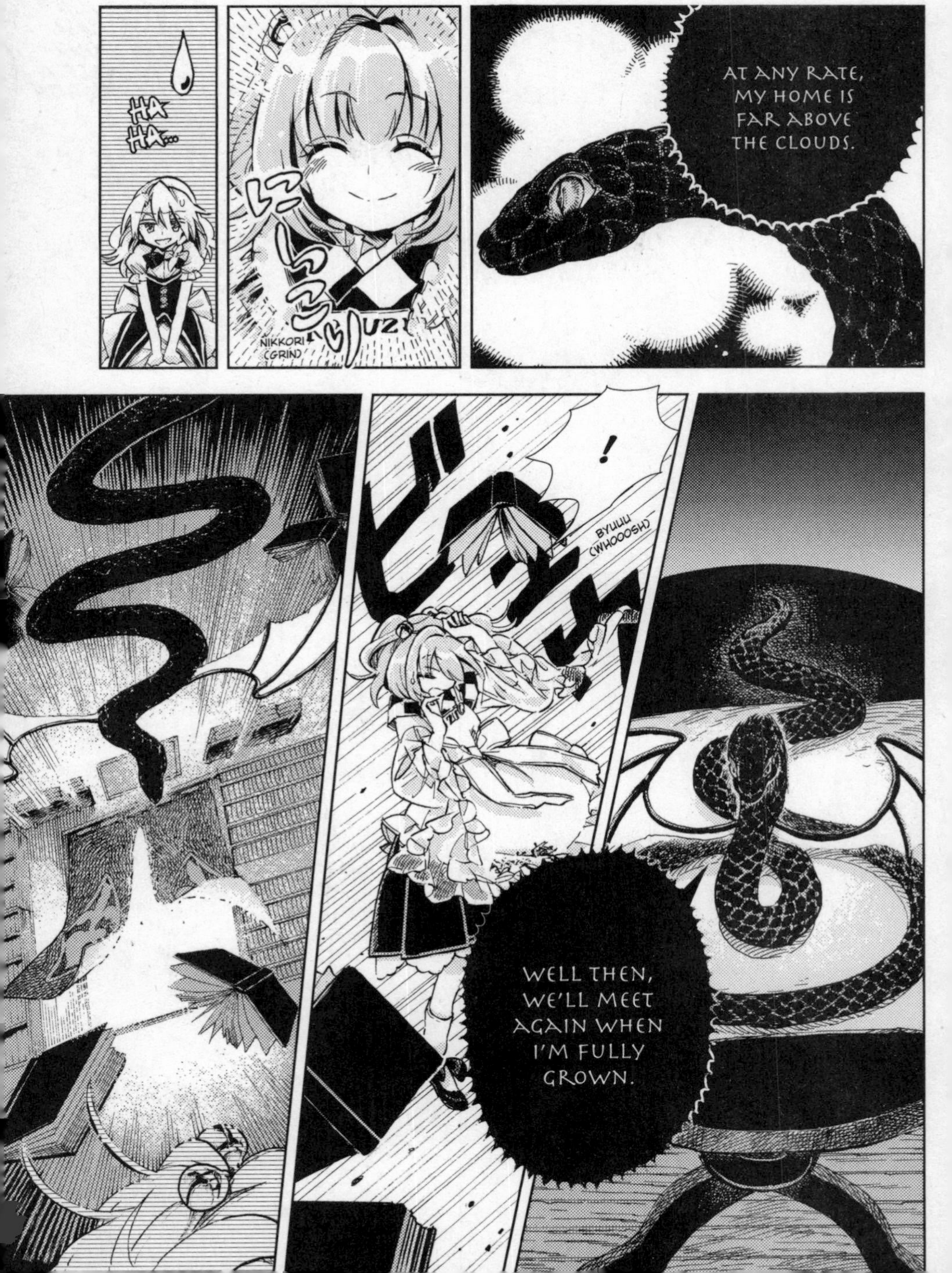
AT ANY RATE, MY HOME IS FAR ABOVE THE CLOUDS.
NIKKORI (GRIN)
HA HA...
WELL THEN, WE'LL MEET AGAIN WHEN I'M FULLY GROWN.
!
BYUUU (WHOOOSH)

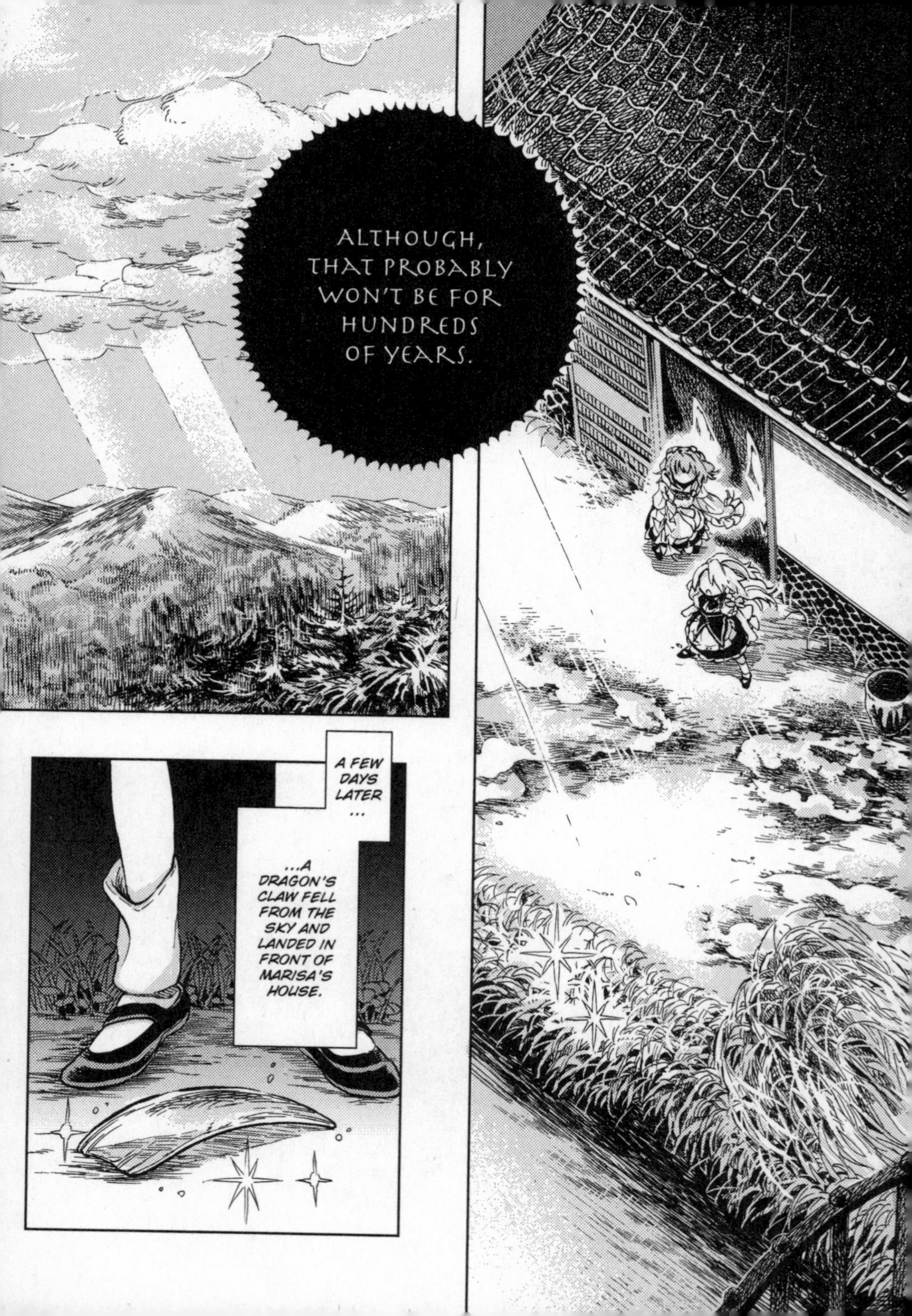
ALTHOUGH, THAT PROBABLY WON'T BE FOR HUNDREDS OF YEARS.
A FEW DAYS LATER ...
...A DRAGON'S CLAW FELL FROM THE SKY AND LANDED IN FRONT OF MARISA'S HOUSE.

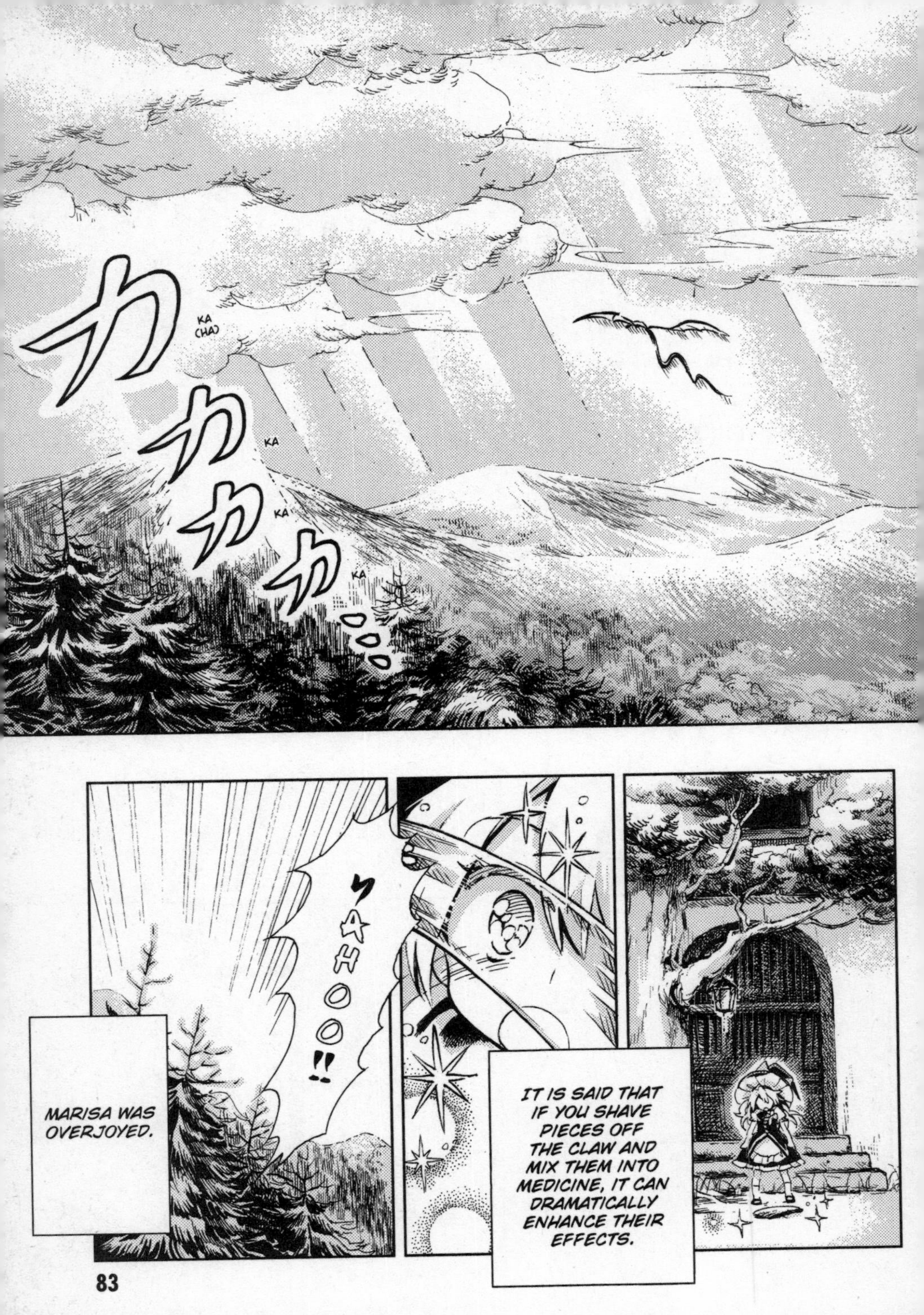

カ
KA (HA)
カ
KA
カ
KA
カ
KA
IT IS SAID THAT IF YOU SHAVE PIECES OFF THE CLAW AND MIX THEM INTO MEDICINE, IT CAN DRAMATICALLY ENHANCE THEIR EFFECTS.
YAHOOO!!
MARISA WAS OVERJOYED.

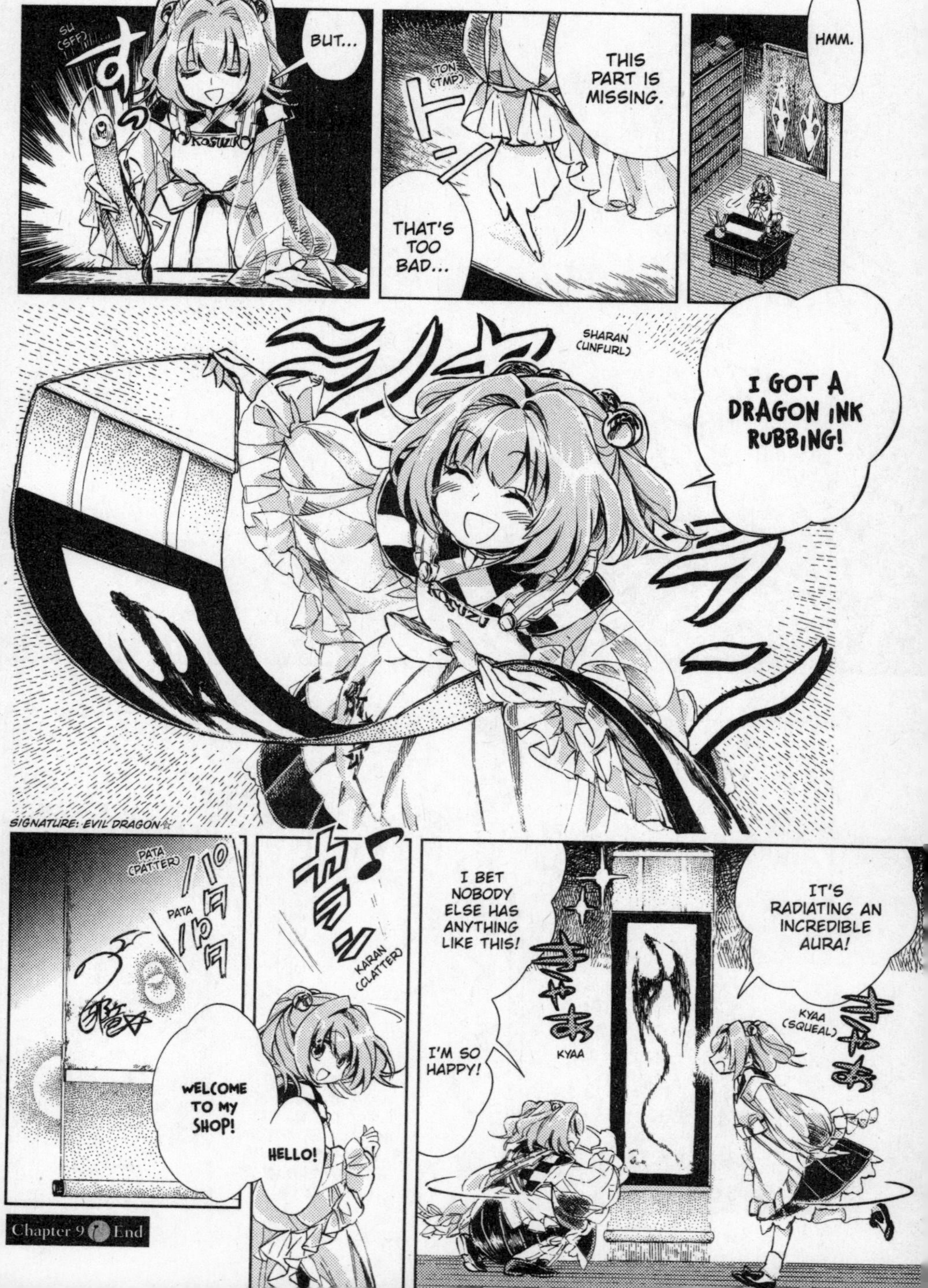
HMM.
THIS PART IS MISSING.
TON (TMP)
THAT'S TOO BAD...
SU (SFF)
BUT...
I GOT A DRAGON INK RUBBING!
SHARAN (UNFURL)
SIGNATURE: EVIL DRAGON
IT'S RADIATING AN INCREDIBLE AURA!
KYAA (SQUEAL)
I BET NOBODY ELSE HAS ANYTHING LIKE THIS!
KYAA
I'M SO HAPPY!
KARAN (CLATTER)
HELLO!
WELCOME TO MY SHOP!
PATA (PATTER)
PATA
Chapter 9 End

Forbidden Scrollery

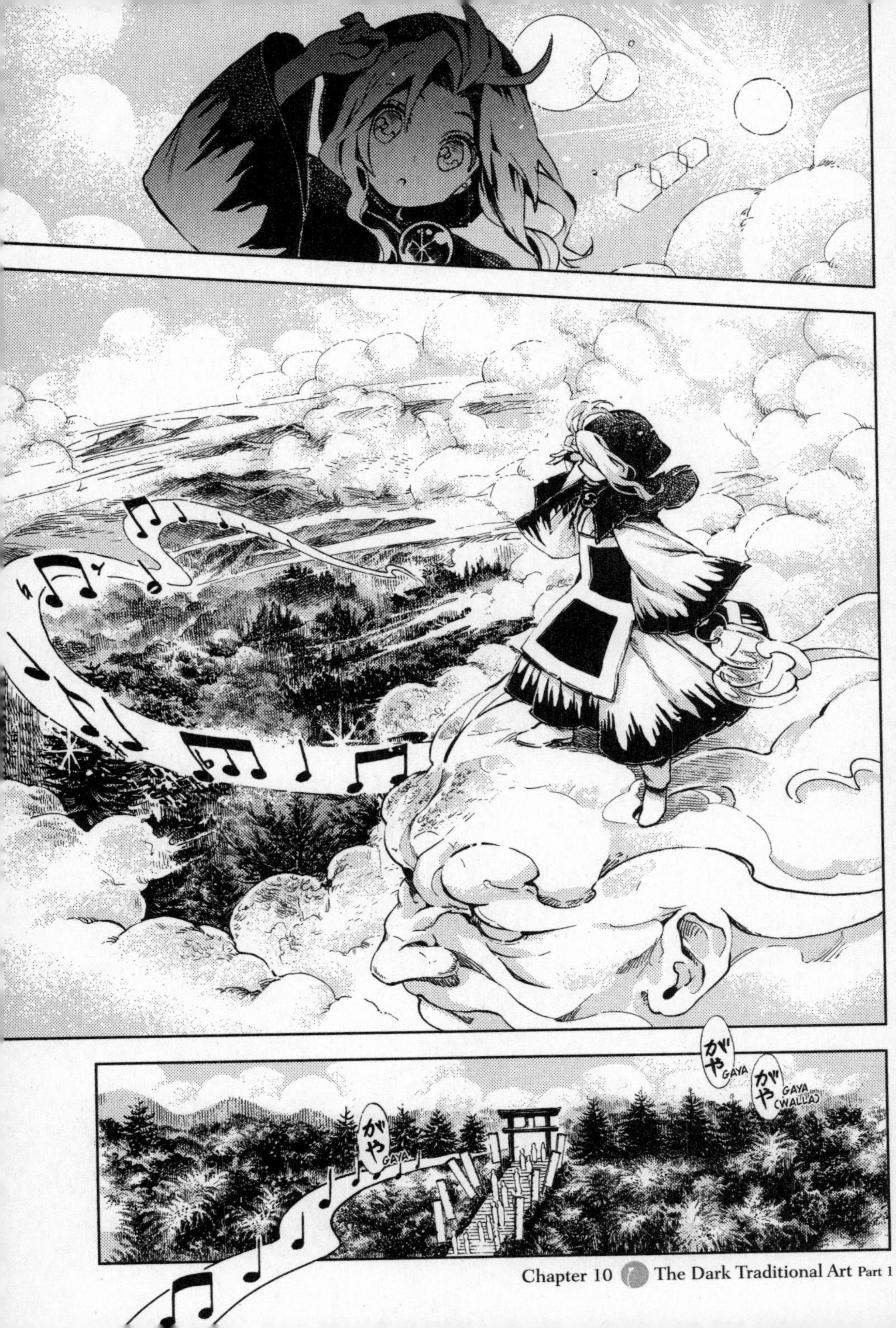
がや GAYA (WALLA)
がや GAYA
がや GAYA

Chapter 10 The Dark Traditional Art Part 1

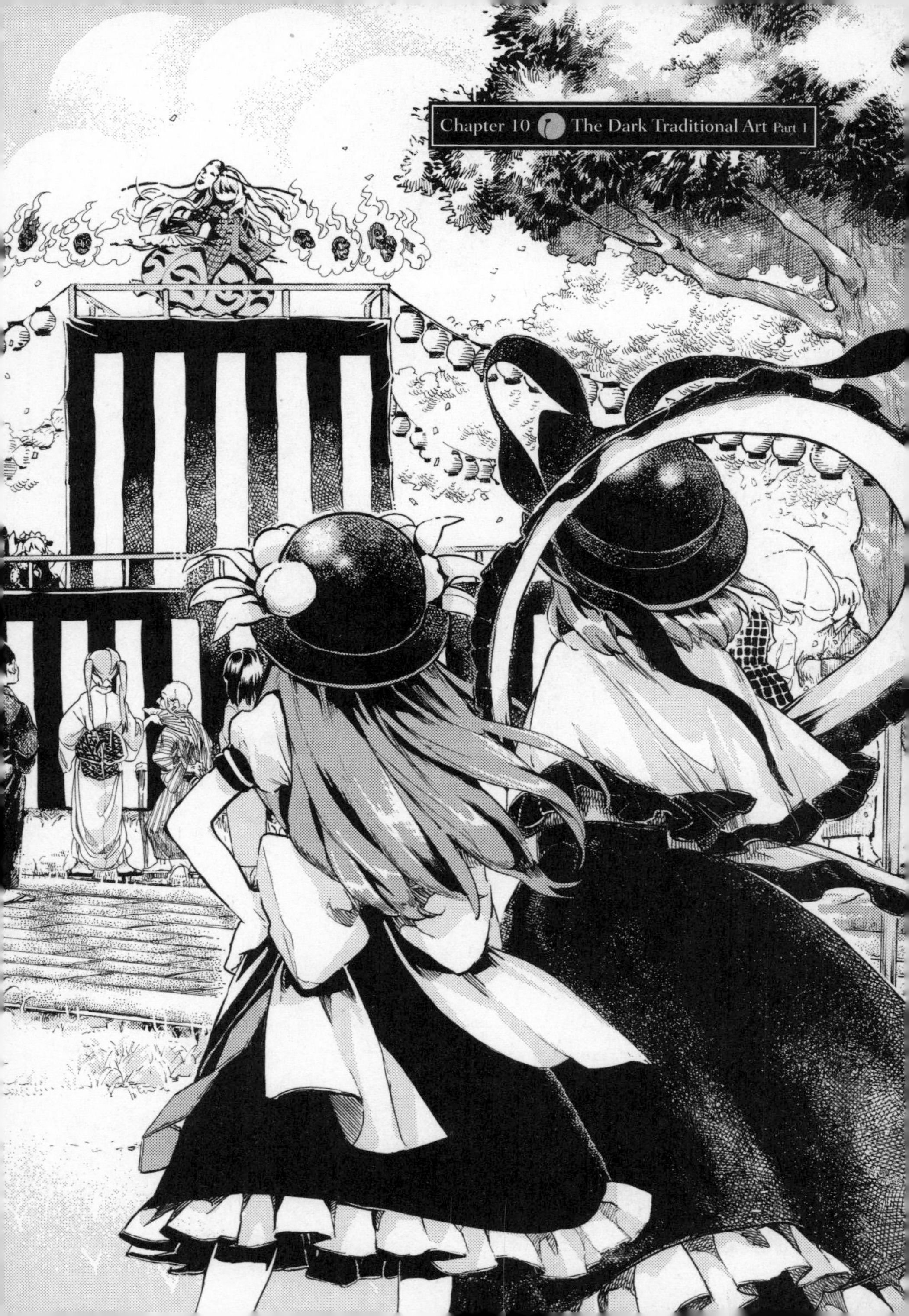
Chapter 10 The Dark Traditional Art Part 1

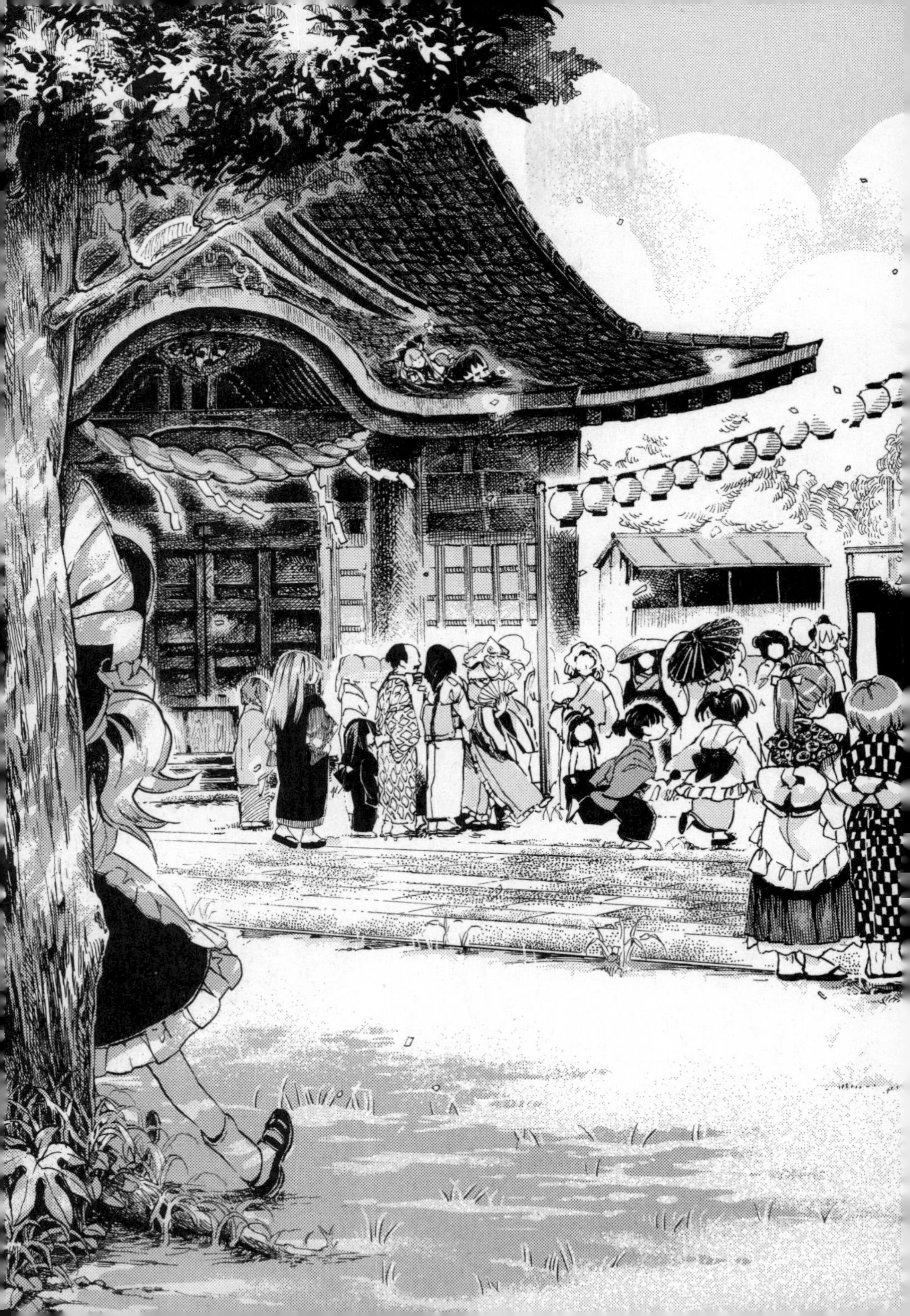

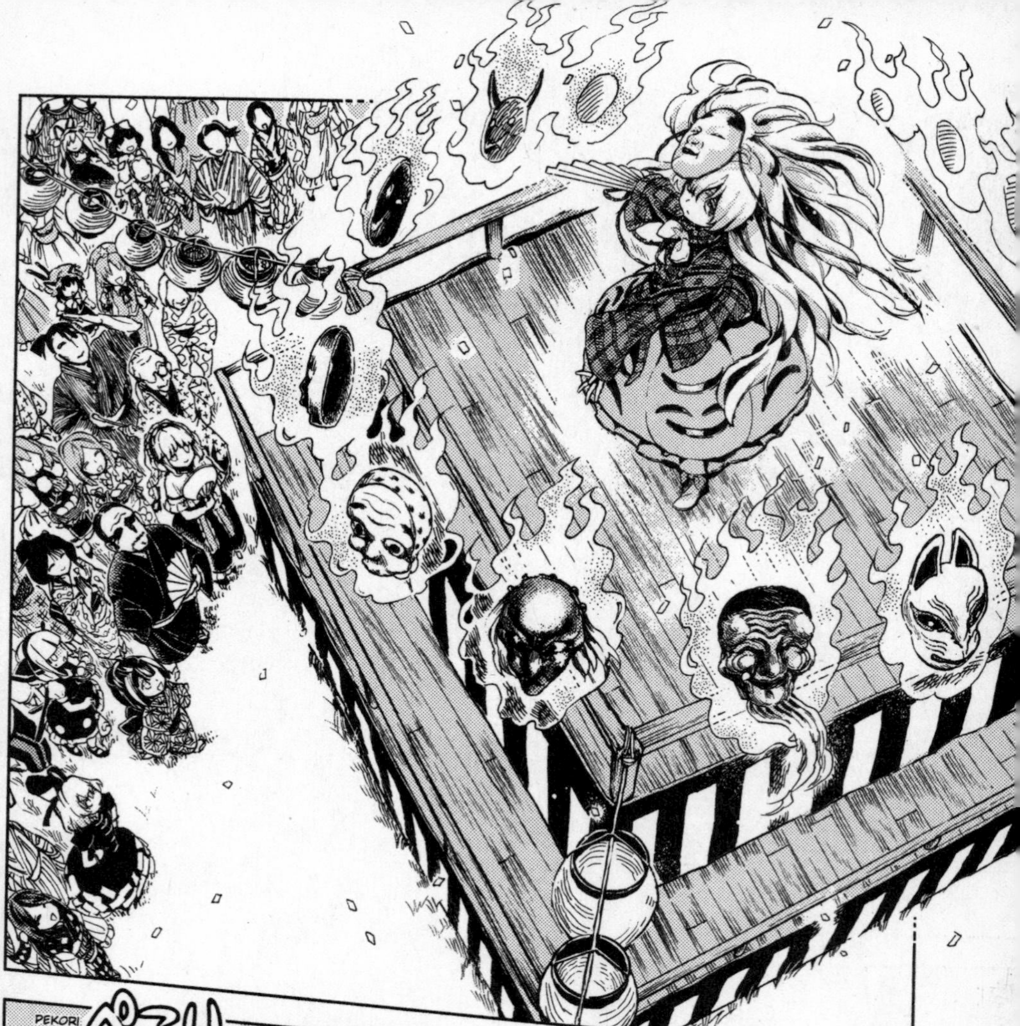

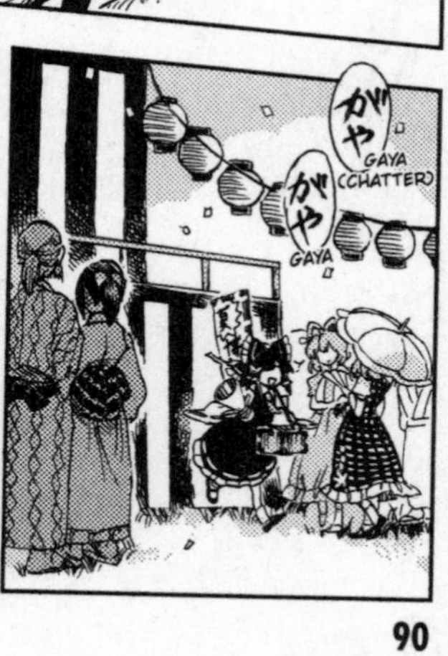
がやGAYA (CHATTER)
がやGAYA

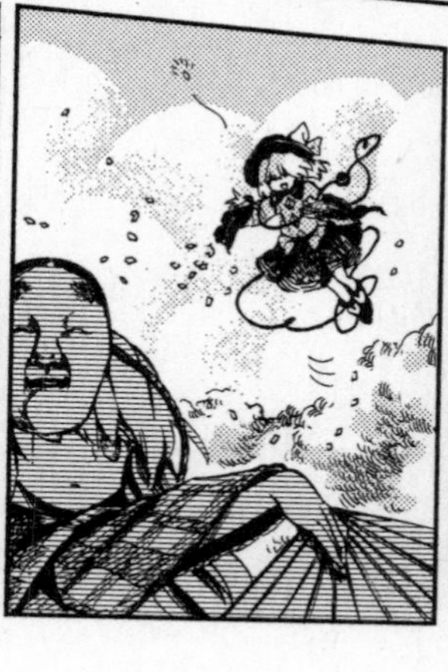

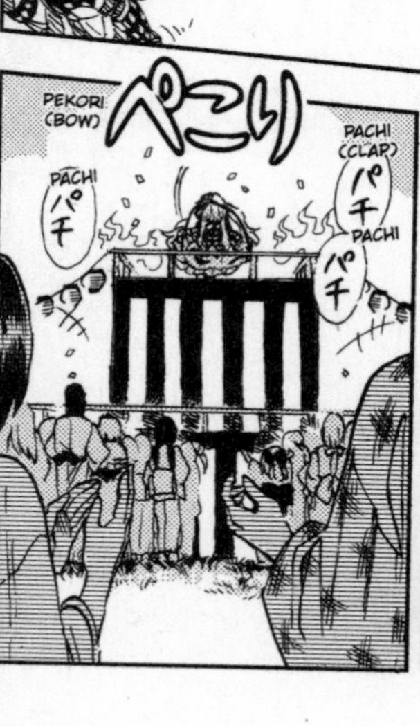
PEKORI (BOW)
ぺこり
パチ PACHI (CLAP)
パチ PACHI
パチ PACHI
パチ

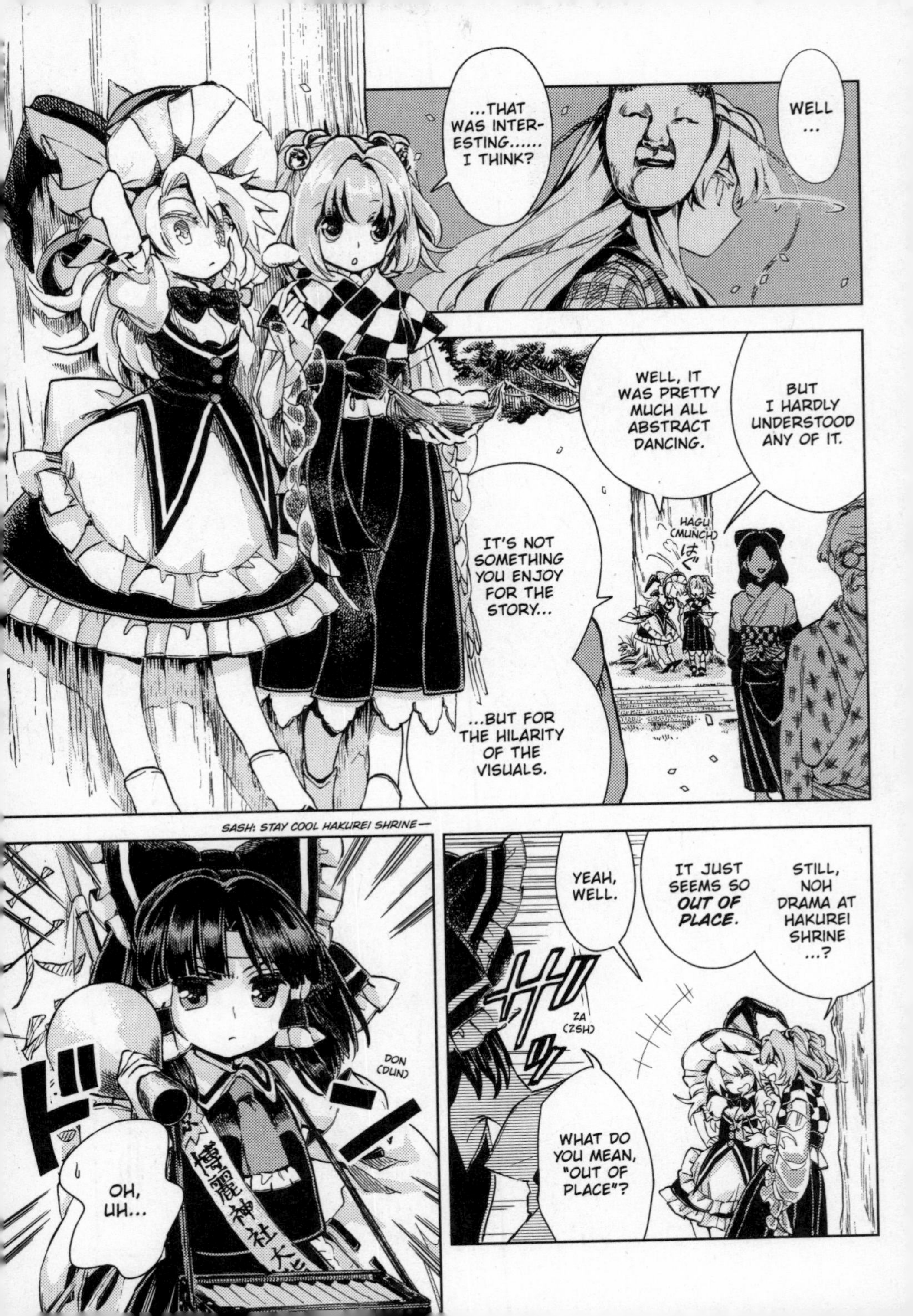
WELL ...
...THAT WAS INTERESTING...... I THINK?
BUT I HARDLY UNDERSTOOD ANY OF IT.
WELL, IT WAS PRETTY MUCH ALL ABSTRACT DANCING.
HAGU (MUNCH)
IT'S NOT SOMETHING YOU ENJOY FOR THE STORY...
...BUT FOR THE HILARITY OF THE VISUALS.
SASH: STAY COOL HAKUREI SHRINE—
STILL, NOH DRAMA AT HAKUREI SHRINE ...?
IT JUST SEEMS SO *OUT OF PLACE*.
YEAH, WELL.
ZA (ZSH)
WHAT DO YOU MEAN, "OUT OF PLACE"?
DON (DUN)
OH, UH...

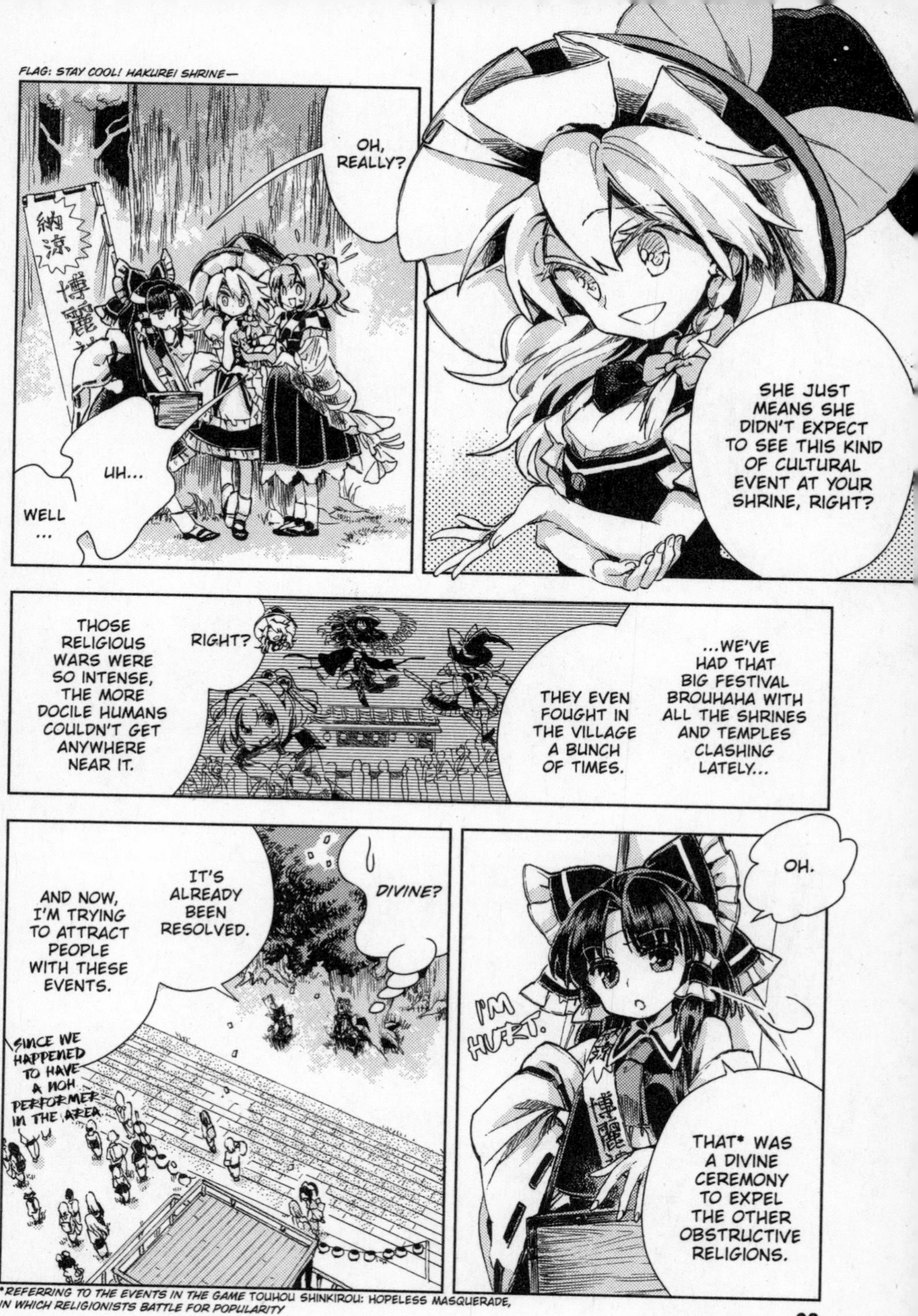
FLAG: STAY COOL! HAKUREI SHRINE—
SHE JUST MEANS SHE DIDN'T EXPECT TO SEE THIS KIND OF CULTURAL EVENT AT YOUR SHRINE, RIGHT?
OH, REALLY?
納涼
博麗
UH...
WELL ...
...WE'VE HAD THAT BIG FESTIVAL BROUHAHA WITH ALL THE SHRINES AND TEMPLES CLASHING LATELY...
THEY EVEN FOUGHT IN THE VILLAGE A BUNCH OF TIMES.
RIGHT?
THOSE RELIGIOUS WARS WERE SO INTENSE, THE MORE DOCILE HUMANS COULDN'T GET ANYWHERE NEAR IT.
OH.
I'M HURT.
THAT* WAS A DIVINE CEREMONY TO EXPEL THE OTHER OBSTRUCTIVE RELIGIONS.
DIVINE?
IT'S ALREADY BEEN RESOLVED.
AND NOW, I'M TRYING TO ATTRACT PEOPLE WITH THESE EVENTS.
SINCE WE HAPPENED TO HAVE A NOH PERFORMER IN THE AREA

*REFERRING TO THE EVENTS IN THE GAME TOUHOU SHINKIROU: HOPELESS MASQUERADE, IN WHICH RELIGIONISTS BATTLE FOR POPULARITY

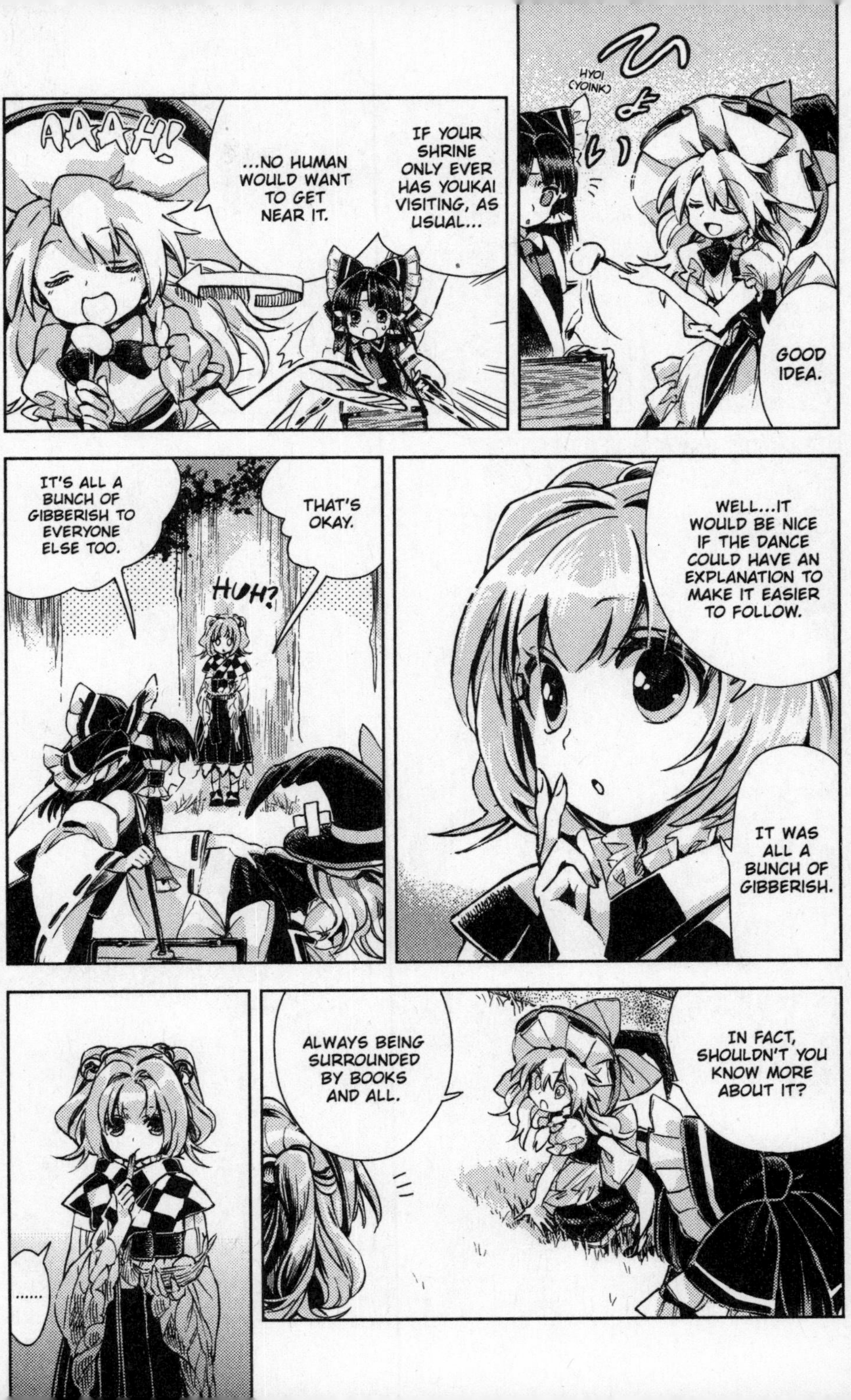
HYOI
(YOINK)
GOOD IDEA.
IF YOUR SHRINE ONLY EVER HAS YOUKAI VISITING, AS USUAL...
...NO HUMAN WOULD WANT TO GET NEAR IT.
AAAH!
WELL...IT WOULD BE NICE IF THE DANCE COULD HAVE AN EXPLANATION TO MAKE IT EASIER TO FOLLOW.
IT WAS ALL A BUNCH OF GIBBERISH.
THAT'S OKAY.
HUH?
IT'S ALL A BUNCH OF GIBBERISH TO EVERYONE ELSE TOO.
IN FACT, SHOULDN'T YOU KNOW MORE ABOUT IT?
ALWAYS BEING SURROUNDED BY BOOKS AND ALL.
......

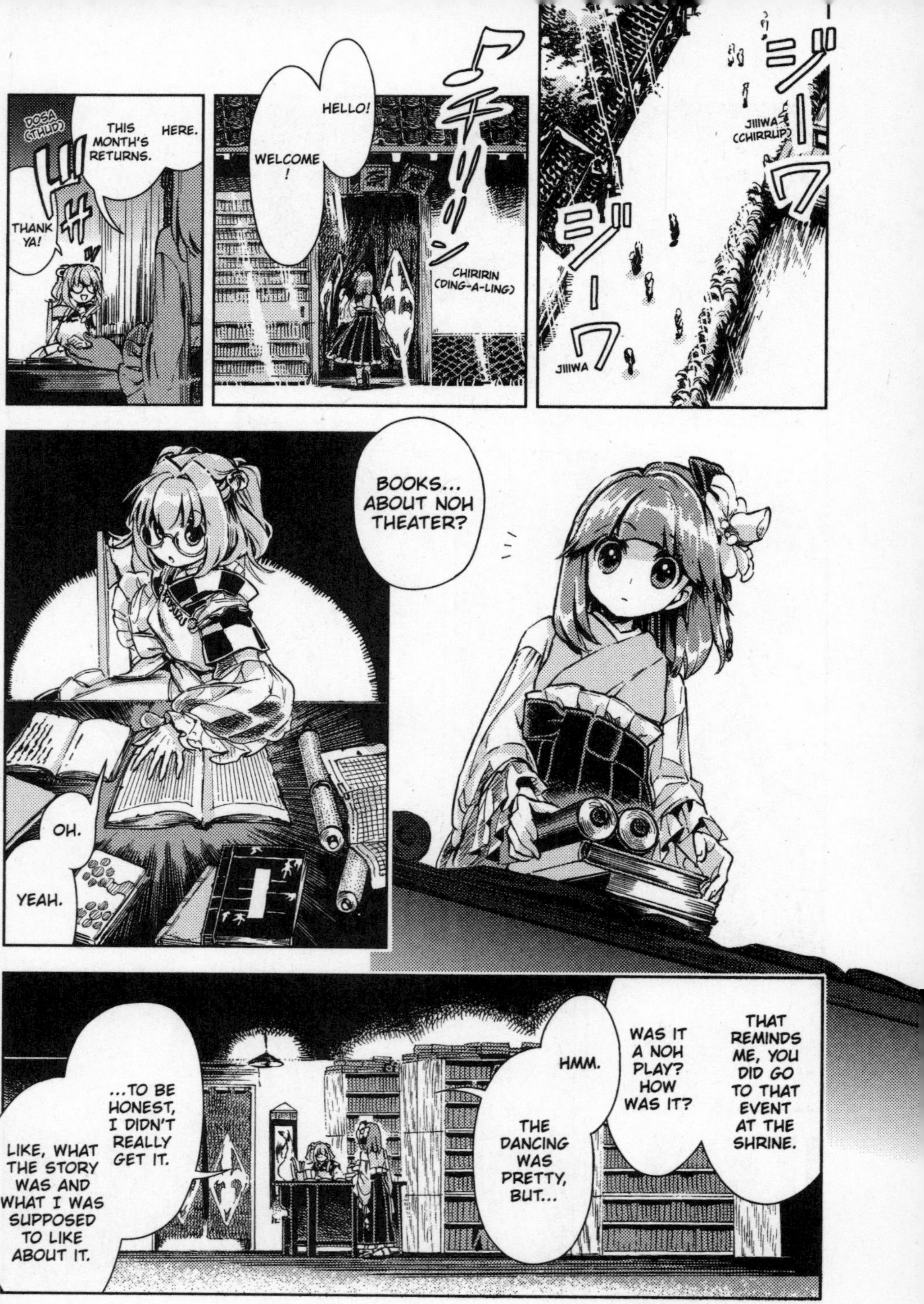
JIIIWA (CHIRRUP)
JIIIWA
CHIRIRIN (DING-A-LING)
HELLO!
WELCOME!
DOSA (THUD)
HERE.
THIS MONTH'S RETURNS.
THANK YA!
BOOKS... ABOUT NOH THEATER?
OH.
YEAH.
THAT REMINDS ME, YOU DID GO TO THAT EVENT AT THE SHRINE.
WAS IT A NOH PLAY? HOW WAS IT?
HMM.
THE DANCING WAS PRETTY, BUT...
...TO BE HONEST, I DIDN'T REALLY GET IT.
LIKE, WHAT THE STORY WAS AND WHAT I WAS SUPPOSED TO LIKE ABOUT IT.

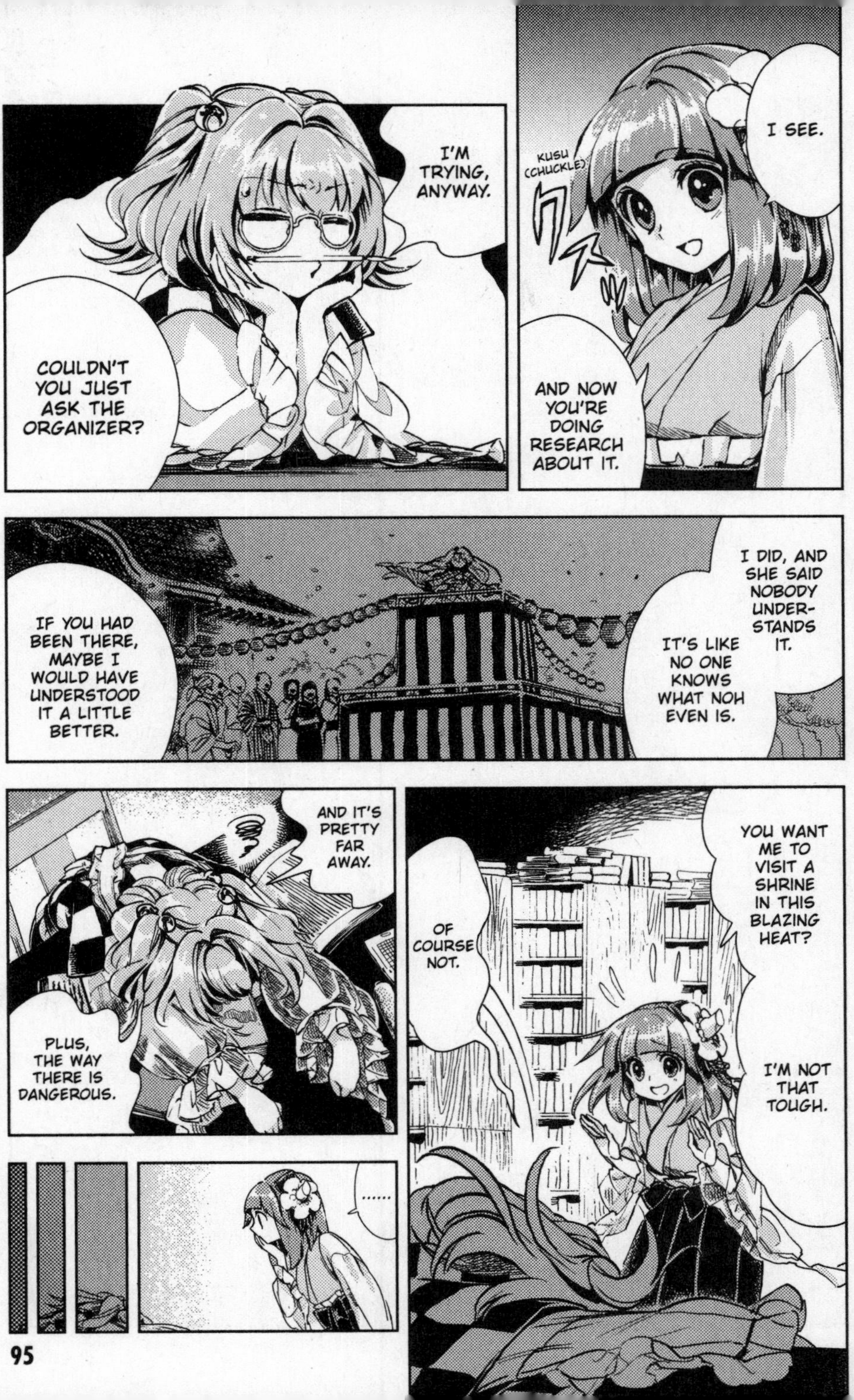
I SEE.
KUSU (CHUCKLE)
AND NOW YOU'RE DOING RESEARCH ABOUT IT.
I'M TRYING, ANYWAY.
COULDN'T YOU JUST ASK THE ORGANIZER?
I DID, AND SHE SAID NOBODY UNDER-STANDS IT.
IT'S LIKE NO ONE KNOWS WHAT NOH EVEN IS.
IF YOU HAD BEEN THERE, MAYBE I WOULD HAVE UNDERSTOOD IT A LITTLE BETTER.
YOU WANT ME TO VISIT A SHRINE IN THIS BLAZING HEAT?
OF COURSE NOT.
I'M NOT THAT TOUGH.
AND IT'S PRETTY FAR AWAY.
PLUS, THE WAY THERE IS DANGEROUS.
......

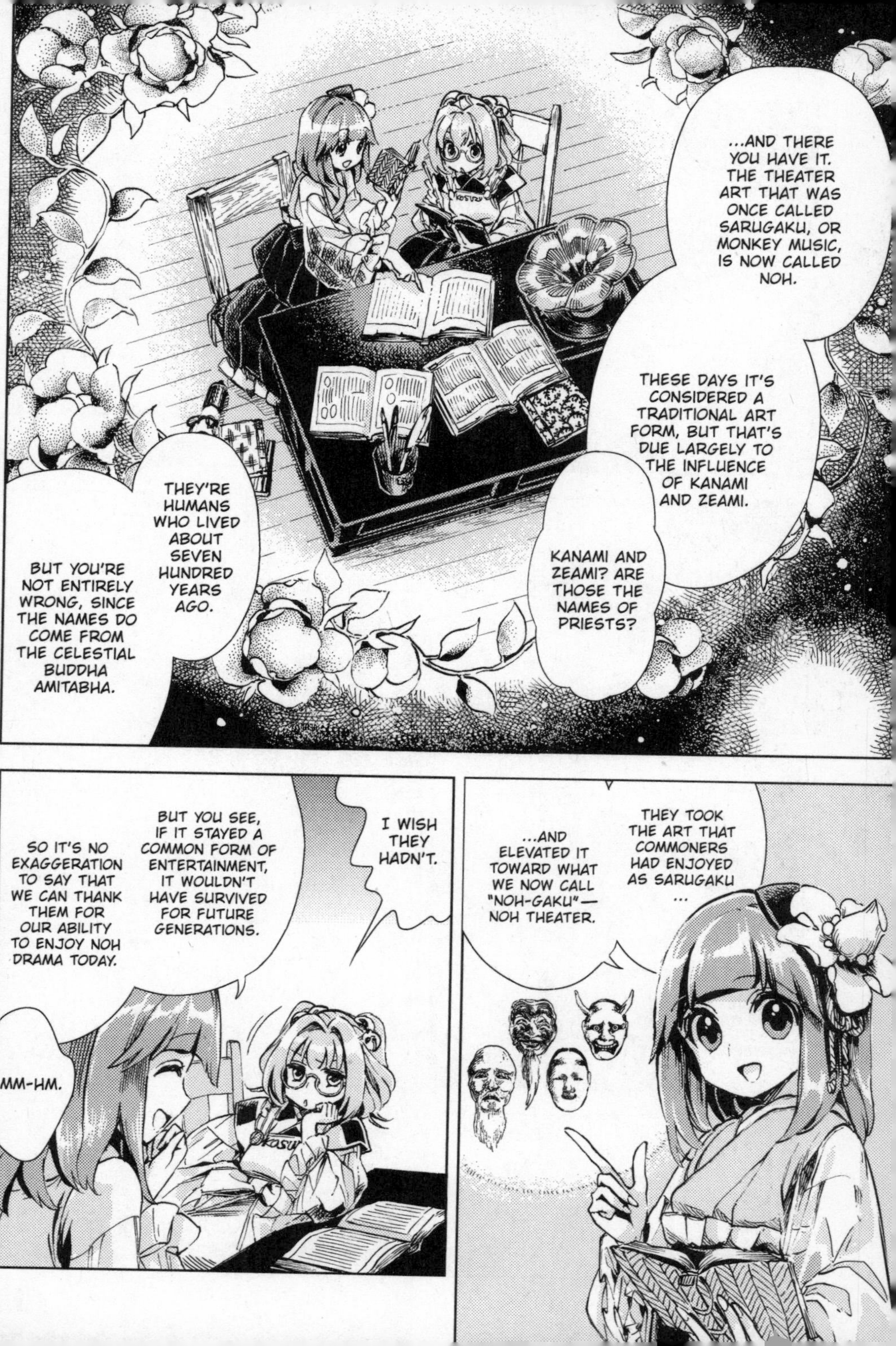
...AND THERE YOU HAVE IT. THE THEATER ART THAT WAS ONCE CALLED SARUGAKU, OR MONKEY MUSIC, IS NOW CALLED NOH.
THESE DAYS IT'S CONSIDERED A TRADITIONAL ART FORM, BUT THAT'S DUE LARGELY TO THE INFLUENCE OF KANAMI AND ZEAMI.
KANAMI AND ZEAMI? ARE THOSE THE NAMES OF PRIESTS?
THEY'RE HUMANS WHO LIVED ABOUT SEVEN HUNDRED YEARS AGO.
BUT YOU'RE NOT ENTIRELY WRONG, SINCE THE NAMES DO COME FROM THE CELESTIAL BUDDHA AMITABHA.
THEY TOOK THE ART THAT COMMONERS HAD ENJOYED AS SARUGAKU...
...AND ELEVATED IT TOWARD WHAT WE NOW CALL "NOH-GAKU"—NOH THEATER.
I WISH THEY HADN'T.
BUT YOU SEE, IF IT STAYED A COMMON FORM OF ENTERTAINMENT, IT WOULDN'T HAVE SURVIVED FOR FUTURE GENERATIONS.
SO IT'S NO EXAGGERATION TO SAY THAT WE CAN THANK THEM FOR OUR ABILITY TO ENJOY NOH DRAMA TODAY.
MM-HM.

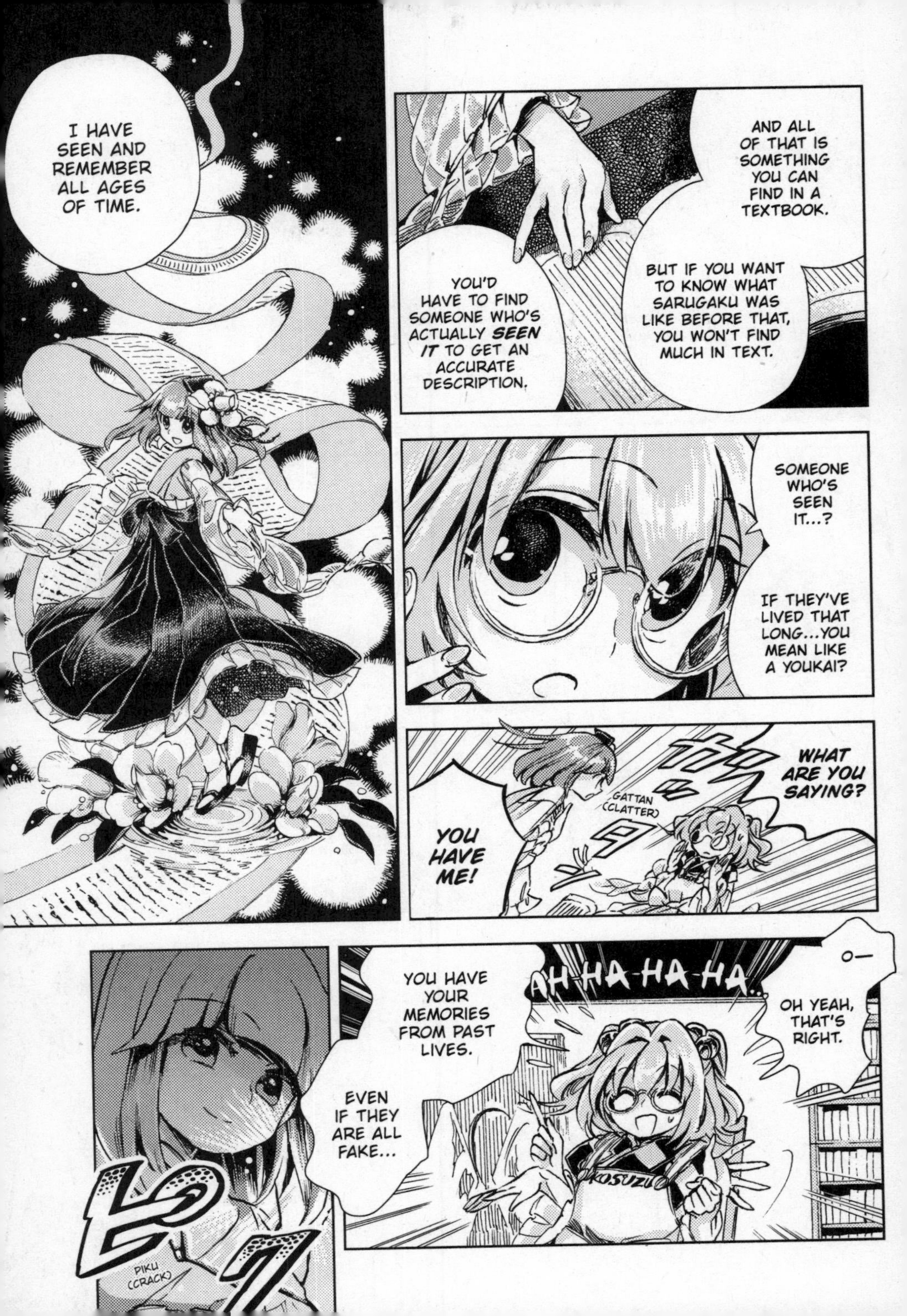
AND ALL OF THAT IS SOMETHING YOU CAN FIND IN A TEXTBOOK.
BUT IF YOU WANT TO KNOW WHAT SARUGAKU WAS LIKE BEFORE THAT, YOU WON'T FIND MUCH IN TEXT.
YOU'D HAVE TO FIND SOMEONE WHO'S ACTUALLY *SEEN IT* TO GET AN ACCURATE DESCRIPTION.
SOMEONE WHO'S SEEN IT...?
IF THEY'VE LIVED THAT LONG...YOU MEAN LIKE A YOUKAI?
WHAT ARE YOU SAYING?
GATTAN (CLATTER)
YOU HAVE ME!
I HAVE SEEN AND REMEMBER ALL AGES OF TIME.
O—
OH YEAH, THAT'S RIGHT.
AH HA HA HA HA
YOU HAVE YOUR MEMORIES FROM PAST LIVES.
EVEN IF THEY ARE ALL FAKE...
PIKU (CRACK)

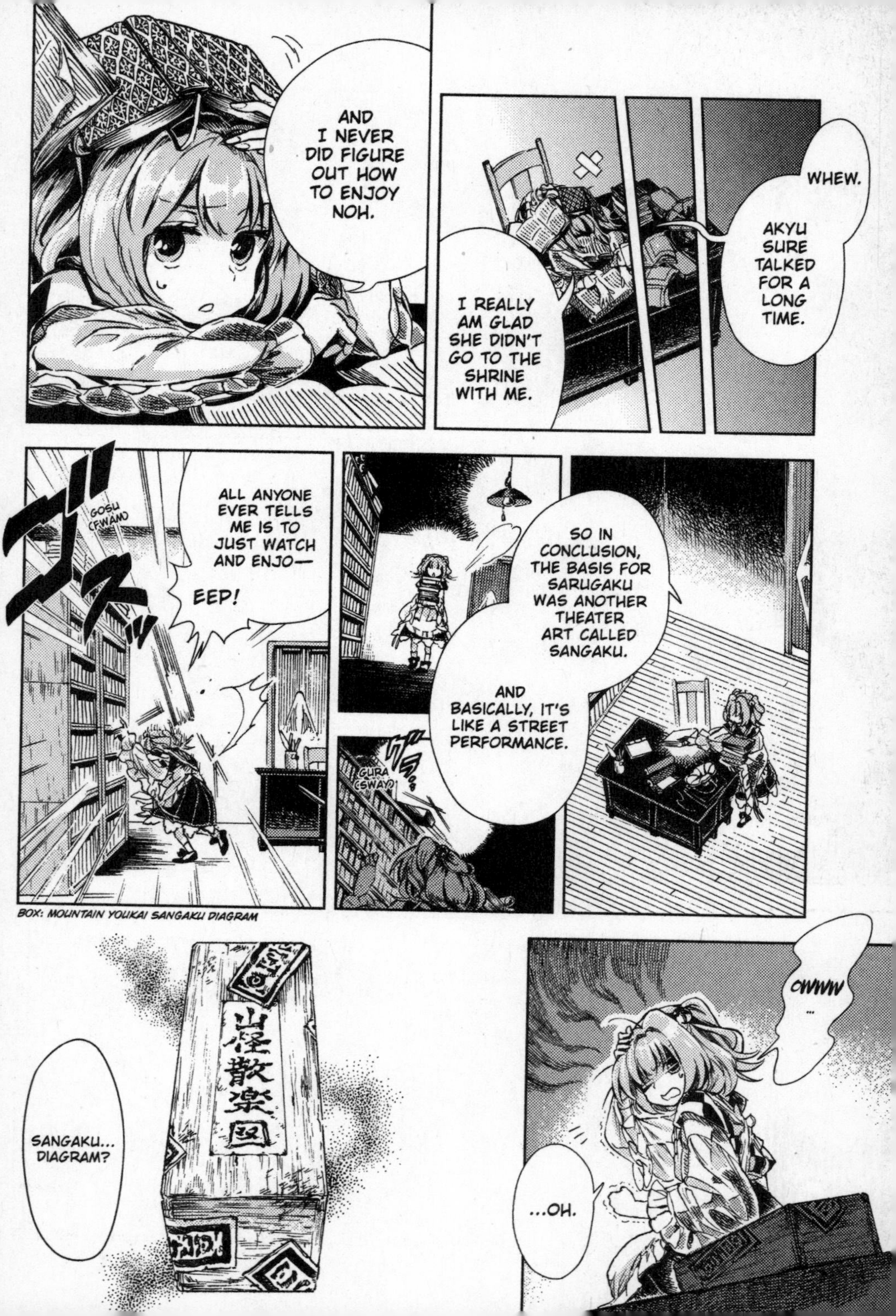
WHEW.
AKYU SURE TALKED FOR A LONG TIME.
I REALLY AM GLAD SHE DIDN'T GO TO THE SHRINE WITH ME.
AND I NEVER DID FIGURE OUT HOW TO ENJOY NOH.
SO IN CONCLUSION, THE BASIS FOR SARUGAKU WAS ANOTHER THEATER ART CALLED SANGAKU.
AND BASICALLY, IT'S LIKE A STREET PERFORMANCE.
GURA (SWAY)
ALL ANYONE EVER TELLS ME IS TO JUST WATCH AND ENJO—
EEP!
GOSU (FWAM)
BOX: MOUNTAIN YOUKAI SANGAKU DIAGRAM
OWWW...
...OH.
山怪散楽図
SANGAKU... DIAGRAM?

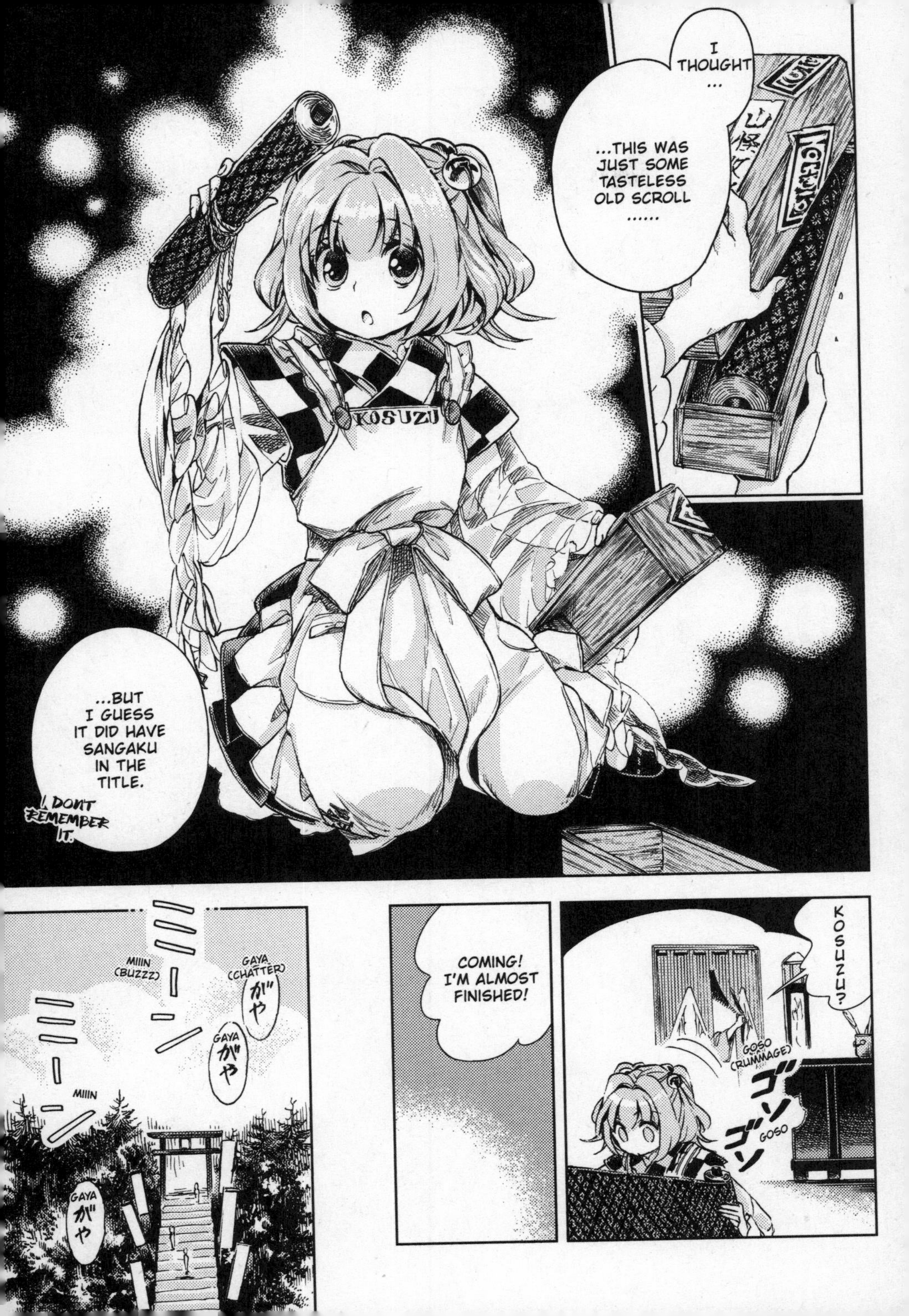
I THOUGHT ...
...THIS WAS JUST SOME TASTELESS OLD SCROLL ......
KOSUZU
...BUT I GUESS IT DID HAVE SANGAKU IN THE TITLE.
I DON'T REMEMBER IT.
KOSUZU?
GOSO (RUMMAGE) ゴソ
ゴソ GOSO
COMING! I'M ALMOST FINISHED!
MIIIN (BUZZZ)
GAYA (CHATTER) がや
GAYA がや
MIIIN
GAYA がや

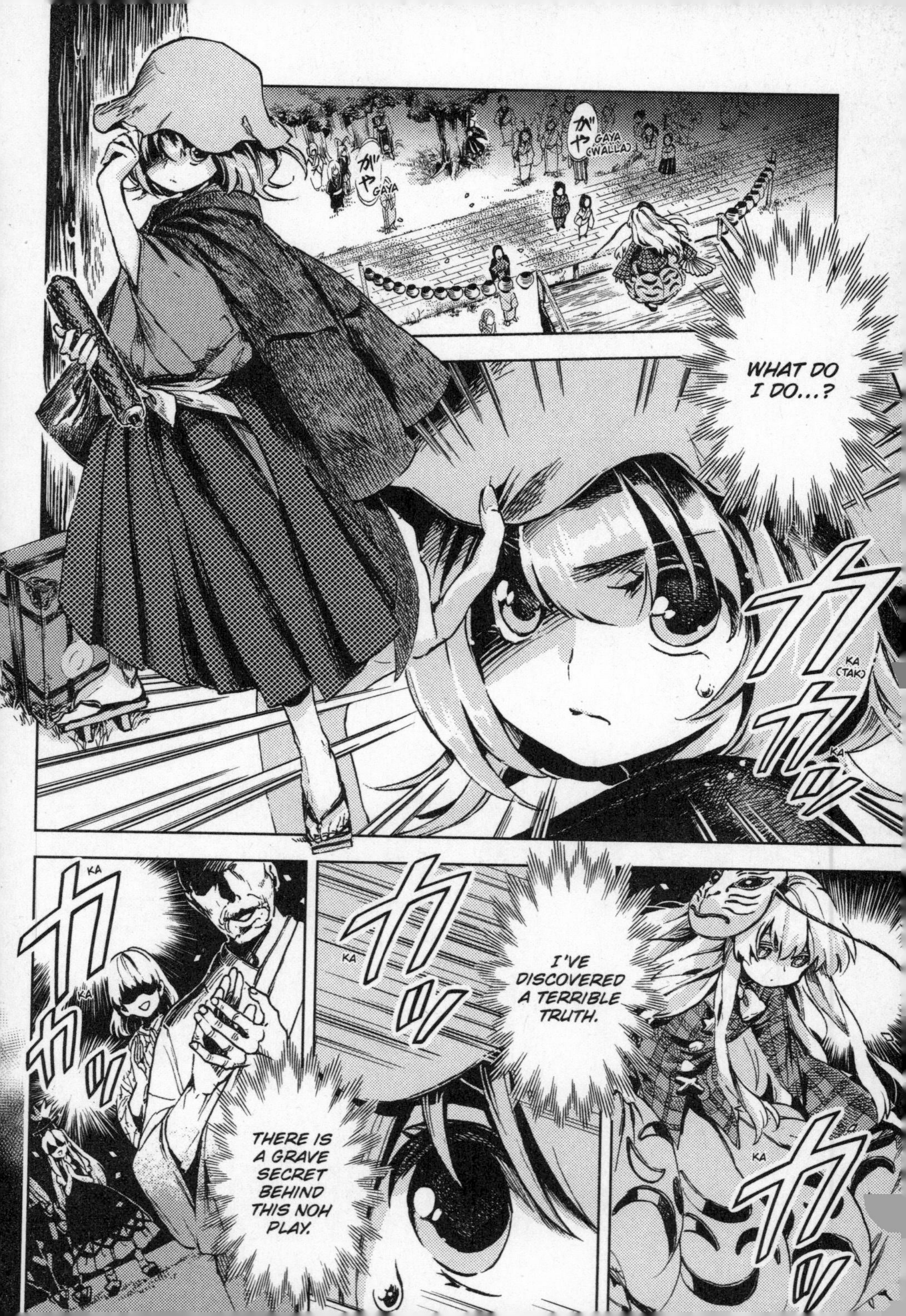

がや
GAYA (WALLA)
がや
GAYA
WHAT DO I DO...?
KA (TAK)
KA
KA
I'VE DISCOVERED A TERRIBLE TRUTH.
KA
KA
KA
THERE IS A GRAVE SECRET BEHIND THIS NOH PLAY.

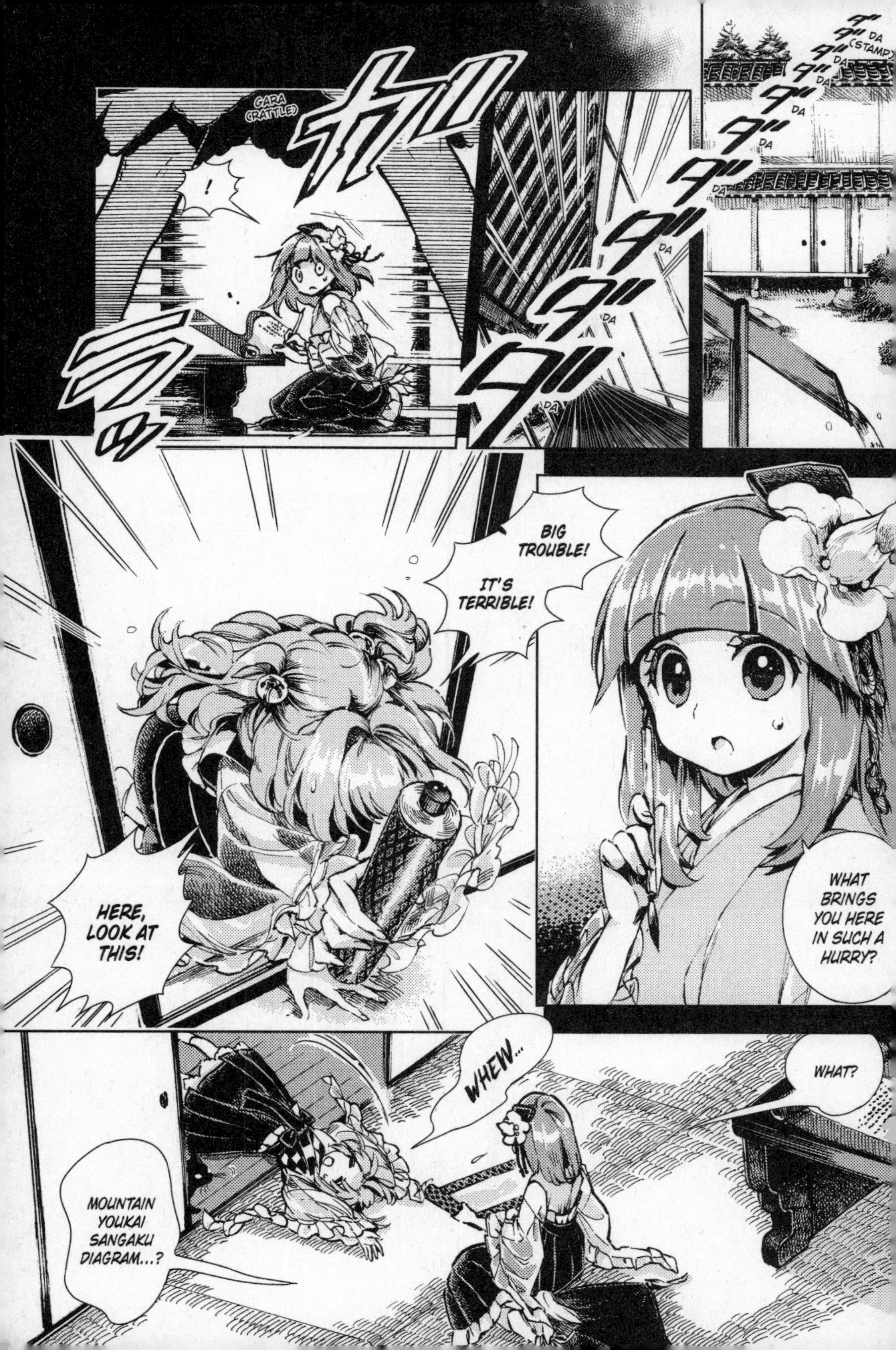

DA (STAMP)
DA
DA
DA
DA
DA
DA
DA
DA
GARA (RATTLE)
!
WHAT BRINGS YOU HERE IN SUCH A HURRY?
BIG TROUBLE!
IT'S TERRIBLE!
HERE, LOOK AT THIS!
WHAT?
WHEW...
MOUNTAIN YOUKAI SANGAKU DIAGRAM...?

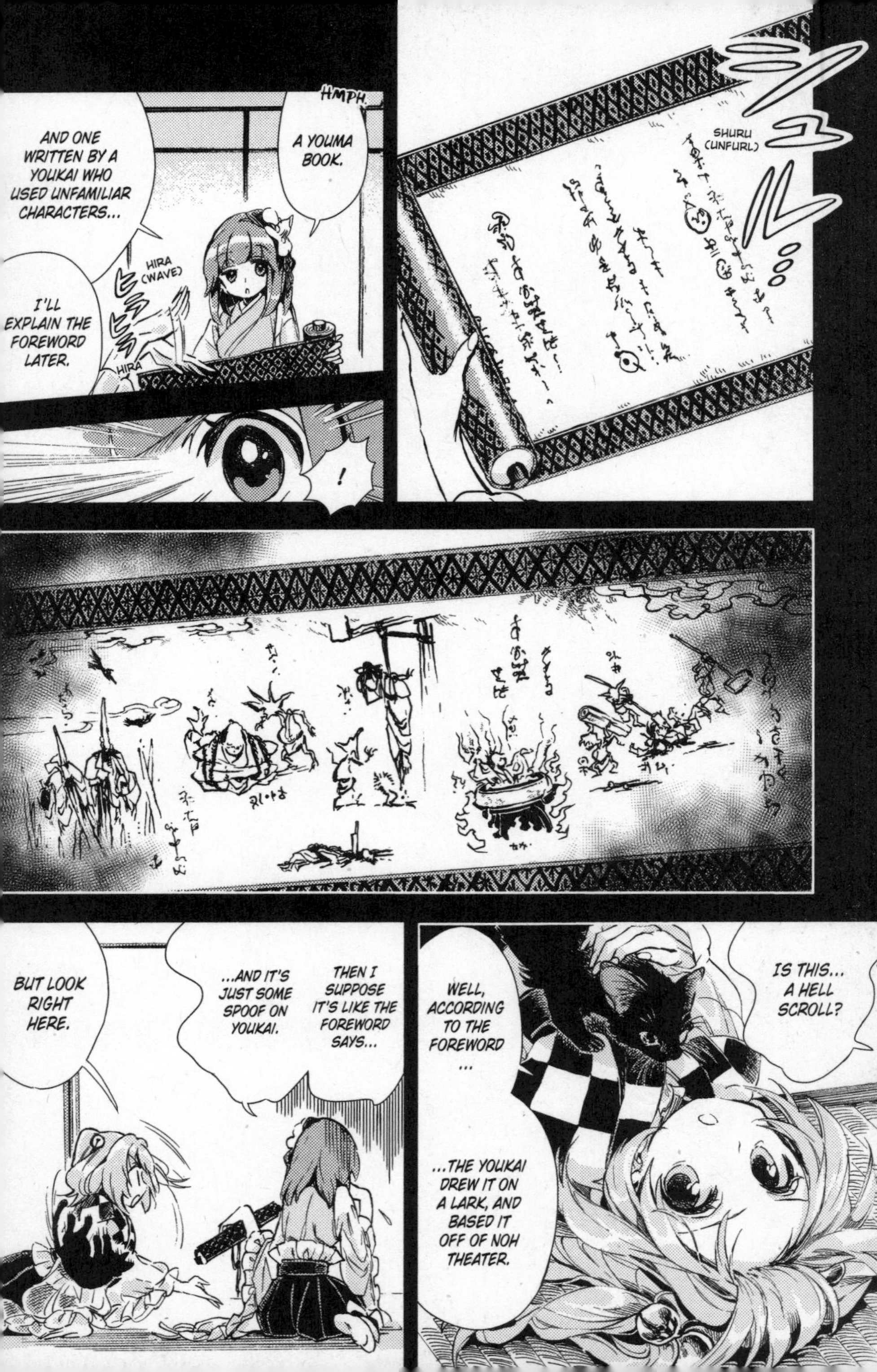
SHURU (UNFURL)
HMPH.
A YOUMA BOOK.
AND ONE WRITTEN BY A YOUKAI WHO USED UNFAMILIAR CHARACTERS...
HIRA (WAVE)
I'LL EXPLAIN THE FOREWORD LATER.
HIRA
!
IS THIS... A HELL SCROLL?
WELL, ACCORDING TO THE FOREWORD...
...THE YOUKAI DREW IT ON A LARK, AND BASED IT OFF OF NOH THEATER.
THEN I SUPPOSE IT'S LIKE THE FOREWORD SAYS...
...AND IT'S JUST SOME SPOOF ON YOUKAI.
BUT LOOK RIGHT HERE.

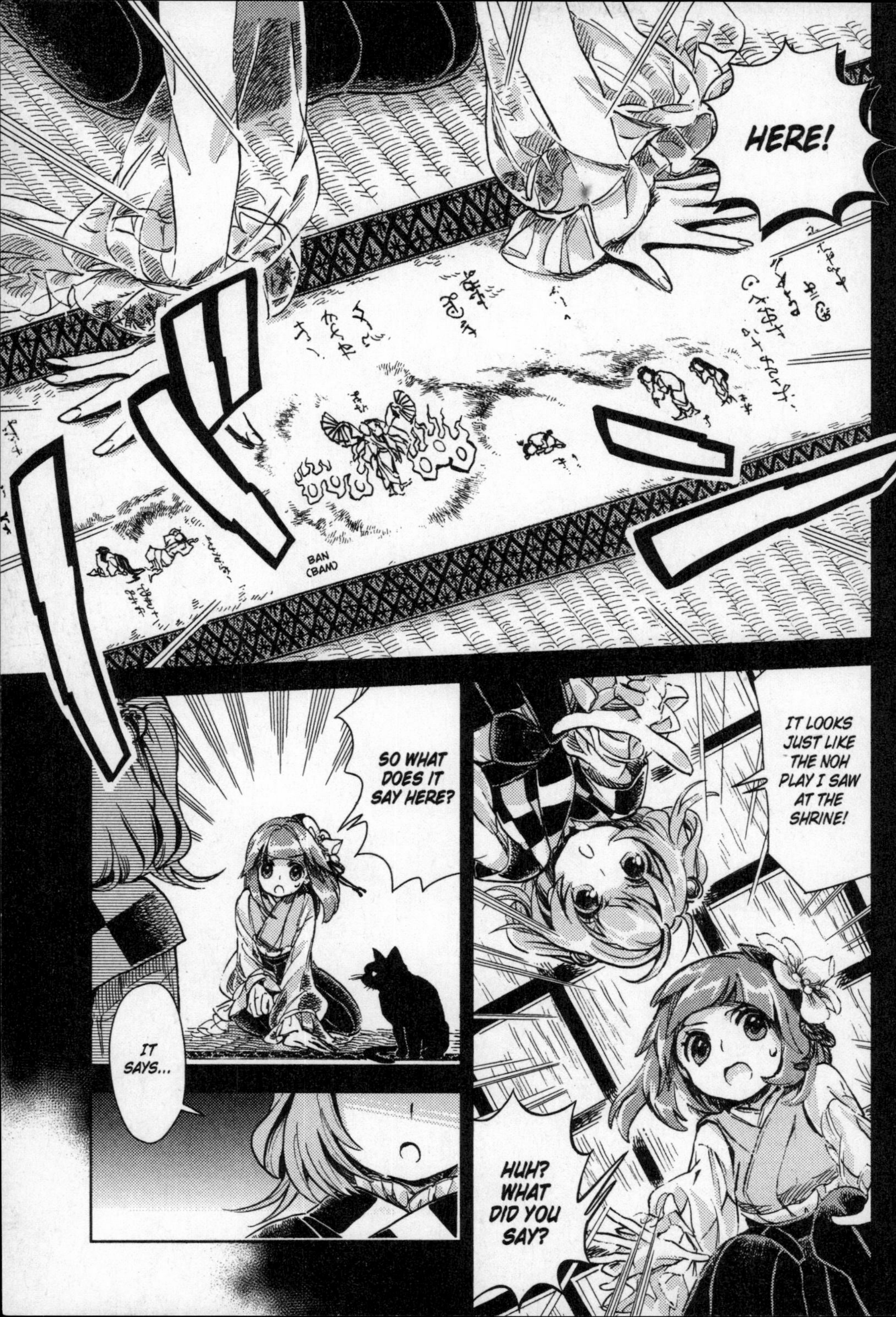
HERE!
BAN (BAM)
IT LOOKS JUST LIKE THE NOH PLAY I SAW AT THE SHRINE!
HUH? WHAT DID YOU SAY?
SO WHAT DOES IT SAY HERE?
IT SAYS...

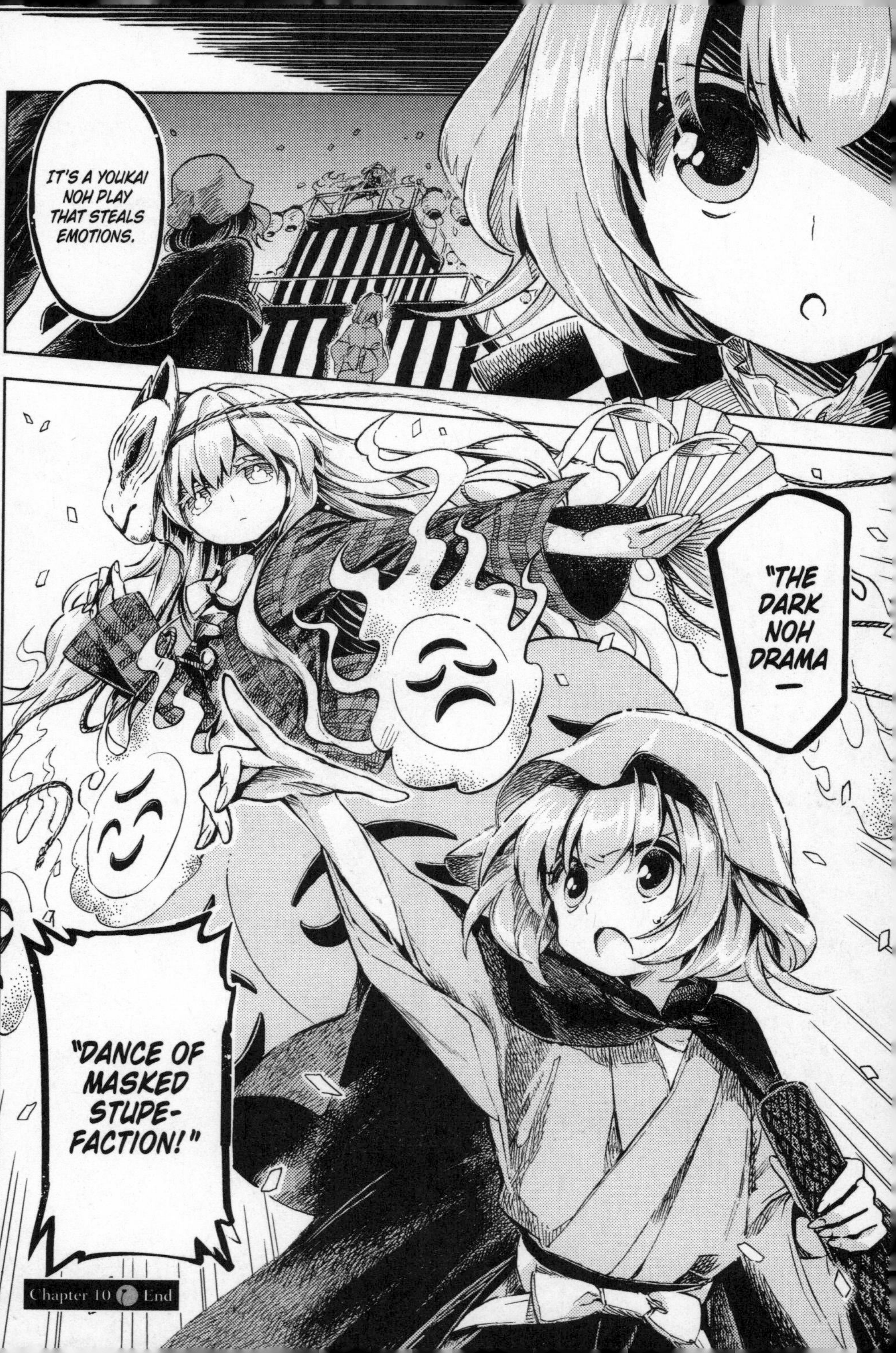
IT'S A YOUKAI NOH PLAY THAT STEALS EMOTIONS.
"THE DARK NOH DRAMA —
"DANCE OF MASKED STUPE-FACTION!"
Chapter 10 End

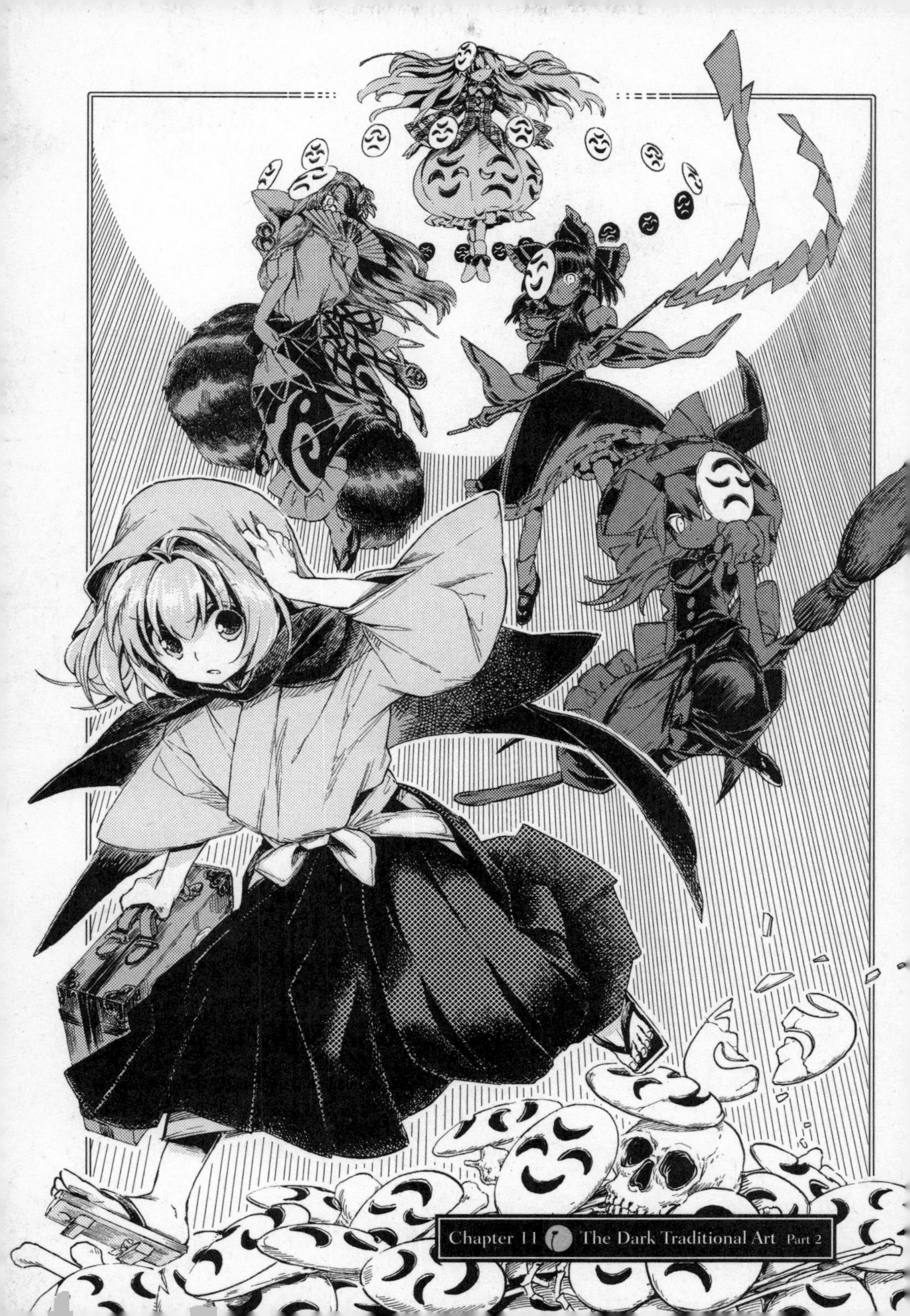
Chapter 11 The Dark Traditional Art Part 2

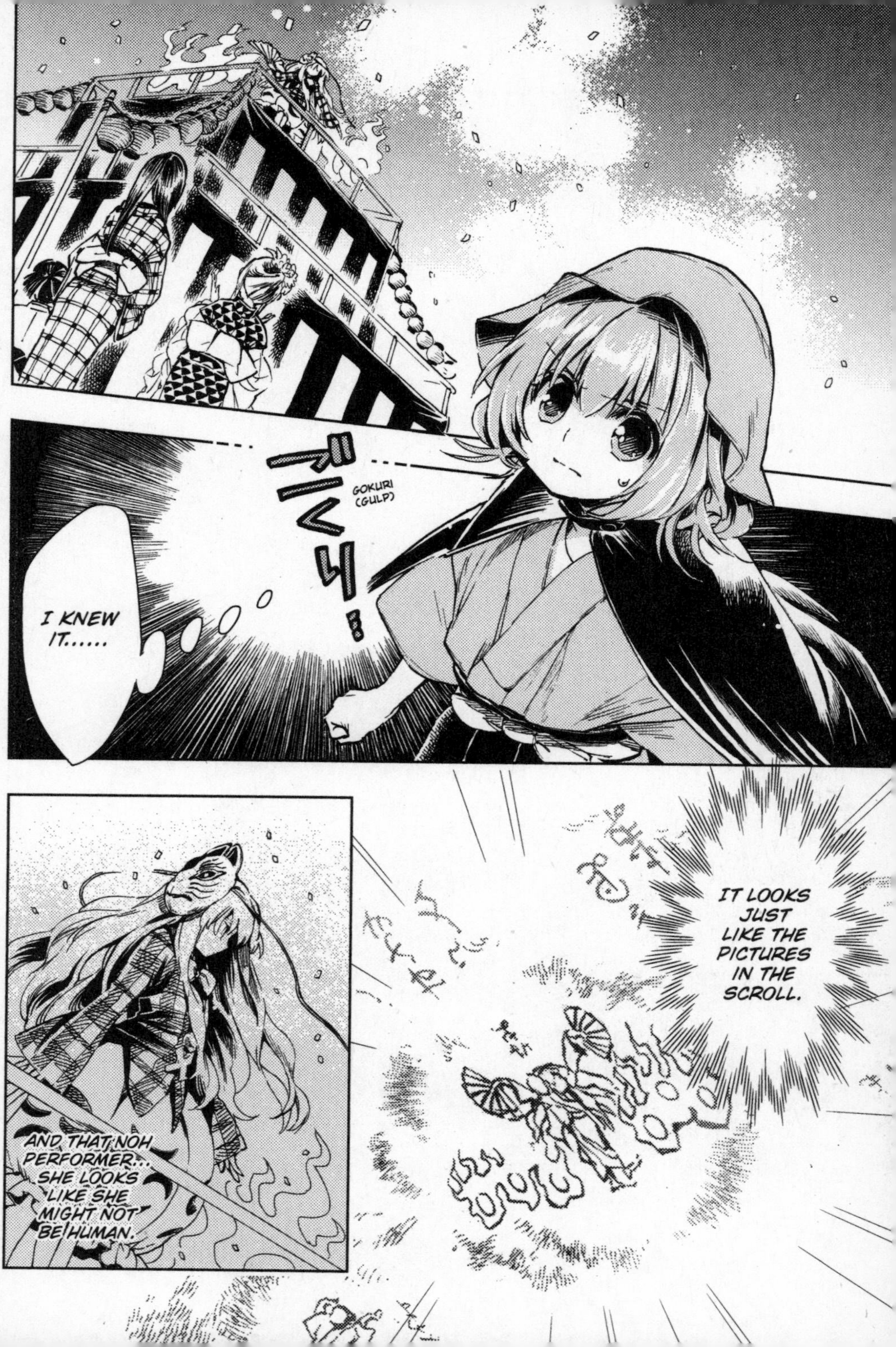
GOKURI (GULP)
I KNEW IT......
IT LOOKS JUST LIKE THE PICTURES IN THE SCROLL.
AND THAT NOH PERFORMER... SHE LOOKS LIKE SHE MIGHT NOT BE HUMAN.

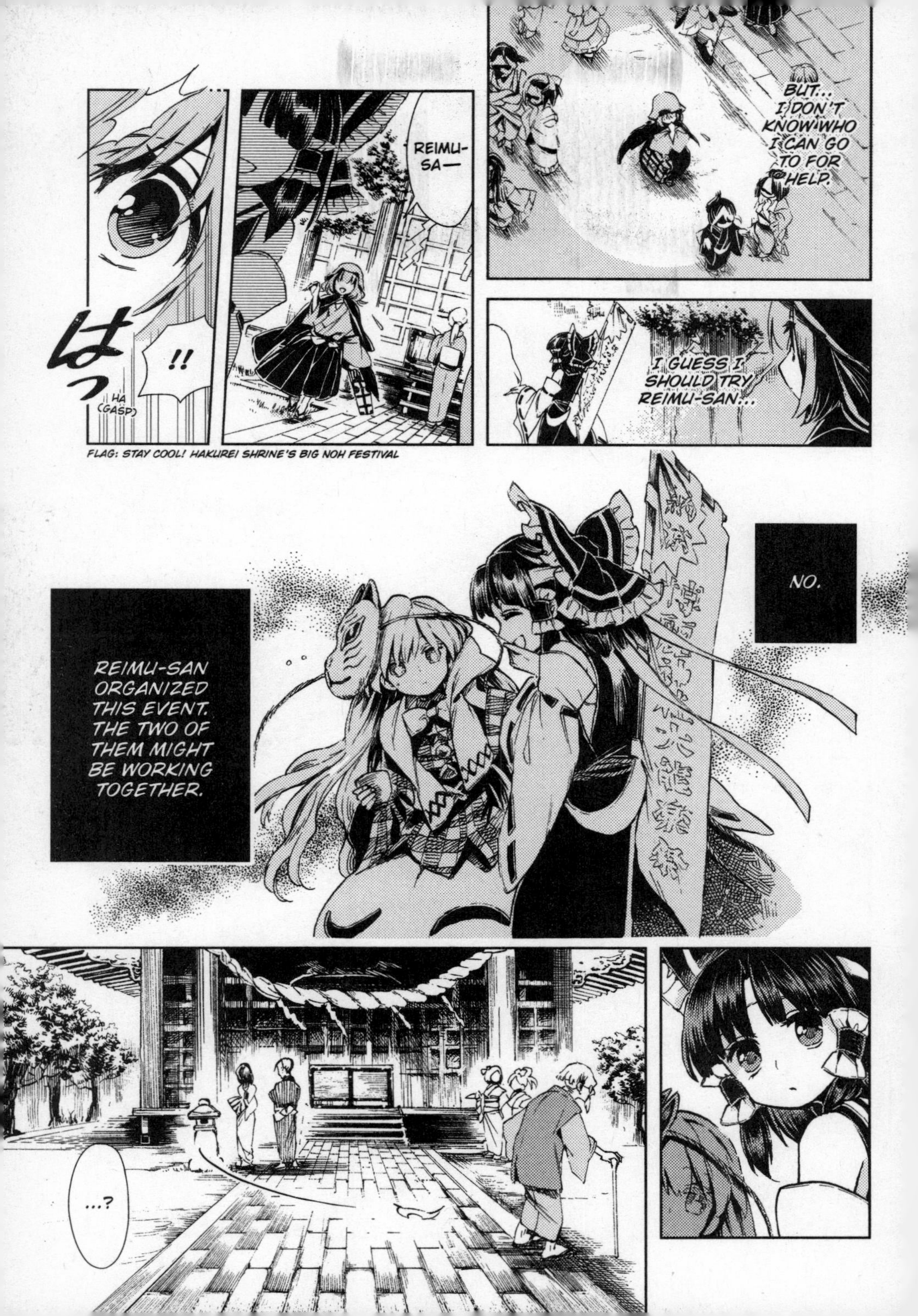
BUT... I DON'T KNOW WHO I CAN GO TO FOR HELP.
I GUESS I SHOULD TRY REIMU-SAN...
REIMU-SA—
!!
はっ
HA (GASP)
FLAG: STAY COOL! HAKUREI SHRINE'S BIG NOH FESTIVAL
NO.
REIMU-SAN ORGANIZED THIS EVENT. THE TWO OF THEM MIGHT BE WORKING TOGETHER.
...?

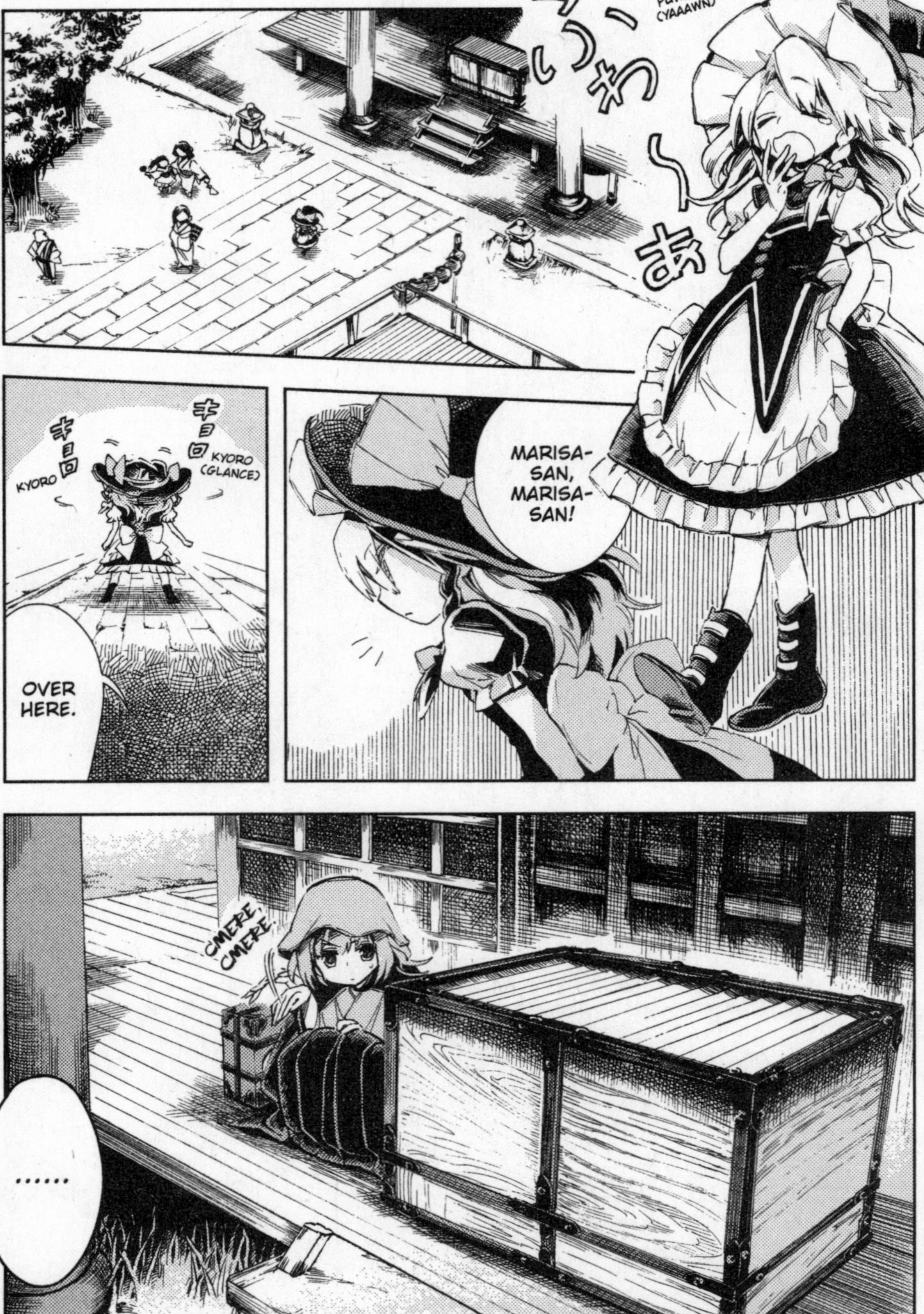
ふわ〜あ
FUWAAA (YAAAWN)
MARISA-SAN, MARISA-SAN!
キョロ
KYORO (GLANCE)
キョロ
KYORO
OVER HERE.
CMERE, CMERE
......

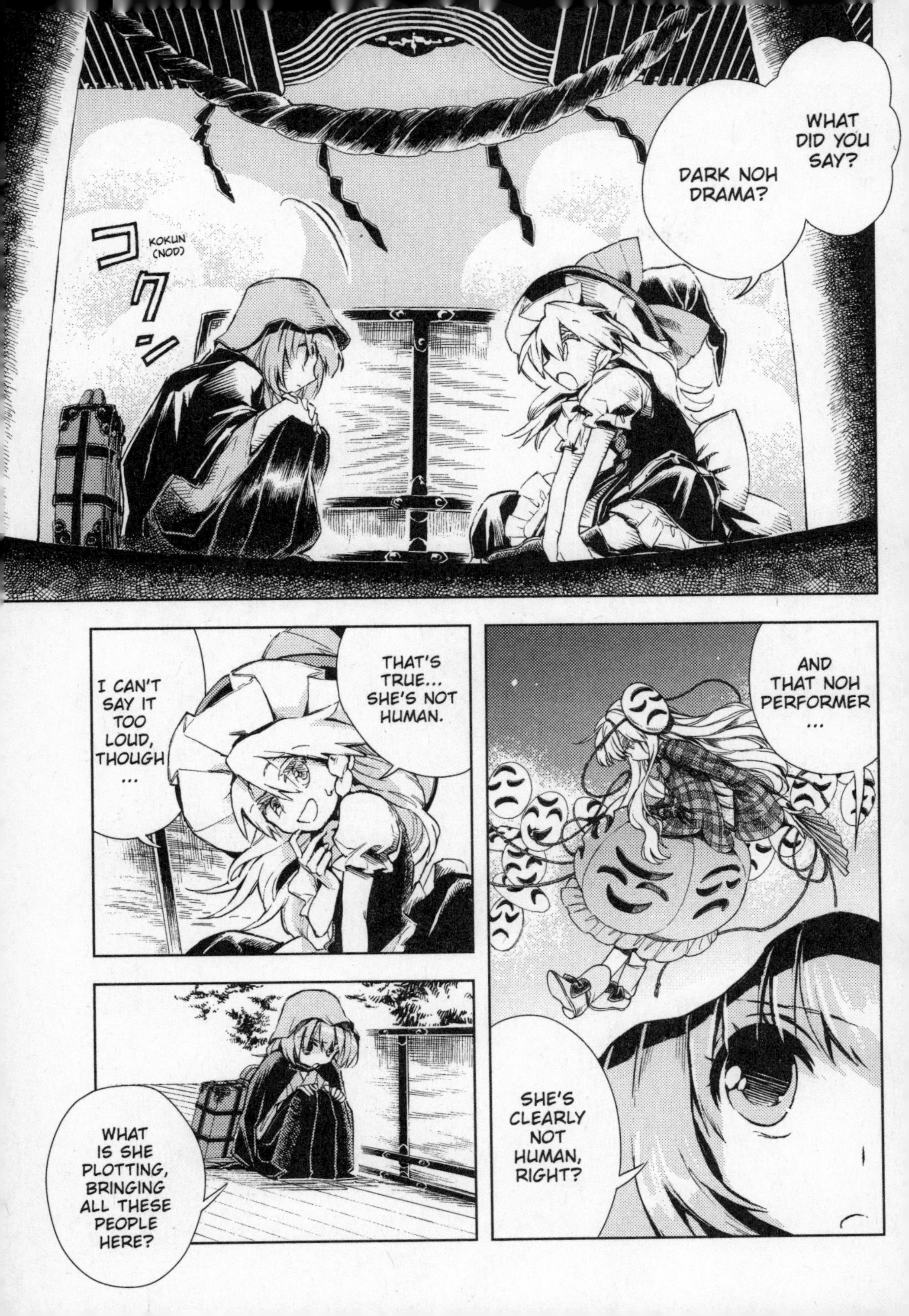
WHAT DID YOU SAY?
DARK NOH DRAMA?
KOKUN (NOD)
AND THAT NOH PERFORMER ...
SHE'S CLEARLY NOT HUMAN, RIGHT?
THAT'S TRUE... SHE'S NOT HUMAN.
I CAN'T SAY IT TOO LOUD, THOUGH ...
WHAT IS SHE PLOTTING, BRINGING ALL THESE PEOPLE HERE?

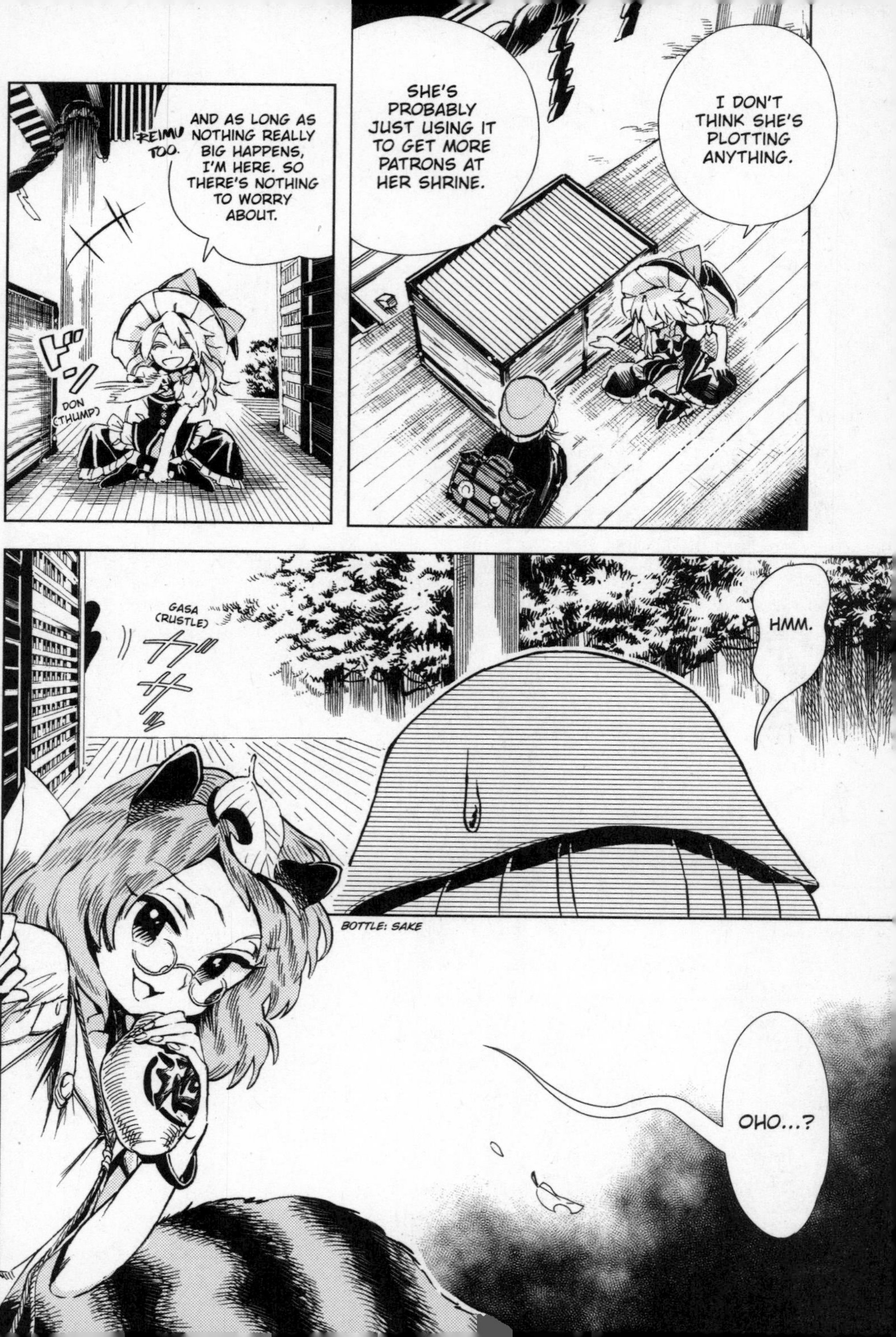
I DON'T THINK SHE'S PLOTTING ANYTHING.
SHE'S PROBABLY JUST USING IT TO GET MORE PATRONS AT HER SHRINE.
AND AS LONG AS NOTHING REALLY BIG HAPPENS, I'M HERE. SO THERE'S NOTHING TO WORRY ABOUT.
REIMU TOO.
DON (THUMP)
HMM.
GASA (RUSTLE)
BOTTLE: SAKE
OHO...?

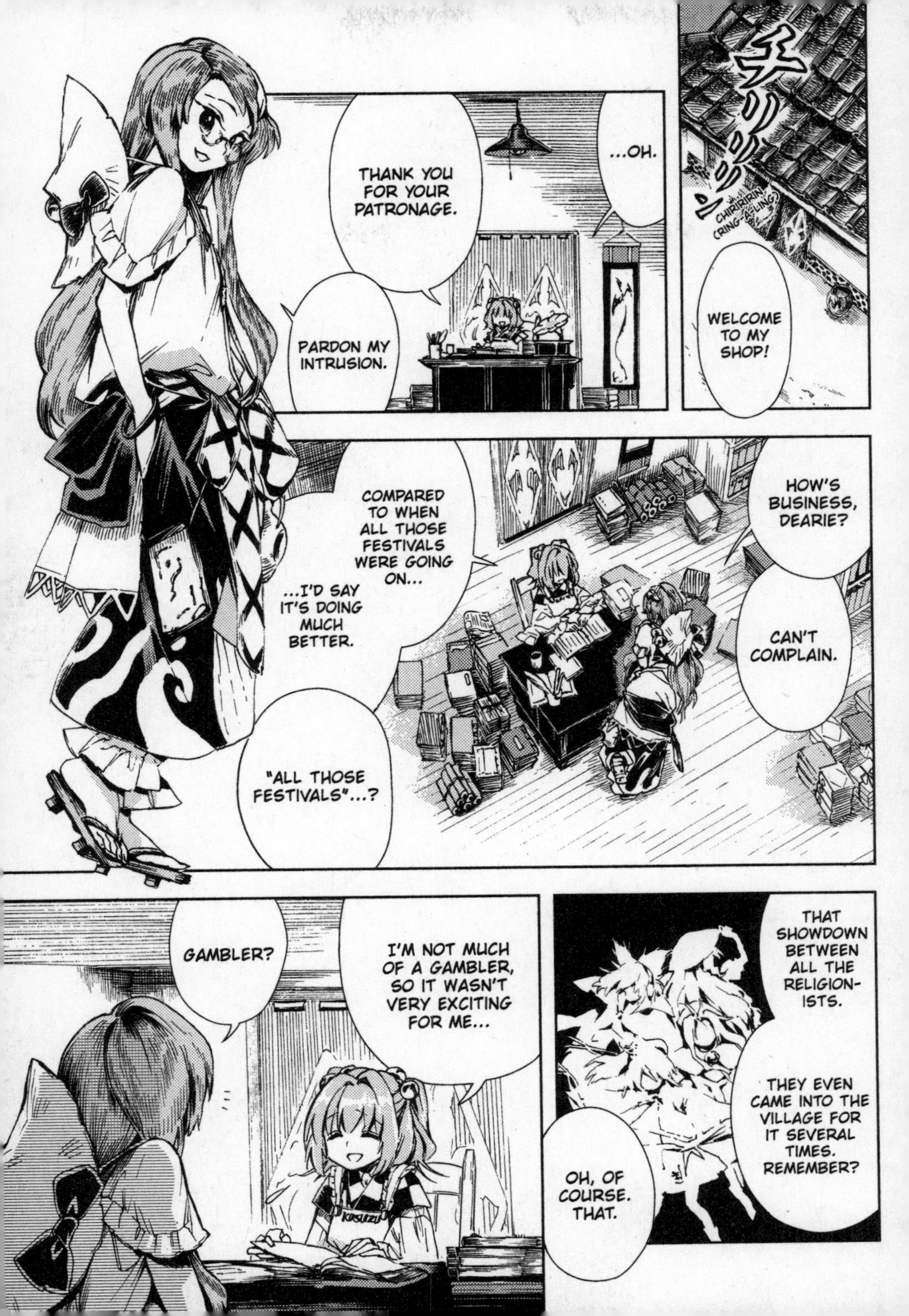
CHIRIRIRIN (RING-A-LING)
WELCOME TO MY SHOP!
...OH.
THANK YOU FOR YOUR PATRONAGE.
PARDON MY INTRUSION.
HOW'S BUSINESS, DEARIE?
CAN'T COMPLAIN.
COMPARED TO WHEN ALL THOSE FESTIVALS WERE GOING ON...
...I'D SAY IT'S DOING MUCH BETTER.
"ALL THOSE FESTIVALS"...?
THAT SHOWDOWN BETWEEN ALL THE RELIGION-ISTS.
THEY EVEN CAME INTO THE VILLAGE FOR IT SEVERAL TIMES. REMEMBER?
OH, OF COURSE. THAT.
I'M NOT MUCH OF A GAMBLER, SO IT WASN'T VERY EXCITING FOR ME...
GAMBLER?

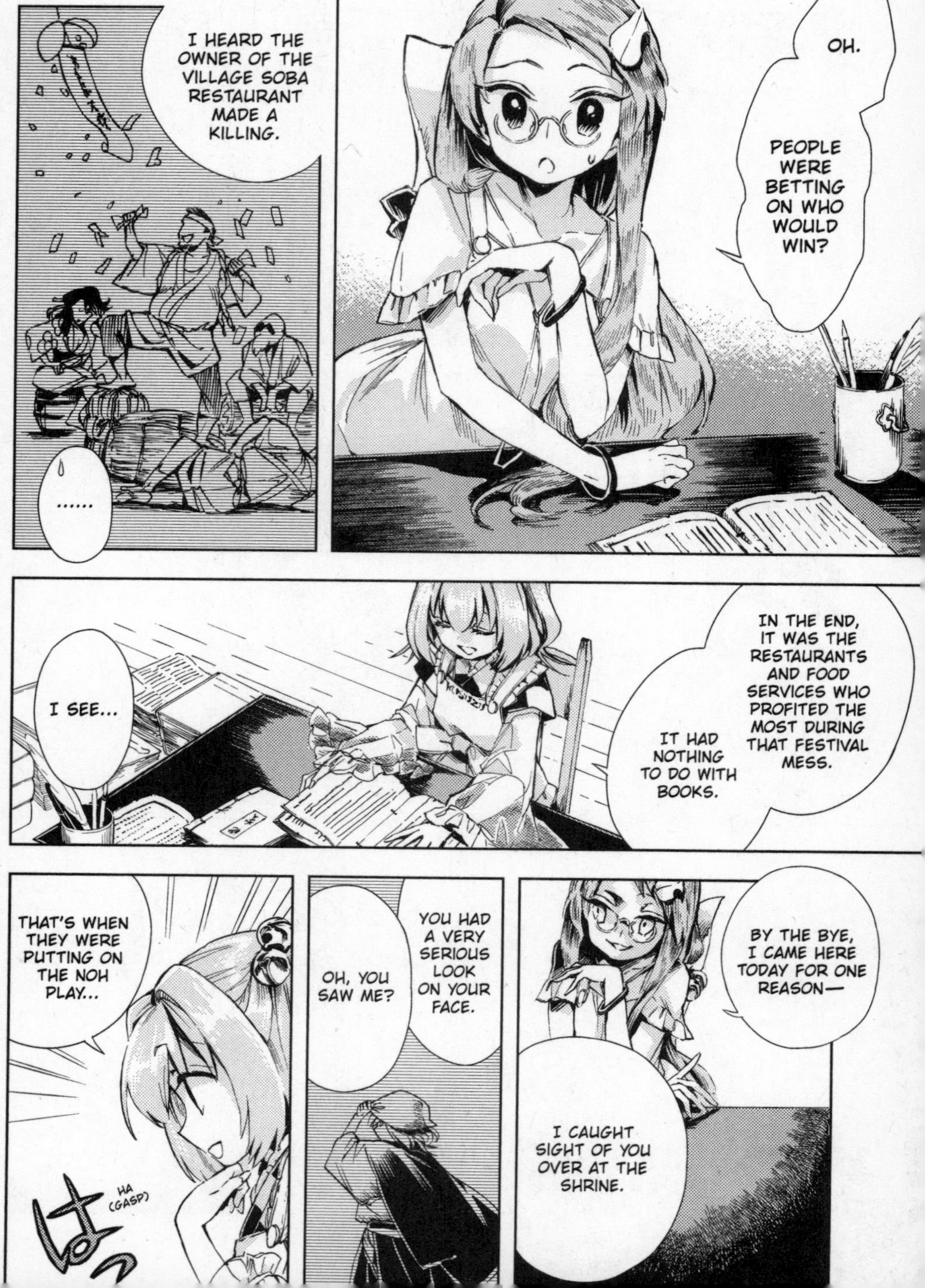
OH.
PEOPLE WERE BETTING ON WHO WOULD WIN?
I HEARD THE OWNER OF THE VILLAGE SOBA RESTAURANT MADE A KILLING.
......
IN THE END, IT WAS THE RESTAURANTS AND FOOD SERVICES WHO PROFITED THE MOST DURING THAT FESTIVAL MESS.
IT HAD NOTHING TO DO WITH BOOKS.
I SEE...
BY THE BYE, I CAME HERE TODAY FOR ONE REASON—
I CAUGHT SIGHT OF YOU OVER AT THE SHRINE.
YOU HAD A VERY SERIOUS LOOK ON YOUR FACE.
OH, YOU SAW ME?
THAT'S WHEN THEY WERE PUTTING ON THE NOH PLAY...
はっ
HA (GASP)

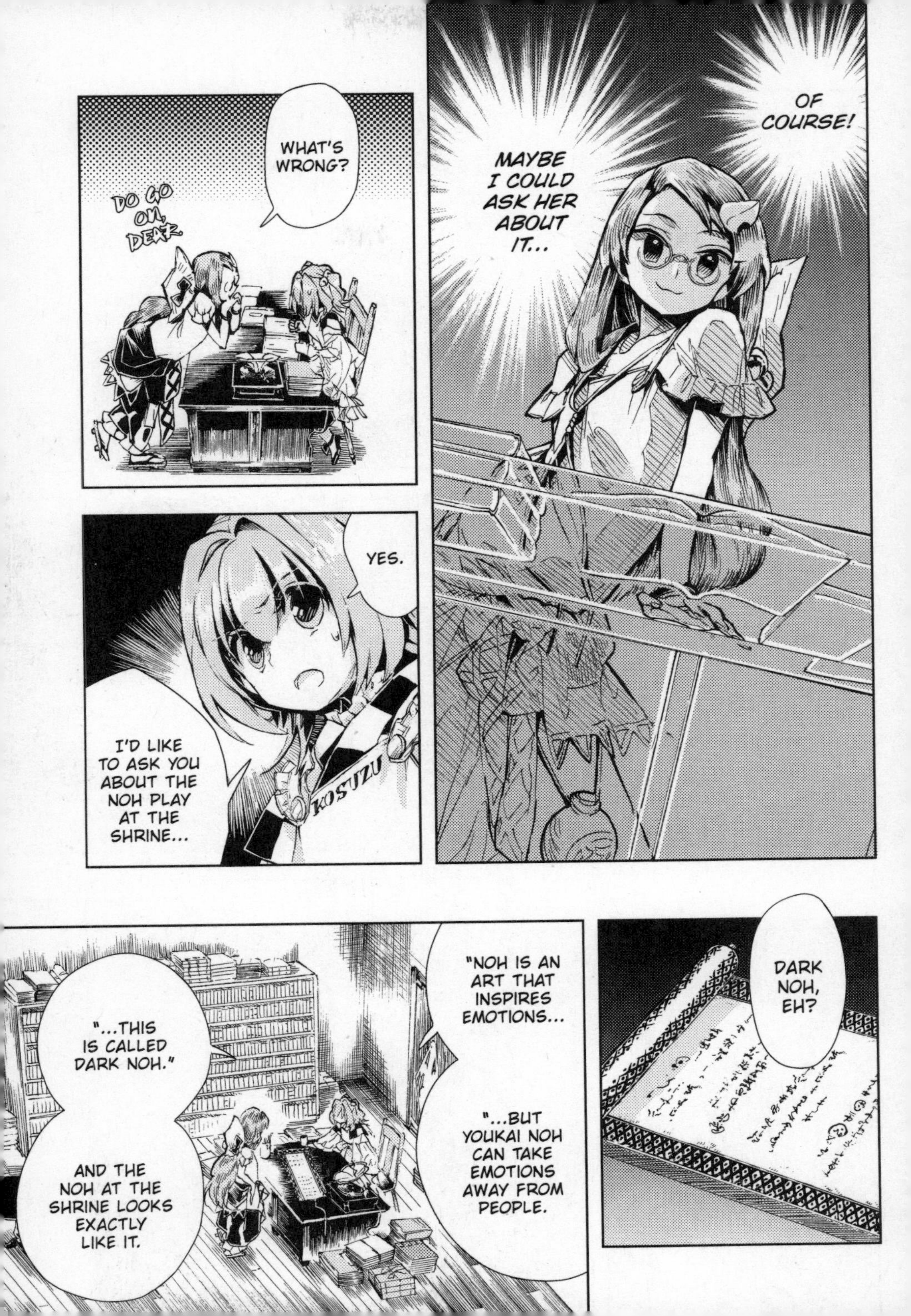
OF COURSE!
MAYBE I COULD ASK HER ABOUT IT...
WHAT'S WRONG?
DO GO ON, DEAR.
YES.
I'D LIKE TO ASK YOU ABOUT THE NOH PLAY AT THE SHRINE...
KOSUZU
DARK NOH, EH?
"NOH IS AN ART THAT INSPIRES EMOTIONS...
"...BUT YOUKAI NOH CAN TAKE EMOTIONS AWAY FROM PEOPLE.
"...THIS IS CALLED DARK NOH."
AND THE NOH AT THE SHRINE LOOKS EXACTLY LIKE IT.

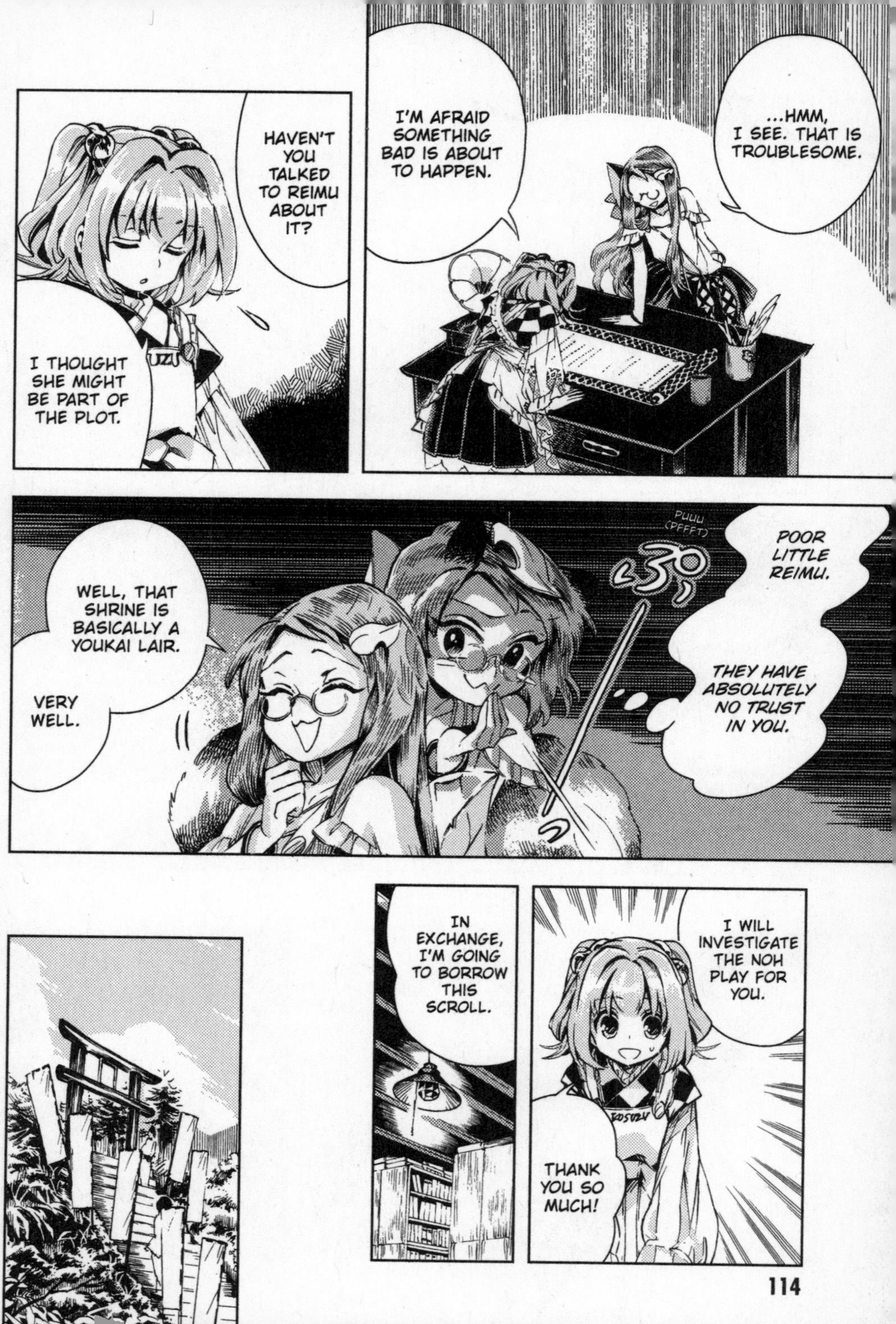
...HMM, I SEE. THAT IS TROUBLESOME.
I'M AFRAID SOMETHING BAD IS ABOUT TO HAPPEN.
HAVEN'T YOU TALKED TO REIMU ABOUT IT?
I THOUGHT SHE MIGHT BE PART OF THE PLOT.
POOR LITTLE REIMU.
PUUU (PFFFT)
THEY HAVE ABSOLUTELY NO TRUST IN YOU.
WELL, THAT SHRINE IS BASICALLY A YOUKAI LAIR.
VERY WELL.
I WILL INVESTIGATE THE NOH PLAY FOR YOU.
THANK YOU SO MUCH!
IN EXCHANGE, I'M GOING TO BORROW THIS SCROLL.

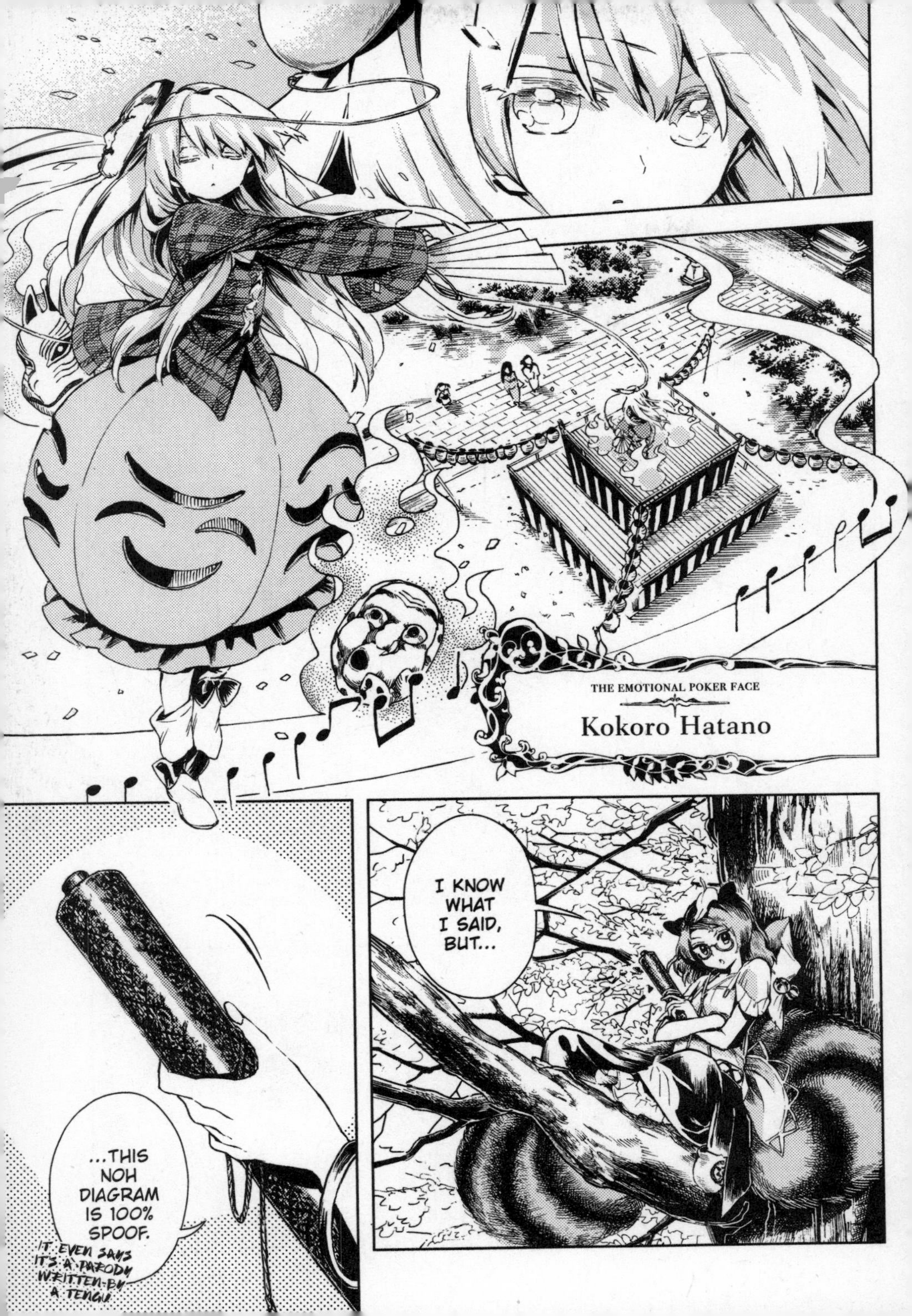
THE EMOTIONAL POKER FACE
Kokoro Hatano
I KNOW WHAT I SAID, BUT...
...THIS NOH DIAGRAM IS 100% SPOOF.
IT EVEN SAYS IT'S A PARODY WRITTEN BY A TENGU!

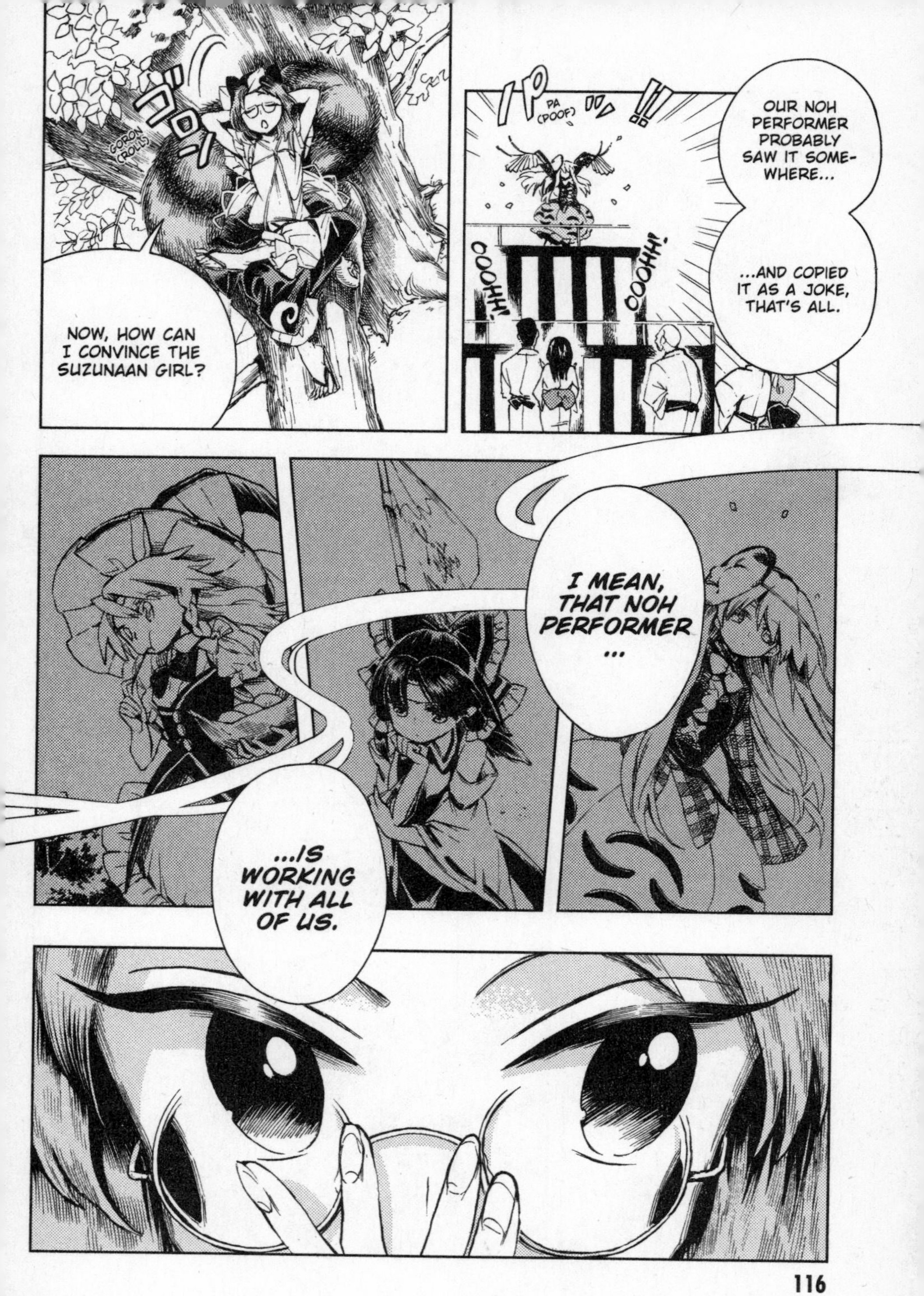
PA (POOF)
OUR NOH PERFORMER PROBABLY SAW IT SOME-WHERE...
OOOHH!
OOOHH!
...AND COPIED IT AS A JOKE, THAT'S ALL.
GORON (ROLLS)
NOW, HOW CAN I CONVINCE THE SUZUNAAN GIRL?
I MEAN, THAT NOH PERFORMER ...
...IS WORKING WITH ALL OF US.

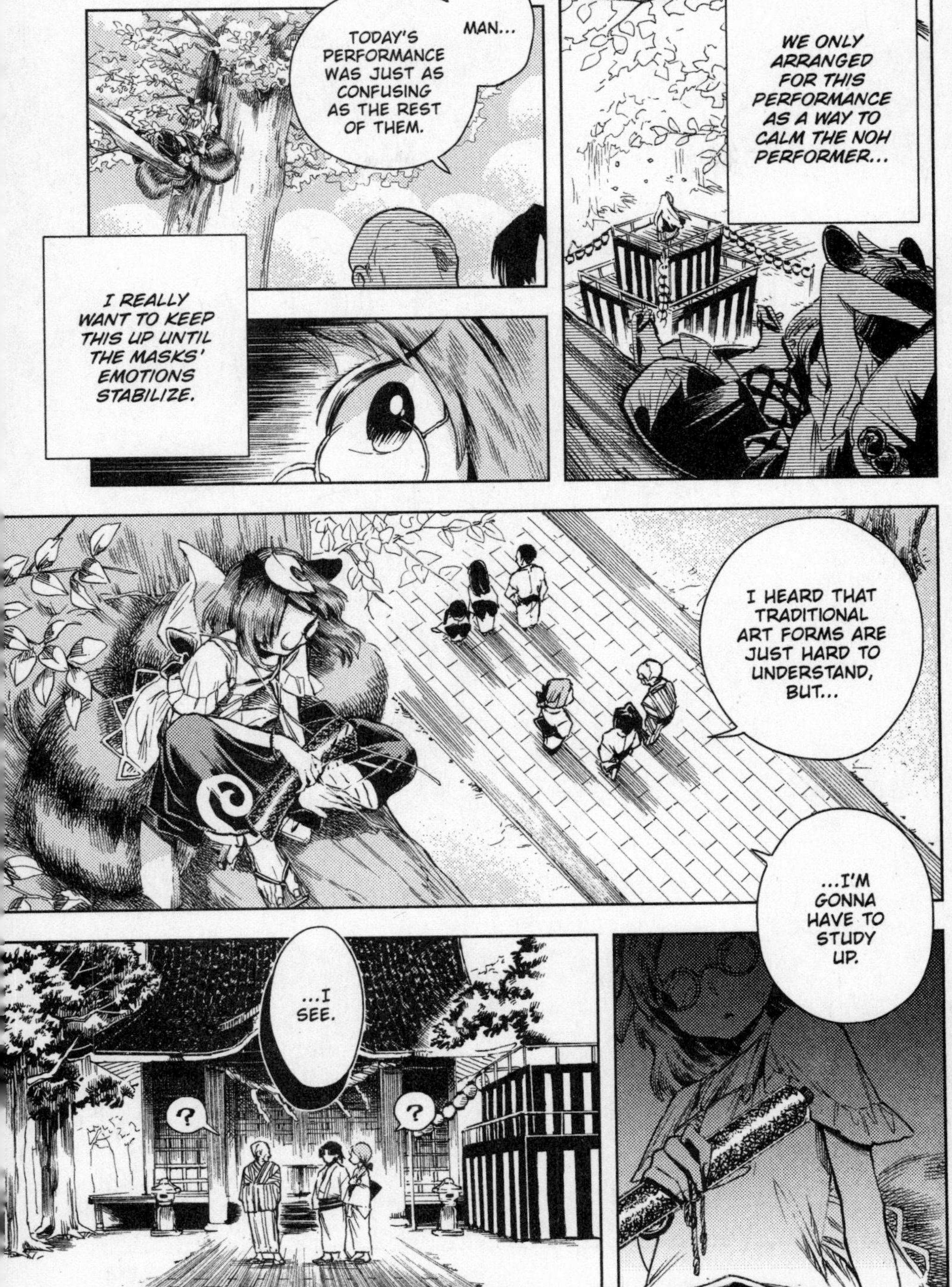
WE ONLY ARRANGED FOR THIS PERFORMANCE AS A WAY TO CALM THE NOH PERFORMER...
MAN... TODAY'S PERFORMANCE WAS JUST AS CONFUSING AS THE REST OF THEM.
I REALLY WANT TO KEEP THIS UP UNTIL THE MASKS' EMOTIONS STABILIZE.
I HEARD THAT TRADITIONAL ART FORMS ARE JUST HARD TO UNDERSTAND, BUT...
...I'M GONNA HAVE TO STUDY UP.
...I SEE.
?
?

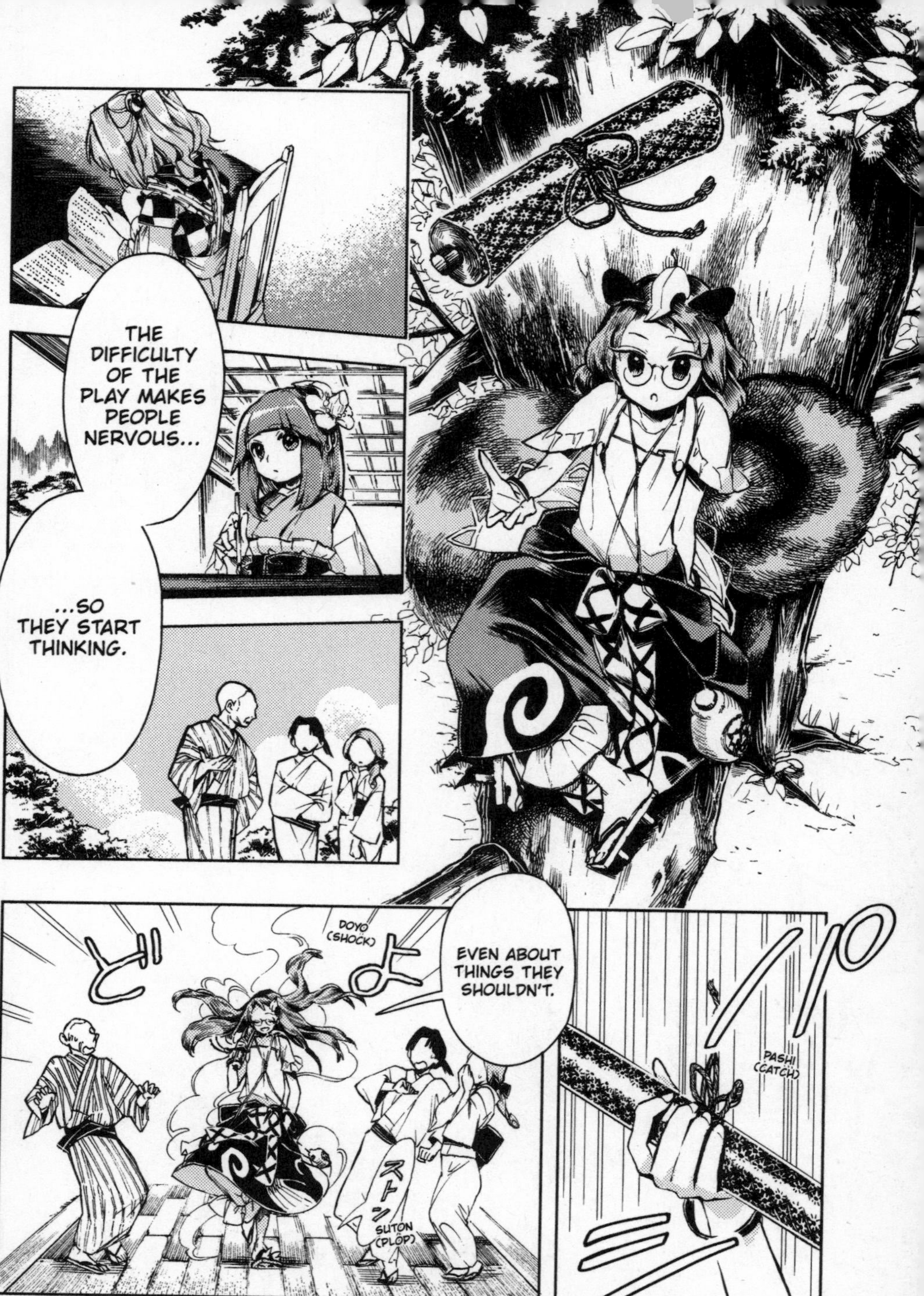
THE DIFFICULTY OF THE PLAY MAKES PEOPLE NERVOUS...
...SO THEY START THINKING.
PASHI (CATCH)
EVEN ABOUT THINGS THEY SHOULDN'T.
DOYO (SHOCK)
ストン
SUTON (PLOP)

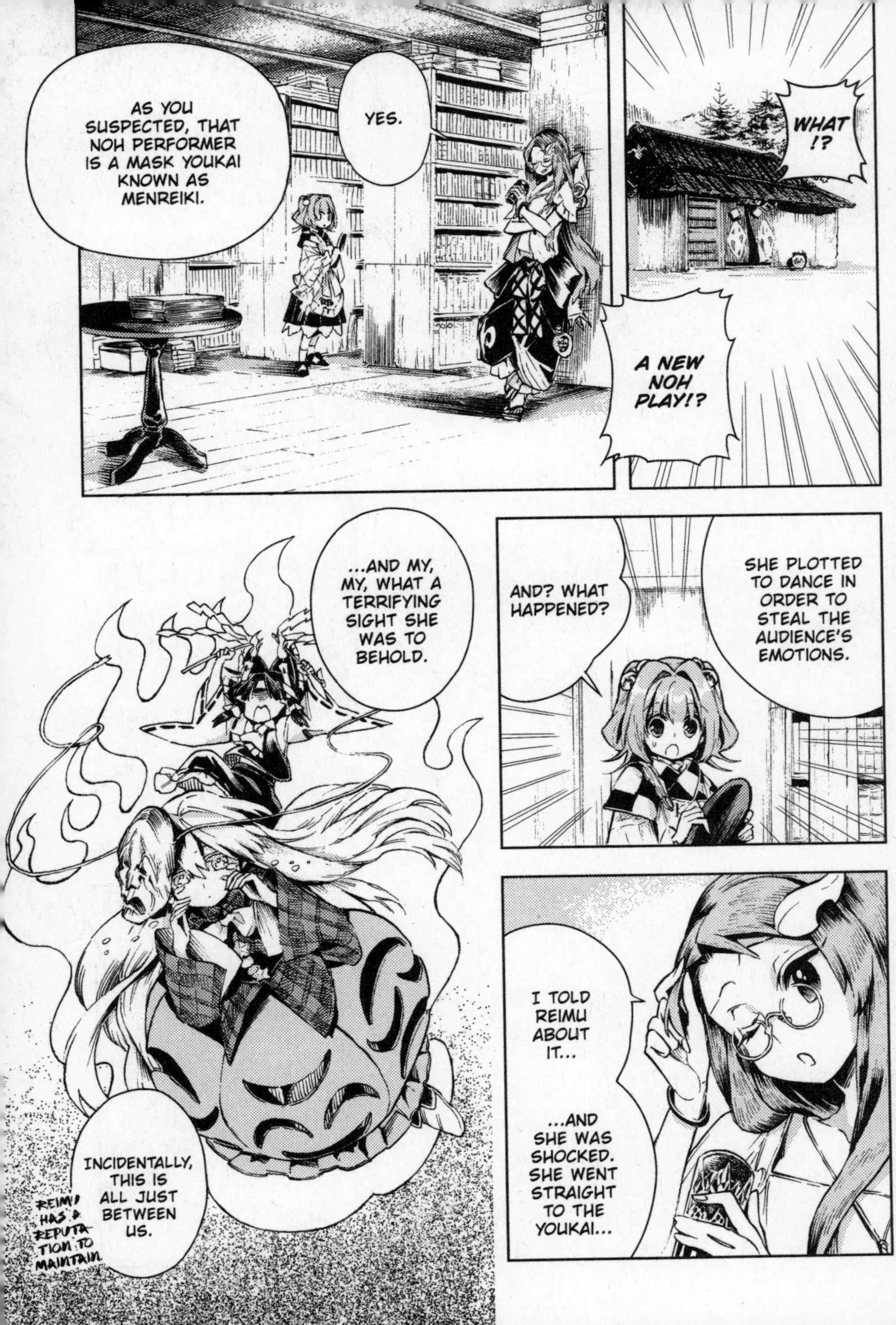
WHAT!?
A NEW NOH PLAY!?
YES.
AS YOU SUSPECTED, THAT NOH PERFORMER IS A MASK YOUKAI KNOWN AS MENREIKI.
SHE PLOTTED TO DANCE IN ORDER TO STEAL THE AUDIENCE'S EMOTIONS.
AND? WHAT HAPPENED?
I TOLD REIMU ABOUT IT...
...AND SHE WAS SHOCKED. SHE WENT STRAIGHT TO THE YOUKAI...
...AND MY, MY, WHAT A TERRIFYING SIGHT SHE WAS TO BEHOLD.
INCIDENTALLY, THIS IS ALL JUST BETWEEN US.
REIMU HAS A REPUTATION TO MAINTAIN.

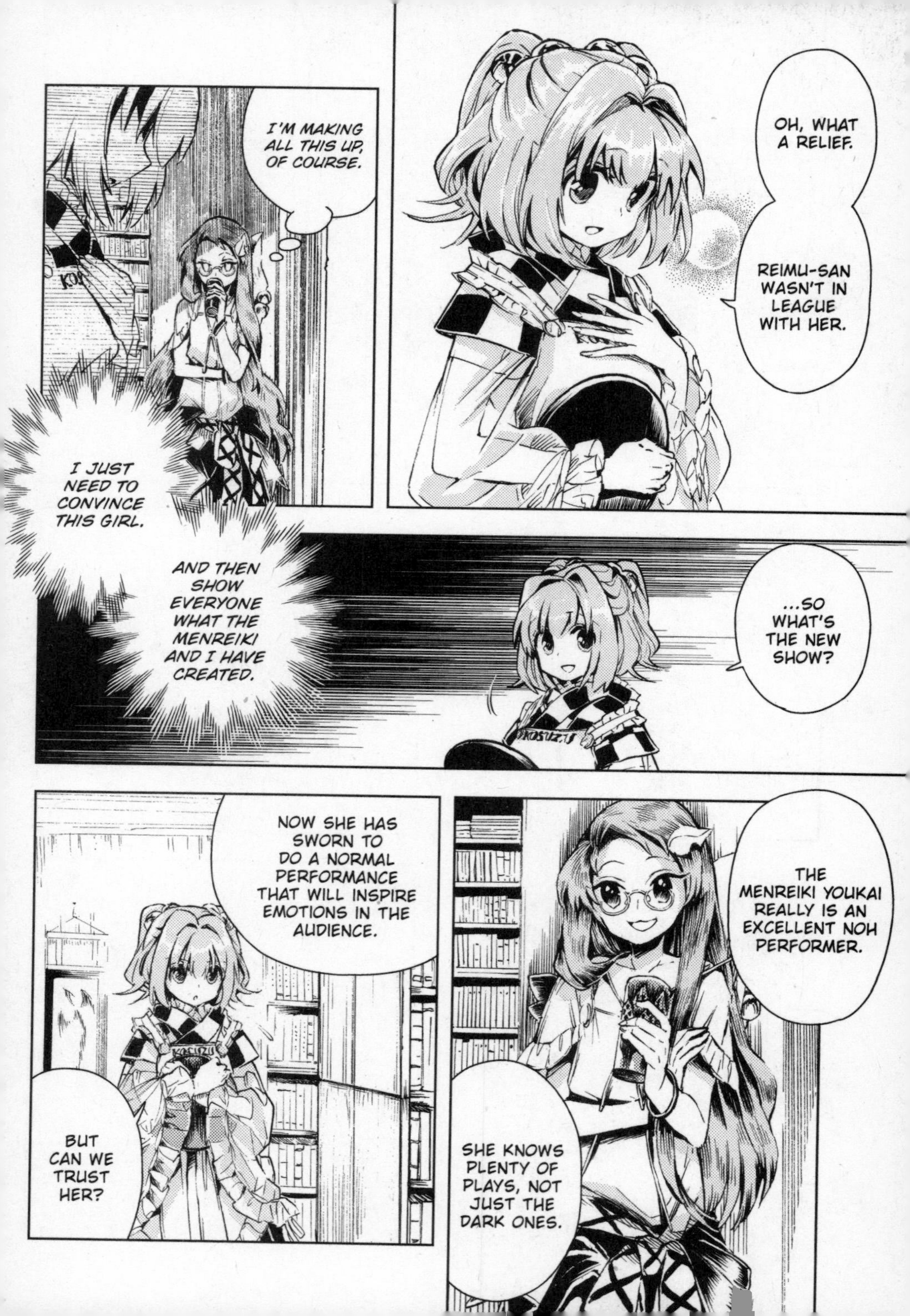
OH, WHAT A RELIEF.
REIMU-SAN WASN'T IN LEAGUE WITH HER.
I'M MAKING ALL THIS UP, OF COURSE.
I JUST NEED TO CONVINCE THIS GIRL.
...SO WHAT'S THE NEW SHOW?
AND THEN SHOW EVERYONE WHAT THE MENREIKI AND I HAVE CREATED.
THE MENREIKI YOUKAI REALLY IS AN EXCELLENT NOH PERFORMER.
SHE KNOWS PLENTY OF PLAYS, NOT JUST THE DARK ONES.
NOW SHE HAS SWORN TO DO A NORMAL PERFORMANCE THAT WILL INSPIRE EMOTIONS IN THE AUDIENCE.
BUT CAN WE TRUST HER?

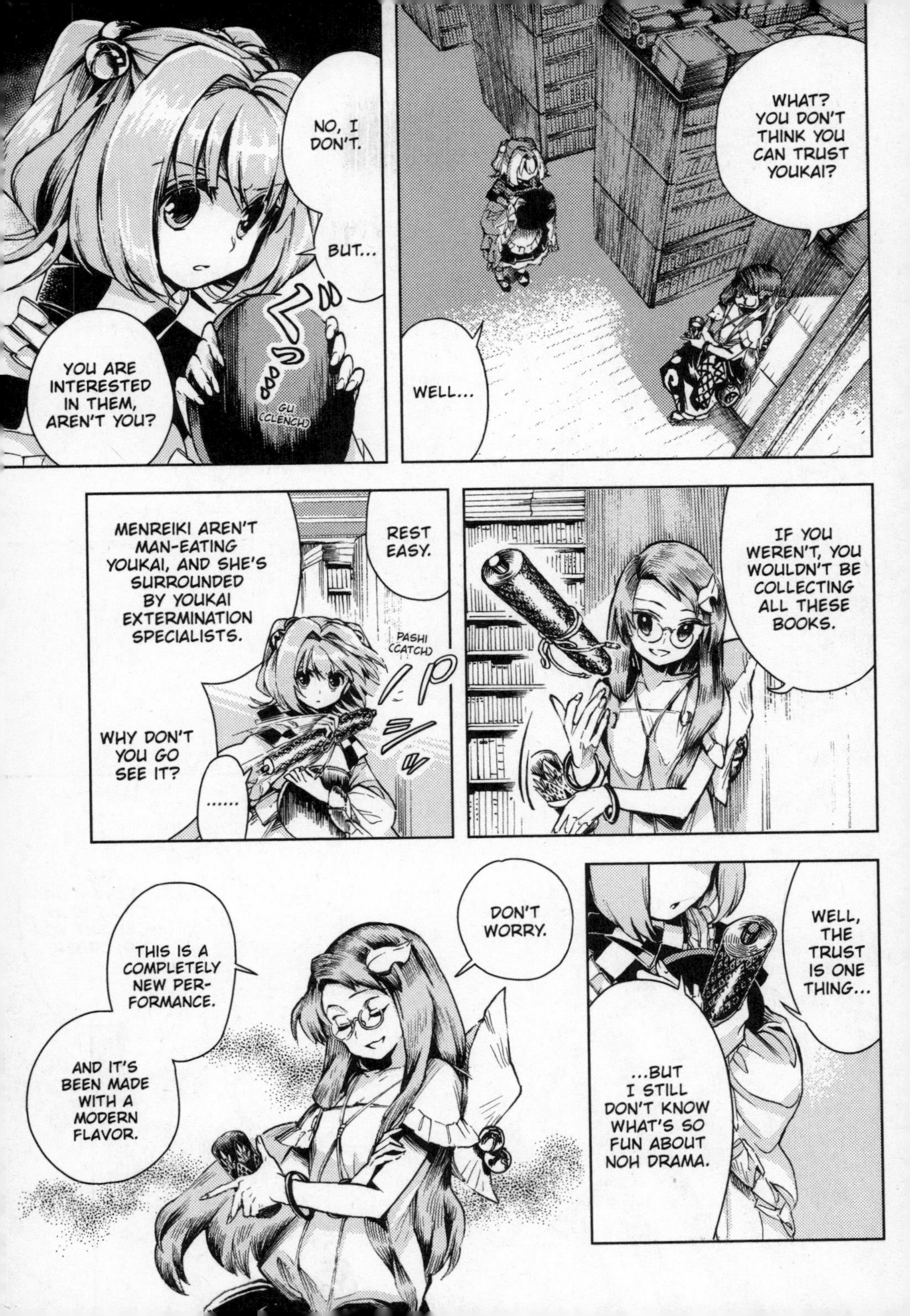
WHAT? YOU DON'T THINK YOU CAN TRUST YOUKAI?
WELL...
NO, I DON'T.
BUT...
YOU ARE INTERESTED IN THEM, AREN'T YOU?
GU (CLENCH)
IF YOU WEREN'T, YOU WOULDN'T BE COLLECTING ALL THESE BOOKS.
REST EASY.
MENREIKI AREN'T MAN-EATING YOUKAI, AND SHE'S SURROUNDED BY YOUKAI EXTERMINATION SPECIALISTS.
PASHI (CATCH)
WHY DON'T YOU GO SEE IT?
......
WELL, THE TRUST IS ONE THING...
...BUT I STILL DON'T KNOW WHAT'S SO FUN ABOUT NOH DRAMA.
DON'T WORRY.
THIS IS A COMPLETELY NEW PER-FORMANCE.
AND IT'S BEEN MADE WITH A MODERN FLAVOR.

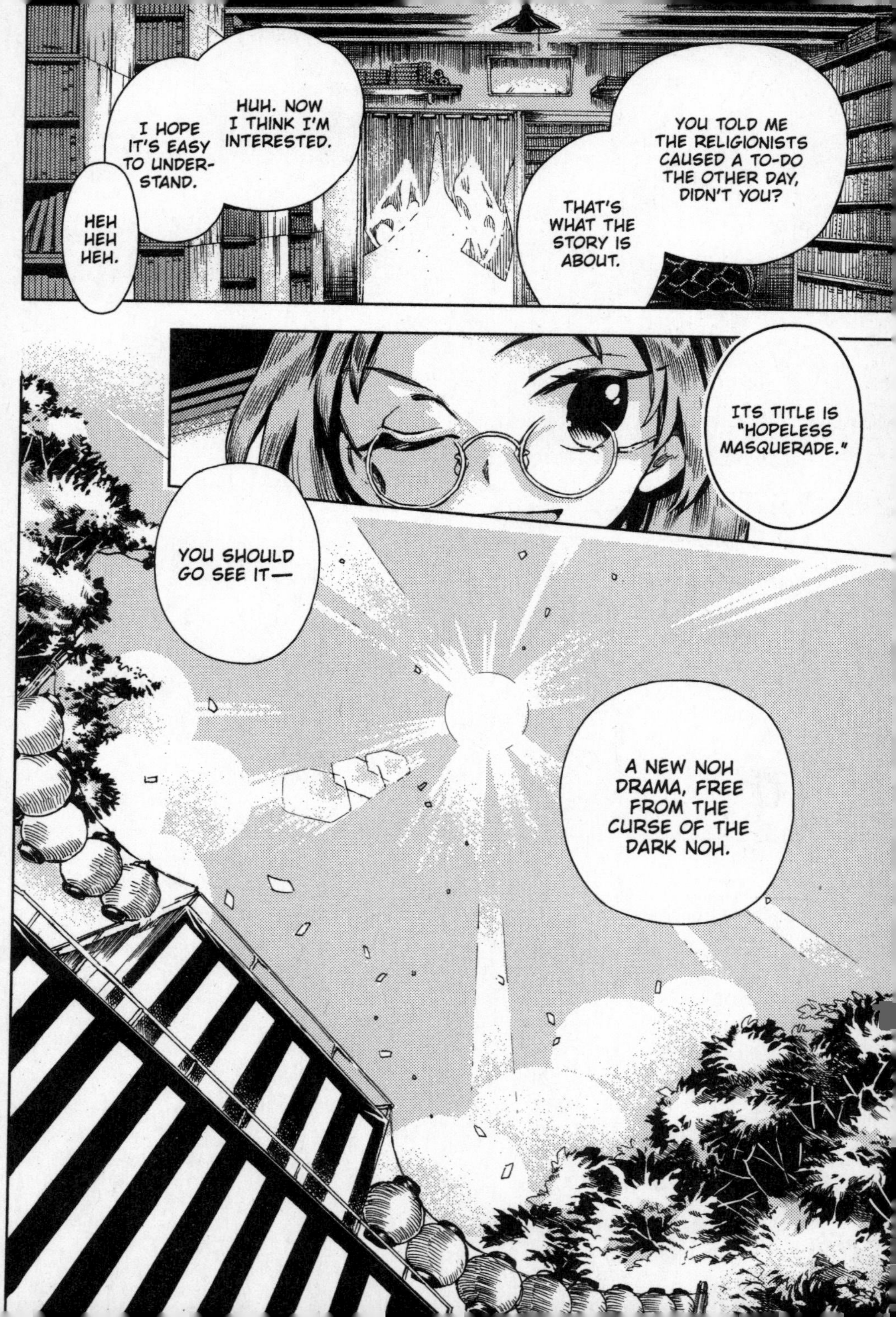
YOU TOLD ME THE RELIGIONISTS CAUSED A TO-DO THE OTHER DAY, DIDN'T YOU?
THAT'S WHAT THE STORY IS ABOUT.
HUH. NOW I THINK I'M INTERESTED.
I HOPE IT'S EASY TO UNDER-STAND.
HEH HEH HEH.
ITS TITLE IS "HOPELESS MASQUERADE."
YOU SHOULD GO SEE IT—
A NEW NOH DRAMA, FREE FROM THE CURSE OF THE DARK NOH.

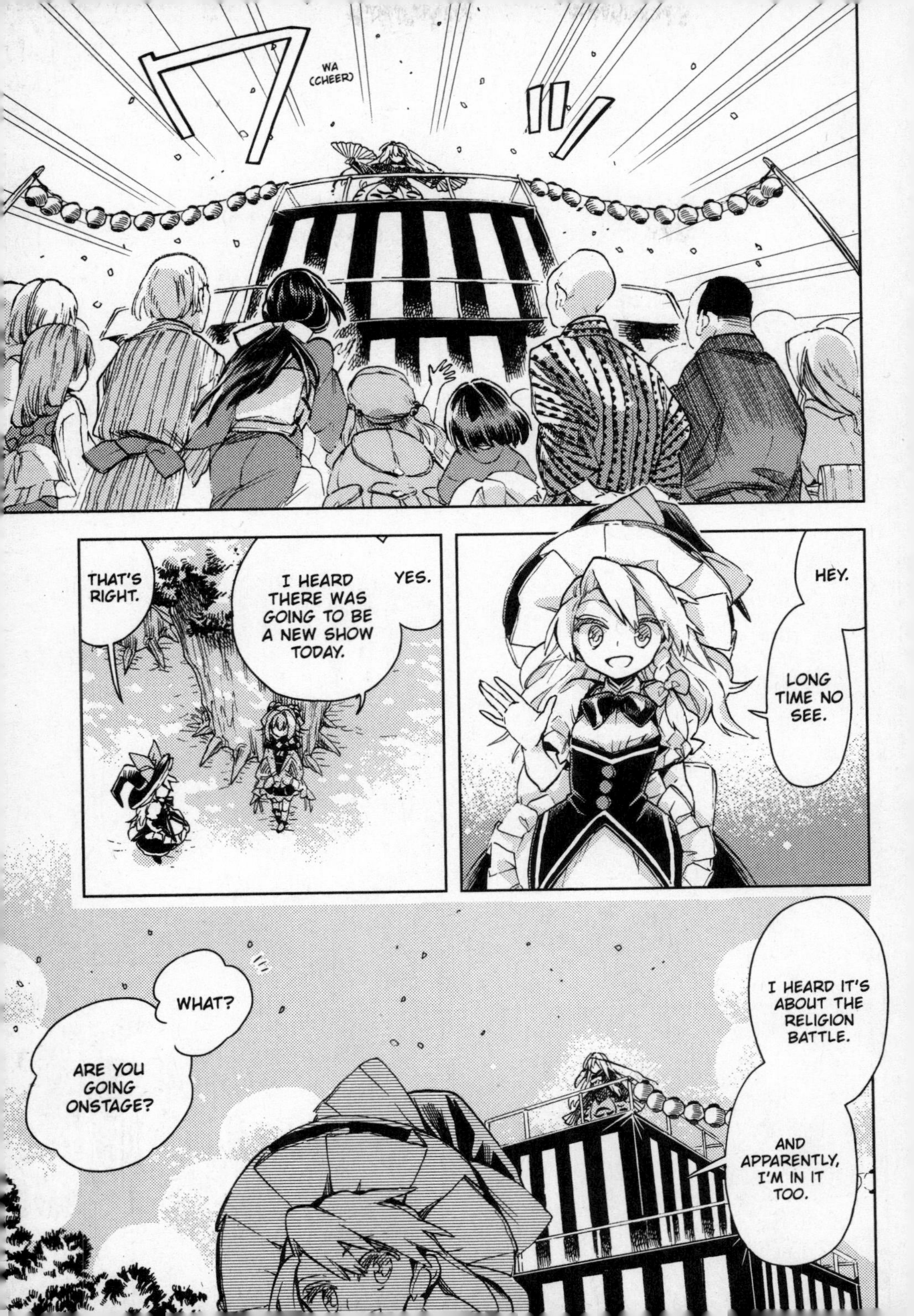
WA (CHEER)
HEY.
LONG TIME NO SEE.
YES.
I HEARD THERE WAS GOING TO BE A NEW SHOW TODAY.
THAT'S RIGHT.
I HEARD IT'S ABOUT THE RELIGION BATTLE.
AND APPARENTLY, I'M IN IT TOO.
WHAT?
ARE YOU GOING ONSTAGE?

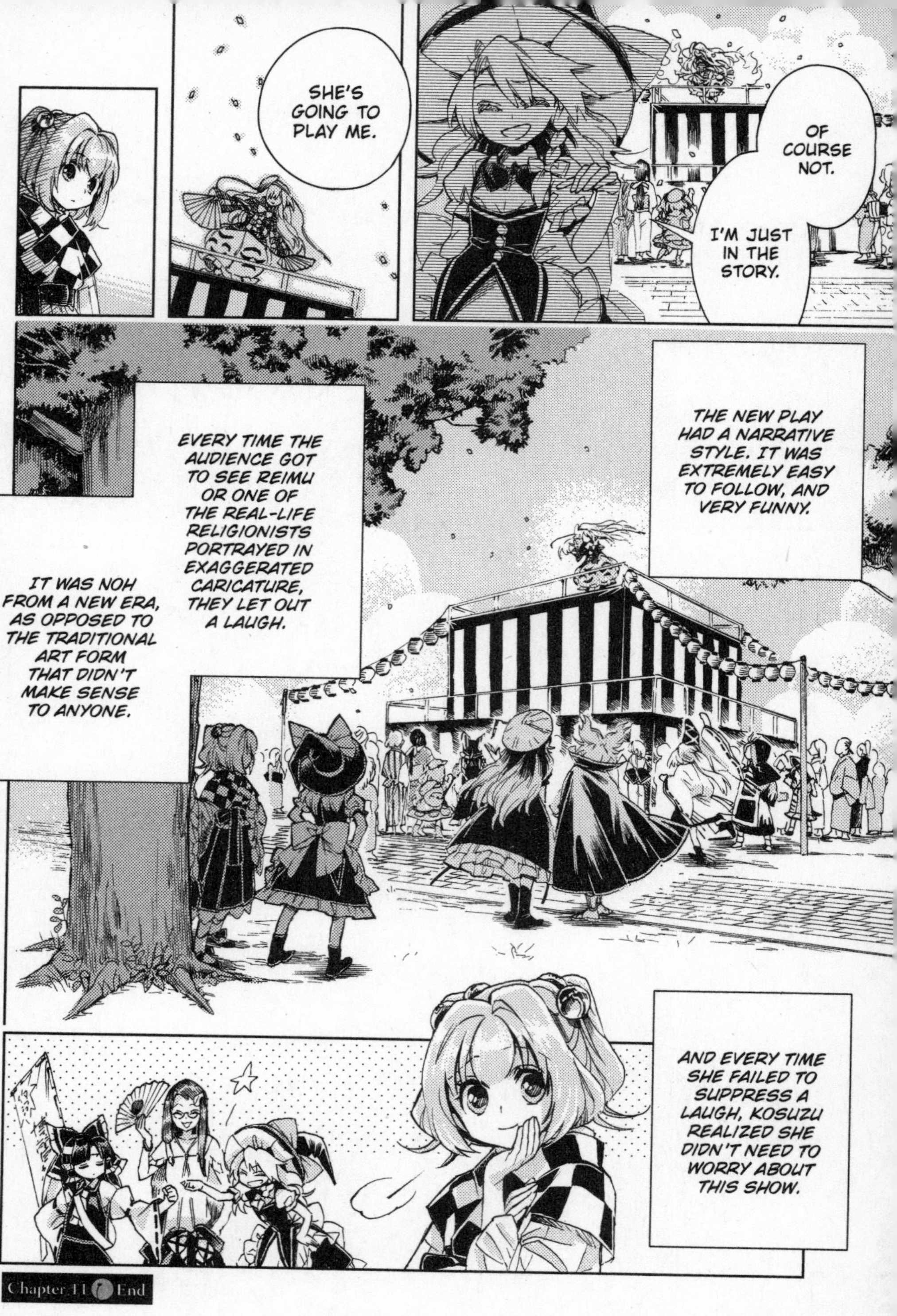
OF COURSE NOT.
I'M JUST IN THE STORY.
SHE'S GOING TO PLAY ME.
THE NEW PLAY HAD A NARRATIVE STYLE. IT WAS EXTREMELY EASY TO FOLLOW, AND VERY FUNNY.
EVERY TIME THE AUDIENCE GOT TO SEE REIMU OR ONE OF THE REAL-LIFE RELIGIONISTS PORTRAYED IN EXAGGERATED CARICATURE, THEY LET OUT A LAUGH.
IT WAS NOH FROM A NEW ERA, AS OPPOSED TO THE TRADITIONAL ART FORM THAT DIDN'T MAKE SENSE TO ANYONE.
AND EVERY TIME SHE FAILED TO SUPPRESS A LAUGH, KOSUZU REALIZED SHE DIDN'T NEED TO WORRY ABOUT THIS SHOW.

Chapter 11 End

Forbidden Scrollery

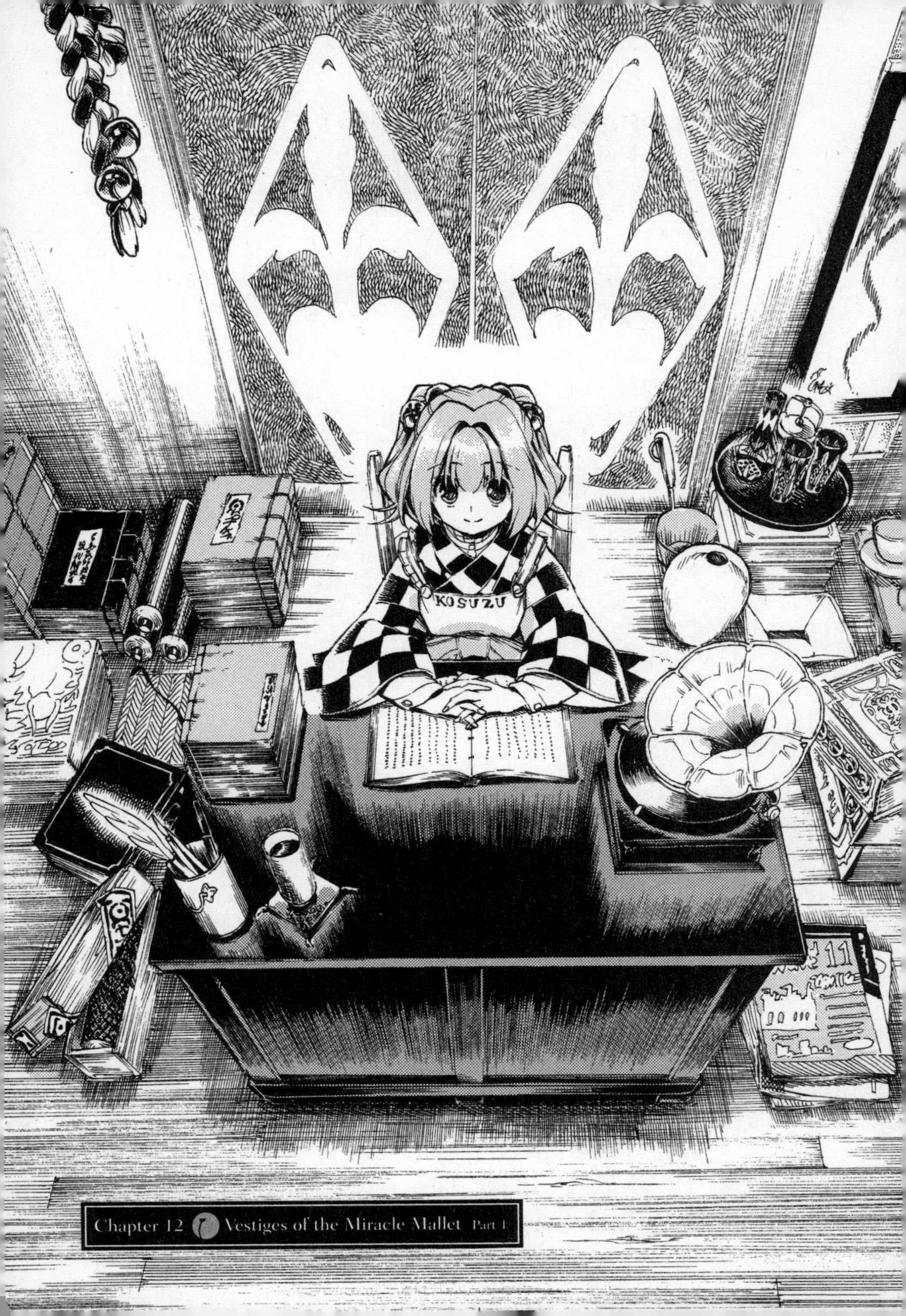
KOSUZU

Chapter 12 Vestiges of the Miracle Mallet Part 1

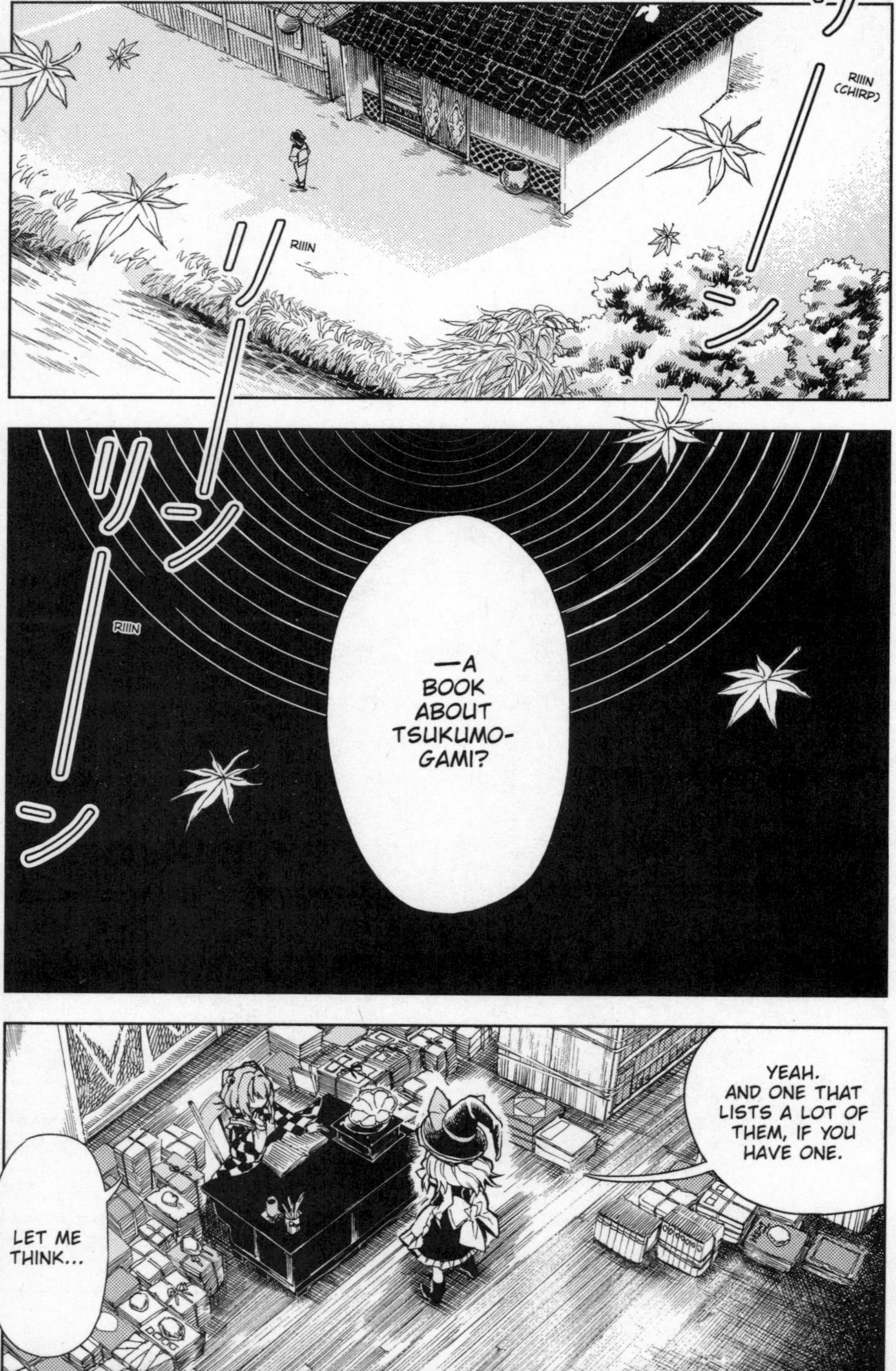
RIIIN (CHIRP)
RIIIN
RIIIN
—A BOOK ABOUT TSUKUMO-GAMI?
YEAH. AND ONE THAT LISTS A LOT OF THEM, IF YOU HAVE ONE.
LET ME THINK...

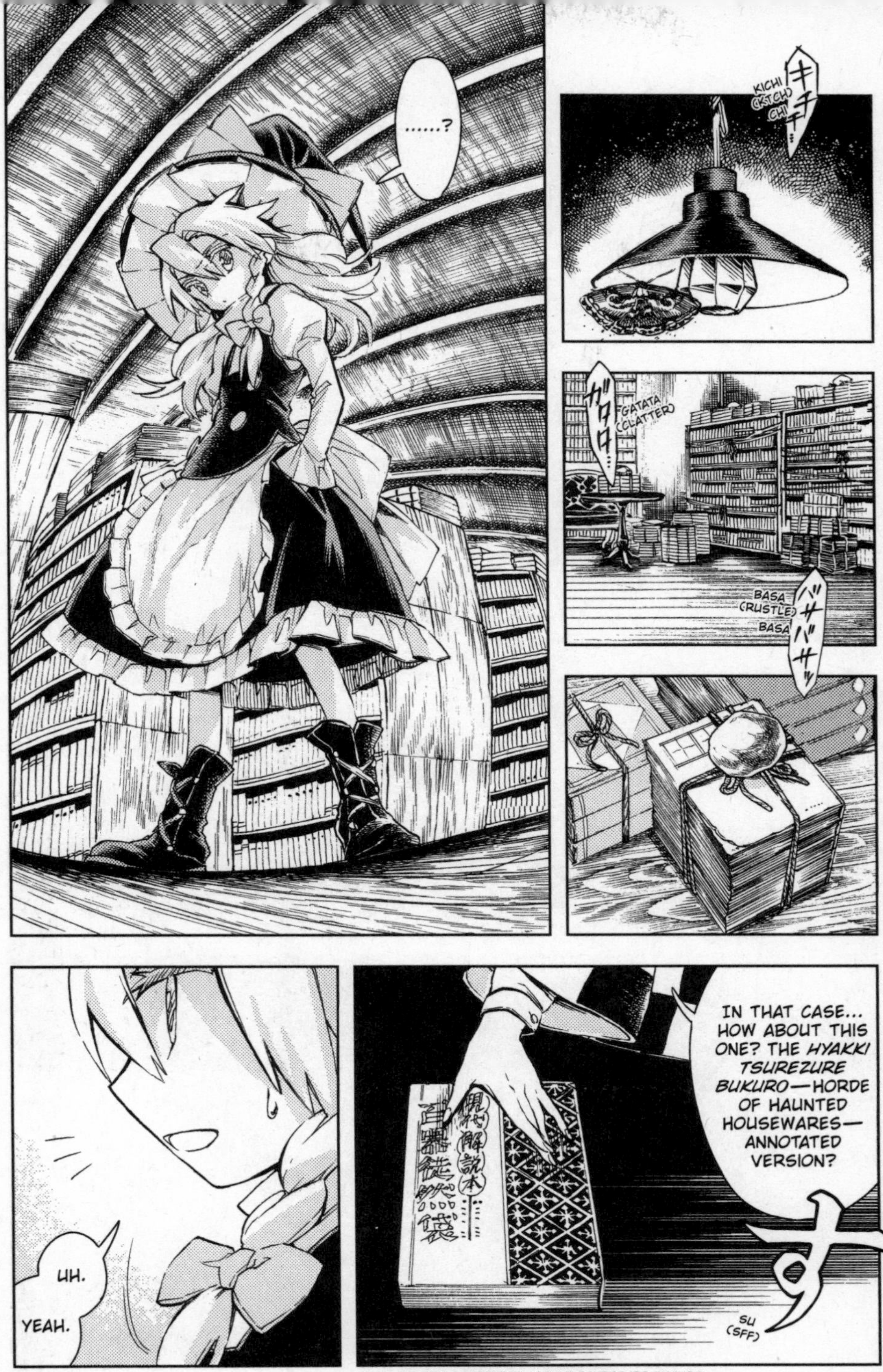
KICHI (KTCH) CHI
GATATA (CLATTER)
BASA (RUSTLE) BASA
......
......?
IN THAT CASE... HOW ABOUT THIS ONE? THE *HYAKKI TSUREZURE BUKURO*—HORDE OF HAUNTED HOUSEWARES—ANNOTATED VERSION?
SU (SFF)
UH.
YEAH.

BOOK: MODERN ANNOTATION, HYAKKI TSUREZURE BUKURO

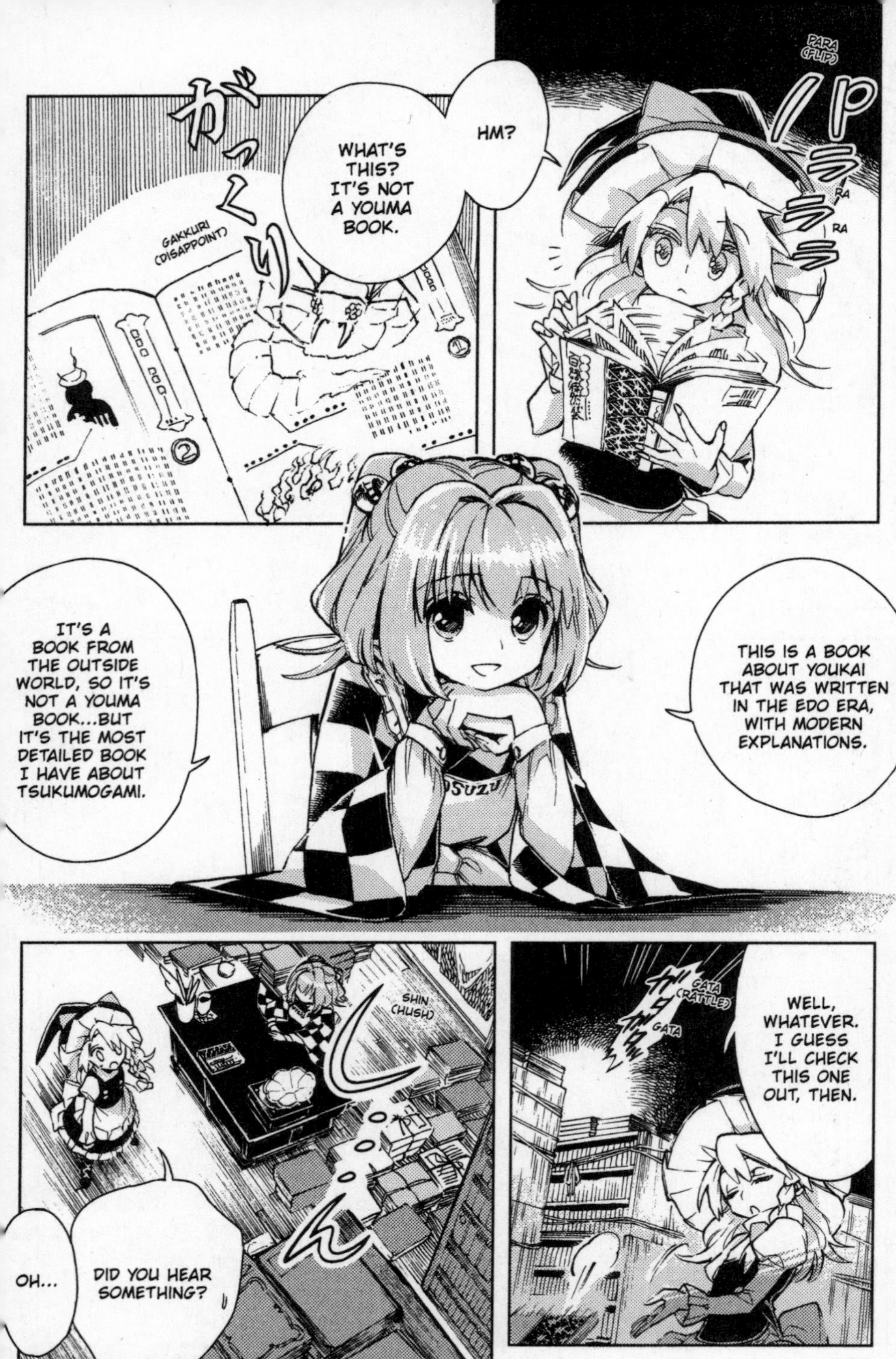
PARA (FLIP)
RA
RA
HM?
WHAT'S THIS? IT'S NOT A YOUMA BOOK.
GAKKURI (DISAPPOINT)
THIS IS A BOOK ABOUT YOUKAI THAT WAS WRITTEN IN THE EDO ERA, WITH MODERN EXPLANATIONS.
IT'S A BOOK FROM THE OUTSIDE WORLD, SO IT'S NOT A YOUMA BOOK...BUT IT'S THE MOST DETAILED BOOK I HAVE ABOUT TSUKUMOGAMI.
KOSUZU
GATA (RATTLE)
GATA
WELL, WHATEVER. I GUESS I'LL CHECK THIS ONE OUT, THEN.
SHIN (HUSH)
DID YOU HEAR SOMETHING?
OH...

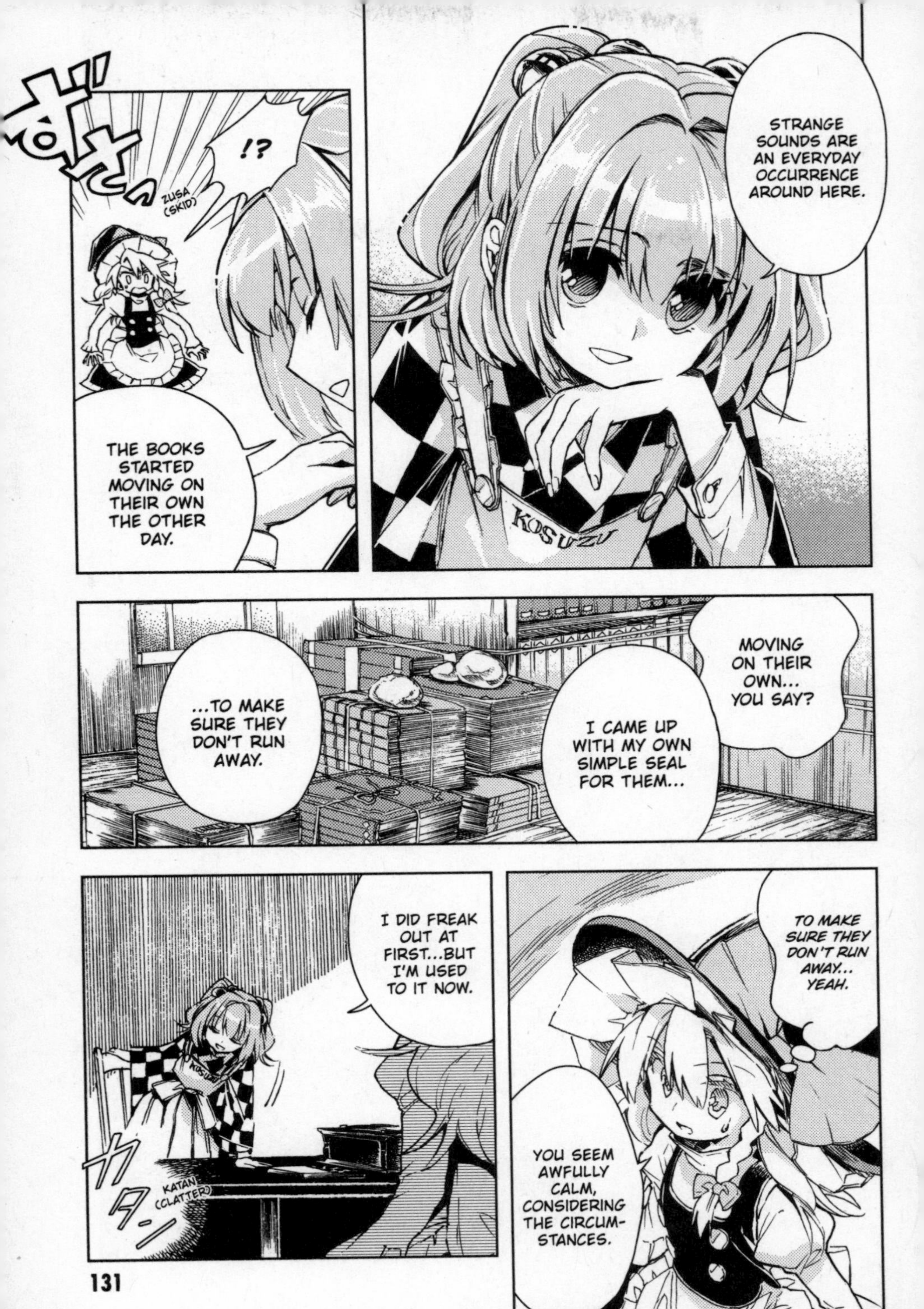
STRANGE SOUNDS ARE AN EVERYDAY OCCURRENCE AROUND HERE.
ZUSA (SKID)
!?
THE BOOKS STARTED MOVING ON THEIR OWN THE OTHER DAY.
MOVING ON THEIR OWN... YOU SAY?
I CAME UP WITH MY OWN SIMPLE SEAL FOR THEM...
...TO MAKE SURE THEY DON'T RUN AWAY.
TO MAKE SURE THEY DON'T RUN AWAY... YEAH.
YOU SEEM AWFULLY CALM, CONSIDERING THE CIRCUM-STANCES.
I DID FREAK OUT AT FIRST...BUT I'M USED TO IT NOW.
KATAN (CLATTER)

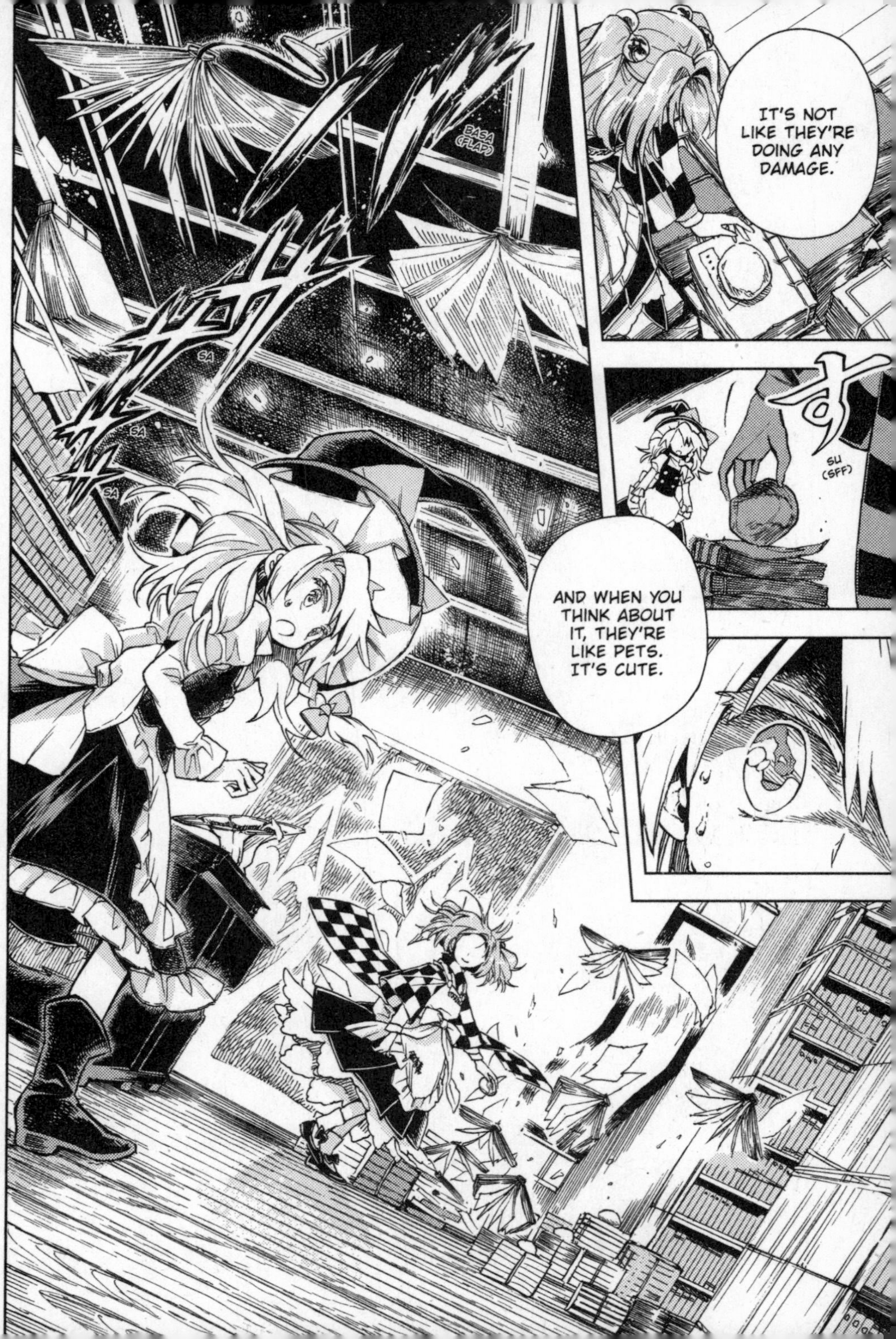
IT'S NOT LIKE THEY'RE DOING ANY DAMAGE.
す
SU (SFF)
AND WHEN YOU THINK ABOUT IT, THEY'RE LIKE PETS. IT'S CUTE.
BASA (FLAP)
SA
SA
SA

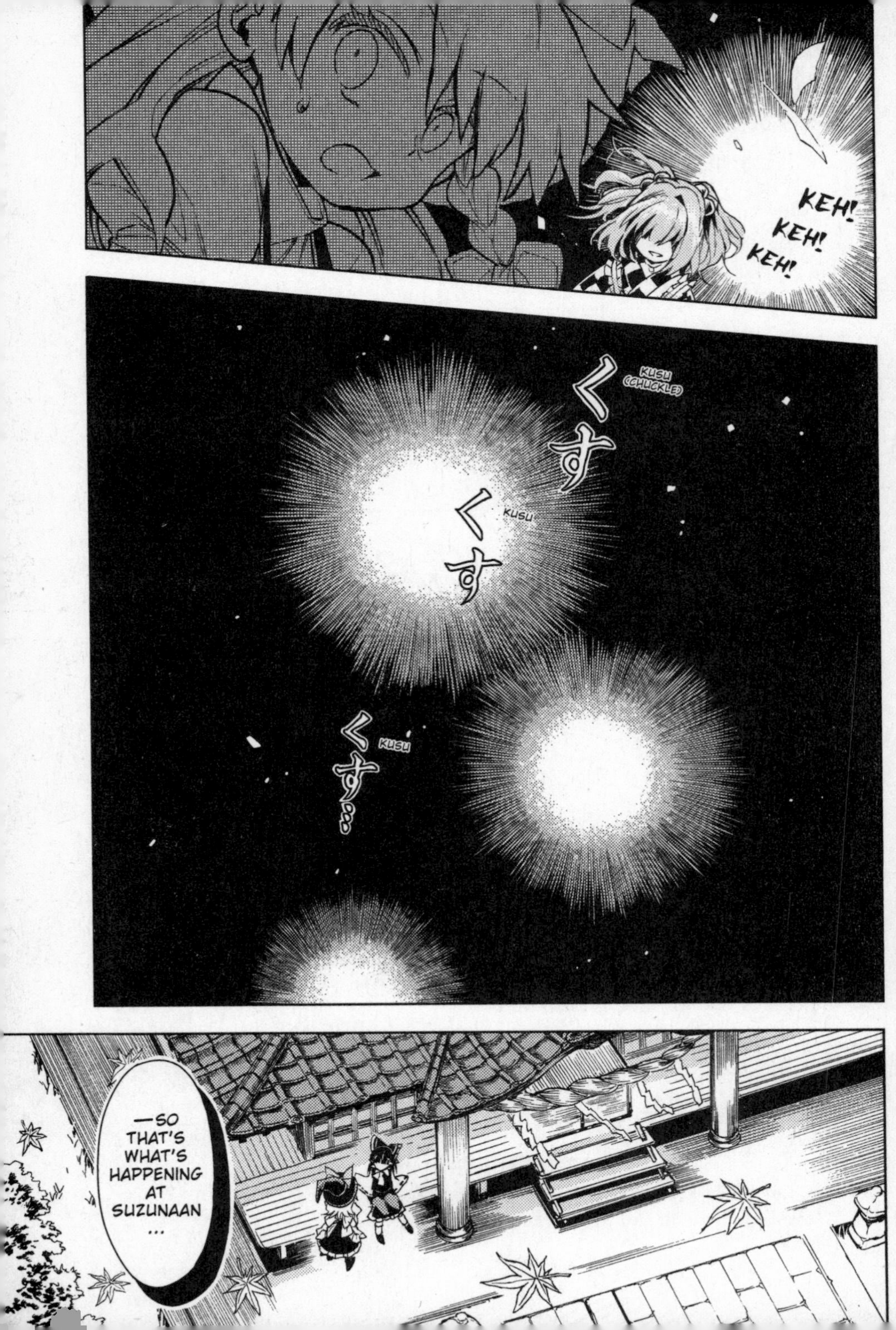
KEH! KEH! KEH!
くす
KUSU (CHUCKLE)
くす
KUSU
くす…
KUSU
—SO THAT'S WHAT'S HAPPENING AT SUZUNAAN...

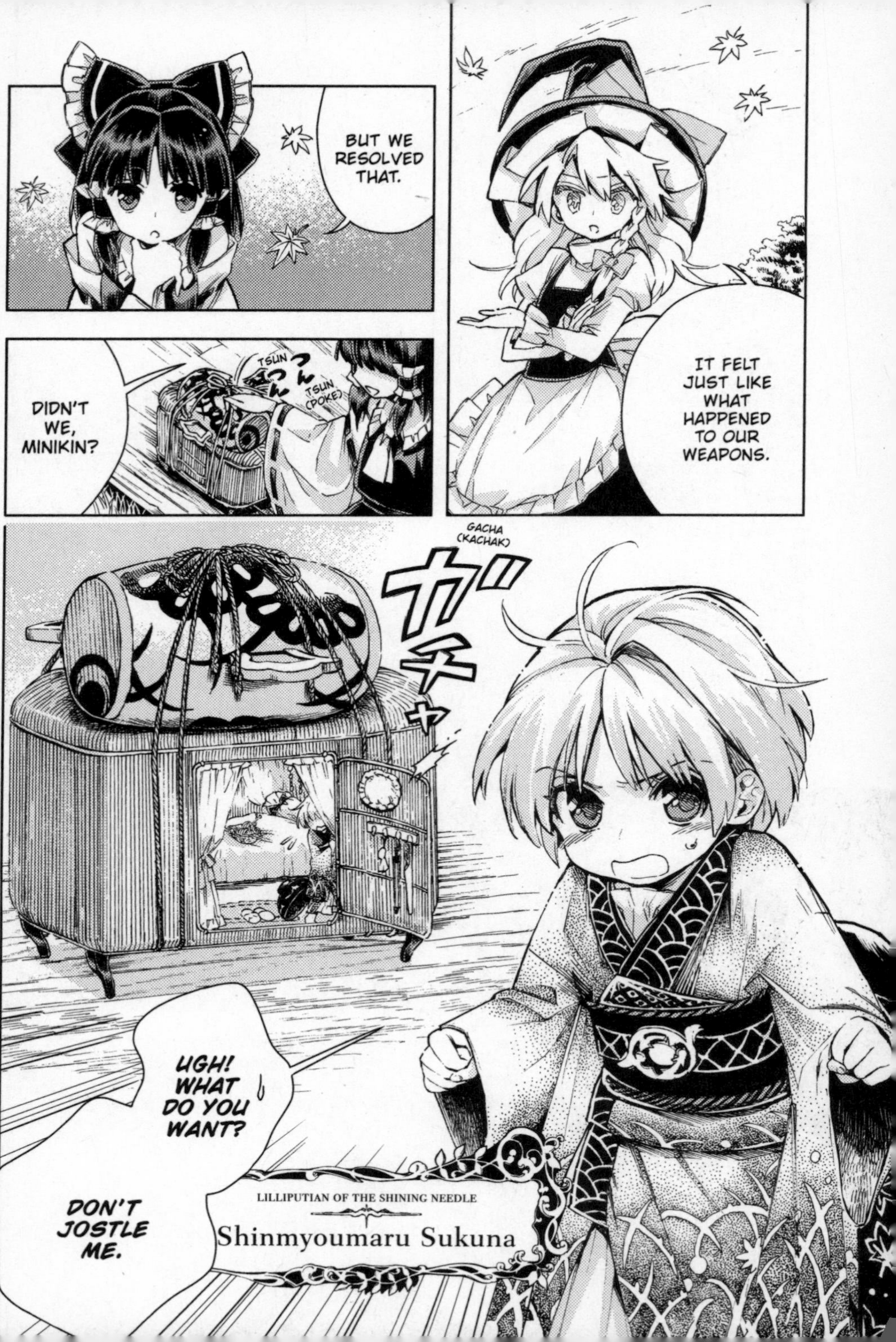
IT FELT JUST LIKE WHAT HAPPENED TO OUR WEAPONS.
BUT WE RESOLVED THAT.
つんつん
TSUN TSUN (POKE)
DIDN'T WE, MINIKIN?
ガチャ
GACHA (KACHAK)
UGH! WHAT DO YOU WANT?
DON'T JOSTLE ME.
LILLIPUTIAN OF THE SHINING NEEDLE
Shinmyoumaru Sukuna

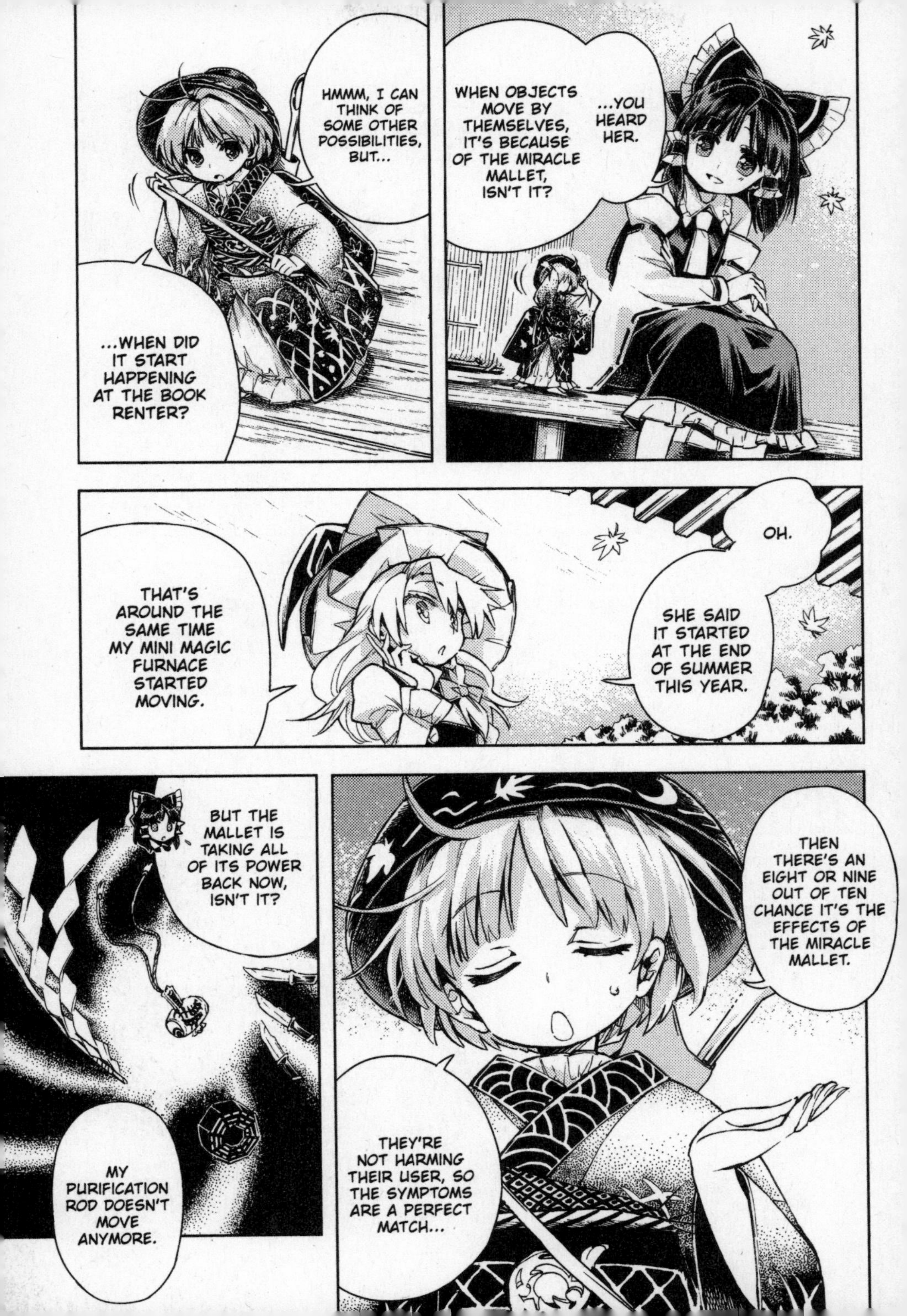
WHEN OBJECTS MOVE BY THEMSELVES, IT'S BECAUSE OF THE MIRACLE MALLET, ISN'T IT?
...YOU HEARD HER.
HMMM, I CAN THINK OF SOME OTHER POSSIBILITIES, BUT...
...WHEN DID IT START HAPPENING AT THE BOOK RENTER?
OH.
SHE SAID IT STARTED AT THE END OF SUMMER THIS YEAR.
THAT'S AROUND THE SAME TIME MY MINI MAGIC FURNACE STARTED MOVING.
THEN THERE'S AN EIGHT OR NINE OUT OF TEN CHANCE IT'S THE EFFECTS OF THE MIRACLE MALLET.
THEY'RE NOT HARMING THEIR USER, SO THE SYMPTOMS ARE A PERFECT MATCH...
BUT THE MALLET IS TAKING ALL OF ITS POWER BACK NOW, ISN'T IT?
MY PURIFICATION ROD DOESN'T MOVE ANYMORE.

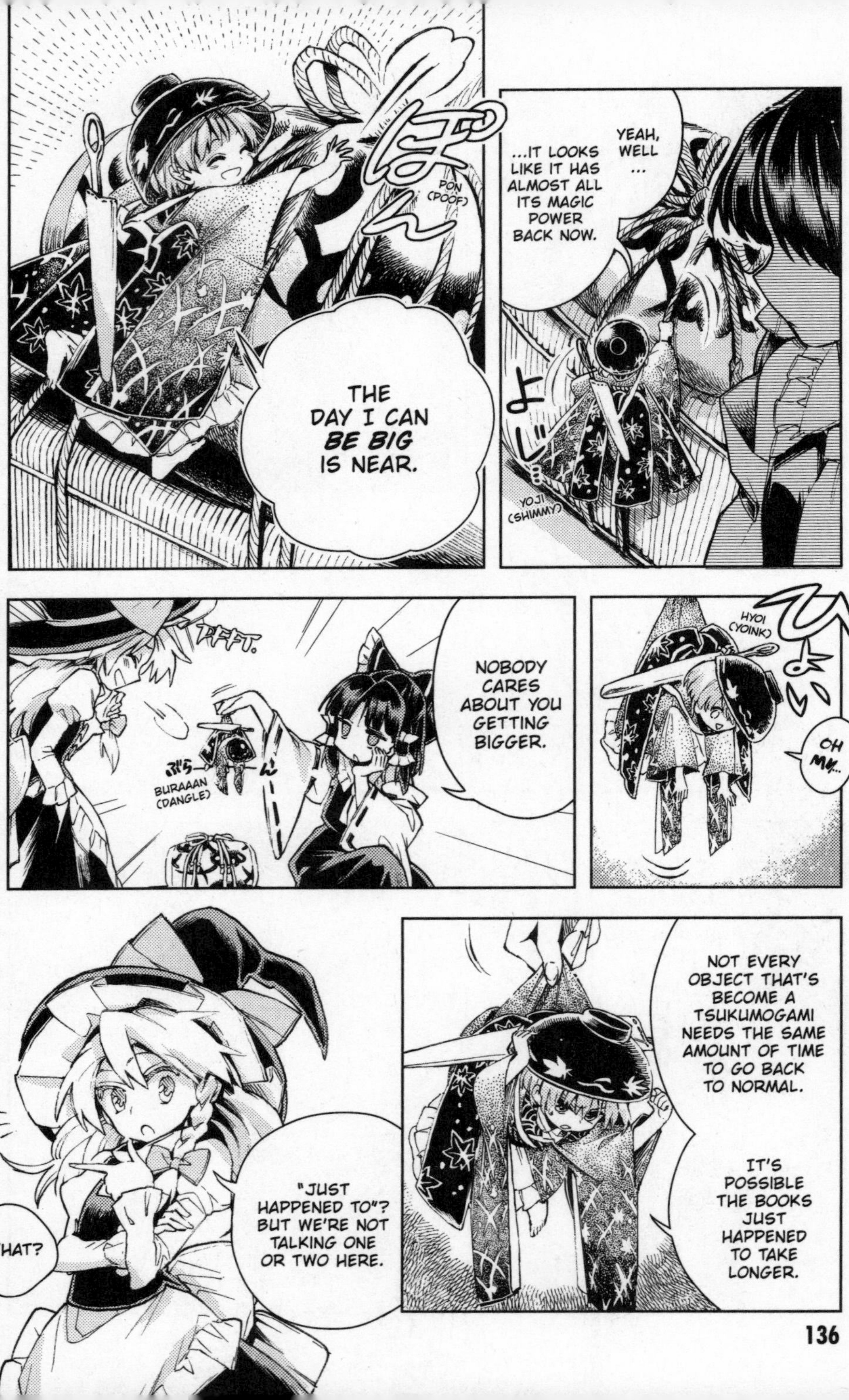
YEAH, WELL ...
...IT LOOKS LIKE IT HAS ALMOST ALL ITS MAGIC POWER BACK NOW.
よじ
YOJI (SHIMMY)
ぽん
PON (POOF)
THE DAY I CAN *BE BIG* IS NEAR.
ひょい
HYOI (YOINK)
OH MY...
NOBODY CARES ABOUT YOU GETTING BIGGER.
ぶら〜ん
BURAAAN (DANGLE)
PFFT.
NOT EVERY OBJECT THAT'S BECOME A TSUKUMOGAMI NEEDS THE SAME AMOUNT OF TIME TO GO BACK TO NORMAL.
IT'S POSSIBLE THE BOOKS JUST HAPPENED TO TAKE LONGER.
WHAT?
"JUST HAPPENED TO"? BUT WE'RE NOT TALKING ONE OR TWO HERE.

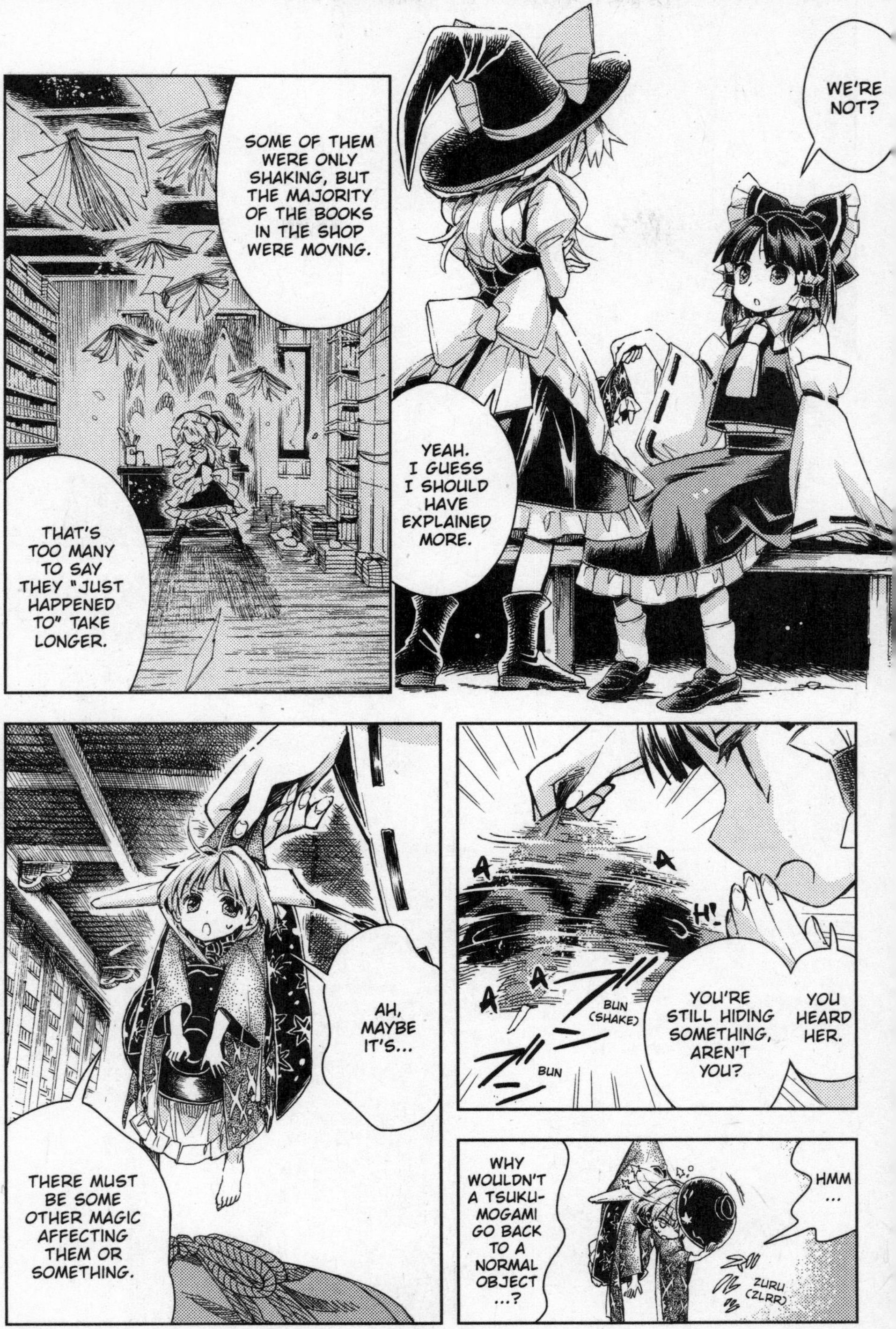
WE'RE NOT?
YEAH. I GUESS I SHOULD HAVE EXPLAINED MORE.
SOME OF THEM WERE ONLY SHAKING, BUT THE MAJORITY OF THE BOOKS IN THE SHOP WERE MOVING.
THAT'S TOO MANY TO SAY THEY "JUST HAPPENED TO" TAKE LONGER.
YOU HEARD HER.
YOU'RE STILL HIDING SOMETHING, AREN'T YOU?
A A H!
A A A
BUN (SHAKE)
BUN
HMM ...
WHY WOULDN'T A TSUKU-MOGAMI GO BACK TO A NORMAL OBJECT ...?
ZURU (ZLRR)
AH, MAYBE IT'S...
THERE MUST BE SOME OTHER MAGIC AFFECTING THEM OR SOMETHING.

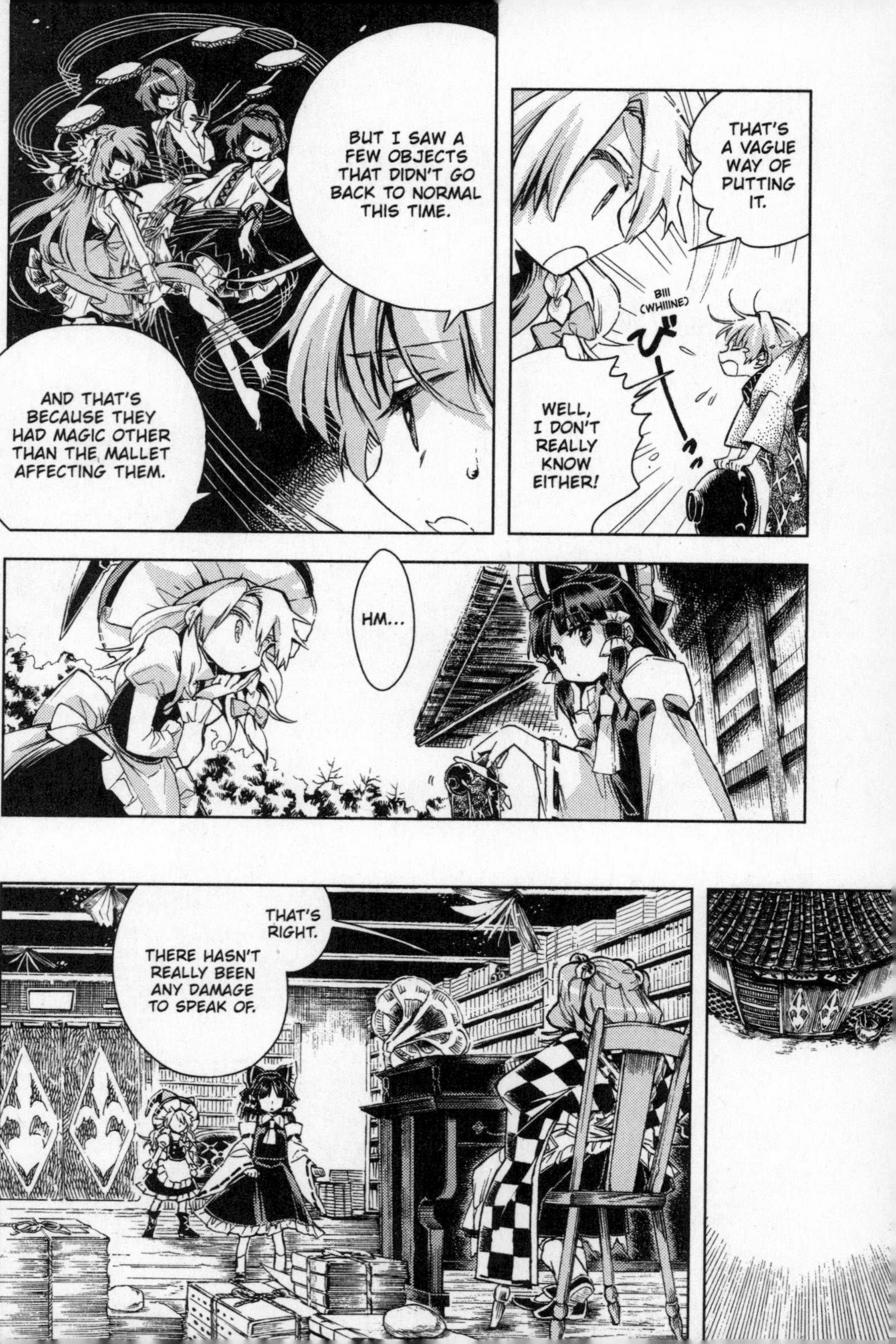
THAT'S A VAGUE WAY OF PUTTING IT.
BIII (WHIIINE)
WELL, I DON'T REALLY KNOW EITHER!
BUT I SAW A FEW OBJECTS THAT DIDN'T GO BACK TO NORMAL THIS TIME.
AND THAT'S BECAUSE THEY HAD MAGIC OTHER THAN THE MALLET AFFECTING THEM.
HM...
THAT'S RIGHT.
THERE HASN'T REALLY BEEN ANY DAMAGE TO SPEAK OF.

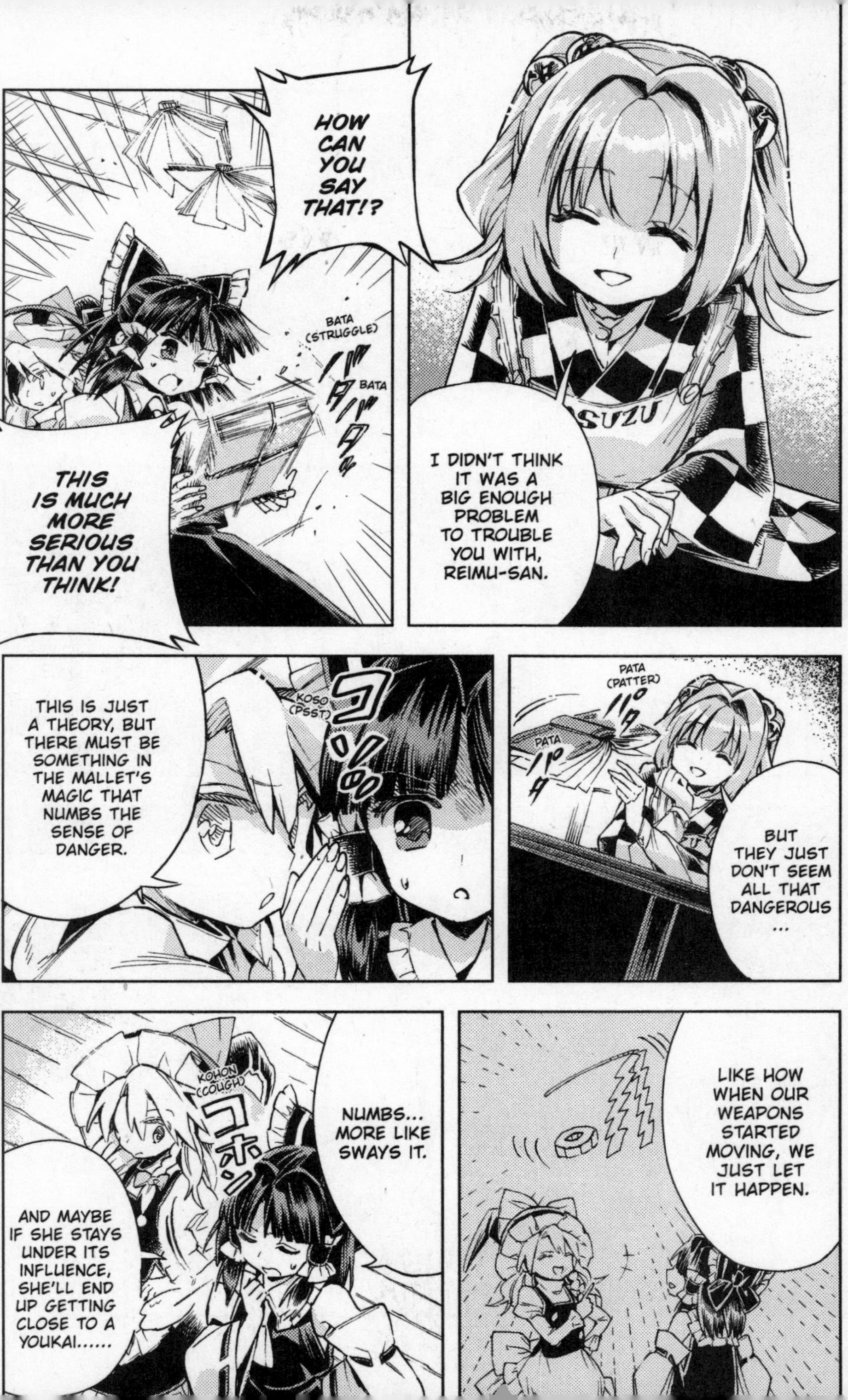
I DIDN'T THINK IT WAS A BIG ENOUGH PROBLEM TO TROUBLE YOU WITH, REIMU-SAN.
HOW CAN YOU SAY THAT!?
BATA (STRUGGLE)
BATA
THIS IS MUCH MORE SERIOUS THAN YOU THINK!
PATA (PATTER)
PATA
BUT THEY JUST DON'T SEEM ALL THAT DANGEROUS ...
KOSO (PSSST)
THIS IS JUST A THEORY, BUT THERE MUST BE SOMETHING IN THE MALLET'S MAGIC THAT NUMBS THE SENSE OF DANGER.
LIKE HOW WHEN OUR WEAPONS STARTED MOVING, WE JUST LET IT HAPPEN.
NUMBS... MORE LIKE SWAYS IT.
KOHON (COUGH)
AND MAYBE IF SHE STAYS UNDER ITS INFLUENCE, SHE'LL END UP GETTING CLOSE TO A YOUKAI......

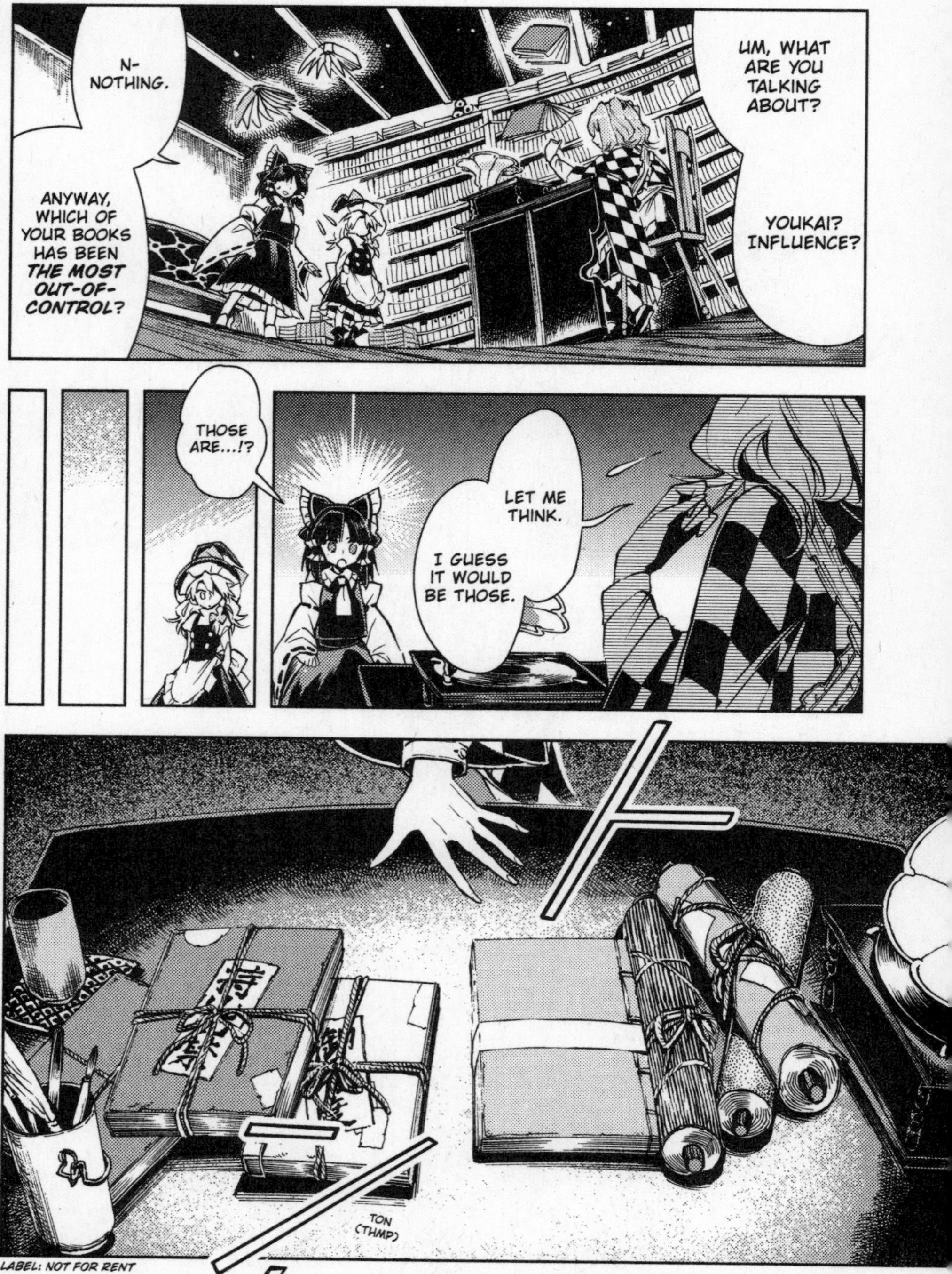
UM, WHAT ARE YOU TALKING ABOUT?
YOUKAI? INFLUENCE?
N-NOTHING.
ANYWAY, WHICH OF YOUR BOOKS HAS BEEN *THE MOST OUT-OF-CONTROL*?
LET ME THINK.
I GUESS IT WOULD BE THOSE.
THOSE ARE...!?
TON (THMP)

LABEL: NOT FOR RENT

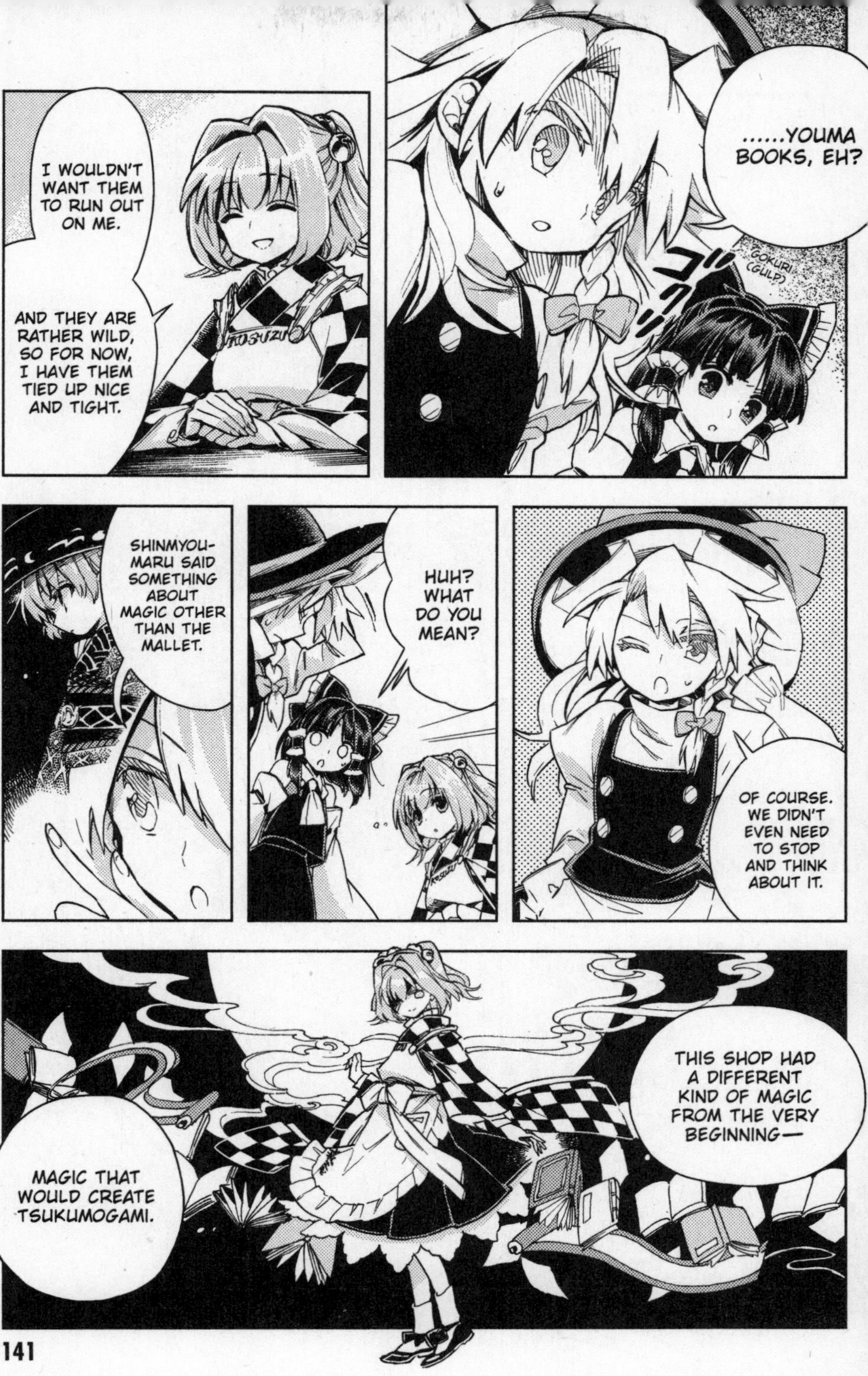

......YOUMA BOOKS, EH?
GOKURI (GULP)
I WOULDN'T WANT THEM TO RUN OUT ON ME.
AND THEY ARE RATHER WILD, SO FOR NOW, I HAVE THEM TIED UP NICE AND TIGHT.
OF COURSE. WE DIDN'T EVEN NEED TO STOP AND THINK ABOUT IT.
HUH? WHAT DO YOU MEAN?
SHINMYOU-MARU SAID SOMETHING ABOUT MAGIC OTHER THAN THE MALLET.
THIS SHOP HAD A DIFFERENT KIND OF MAGIC FROM THE VERY BEGINNING—
MAGIC THAT WOULD CREATE TSUKUMOGAMI.

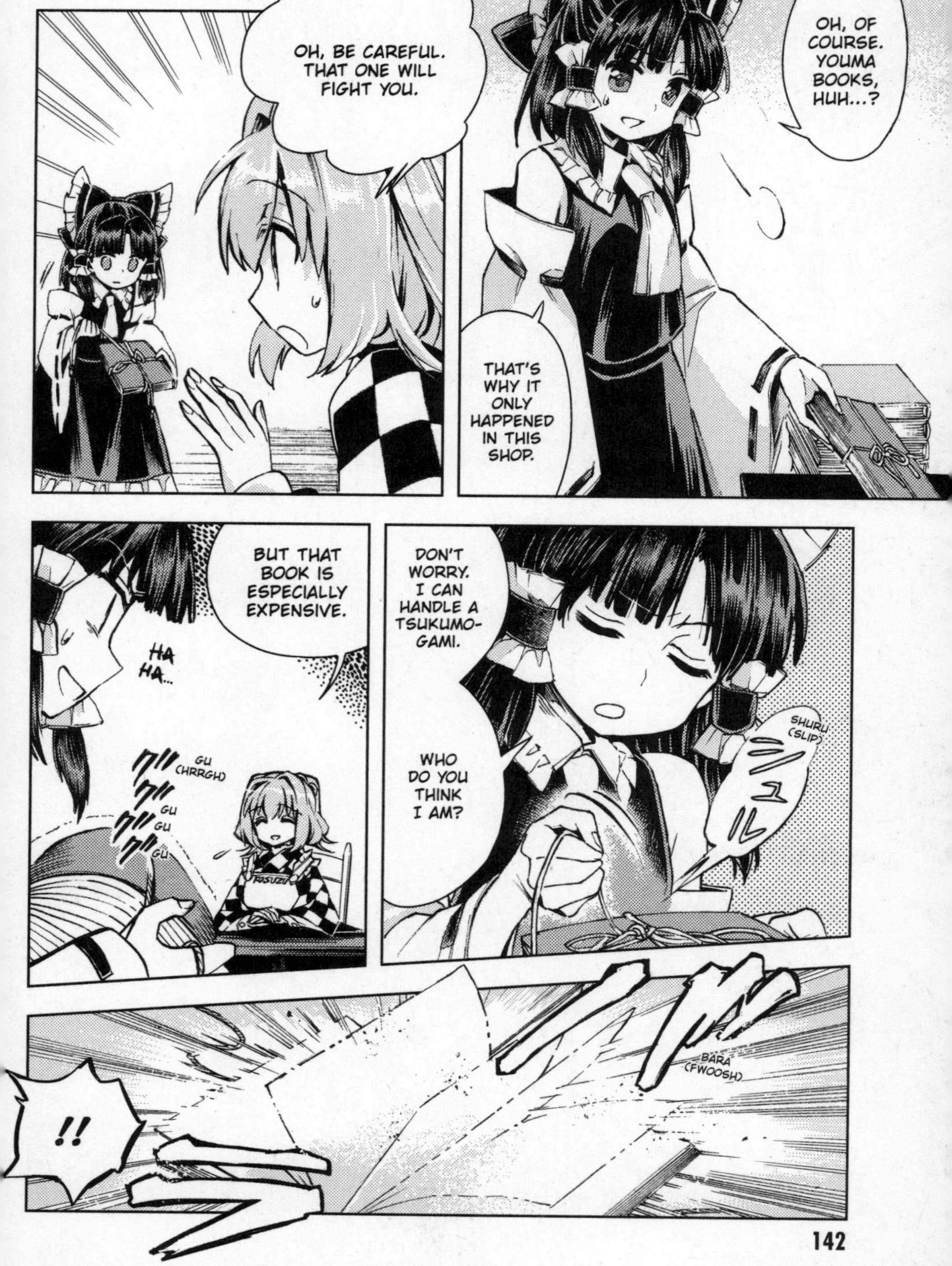
OH, OF COURSE. YOUMA BOOKS, HUH...?
THAT'S WHY IT ONLY HAPPENED IN THIS SHOP.
OH, BE CAREFUL. THAT ONE WILL FIGHT YOU.
DON'T WORRY. I CAN HANDLE A TSUKUMO-GAMI.
SHURU (SLIP)
WHO DO YOU THINK I AM?
BUT THAT BOOK IS ESPECIALLY EXPENSIVE.
HA HA...
GU (HRRGH)
GU
GU
GU
BARA (FWOOSH)
!!

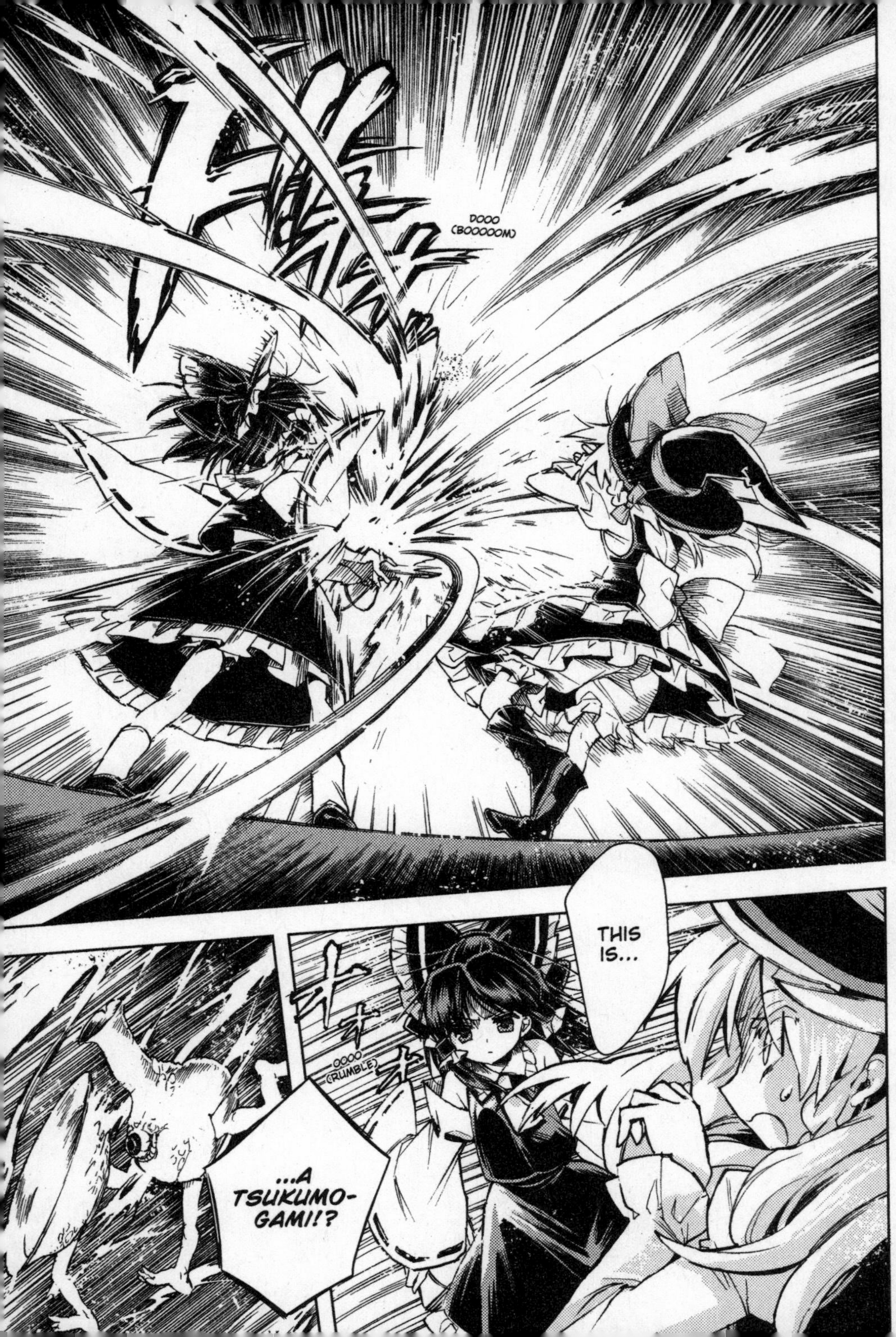
DOOO
(BOOOOOM)
THIS IS...
OOOO
(RUMBLE)
...A TSUKUMO-GAMI!?

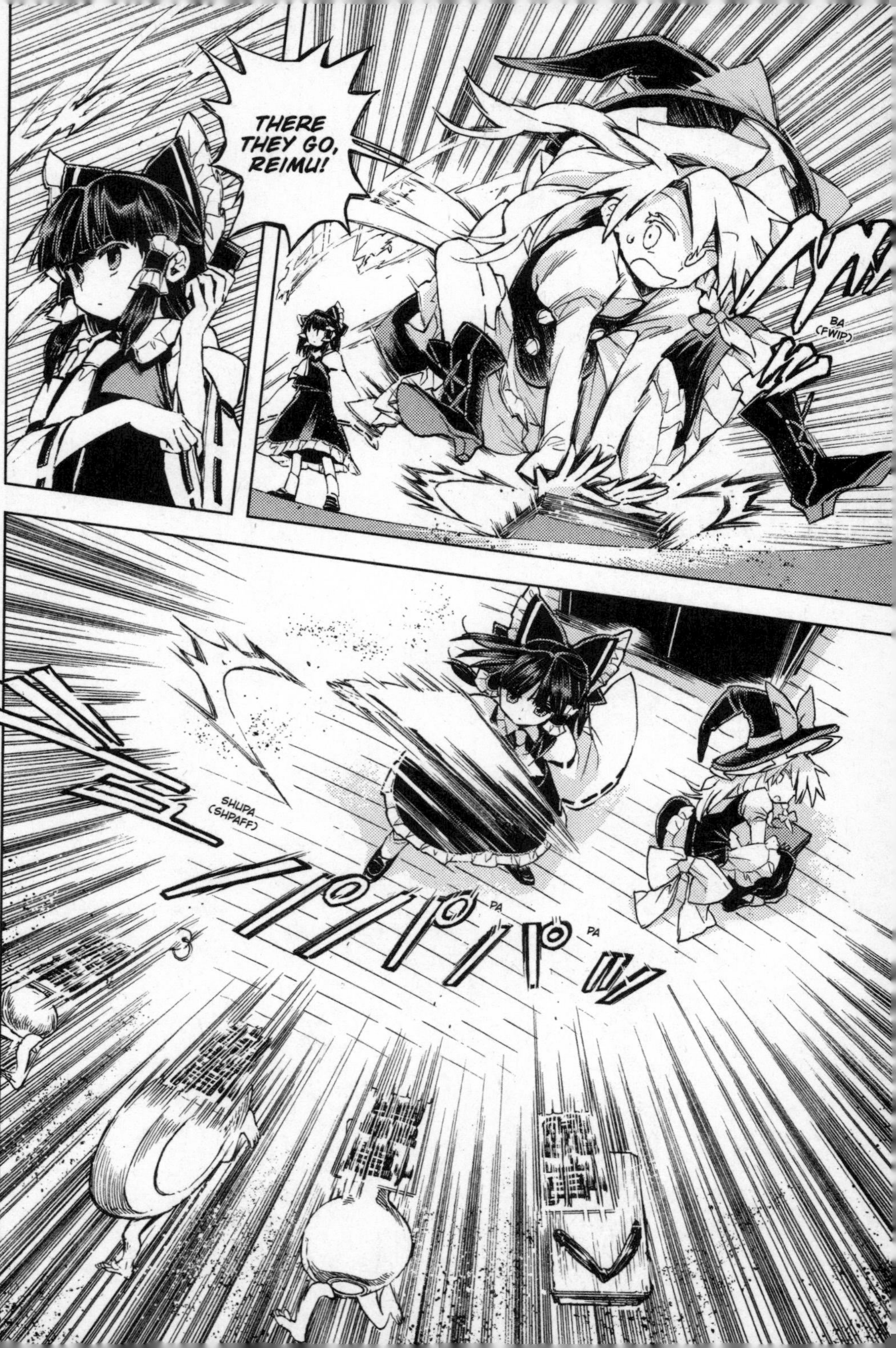
THERE THEY GO, REIMU!
BA (FWIP)
SHUPA (SHPAFF)
PA
PA

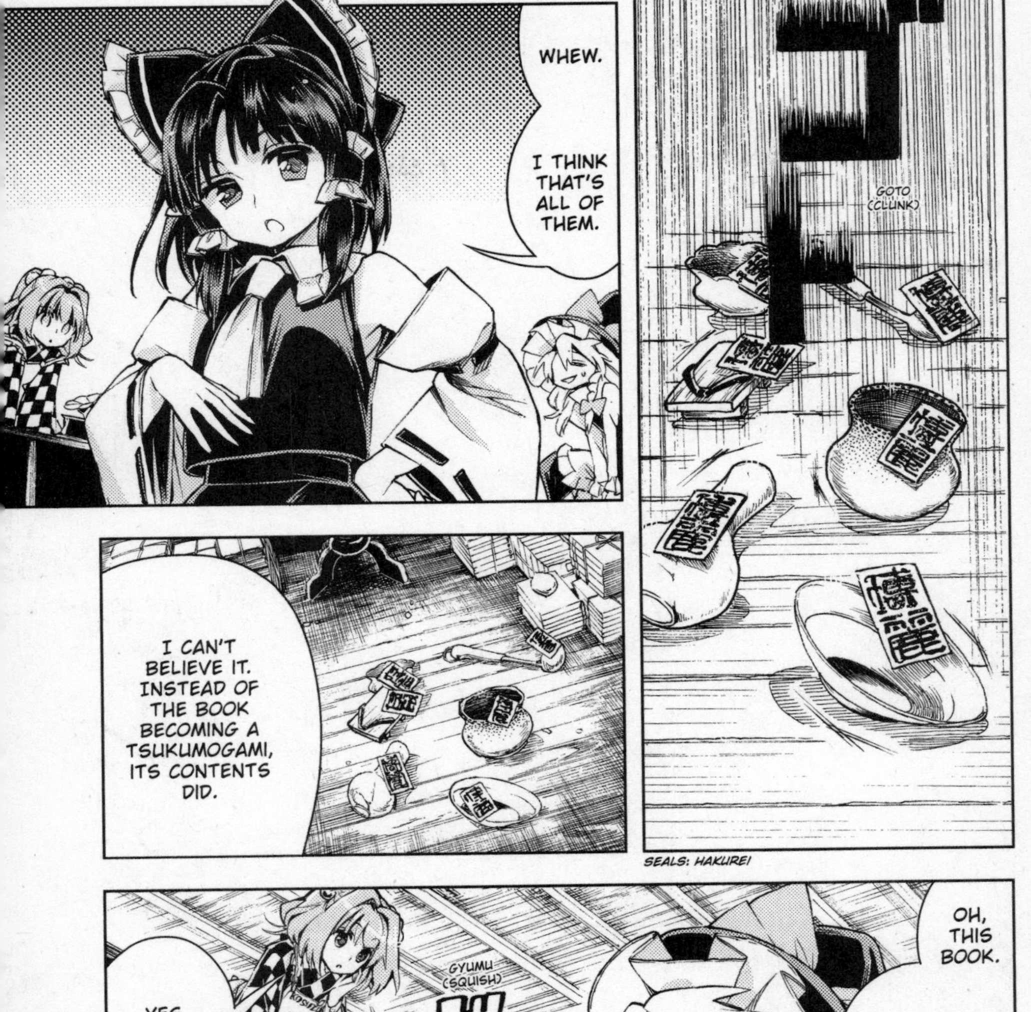
GOTO
(CLUNK)
SEALS: HAKUREI
WHEW.
I THINK THAT'S ALL OF THEM.
I CAN'T BELIEVE IT. INSTEAD OF THE BOOK BECOMING A TSUKUMOGAMI, ITS CONTENTS DID.
OH, THIS BOOK.
DIDN'T YOU SAY THIS ONE HAD YOUKAI SEALED INSIDE IT?
GYUMU
(SQUISH)
YES, THAT'S RIGHT.
BUT THEY'VE NEVER GONE BERSERK INSIDE THE BOOK BEFORE...

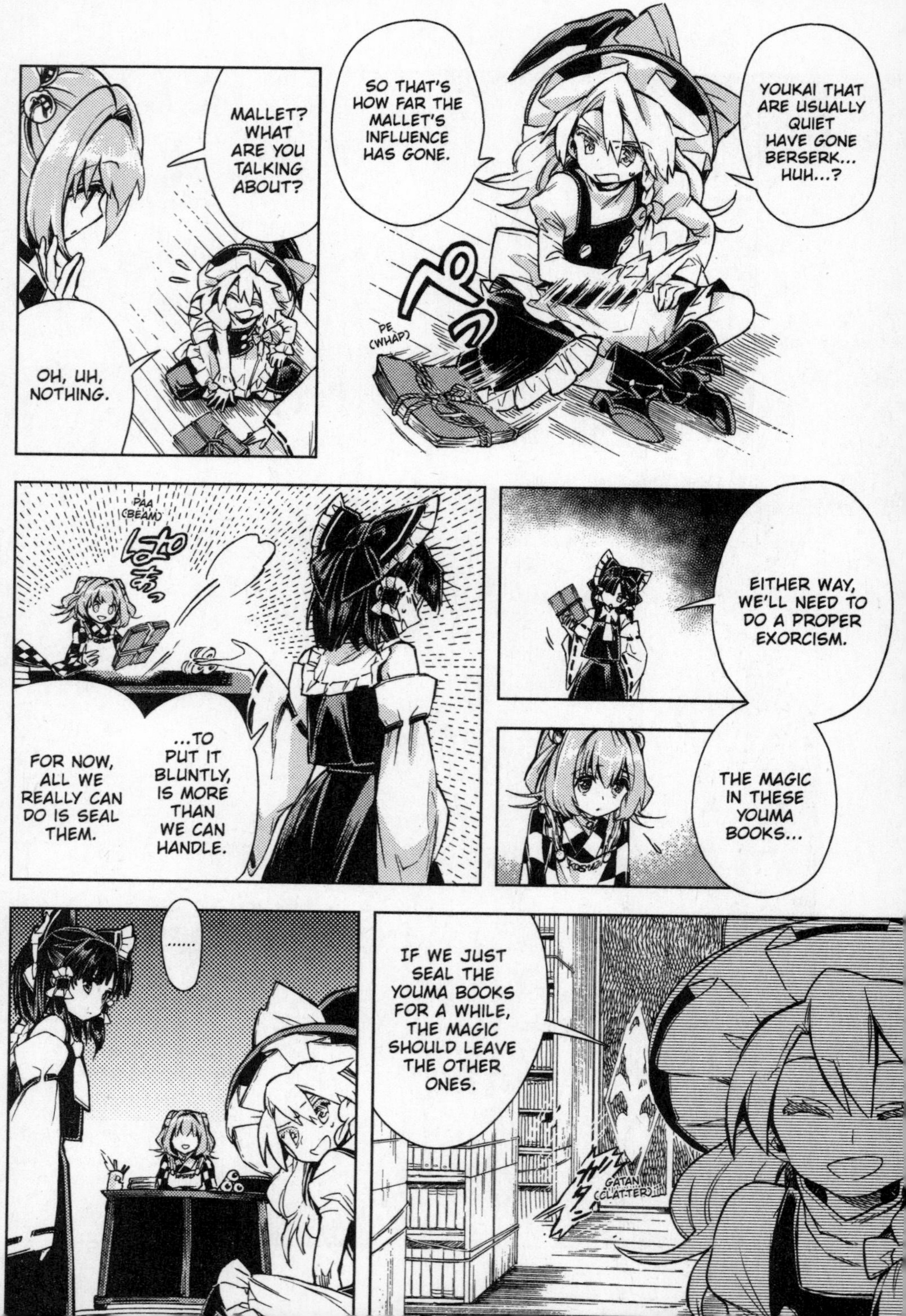
YOUKAI THAT ARE USUALLY QUIET HAVE GONE BERSERK... HUH...?
SO THAT'S HOW FAR THE MALLET'S INFLUENCE HAS GONE.
PE (WHAP)
MALLET? WHAT ARE YOU TALKING ABOUT?
OH, UH, NOTHING.
EITHER WAY, WE'LL NEED TO DO A PROPER EXORCISM.
THE MAGIC IN THESE YOUMA BOOKS...
...TO PUT IT BLUNTLY, IS MORE THAN WE CAN HANDLE.
PAA (BEAM)
FOR NOW, ALL WE REALLY CAN DO IS SEAL THEM.
IF WE JUST SEAL THE YOUMA BOOKS FOR A WHILE, THE MAGIC SHOULD LEAVE THE OTHER ONES.
GATAN (CLATTER)
......

BUT IT MIGHT GET A LITTLE NOISY IN HERE FOR A WHILE.

HA HA HA...

......

......

SHURU
(SHRR)

RU

RU

RU

RU

RU

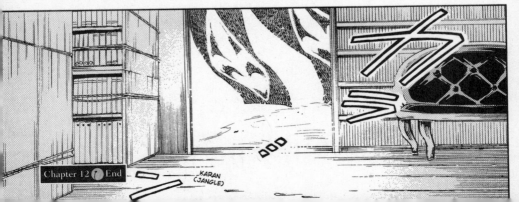

KARAN
(JANGLE)

TRANSLATION NOTES

GENERAL

Certain character names, such as Kokoro Hatano, are also commonly rendered differently, i.e., Hatano-Kokoro, literally "Kokoro of the Hata." This English edition renders names as given name first in order to avoid confusion.

The character names also frequently contain references or certain meanings due to how they're written in Japanese.

Kokoro Hatano: Kokoro is named after Kawakatsu Hatano (aka Hata-no-Kawakatsu), the founder of sarugaku—the precursor of noh.

Shinmyoumaru Sukuna: "Shinmyoumaru" is written with the Japanese characters for "needle" and "subtle," referring to her skill with her signature item, the Shining Needle. "Sukuna" means "small name," referring to her small stature.

Remilia Scarlet: Her name is mainly to give a Western feel to the character, as she actually comes from the normal human world—not Gensokyo.

Patchouli Knowledge: Another character whose name has no Japanese characters. "Patchouli" refers to the flower of the same name, while "Knowledge" is from her fondness for books.

PAGE 15

Orochi: Also known as Yamata-no-Orochi, Orochi is a famous *uwabami* (giant serpent) of Japanese legend. It would come yearly and demand one of the daughters of Ashi-nazuchi as sacrifice. When the time came for him to eat the eighth daughter, the god Susanoo appeared and rescued her by slaying the serpent. Her name was Princess Kushinada.

PAGE 17

Mirin: Mirin is a weak rice wine used as a condiment, like sugar or soy sauce.

Page 18

Flower viewing: A popular tradition in Japan is to admire the beautiful yet fleeting cherry blossoms, which bloom for about a month and then scatter in the wind. It is customary to get together for a flower viewing picnic, where alcohol is one of the main items on the menu.

Page 28

Spring is coming: Here, Marisa is singing a Japanese nursery rhyme called "Haru ga Kita," which technically translates to "Spring Has Come," but "spring is coming" is easier to fit into the melody. The song asks where spring is now and goes on to say that it is in the mountains, the village, and the field too.

Page 47

Oinari-san's hood: Inari (or Oinari) is another name for Uka-no-Mitama, the god of agriculture, who is often represented as, or by, a fox. Shrines to Inari are adorned with fox statues wearing red kerchiefs.

PAGE 84

Ink rubbing: Also known as *gyotaku*, this is a form of nature printing in which the subject will be covered with ink, then pressed against paper to create an image.

PAGE 91

Noh: Noh is a classical Japanese form of drama. It typically involves stories of the supernatural and the use of multiple masks—fitting for Kokoro.

PAGE 102

Hell scroll: A hell scroll is a picture scroll depicting scenes from hell. Similar to Dante's *Inferno*, it showcases greater and greater levels of hell.

Page 135

Mini magic furnace: Specifically, Marisa's mini magic furnace is a *hakkero*. Usually translated as an "eight trigram furnace," it is inscribed with the eight trigrams of Taoist cosmology, which represent the fundamental principles of reality.

PAGE 166

"Never put on shoes in a melon field, never adjust your hat under a plum tree": This is a proverb about avoiding behavior that seems inappropriate.

PAGE 177

Throwing masks: Touhou games are primarily vertical-style shooters where characters fire volleys of projectiles, in the tradition of titles such as *R-Type* and *Gradius*. Kokoro's barrage of masks is a direct reference to this, though her source game, *Hopeless Masquerade*, is more of a fighting game.

Forbidden Scrollery

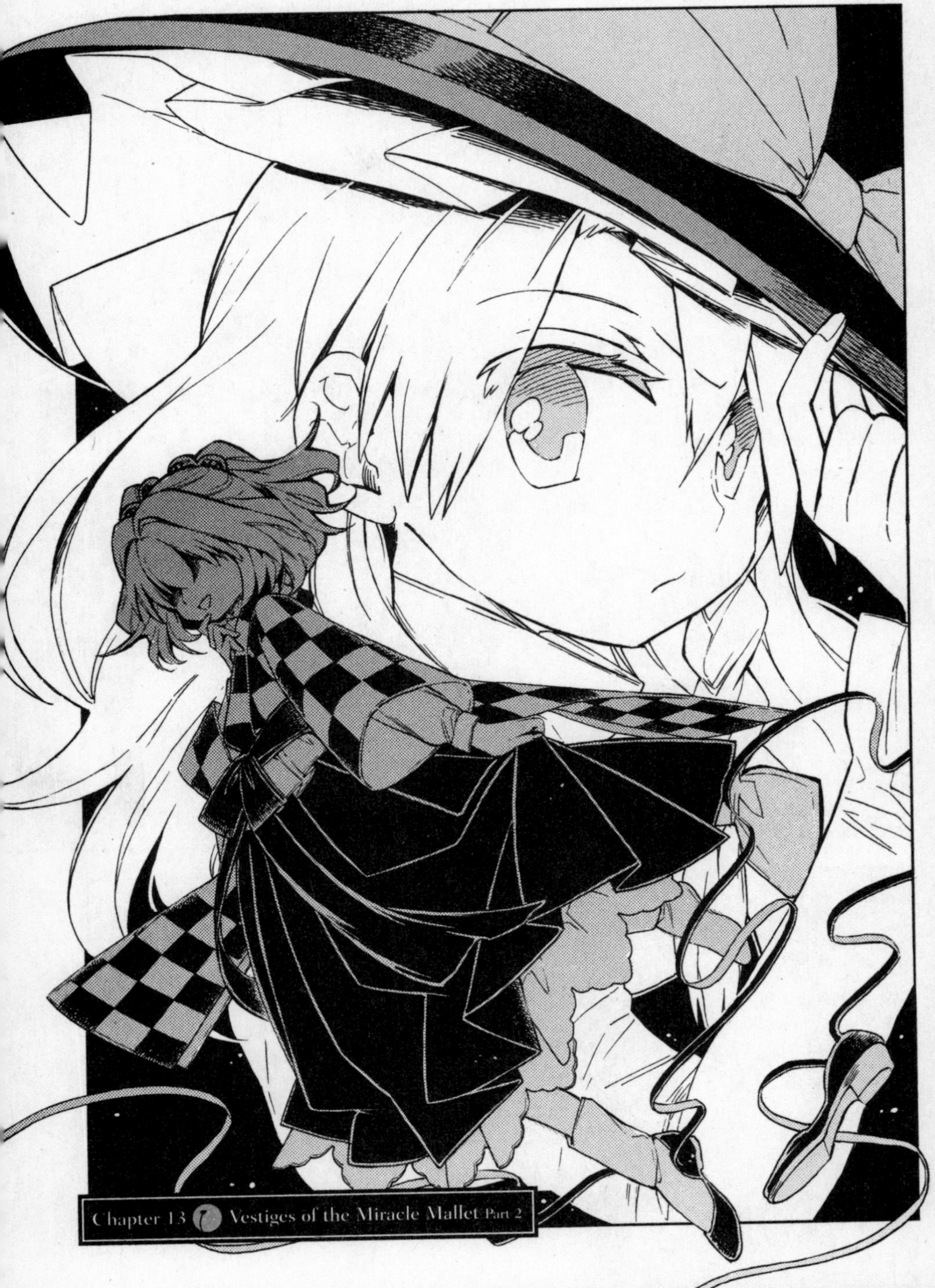

Chapter 13 Vestiges of the Miracle Mallet Part 2

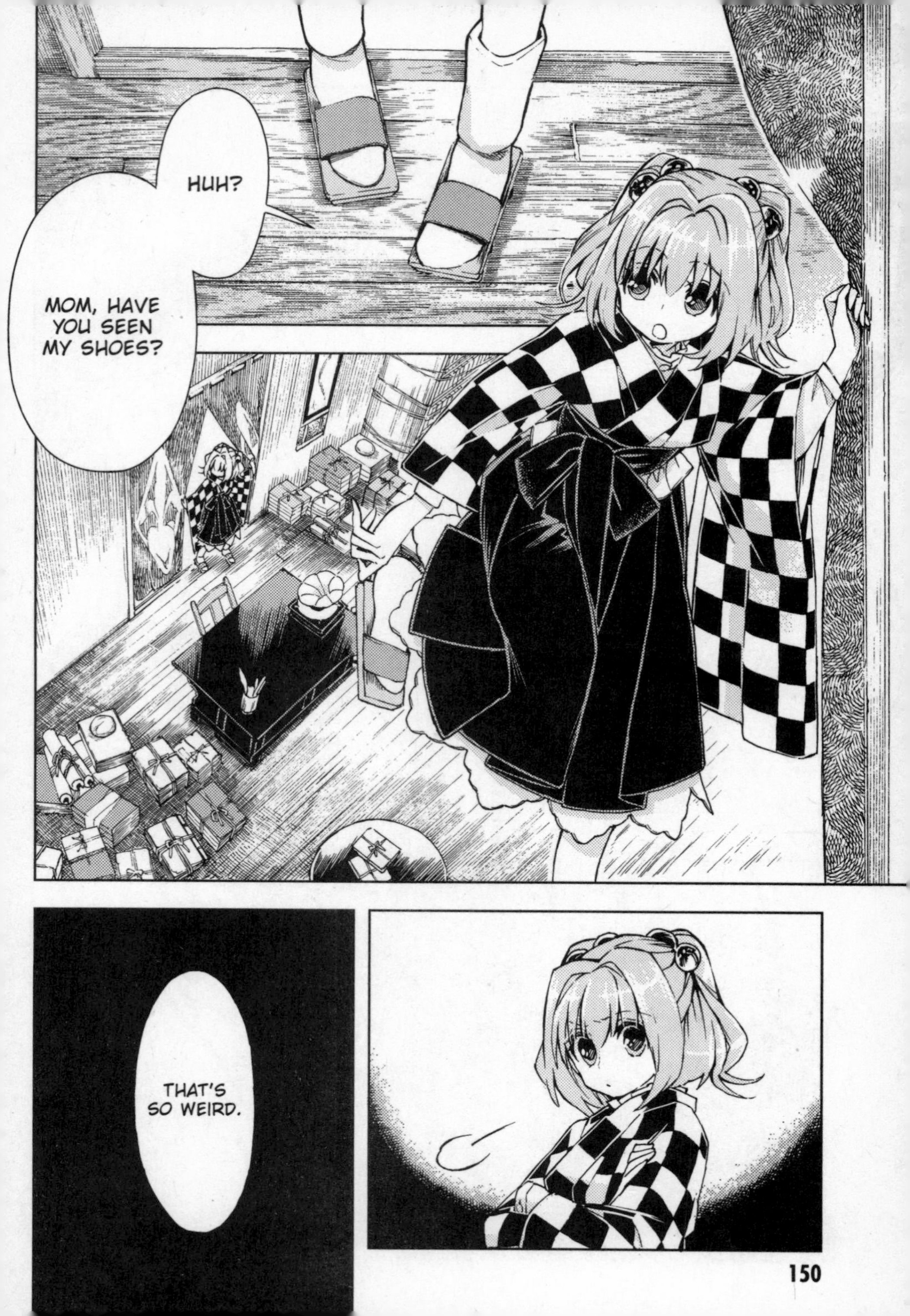
HUH?
MOM, HAVE YOU SEEN MY SHOES?
THAT'S SO WEIRD.

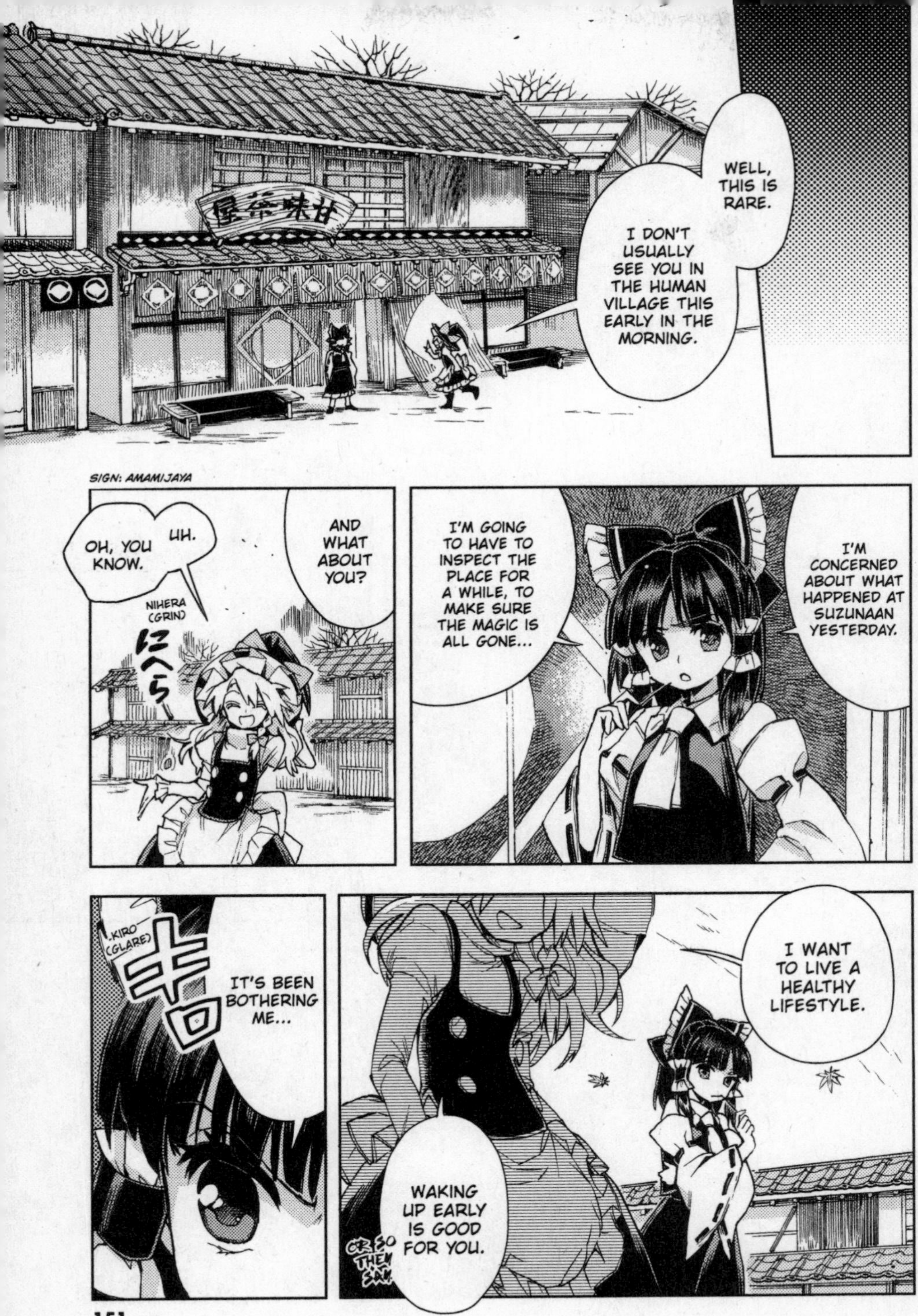
甘味茶屋
WELL, THIS IS RARE.
I DON'T USUALLY SEE YOU IN THE HUMAN VILLAGE THIS EARLY IN THE MORNING.
SIGN: AMAMIJAYA
I'M CONCERNED ABOUT WHAT HAPPENED AT SUZUNAAN YESTERDAY.
I'M GOING TO HAVE TO INSPECT THE PLACE FOR A WHILE, TO MAKE SURE THE MAGIC IS ALL GONE...
AND WHAT ABOUT YOU?
UH.
OH, YOU KNOW.
NIHERA (GRIN)
にへら
I WANT TO LIVE A HEALTHY LIFESTYLE.
WAKING UP EARLY IS GOOD FOR YOU.
KIRO (GLARE)
キロ
IT'S BEEN BOTHERING ME...

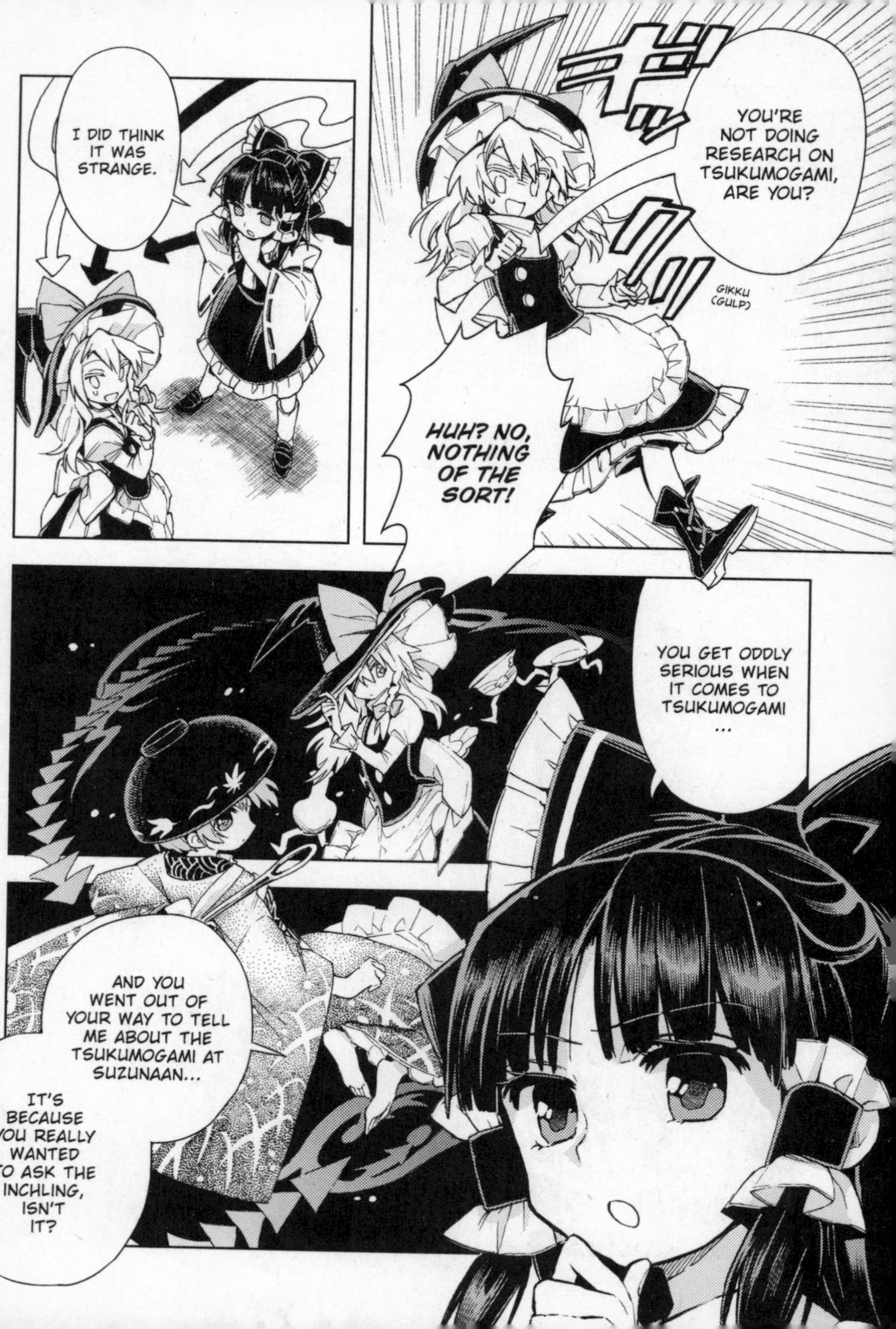
YOU'RE NOT DOING RESEARCH ON TSUKUMOGAMI, ARE YOU?
GIKKU (GULP)
HUH? NO, NOTHING OF THE SORT!
I DID THINK IT WAS STRANGE.
YOU GET ODDLY SERIOUS WHEN IT COMES TO TSUKUMOGAMI ...
AND YOU WENT OUT OF YOUR WAY TO TELL ME ABOUT THE TSUKUMOGAMI AT SUZUNAAN...
IT'S BECAUSE YOU REALLY WANTED TO ASK THE INCHLING, ISN'T IT?

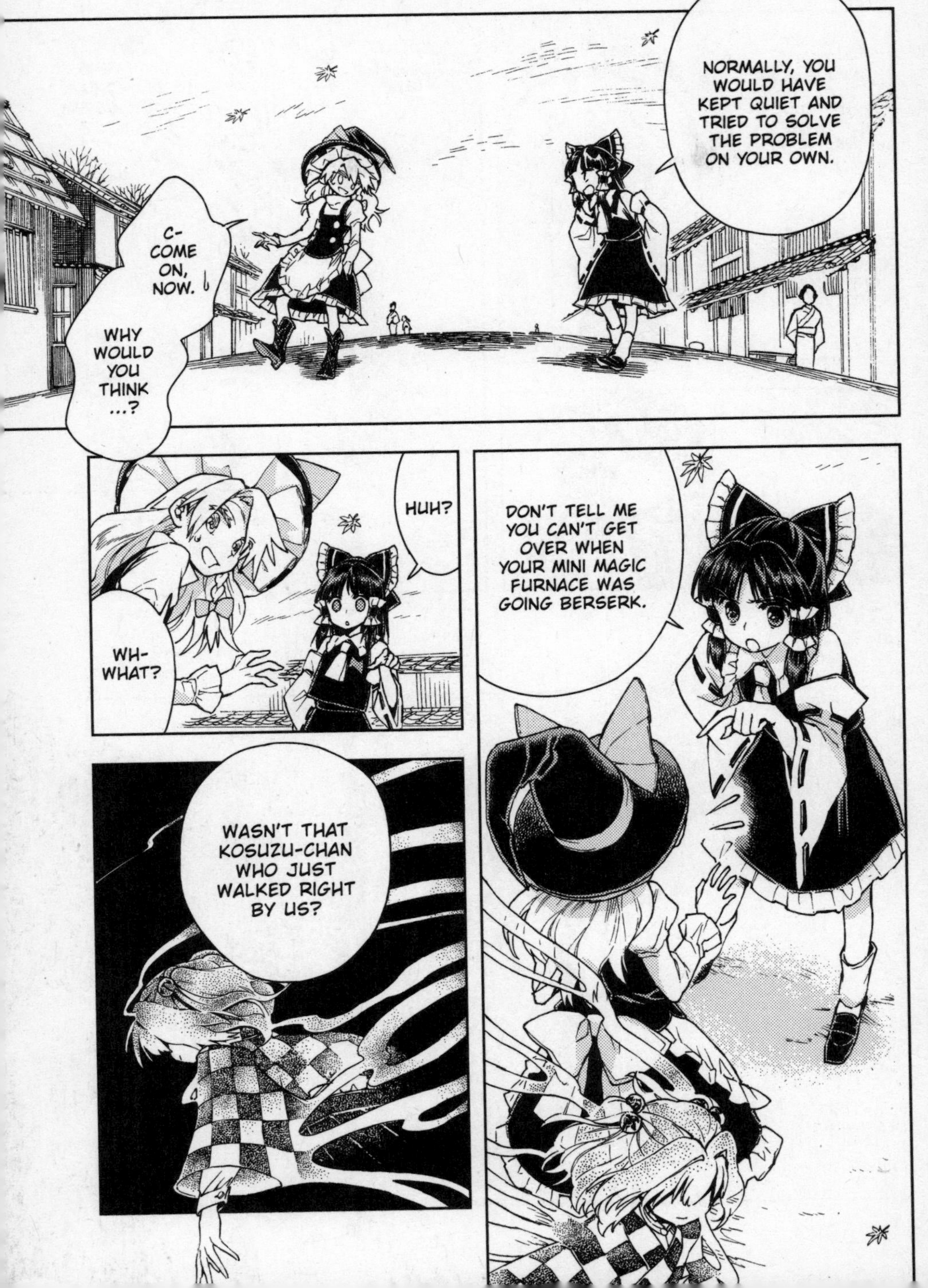
NORMALLY, YOU WOULD HAVE KEPT QUIET AND TRIED TO SOLVE THE PROBLEM ON YOUR OWN.
C- COME ON, NOW.
WHY WOULD YOU THINK ...?
DON'T TELL ME YOU CAN'T GET OVER WHEN YOUR MINI MAGIC FURNACE WAS GOING BERSERK.
HUH?
WH- WHAT?
WASN'T THAT KOSUZU-CHAN WHO JUST WALKED RIGHT BY US?

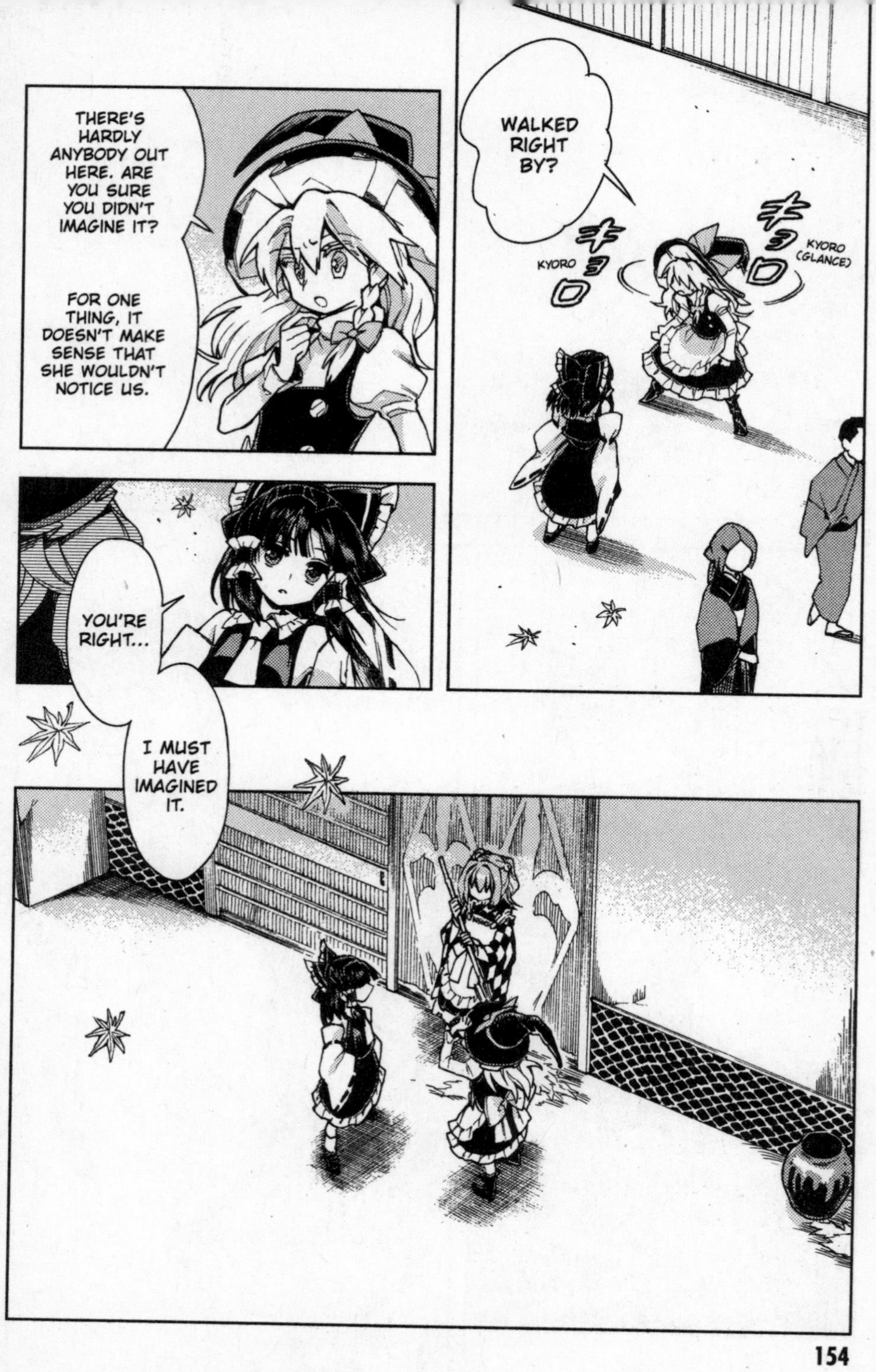
WALKED RIGHT BY?
キョロ
KYORO (GLANCE)
キョロ
KYORO
THERE'S HARDLY ANYBODY OUT HERE. ARE YOU SURE YOU DIDN'T IMAGINE IT?
FOR ONE THING, IT DOESN'T MAKE SENSE THAT SHE WOULDN'T NOTICE US.
YOU'RE RIGHT...
I MUST HAVE IMAGINED IT.

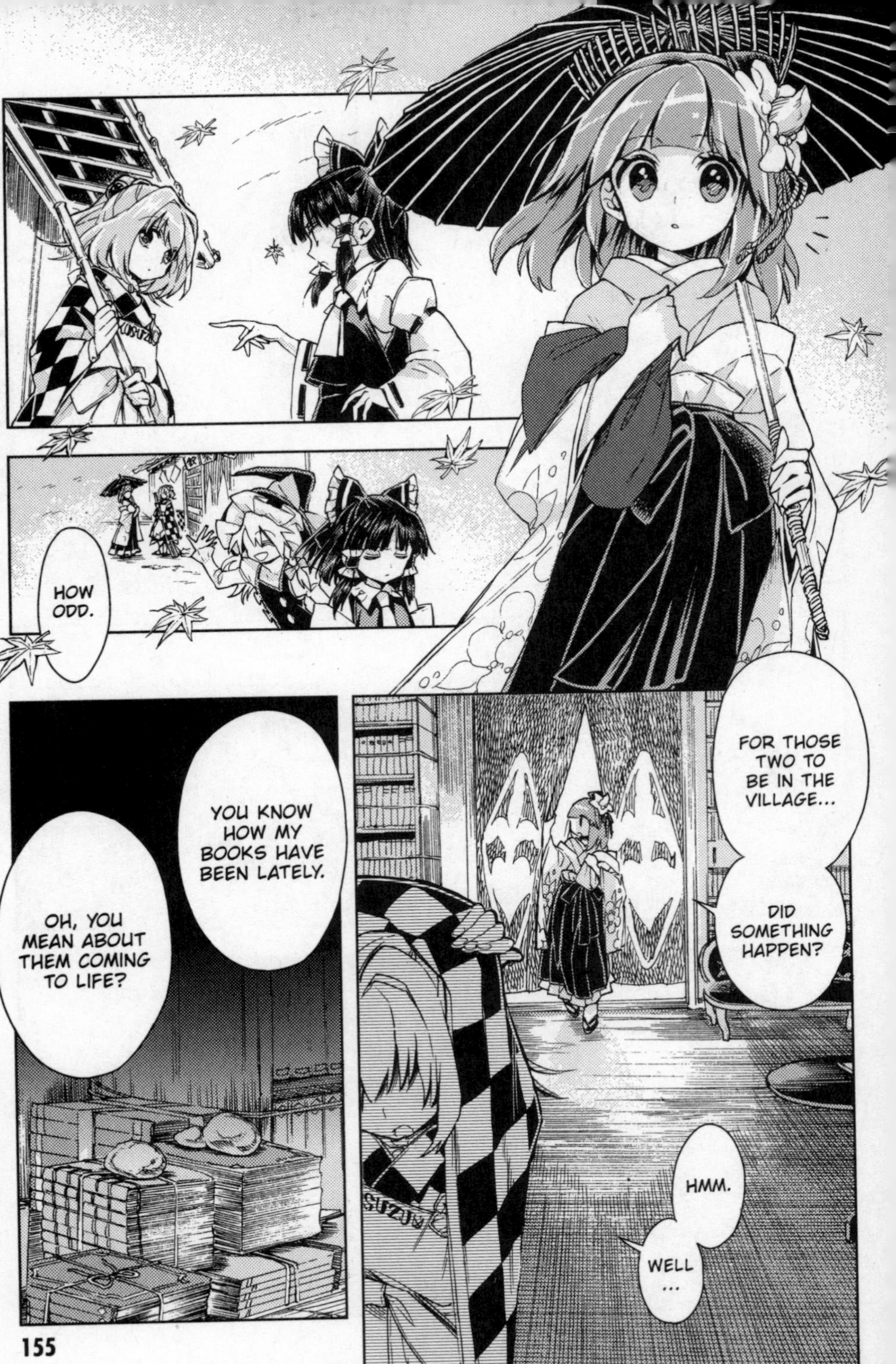
HOW ODD.
FOR THOSE TWO TO BE IN THE VILLAGE...
DID SOMETHING HAPPEN?
HMM.
WELL ...
YOU KNOW HOW MY BOOKS HAVE BEEN LATELY.
OH, YOU MEAN ABOUT THEM COMING TO LIFE?

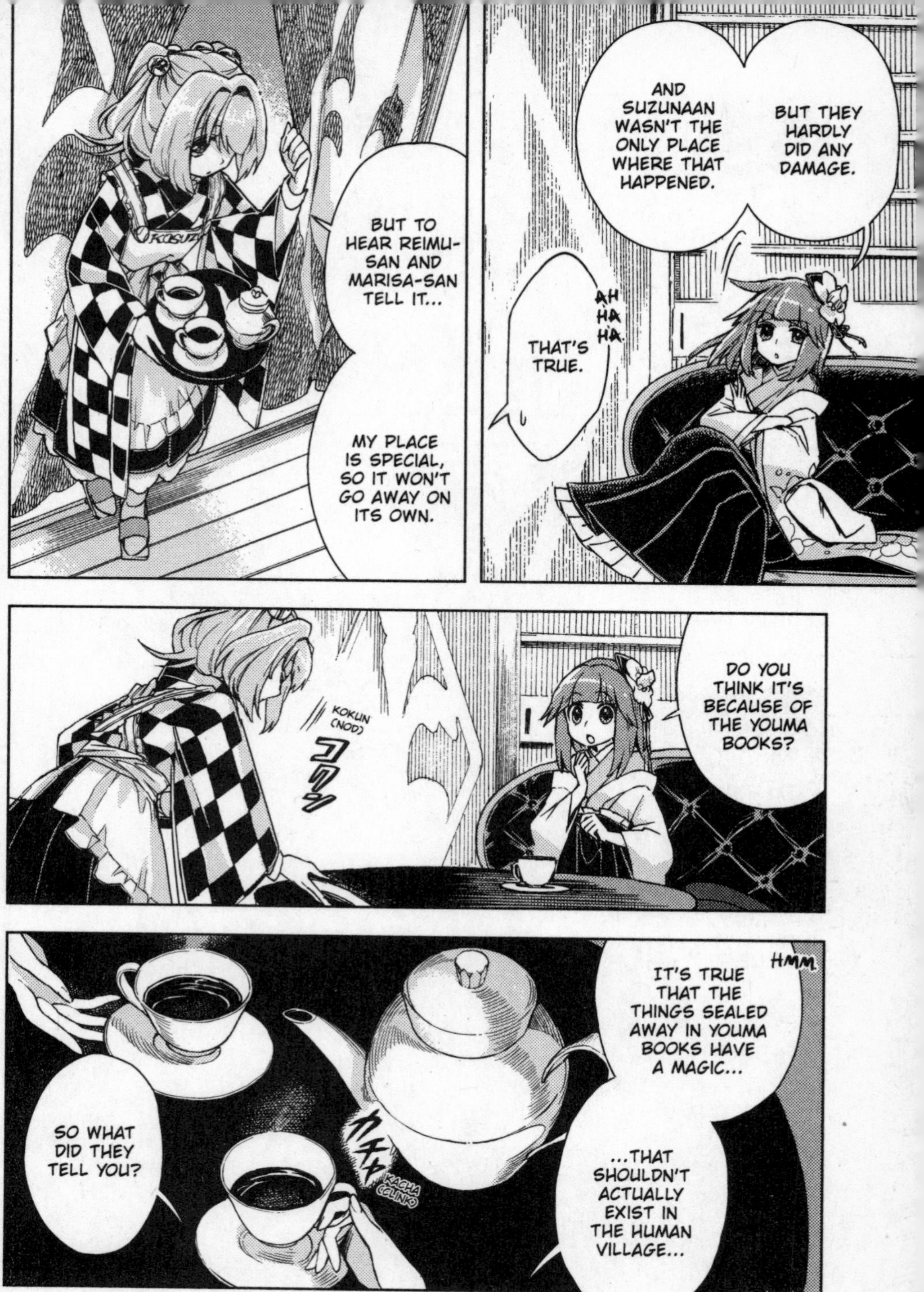
BUT THEY HARDLY DID ANY DAMAGE.
AND SUZUNAAN WASN'T THE ONLY PLACE WHERE THAT HAPPENED.
AH HA HA
THAT'S TRUE.
BUT TO HEAR REIMU-SAN AND MARISA-SAN TELL IT...
MY PLACE IS SPECIAL, SO IT WON'T GO AWAY ON ITS OWN.
DO YOU THINK IT'S BECAUSE OF THE YOUMA BOOKS?
KOKUN (NOD)
HMM.
IT'S TRUE THAT THE THINGS SEALED AWAY IN YOUMA BOOKS HAVE A MAGIC...
...THAT SHOULDN'T ACTUALLY EXIST IN THE HUMAN VILLAGE...
KACHA (CLINK)
SO WHAT DID THEY TELL YOU?

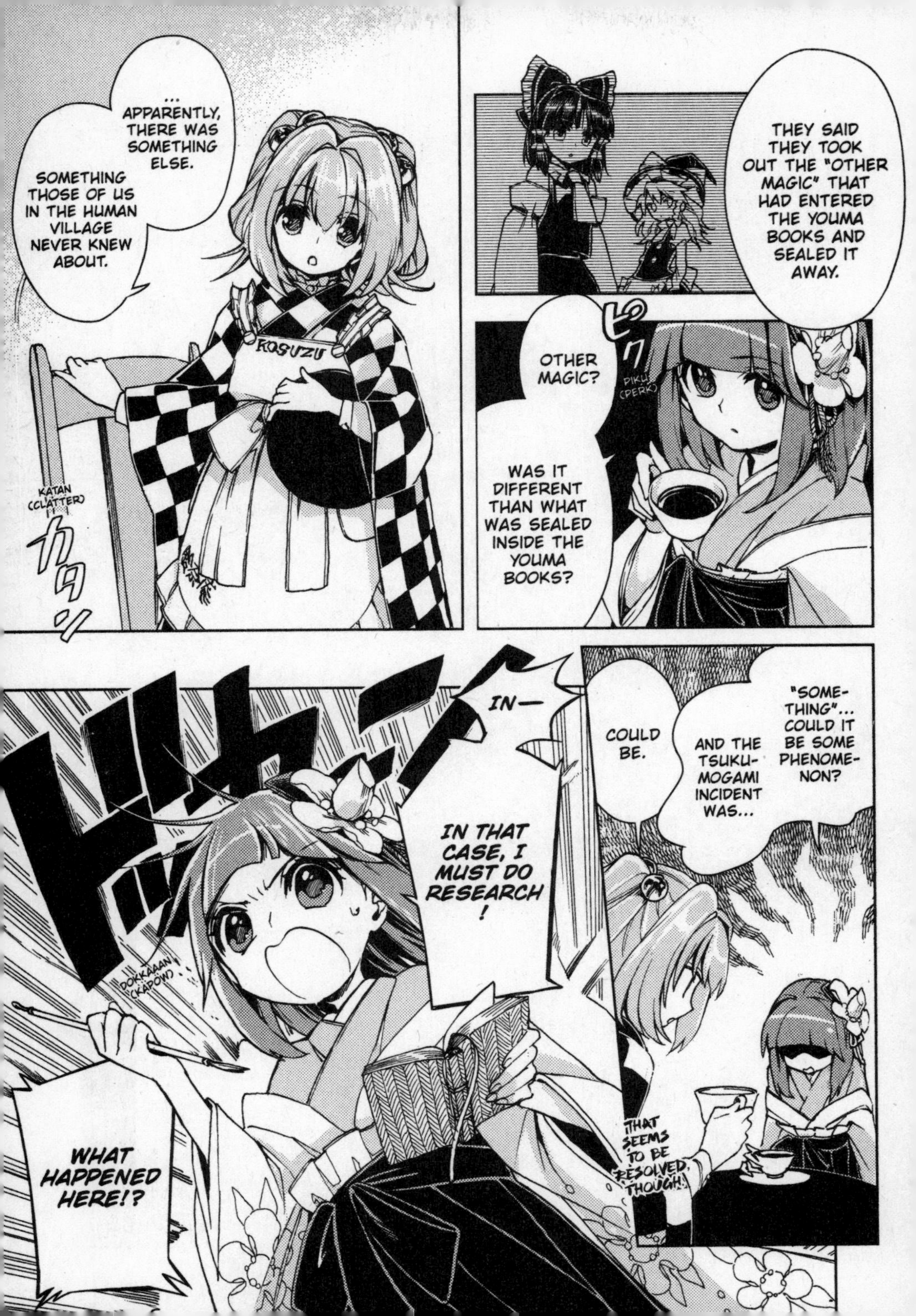
THEY SAID THEY TOOK OUT THE "OTHER MAGIC" THAT HAD ENTERED THE YOUMA BOOKS AND SEALED IT AWAY.
OTHER MAGIC?
PIKU (PERK)
WAS IT DIFFERENT THAN WHAT WAS SEALED INSIDE THE YOUMA BOOKS?
... APPARENTLY, THERE WAS SOMETHING ELSE.
SOMETHING THOSE OF US IN THE HUMAN VILLAGE NEVER KNEW ABOUT.
KOSUZU
KATAN (CLATTER)
"SOME-THING"... COULD IT BE SOME PHENOME-NON?
AND THE TSUKU-MOGAMI INCIDENT WAS...
COULD BE.
THAT SEEMS TO BE RESOLVED, THOUGH!
IN—
IN THAT CASE, I MUST DO RESEARCH!
DOKKAAAN (KAPOW)
WHAT HAPPENED HERE!?

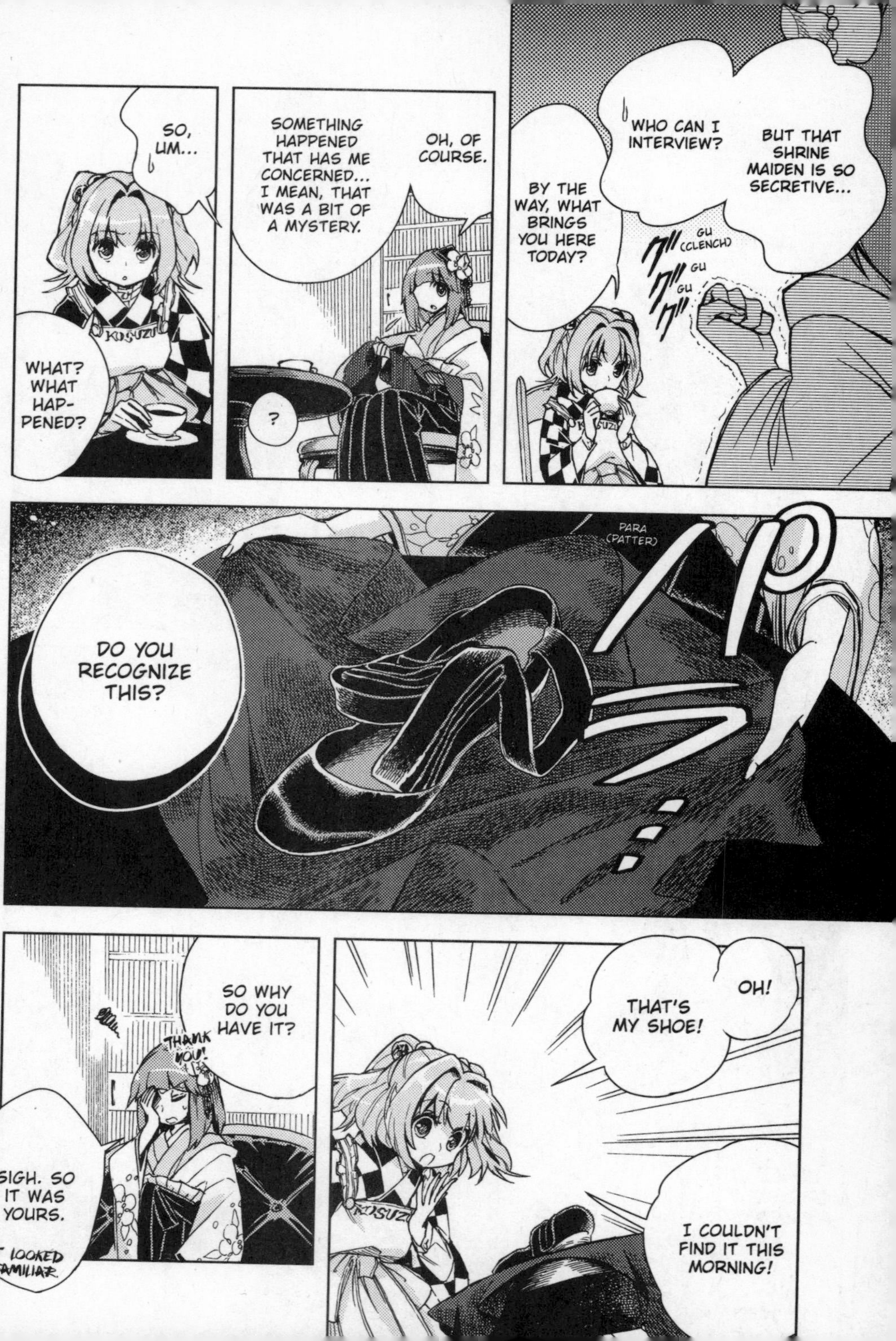
BUT THAT SHRINE MAIDEN IS SO SECRETIVE...
WHO CAN I INTERVIEW?
GU (CLENCH) GU GU
BY THE WAY, WHAT BRINGS YOU HERE TODAY?
OH, OF COURSE.
SOMETHING HAPPENED THAT HAS ME CONCERNED... I MEAN, THAT WAS A BIT OF A MYSTERY.
?
SO, UM...
WHAT? WHAT HAP-PENED?
PARA (PATTER)
DO YOU RECOGNIZE THIS?
OH!
THAT'S MY SHOE!
I COULDN'T FIND IT THIS MORNING!
SO WHY DO YOU HAVE IT?
THANK YOU!
SIGH. SO IT WAS YOURS.
IT LOOKED FAMILIAR

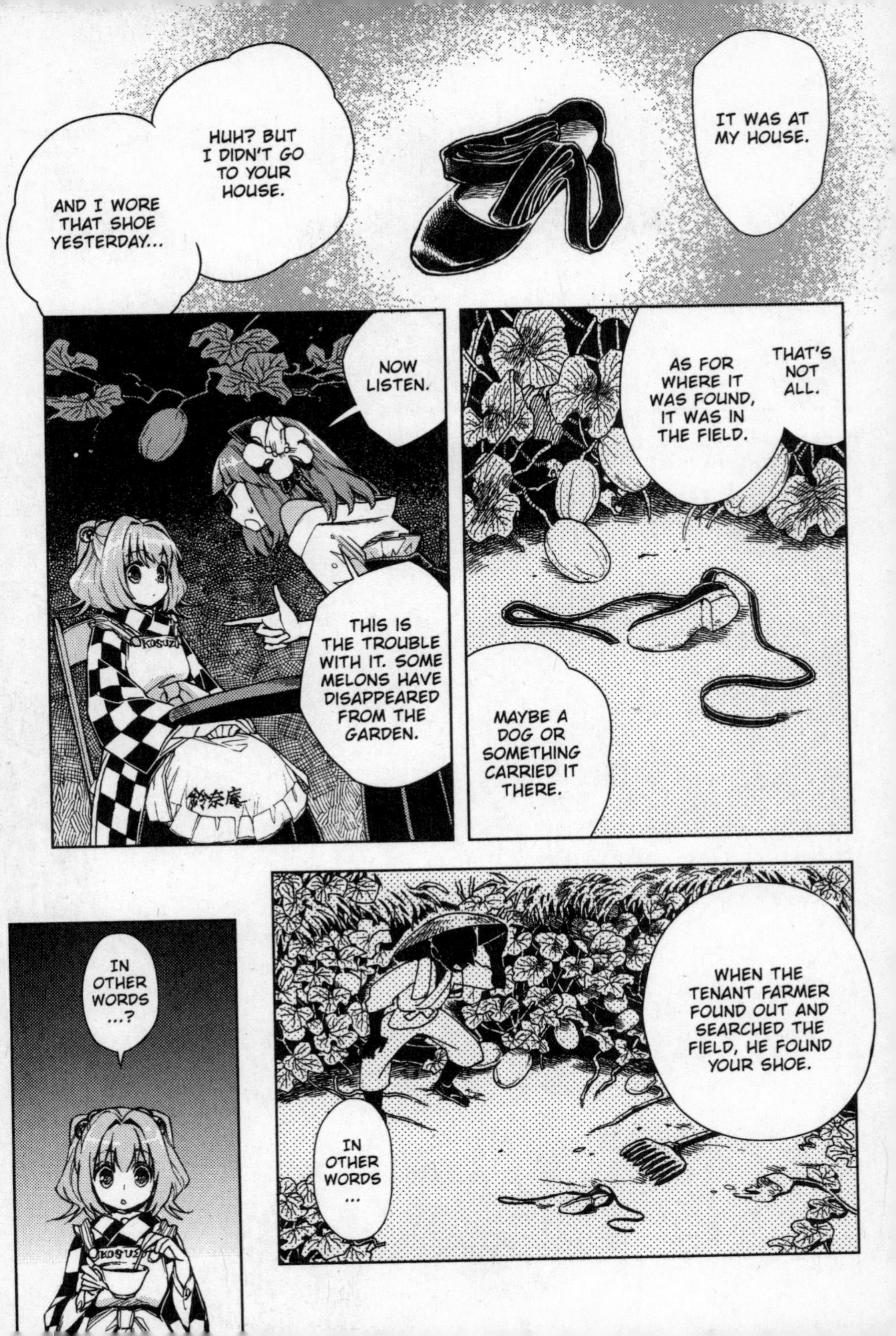
IT WAS AT MY HOUSE.
HUH? BUT I DIDN'T GO TO YOUR HOUSE.
AND I WORE THAT SHOE YESTERDAY...
THAT'S NOT ALL.
AS FOR WHERE IT WAS FOUND, IT WAS IN THE FIELD.
MAYBE A DOG OR SOMETHING CARRIED IT THERE.
NOW LISTEN.
THIS IS THE TROUBLE WITH IT. SOME MELONS HAVE DISAPPEARED FROM THE GARDEN.
WHEN THE TENANT FARMER FOUND OUT AND SEARCHED THE FIELD, HE FOUND YOUR SHOE.
IN OTHER WORDS ...
IN OTHER WORDS ...?

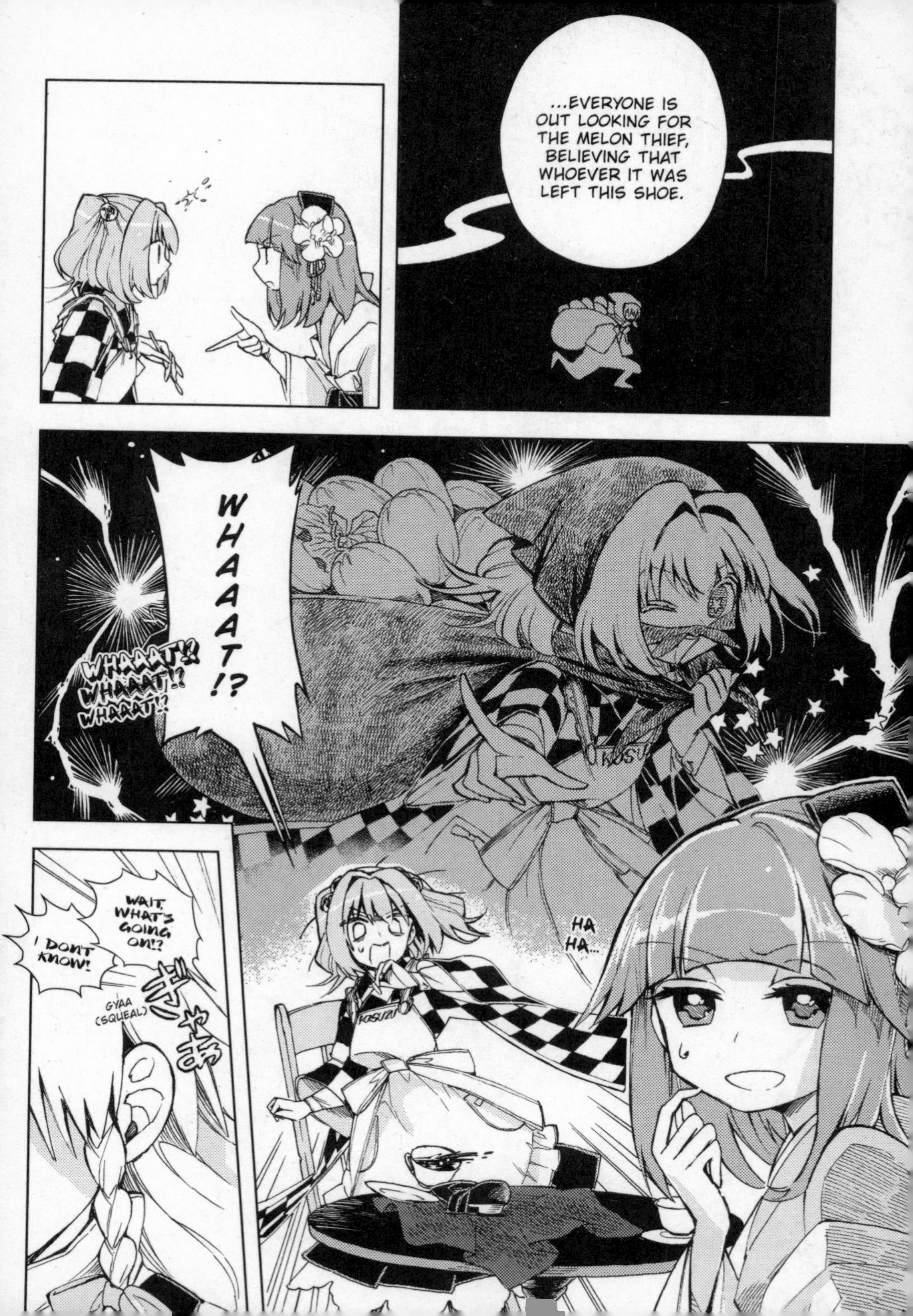
...EVERYONE IS OUT LOOKING FOR THE MELON THIEF, BELIEVING THAT WHOEVER IT WAS LEFT THIS SHOE.
WHAAAAT!?
WHAAAT!? WHAAAT!? WHAAAT!?
KOSU
HA HA...
KOSUZU
WAIT, WHAT'S GOING ON!?
I DON'T KNOW!
GYAA (SQUEAL)

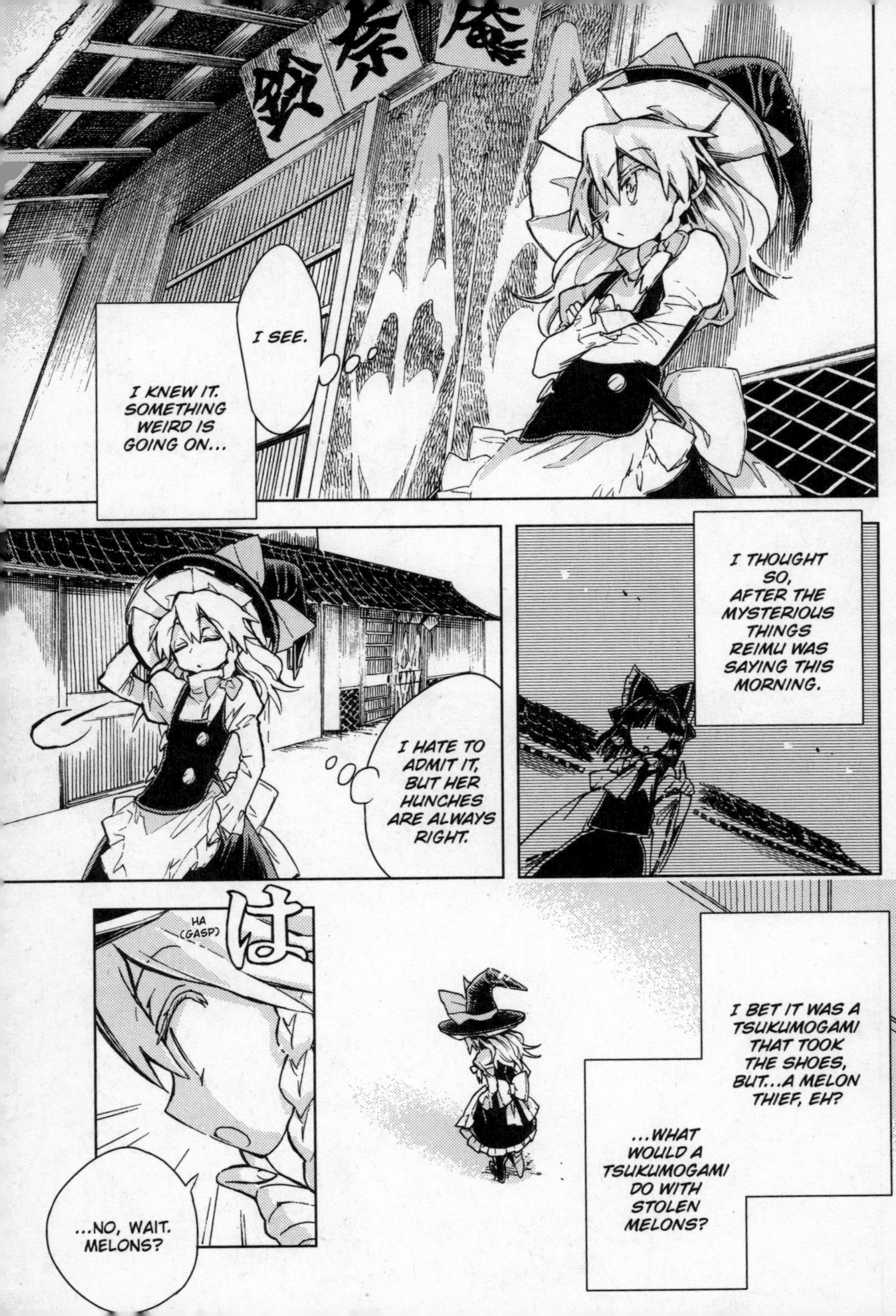
I SEE.
I KNEW IT. SOMETHING WEIRD IS GOING ON...
I THOUGHT SO, AFTER THE MYSTERIOUS THINGS REIMU WAS SAYING THIS MORNING.
I HATE TO ADMIT IT, BUT HER HUNCHES ARE ALWAYS RIGHT.
I BET IT WAS A TSUKUMOGAMI THAT TOOK THE SHOES, BUT...A MELON THIEF, EH?
...WHAT WOULD A TSUKUMOGAMI DO WITH STOLEN MELONS?
は
HA (GASP)
...NO, WAIT. MELONS?

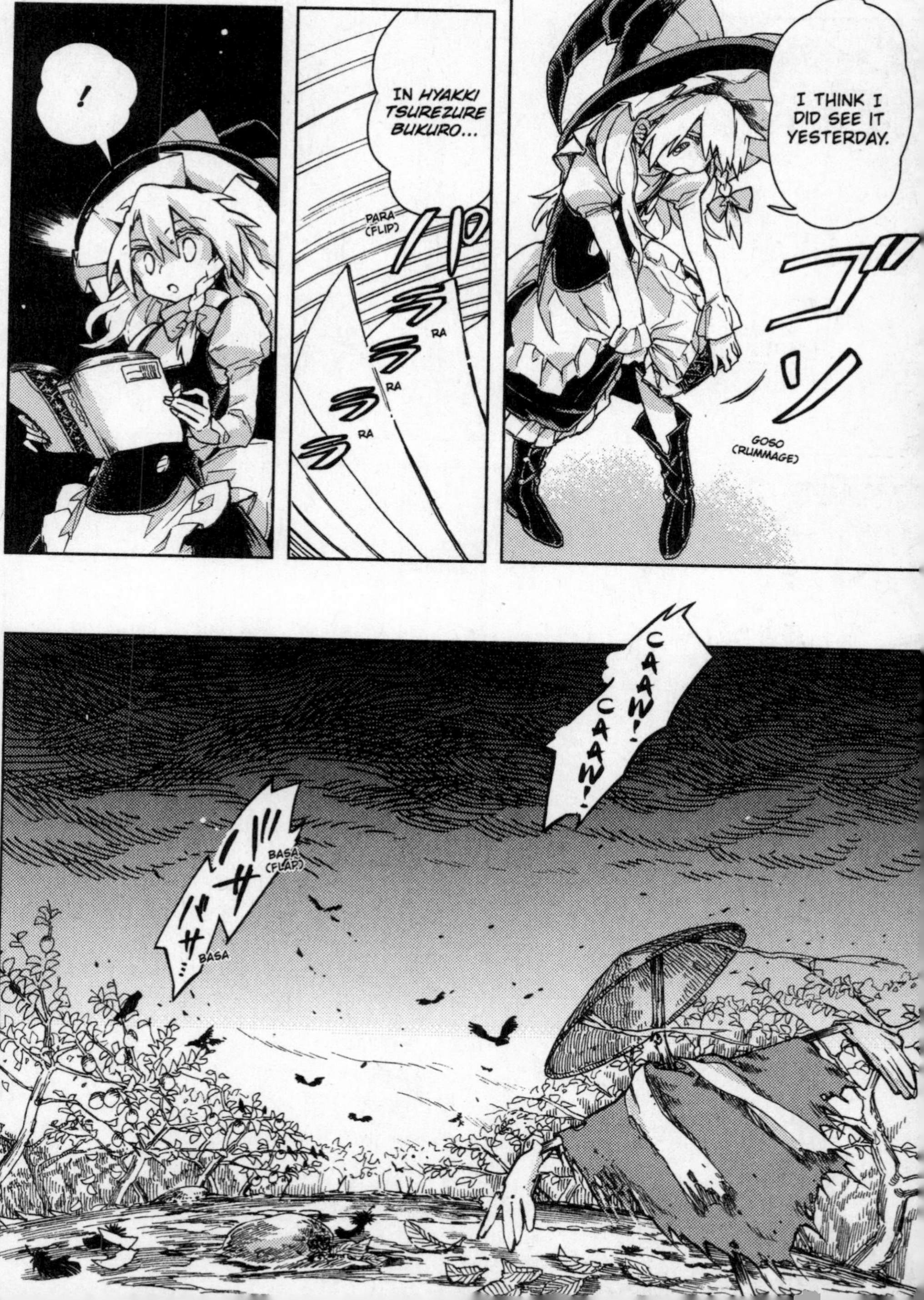
I THINK I DID SEE IT YESTERDAY.
GOSO (RUMMAGE)
IN HYAKKI TSUREZURE BUKURO...
PARA (FLIP)
RA
RA
RA
!
CAAAW! CAAAW!
BASA (FLAP)
BASA

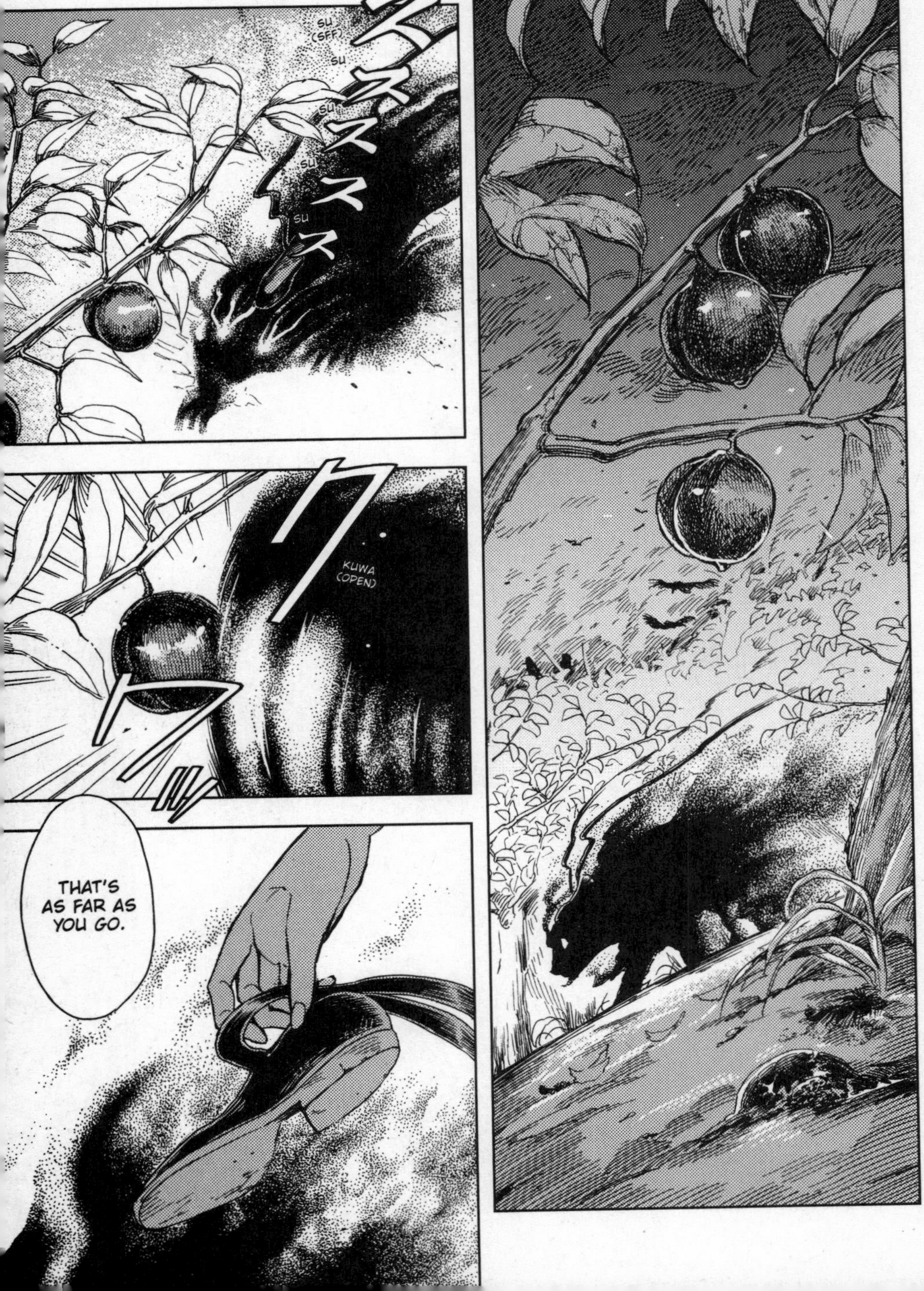
SU (SFF)
SU
SU
SU
SU
KUWA (OPEN)
THAT'S AS FAR AS YOU GO.

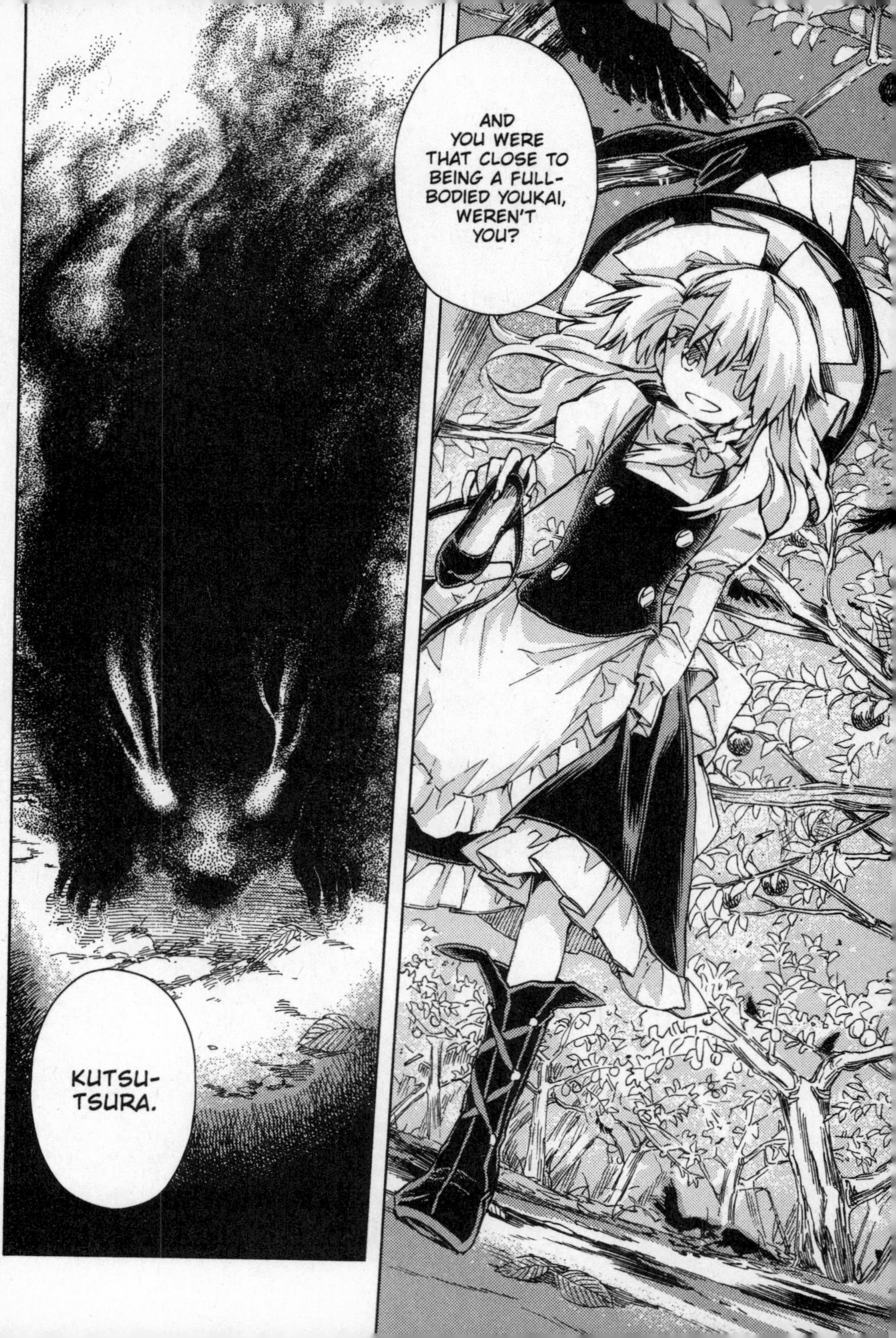
AND YOU WERE THAT CLOSE TO BEING A FULL-BODIED YOUKAI, WEREN'T YOU?
KUTSU-TSURA.

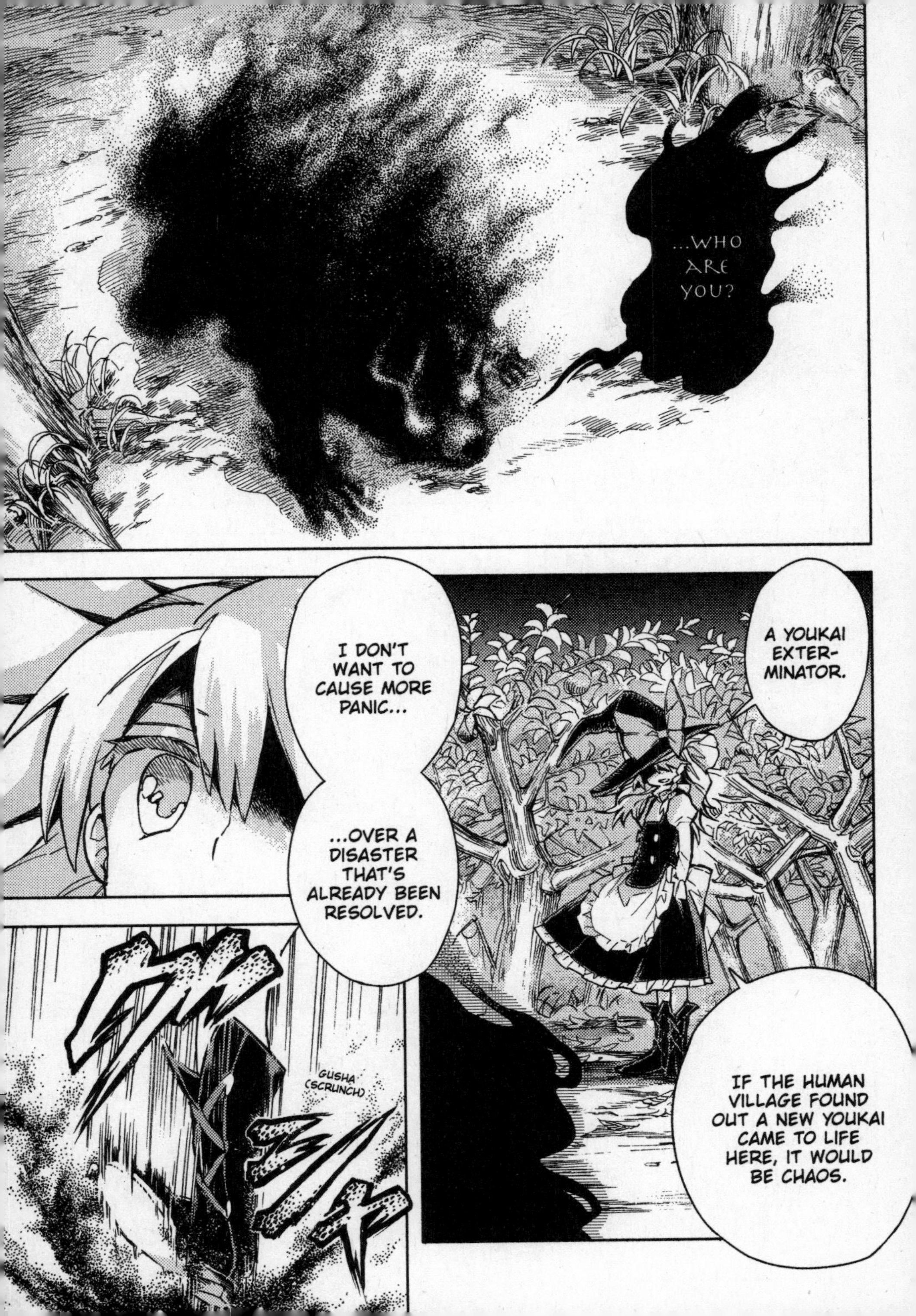
...WHO ARE YOU?
A YOUKAI EXTER-MINATOR.
I DON'T WANT TO CAUSE MORE PANIC...
...OVER A DISASTER THAT'S ALREADY BEEN RESOLVED.
IF THE HUMAN VILLAGE FOUND OUT A NEW YOUKAI CAME TO LIFE HERE, IT WOULD BE CHAOS.
GUSHA (SCRUNCH)

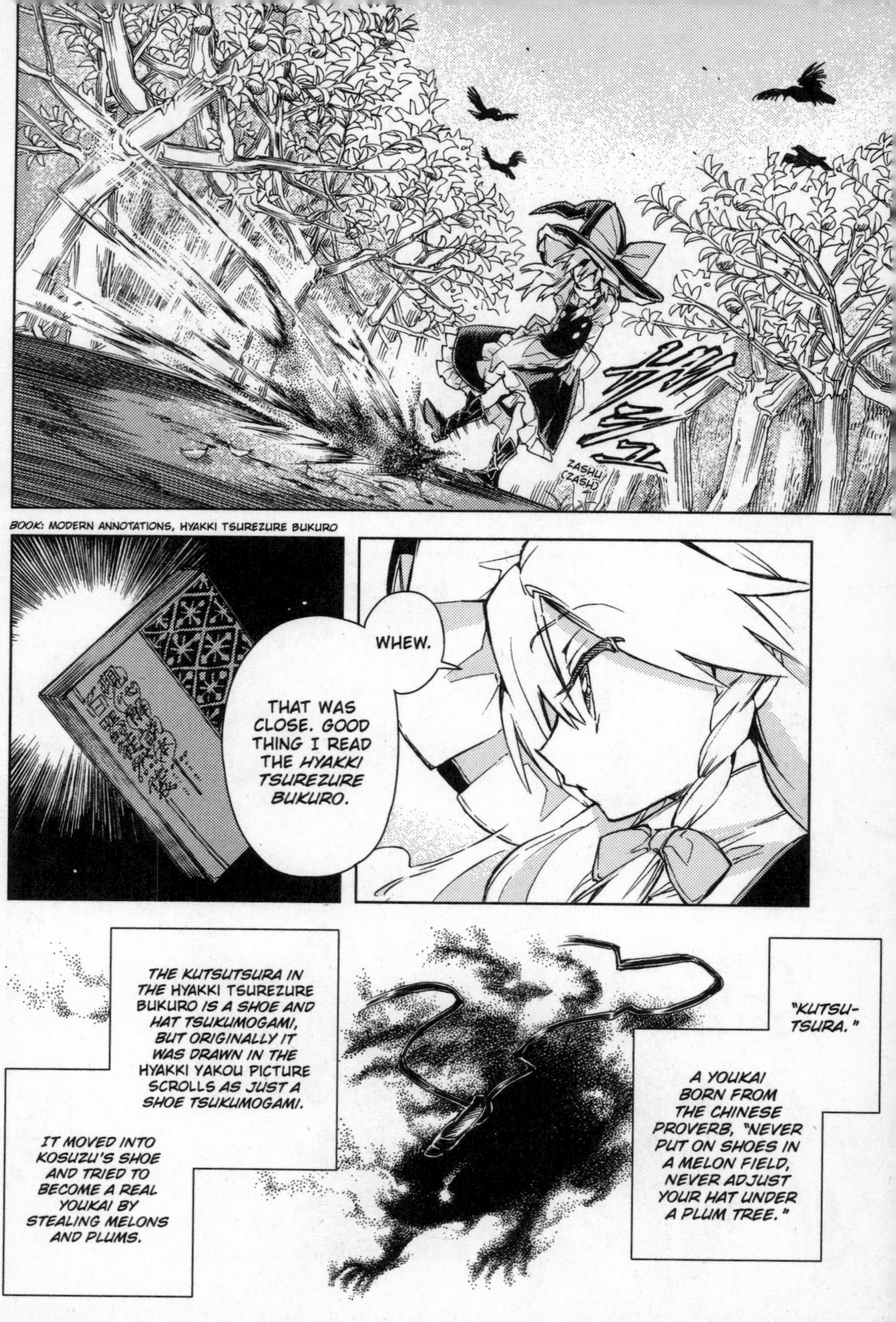
ZASHU (ZASH)
BOOK: MODERN ANNOTATIONS, HYAKKI TSUREZURE BUKURO
WHEW.
THAT WAS CLOSE. GOOD THING I READ THE *HYAKKI TSUREZURE BUKURO*.
"KUTSU-TSURA."
A YOUKAI BORN FROM THE CHINESE PROVERB, "NEVER PUT ON SHOES IN A MELON FIELD, NEVER ADJUST YOUR HAT UNDER A PLUM TREE."
THE KUTSUTSURA IN THE HYAKKI TSUREZURE BUKURO IS A SHOE AND HAT TSUKUMOGAMI, BUT ORIGINALLY IT WAS DRAWN IN THE HYAKKI YAKOU PICTURE SCROLLS AS JUST A SHOE TSUKUMOGAMI.
IT MOVED INTO KOSUZU'S SHOE AND TRIED TO BECOME A REAL YOUKAI BY STEALING MELONS AND PLUMS.

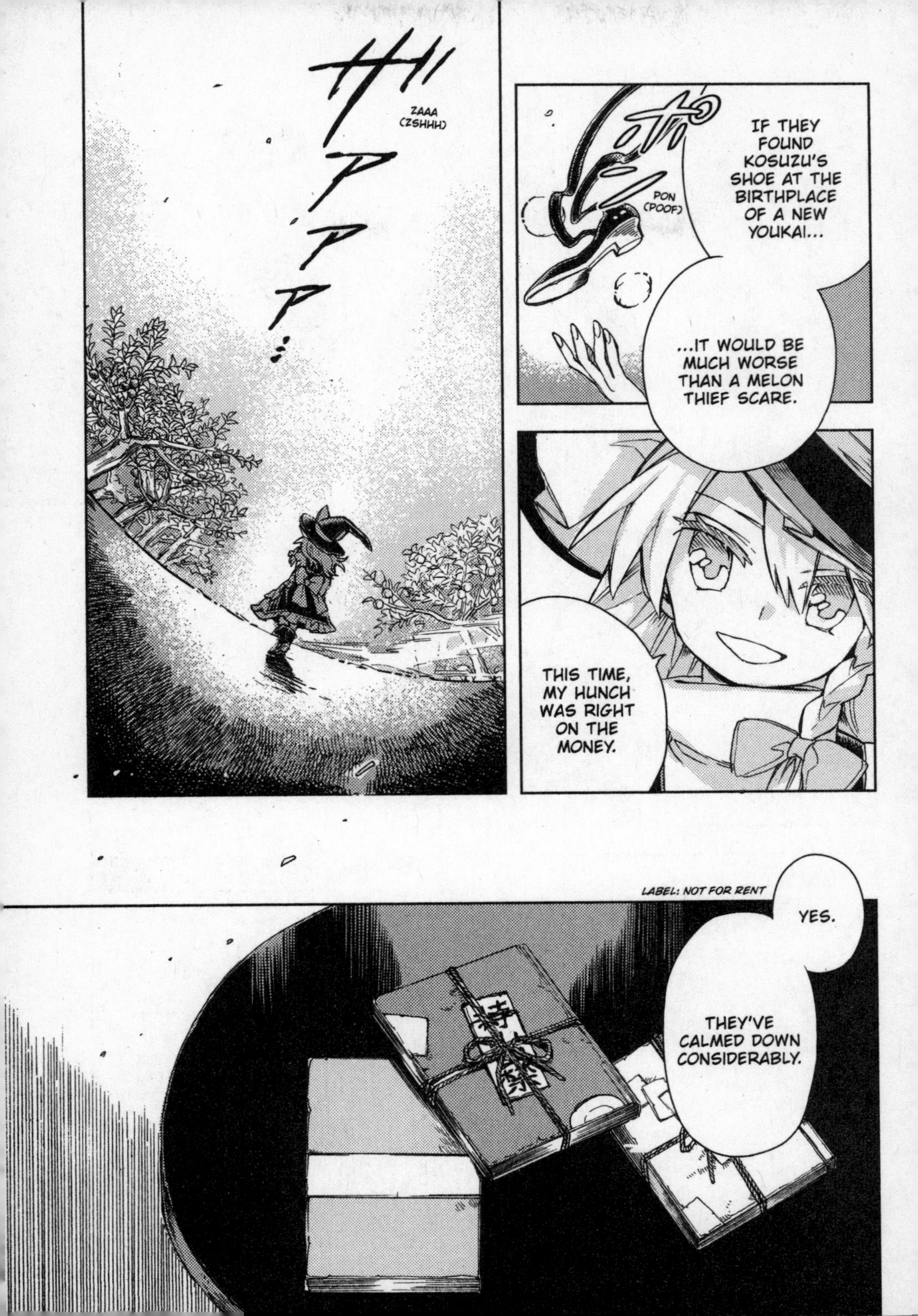
PON (POOF)
IF THEY FOUND KOSUZU'S SHOE AT THE BIRTHPLACE OF A NEW YOUKAI...
...IT WOULD BE MUCH WORSE THAN A MELON THIEF SCARE.
THIS TIME, MY HUNCH WAS RIGHT ON THE MONEY.
ZAAA (ZSHHH)
LABEL: NOT FOR RENT
YES.
THEY'VE CALMED DOWN CONSIDERABLY.

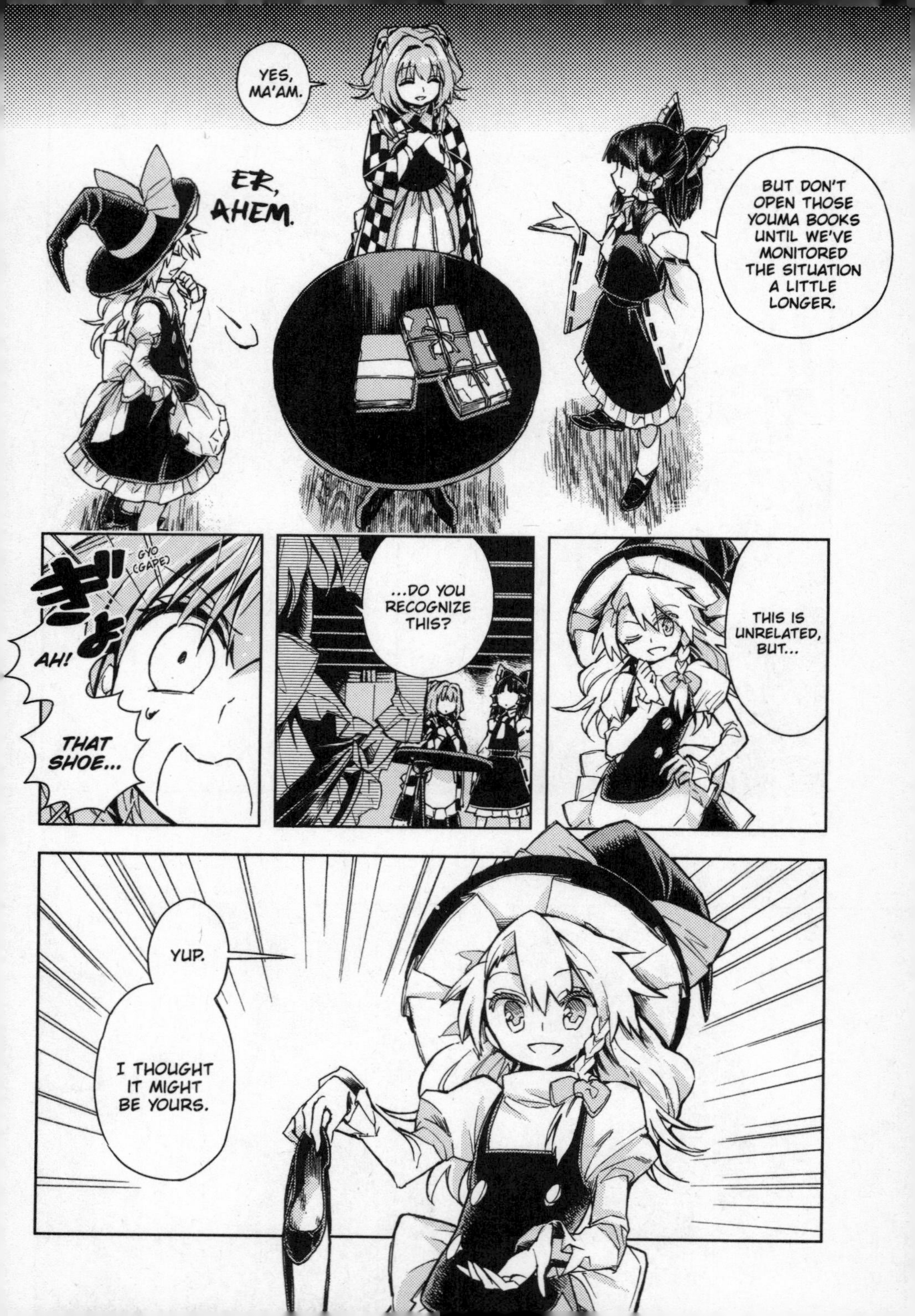
BUT DON'T OPEN THOSE YOUMA BOOKS UNTIL WE'VE MONITORED THE SITUATION A LITTLE LONGER.
YES, MA'AM.
ER, AHEM.
THIS IS UNRELATED, BUT...
...DO YOU RECOGNIZE THIS?
ぎょ
GYO (GAPE)
AH!
THAT SHOE...
YUP.
I THOUGHT IT MIGHT BE YOURS.

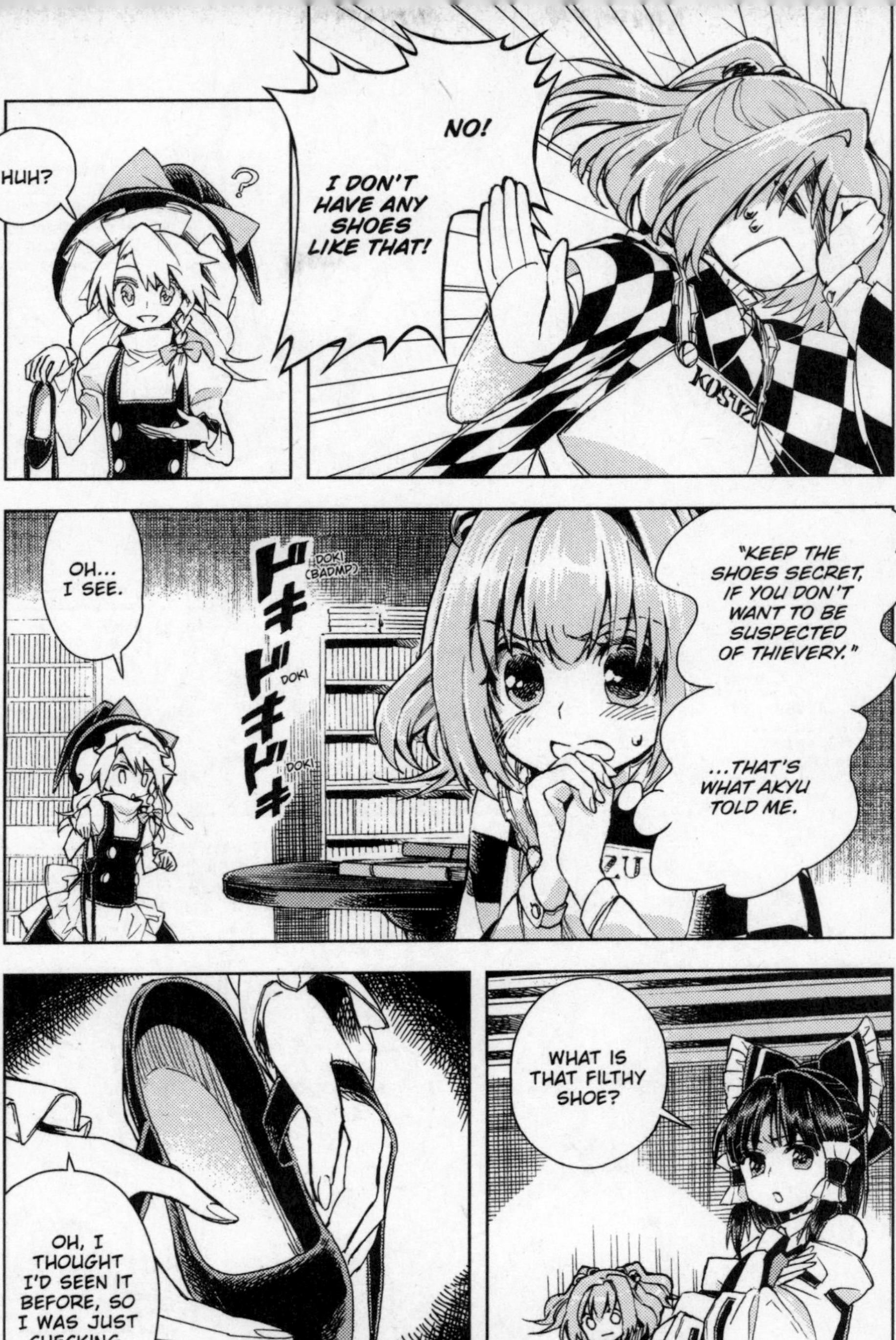
NO!
I DON'T HAVE ANY SHOES LIKE THAT!
HUH?
?
"KEEP THE SHOES SECRET, IF YOU DON'T WANT TO BE SUSPECTED OF THIEVERY."
...THAT'S WHAT AKYU TOLD ME.
DOKI (BADMP)
DOKI
DOKI
OH... I SEE.
WHAT IS THAT FILTHY SHOE?
OH, I THOUGHT I'D SEEN IT BEFORE, SO I WAS JUST CHECKING.

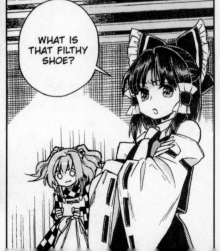

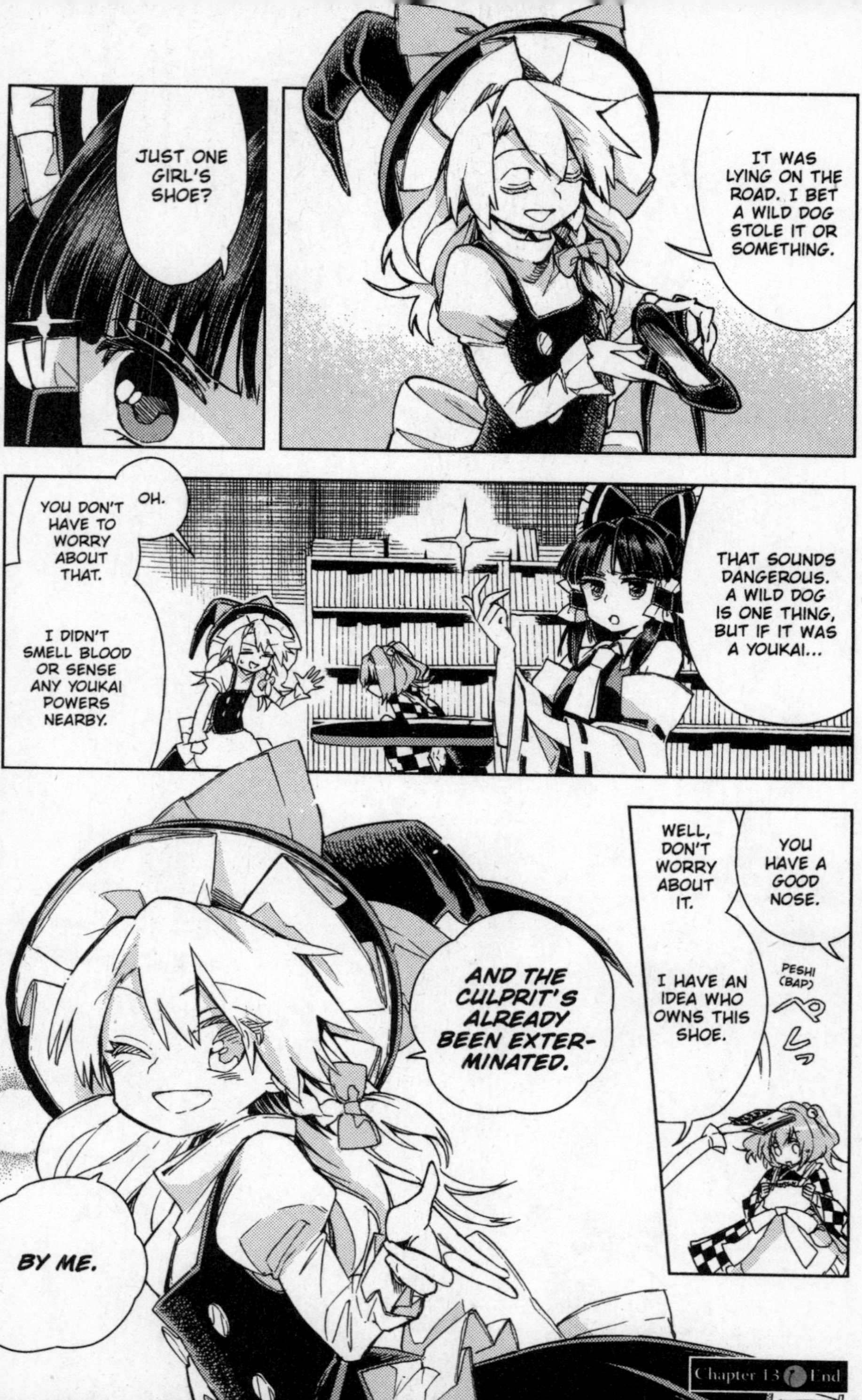
IT WAS LYING ON THE ROAD. I BET A WILD DOG STOLE IT OR SOMETHING.
JUST ONE GIRL'S SHOE?
THAT SOUNDS DANGEROUS. A WILD DOG IS ONE THING, BUT IF IT WAS A YOUKAI...
OH.
YOU DON'T HAVE TO WORRY ABOUT THAT.
I DIDN'T SMELL BLOOD OR SENSE ANY YOUKAI POWERS NEARBY.
YOU HAVE A GOOD NOSE.
WELL, DON'T WORRY ABOUT IT.
I HAVE AN IDEA WHO OWNS THIS SHOE.
PESHI (BAP)
AND THE CULPRIT'S ALREADY BEEN EXTER-MINATED.
BY ME.
Chapter 13 End

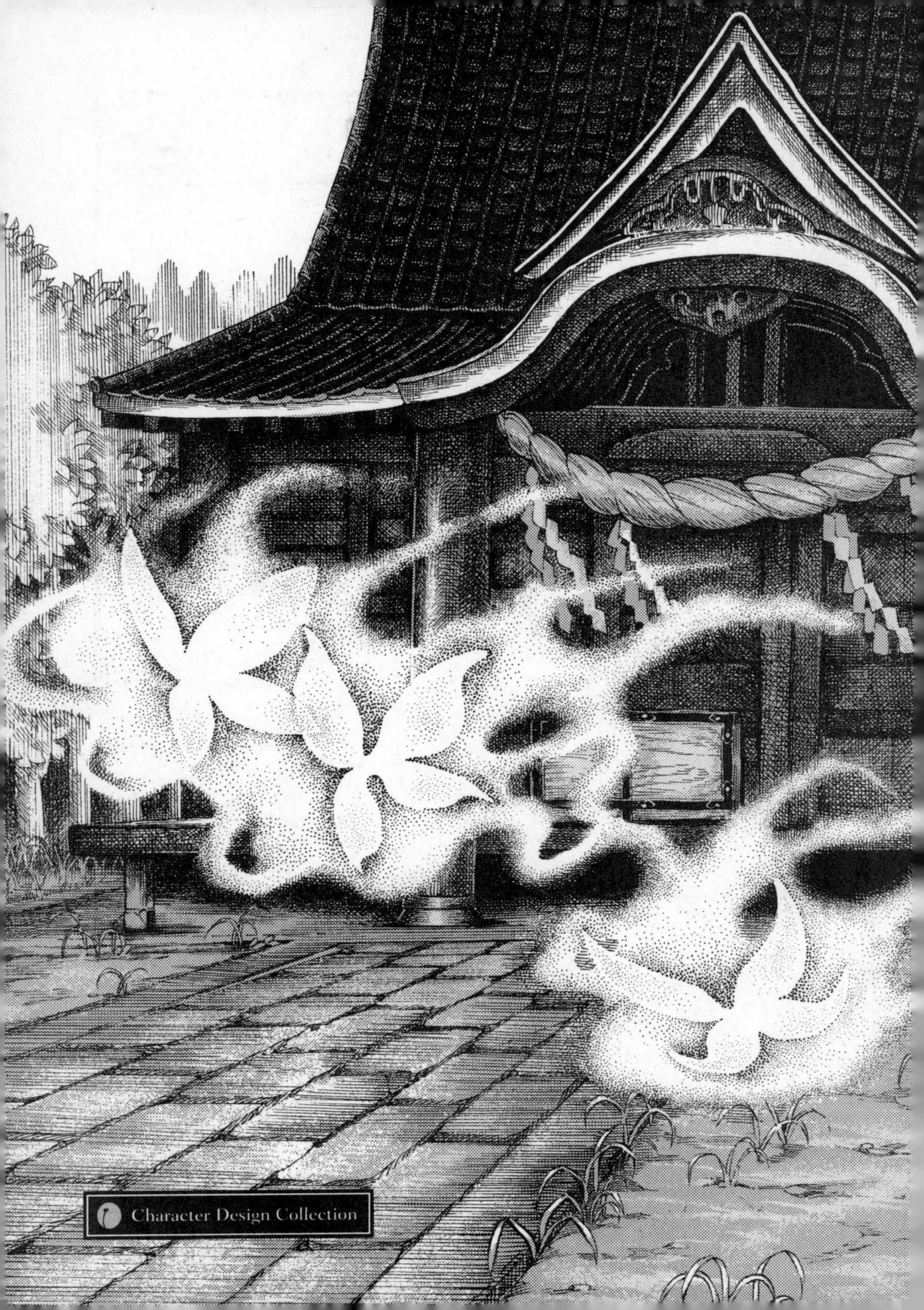
Character Design Collection

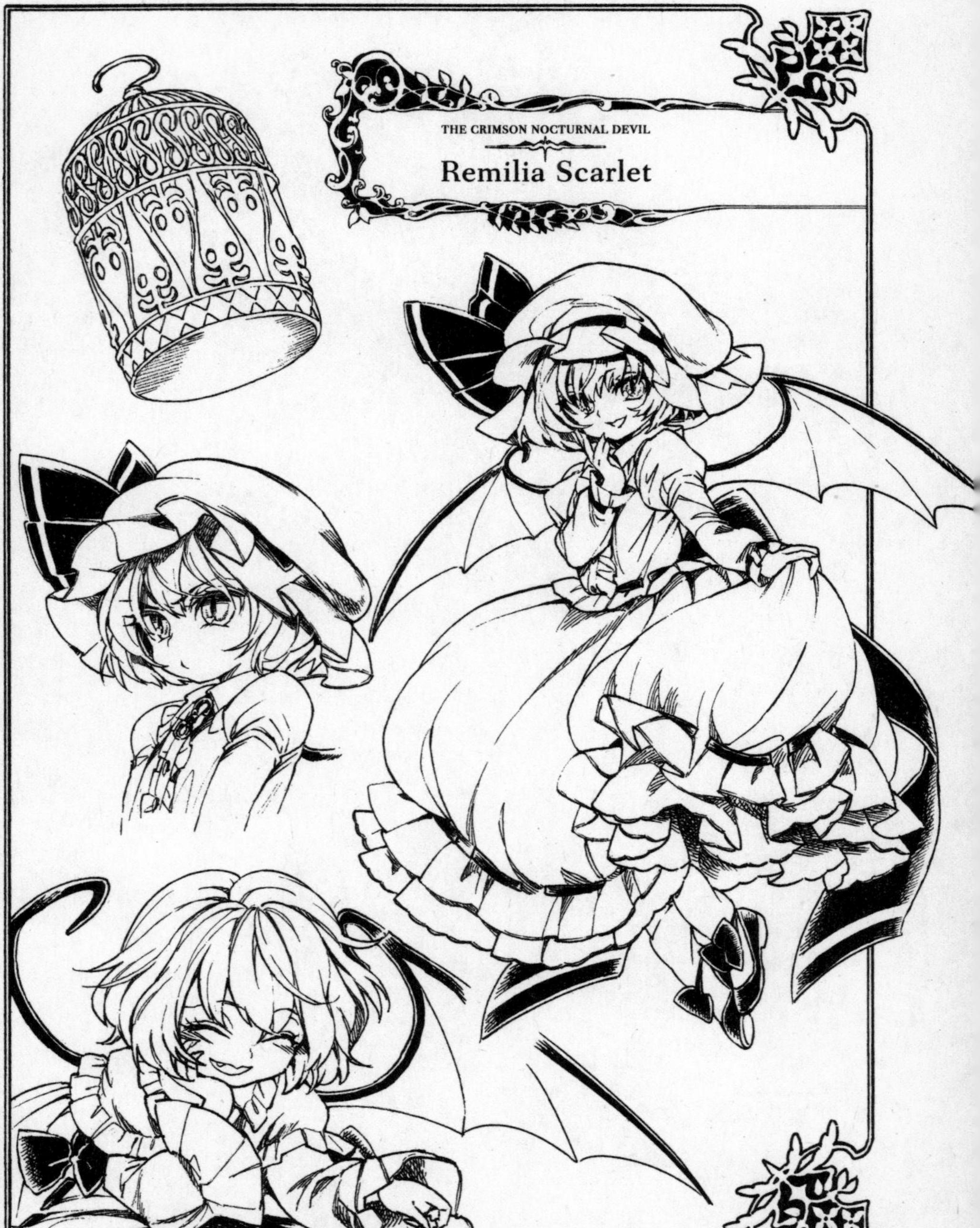
THE CRIMSON NOCTURNAL DEVIL
Remilia Scarlet

THE EMOTIONAL POKER FACE

Kokoro Hatano

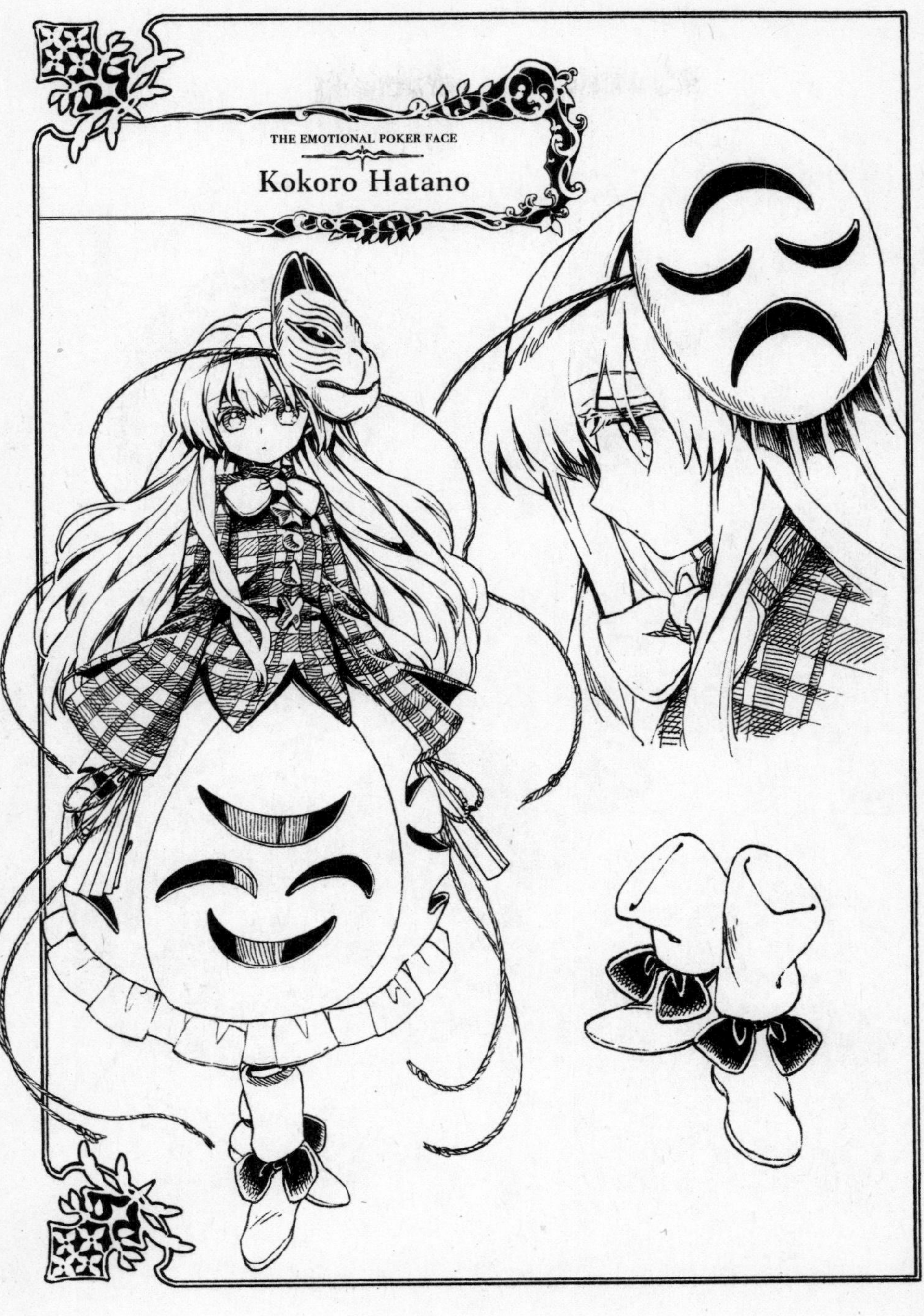

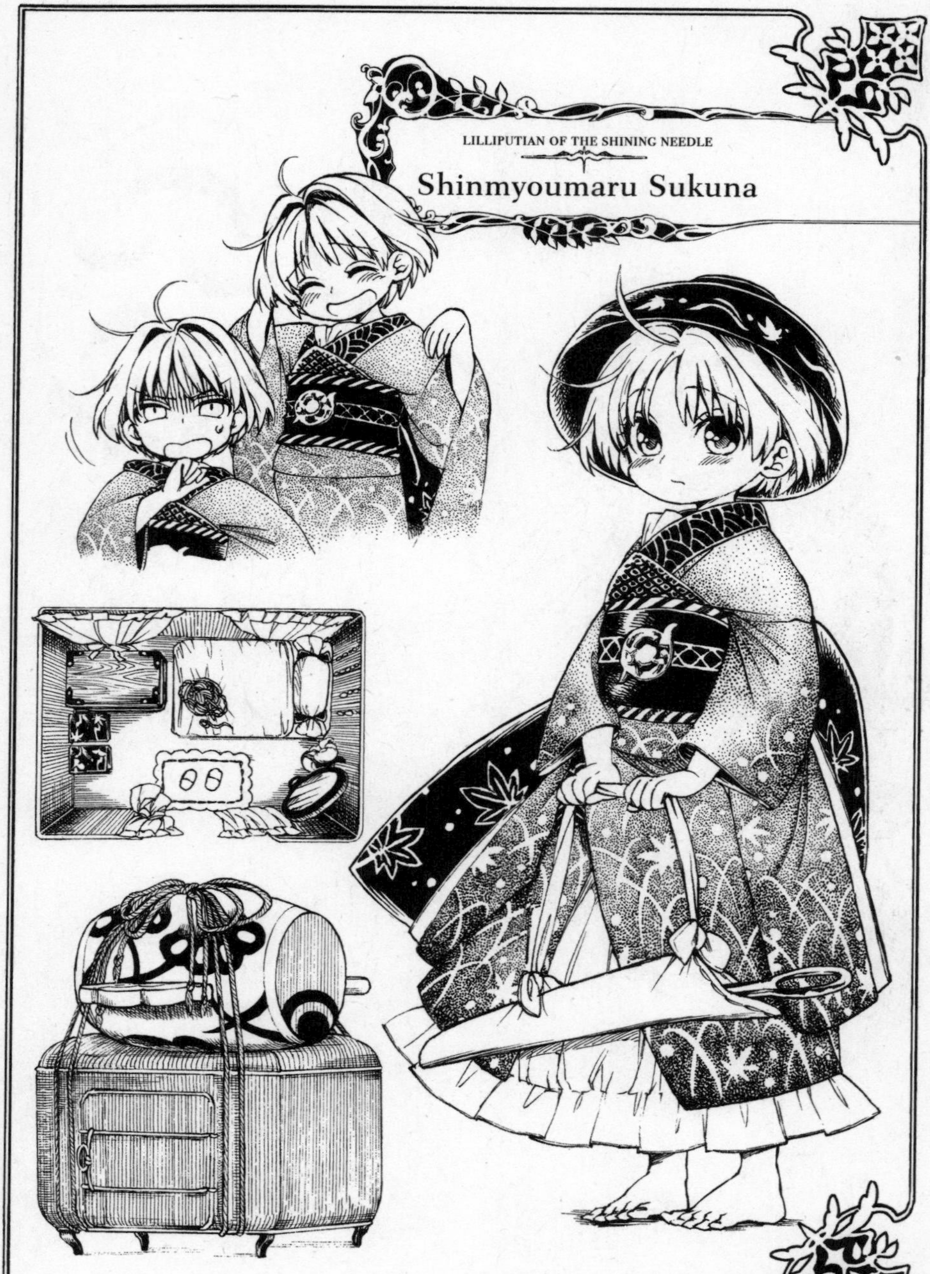
LILLIPUTIAN OF THE SHINING NEEDLE
Shinmyoumaru Sukuna

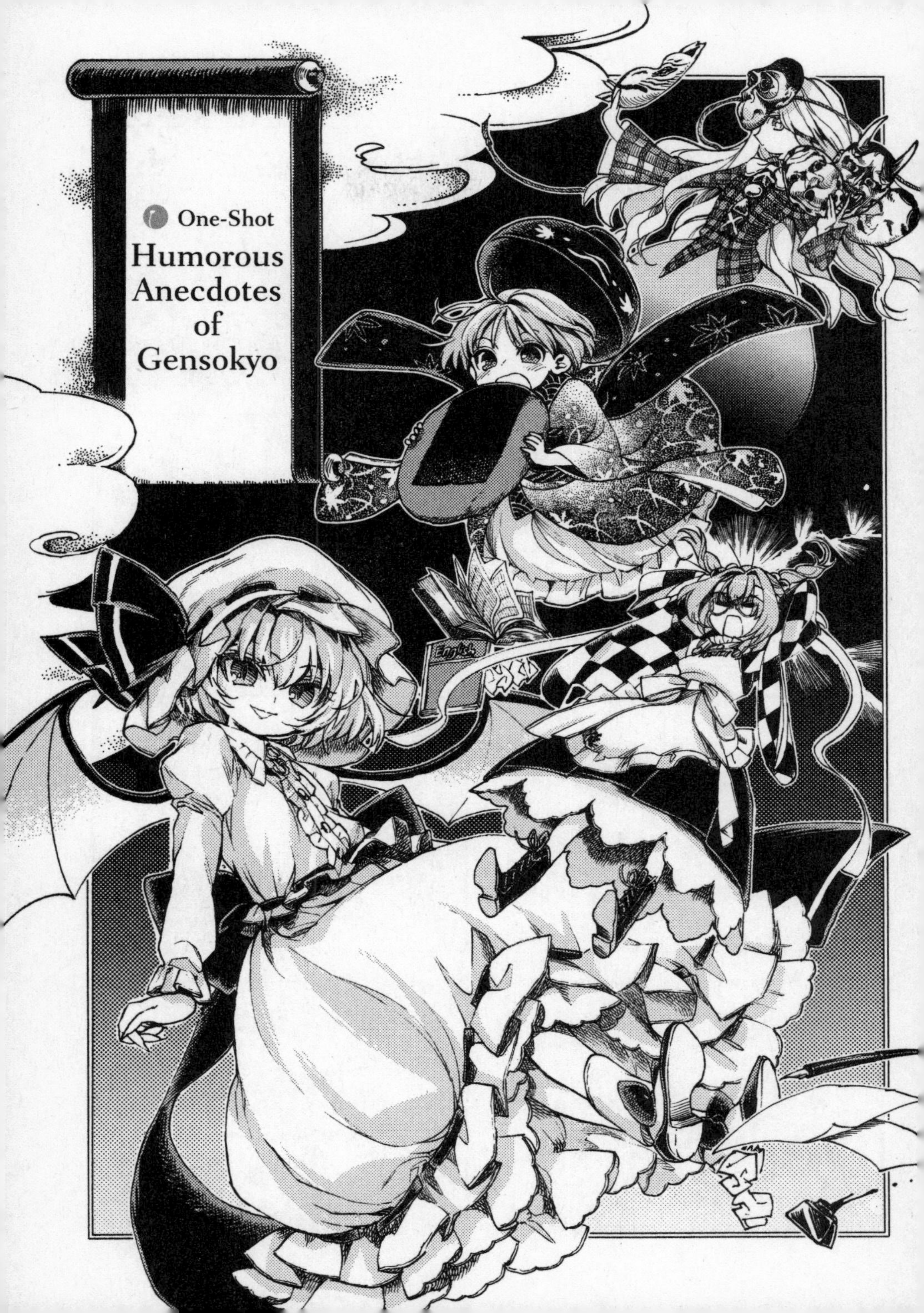
One-Shot
Humorous Anecdotes of Gensokyo

CORRESPONDENCE

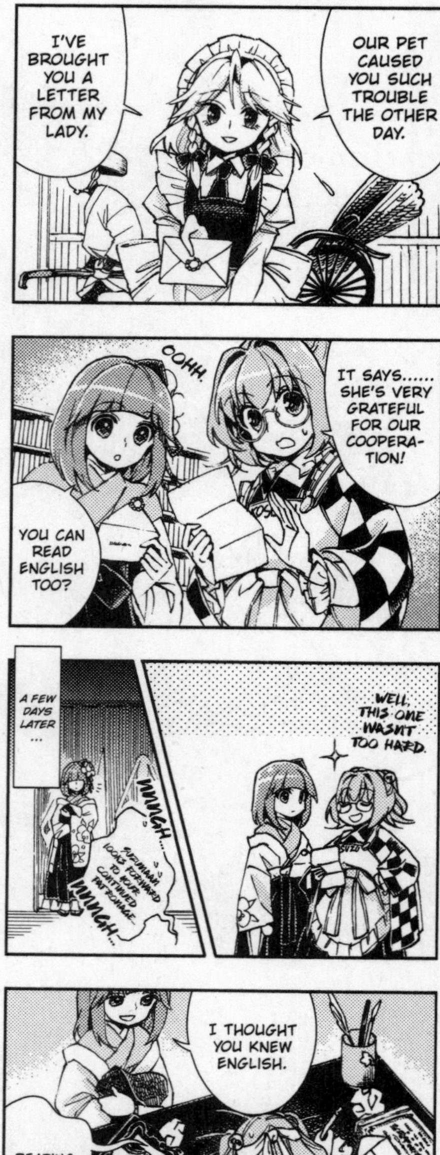
OUR PET CAUSED YOU SUCH TROUBLE THE OTHER DAY.
I'VE BROUGHT YOU A LETTER FROM MY LADY.
IT SAYS...... SHE'S VERY GRATEFUL FOR OUR COOPERATION!
OOHH.
YOU CAN READ ENGLISH TOO?
WELL, THIS ONE WASN'T TOO HARD.
A FEW DAYS LATER ...
NNNGH...
SUZUNAAN LOOKS FORWARD TO YOUR CONTINUED PATRONAGE...
NNNGH...
I THOUGHT YOU KNEW ENGLISH.
READING AND WRITING ARE TWO DIFFERENT THINGS!

BOOKS: ABC DICTIONARY, ENGLISH WRITING

TUPAI

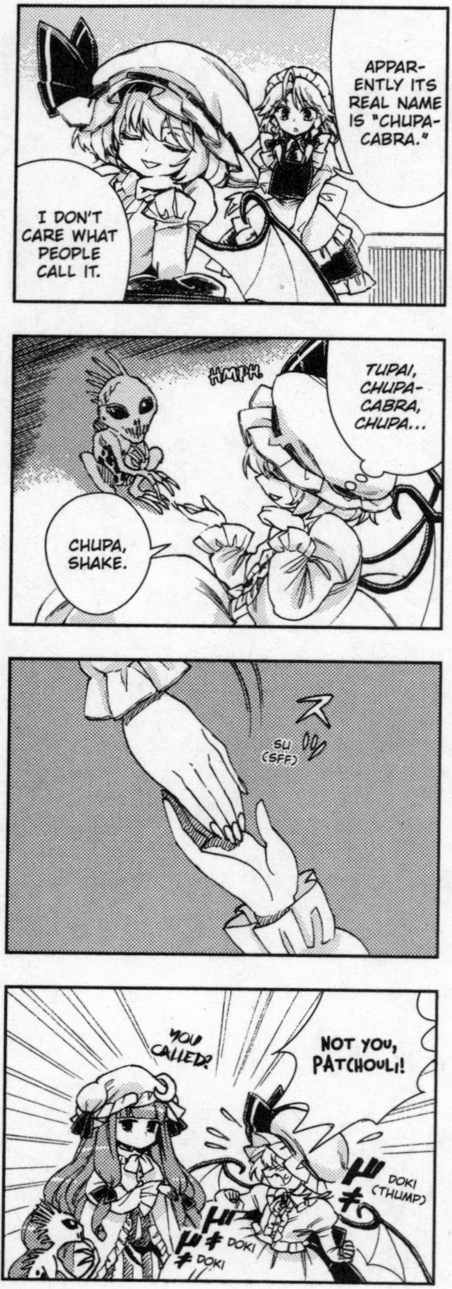
APPARENTLY ITS REAL NAME IS "CHUPACABRA."
I DON'T CARE WHAT PEOPLE CALL IT.
TUPAI, CHUPACABRA, CHUPA...
HMPH.
CHUPA, SHAKE.
スッ
SU (SFF)
NOT YOU, PATCHOULI!
YOU CALLED?
DOKI (THUMP)
DOKI
DOKI

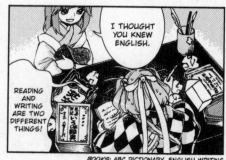

EMOTIONAL EXPRESSION

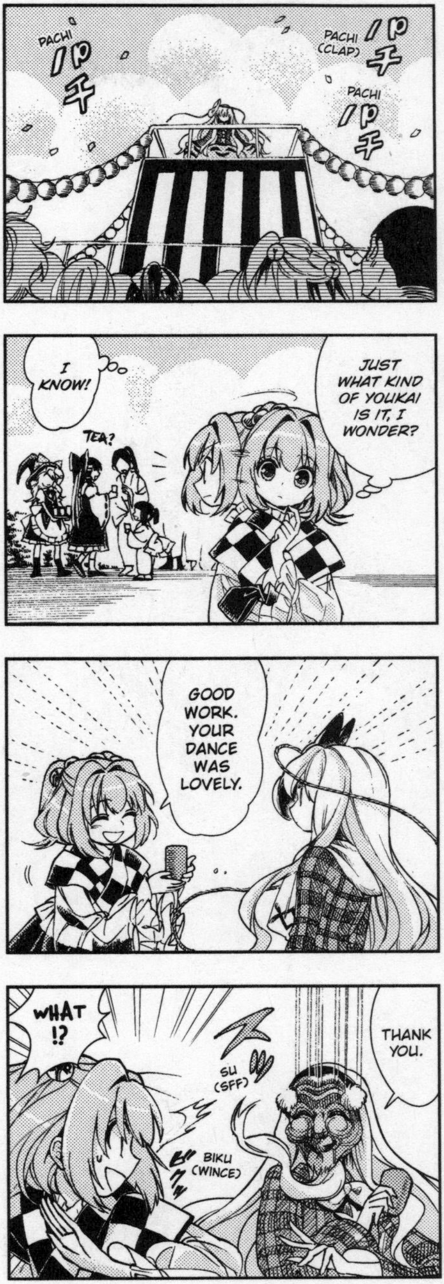
PACHI (CLAP)
PACHI
PACHI
JUST WHAT KIND OF YOUKAI IS IT, I WONDER?
TEA?
I KNOW!
GOOD WORK. YOUR DANCE WAS LOVELY.
THANK YOU.
SU (SFF)
BIKU (WINCE)
WHAT!?

INTEREST

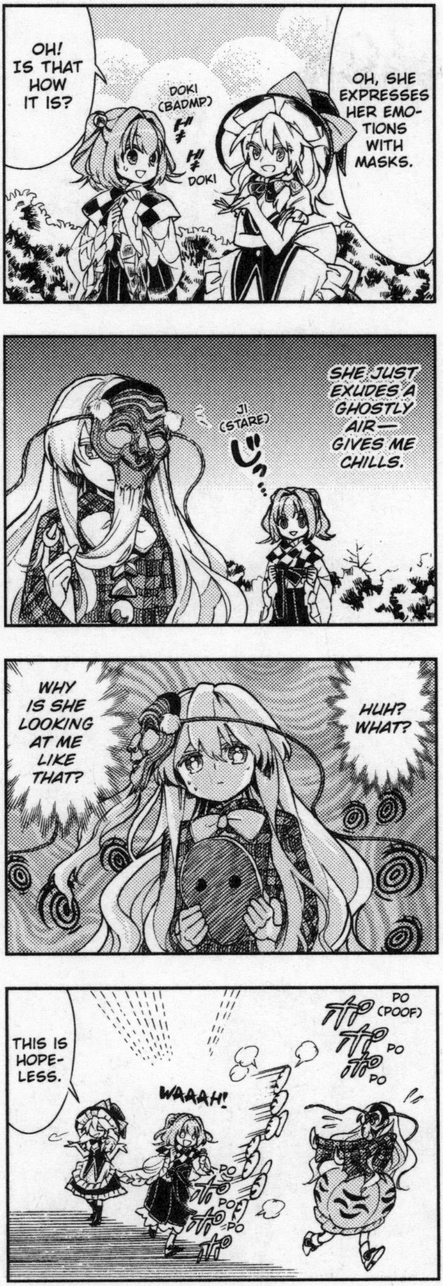
OH, SHE EXPRESSES HER EMOTIONS WITH MASKS.
DOKI (BADMP)
DOKI
OH! IS THAT HOW IT IS?
SHE JUST EXUDES A GHOSTLY AIR— GIVES ME CHILLS.
JI (STARE)
HUH? WHAT?
WHY IS SHE LOOKING AT ME LIKE THAT?
PO (POOF)
PO
PO
WAAAH!
PO
PO
PO
THIS IS HOPELESS.

THE MALLET'S

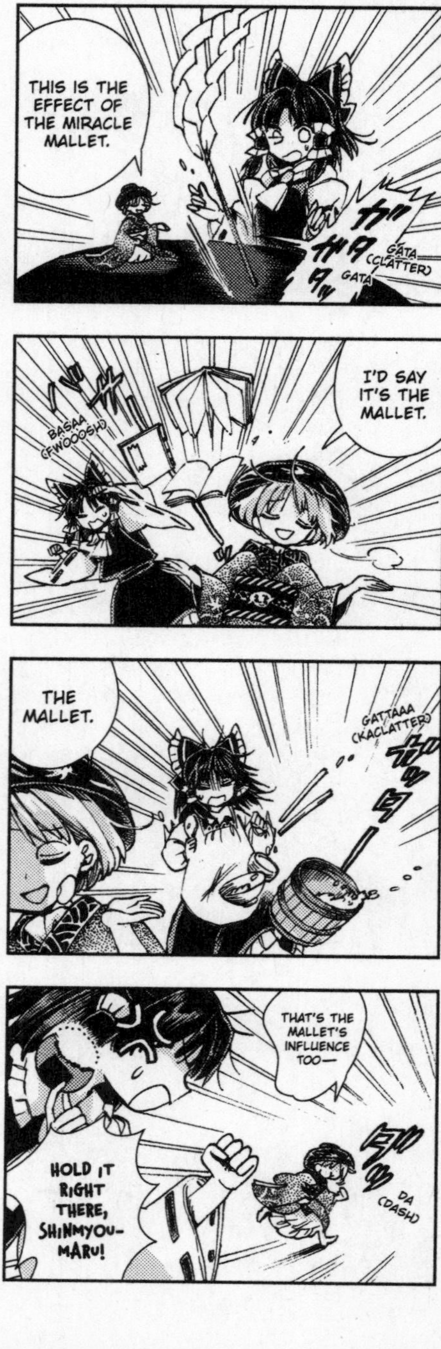
THIS IS THE EFFECT OF THE MIRACLE MALLET.
GATA (CLATTER) GATA
I'D SAY IT'S THE MALLET.
BASAA (FWOOOSH)
THE MALLET.
GATTAAA (KACLATTER)
THAT'S THE MALLET'S INFLUENCE TOO—
HOLD IT RIGHT THERE, SHINMYOU-MARU!
DA (DASH)

GRATITUDE

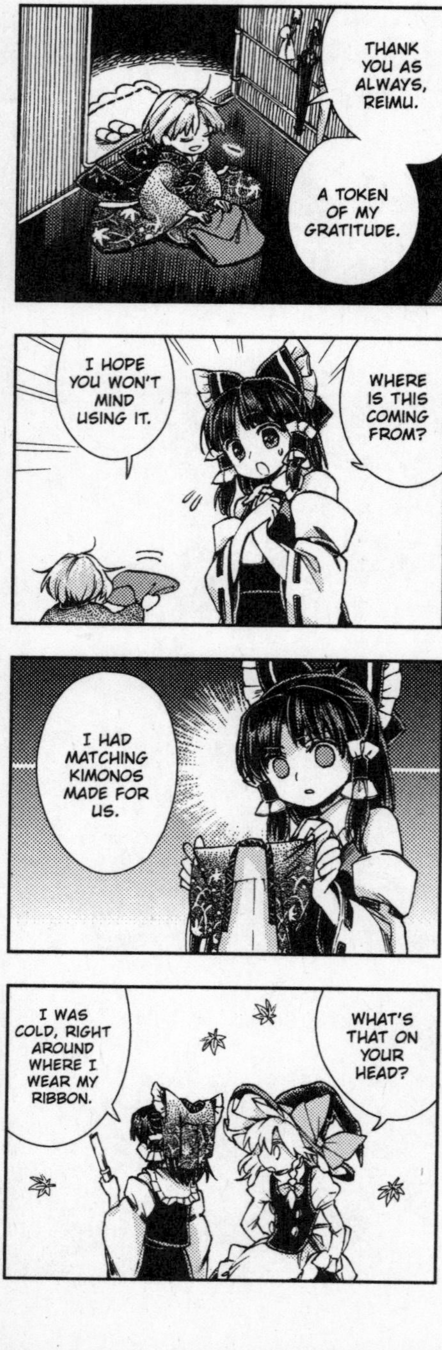
THANK YOU AS ALWAYS, REIMU.
A TOKEN OF MY GRATITUDE.
WHERE IS THIS COMING FROM?
I HOPE YOU WON'T MIND USING IT.
I HAD MATCHING KIMONOS MADE FOR US.
WHAT'S THAT ON YOUR HEAD?
I WAS COLD, RIGHT AROUND WHERE I WEAR MY RIBBON.

ZUN

Hello, ZUN here. Thank you very much for picking up Volume 2 of *Forbidden Scrollery*.

This time, we have new game characters like Kokoro and Shinmyoumaru. There's not a lot of explanation about who they are, so if you're curious, please play *Hopeless Masquerade* and *Double Dealing Character*.

With more characters in Volume 2, it's starting to take on that chaotic feeling you always get from the Touhou games. I'm worried about what kinds of characters and stories I should have Moe Harukawa-san draw.

Well, I hope to see you again in Volume 3 or in *Comp Ace*.

Moe Harukawa

Hello, I am the artist, Harukawa.

I don't get a lot of instructions for what to draw for the cover of each chapter, so I draw whatever I want.

For the cover of Chapter 12, partly to represent the series' first anniversary, I drew books, scrolls, and little items that have shown up in the previous chapters. If you have some spare time, please try to find them all.

To ZUN-san, who writes up the story outline for me every month despite his busy schedule, my editor who came up with the outline and rough draft for the Kokoro four-panel comics, and all of you who read this book, thank you very much.

I will continue to do my best to deliver the atmosphere of Gensokyo to you readers.

4-18

Forbidden Scrollery

2

⸓STORY⸍
ZUN

⸓ART⸍
Moe Harukawa

TRANSLATION: ALETHEA NIBLEY AND ATHENA NIBLEY
LETTERING: ALEXIS ECKERMAN

TOUHOU SUZUNA AN ~Forbidden Scrollery. Vol. 2
© Team Shanghai Alice © Moe HARUKAWA 2014
First published in Japan in 2014 by KADOKAWA CORPORATION, Tokyo.
English translation rights arranged with KADOKAWA CORPORATION, Tokyo through TUTTLE-MORI AGENCY, Inc., Tokyo.

English translation © 2018 by Yen Press, LLC

Yen Press
1290 Avenue of the Americas
New York, NY 10104

VISIT US AT YENPRESS.COM

facebook.com/yenpress
twitter.com/yenpress

yenpress.tumblr.com
instagram.com/yenpress

First Yen Press Edition: March 2018

Yen Press is an imprint of Yen Press, LLC.
The Yen Press name and logo are trademarks of Yen Press, LLC.

Library of Congress Control Number: 2017949553

ISBNs: 978-0-316-51190-2 (paperback)
978-0-316-51200-8 (ebook)

10 9 8 7 6 5 4 3 2 1

BVG

Printed in the United States of America